Secrets and Lies:

The Shocking Truth About Recent Australian Aboriginal History, A Memoir (First Nations True Stories Series)

By

Barbara Miller

WARNING

Aboriginal and Torres Strait Islander readers are advised that the following book contains images and names of people who have died.

Barbara Miller /Barbara Miller Books
PO Box 425 Westcourt
Cairns, Australia 4870
www.barbara-miller-books.com

Ordering Information:
Quantity sales. Special discounts are available on quantity purchases by corporations, associations, and others. For details, contact the "Special Sales Department" at the address above.

Secrets and Lies: The Shocking Truth of Recent Australian Aboriginal History, A Memoir /Barbara Miller
—1st ed.
ISBN paperback 978-0-6488709-2-0
ISBN kindle 978-0-6488709-1-3

DOWNLOAD FREE GIFT NOW

Just to thank you for buying my book, I would like to give you a 14-page PDF of the hidden history of the first contact of Europeans with Australian Aborigines. It is the untold story that is not in your school text books. Hear from Aborigines who have had the story passed down through generations and from the explorers.

For information on my other books go to – www.barbara-miller-books.com

TO DOWNLOAD GO TO

http://eepurl.com/dn69ab

You can help me by posting a review on Amazon. Thanks in advance. Here is the link https://www.amazon.com/dp/B095SDW3LY

Check out the following books!

www.barbara-miller-books.com

Dedication and Acknowledgements

I would like to dedicate this book to the God of Abraham, Isaac and Jacob and His Messiah who has given me the vision, inspiration and perseverance to write this history and memoir. I would also like to dedicate this book to my husband Norman, the love of my life who has encouraged and supported me and helped make the time for me to write and to my dear son Michael and granddaughter Jaydah. I hope that this will be an inheritance for them.

I also dedicate this book to my parents, Mervyn and Joyce Russell, my brother Greg Russell and his family, Norman's parents, Barclay and Shirley Miller, their children Thomas, Colleen, Lillian, Joanne and Deborah and their spouses and children. I also dedicate this book to my first husband, Mick Miller and his parents Mick and Cissy Miller and their children Marge, Timer, Betty, Margaret and Annie and their spouses and children. This book is also dedicated to Mick's children Lydia, Marilyn and Jenny and Jenny's children. All have been a source of inspiration and love and both Miller families have dedicated their lives to the advancement of First Nations People.

It is a privilege to dedicate this book to all the First Nations leaders whose inspiring stories are covered in this book which gives them a voice and legacy. Many have passed on but their stories will live on as an inspiration to many.

Thanks to Tony Crofts for dedicated editing, Polgarus for formatting, 100 Covers for the cover design and Susan Jagannath for help with the title. I am grateful to the following people for wonderful reviews – Judy Atkinson, Greg McIntyre, Christine Howes and Paul Richards.

Again, thanks to David Jack for work on old photographs. As some original photos were lost, I had to rely on copies from the newspaper I edited *NQ Messagestick*. Thanks to Alex Shaland for photos of Chicago and Fairfax and Newspix for photos from newspapers. Thanks also to my beloved husband Norman who took many photos. Thanks also to friends who pray for me.

Contents

Foreword

This explosive book is a gripping read that you will not be able to put down. It tells the hidden history of First Nations people in Australia and particularly in Queensland, her home state. However, it also touches on the internationalization of the struggle for justice of the First Nations people.

The personal and political are interwoven in this book which is a memoir and a history at the same time. Barbara is a walking talking history, mainly because she has lived through and been closely involved with many ups and downs in Aboriginal affairs.

I believe this book is ground-breaking and history-making and it honours many of the First Nations people of Australia whose story needs to be told.

This book is a treasured book that must be read.

By Munganbana Norman Miller, from the First Nations tribes of Jirrbal, Bar-Barrum and Tableland Yidinji

Cairns, 3 June 2021

Preface

This book has been a labor of love as I wanted to tell some of the stories of key events and key people in Aboriginal history that I have been close to. I have profound respect for the people in these pages and I wanted their stories to be told. In some way, to varying degrees, their lives have become entwined with mine.

My memoir, White Woman Black Heart was too long, so in mid-2017, I pulled out about50,000 words written mostly in 2016 and published White Woman Black Heart in March 2018. I planned to use the chapters I took out to write a second memoir and wondered if I would ever get back to it.

Then in November 2020, I had a dream where I was taken to Aurukun Aboriginal community, and saw an elder, a relative by marriage. In my dream, I thought 'but you've passed away'. Then I saw a young Aboriginal girl who I thought might be his great granddaughter. She pointed to a mobile phone of all things and said, "This is your story. You need to tell it." Surprised, I didn't say anything. The next morning, I remembered he dream clearly and that the first few chapters of my unfinished second memoir were about Aurukun. This gave me the inspiration and motivation to pick up the pieces and finish the writing.

Reviews

Secrets and Lies: The Shocking Truth of Recent Aboriginal History, A Memoir, is both a political chronicle and a personal memoir – a journey the young Barbara took into political activism and personal transformation, which became life-long. Barbara Miller shows the political and the personal can be two sides of a life journey of service.

There is critical history in this book from an activist on the inside. Yet the book also shows that political activism is not enough. It must be balanced by personal integrity and pursuit. The journey from the political into the personal, with fulfillment in spiritual practice, is also illuminating. Can we do one without the other? I think not, whatever the spiritual practice is.

Barbara's book bought memories of the days of the Aboriginal Co-ordinating Council (ACC), both of us working at different levels within the ACC to respond to the directions and needs of the old reserve mission controls moving into deeds of grant in trust and 'self-management'. Barbara's political background provided essential insight and sound analysis. Mine saw the failure of the services delivered by a racist regime, with the ACC working to meet their legislative responsibilities. Barbara supported this work through research. Hers has been an inspirational journey of service at many levels.

Judy Atkinson, Emeritus Professor, PhD AM

Secrets and Lies contains exciting examples of the battles by the indigenous people of QLD against a repressive state regime which greedily sought to control their land and their lives in order to exploit the natural resources. They have developed a remarkable capacity for developing relationships with non-indigenous people who have joined them in their struggle. Barbara has been admitted, not only into their confidence, but also into their families and has achieved remarkable advantages for them in those battles.

Paul Richards, lawyer, author of Adventures with Agitators, stories of indigenous battles in the justice system during his half century

Secrets and Lies - A powerful, hard-hitting yarn, from the grassroots of Cape York community-life through to the necessary development of life-changing political activism on Cape York in the 1970s and 80s.

This is a story which needs to be told and has to be taught, with lessons to learn about what should be done, and how it should (and shouldn't) be done.

These yarns are at the roots of what still happens today, in this day and age, making it an essential read for anyone who has ties or in an interest, not just in the Cape York landscape, but across all of Government/Aboriginal politics.

A well-written and fascinating contextual read for anyone with a passion for justice for Aboriginal people.

Christine Howes, FNQ correspondent for *Koori Mail*

This memoire, Secrets and Lies, tells the story of important events in the relationship between the Queensland and Commonwealth Governments and Aboriginal people on Aurukun and Mornington Island and their struggle to maintain control of their lives in the face of paternalism and racism. It does so from the perspective of the author, who had a unique opportunity to observe the events in which Aboriginal leaders participated and recount the conversations which occurred at meetings between community members and with politicians who played key roles in these events along with what was played out in the public arena and recorded in the media.

It paints an intimate picture of the individuals involved and brings to life the impact which actions of Government have had upon them at a personal and structural level. It provides a detailed insight into how a grass-roots activist organisation, the North Queensland Land Council, with a charismatic leader, Mick Miller, was able to operate in a regional, State, national and international arena in its advocacy of self-determination for Aboriginal people.

It traces the history of on-going advocacy of the author for Aboriginal people and the challenges they face through various changes of direction in her personal life. It is a unique and valuable record of the observations and participation of the author in activism which has as its unwavering focus a dedication to the cause of social justice for Indigenous people.

Greg McIntyre SC, Barrister, Michael Kirby Chambers Perth, Lawyer for the Mabo Case

Map Of Cape York, Australia

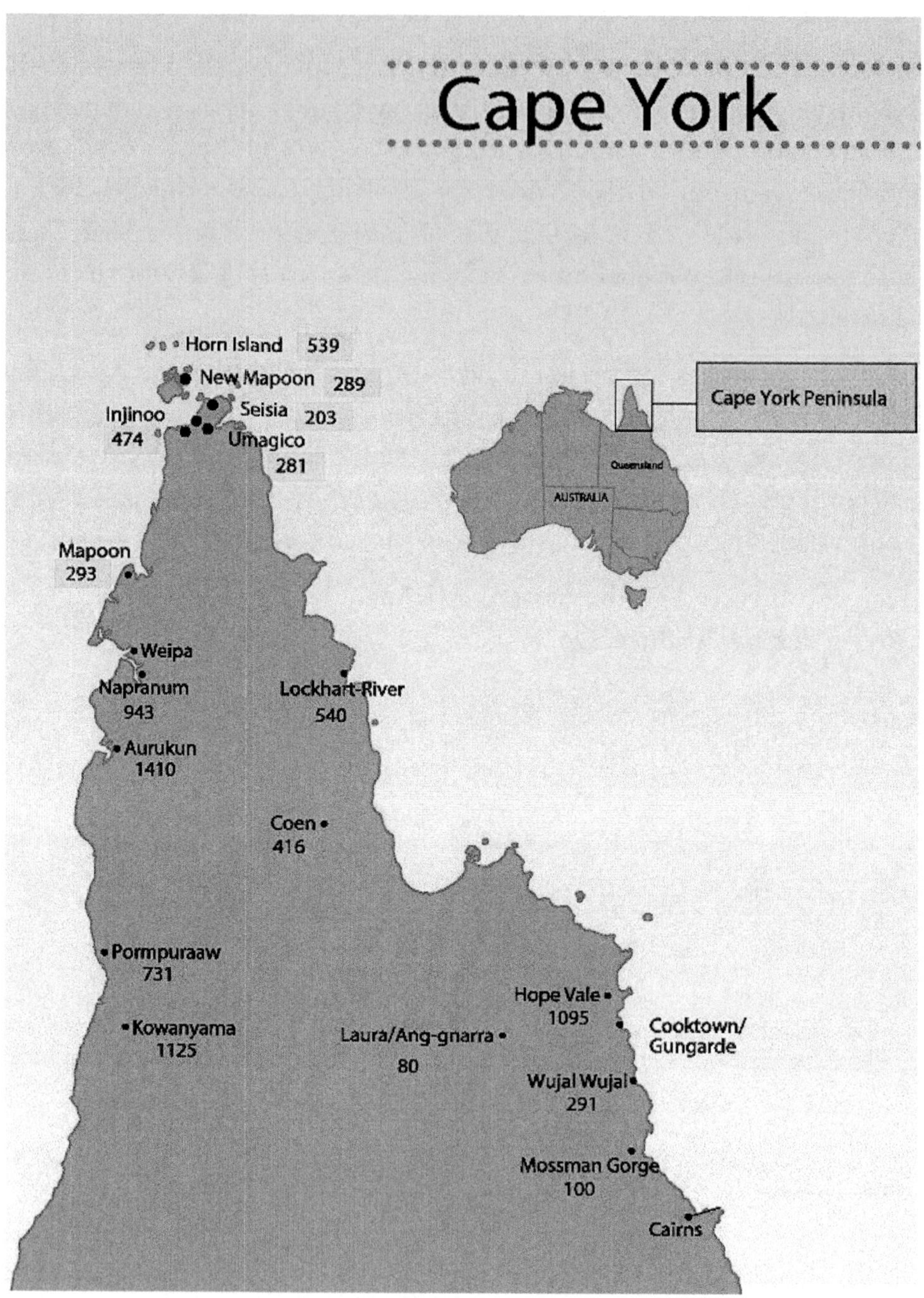

Map of Cape York Indigenous Communities by researchgate.com

Chapter 1

Aurukun and Mornington Island Takeover

A transistor radio sits on the dirt beside a campfire with charred black billy cans ready for use. The radio is their only link to the outside world. A few dogs lie around in the sun. Some women sit on the ground under the shade of a mango tree to escape the heat of the day.

The music blaring from the radio gives way to a startling news report. The Queensland government plans to throw the church out of this Aboriginal mission and take over its administration. The news circulates quickly around Aurukun by word of mouth. The community is in shock. They have not been consulted, nor have their Aboriginal council. The government has two communities in its sights: Mornington Island and Aurukun,

Mornington Island, in the Gulf of Carpentaria NE Australia, is the largest of 22 islands that form the Wellesley Islands group. It is flat and skirted by mangrove forests. The Lardil tribe are the traditional owners and the Bentinck Islanders were moved here after the 1947 cyclone. A cyclone-prone island itself, most people live in the largest town, which is Gununa. In 1978, there are 681 people living on this beautiful tropical island.

Aurukun, on the west coast of Cape York Peninsula NE Australia, is the traditional homeland of the Wik, Wik Way and Kugu people and the main language is Wik Mungkan. Still today, nearly 90% of the people speak a traditional Indigenous language at home. Traditional culture is strong because it was not undermined, as in most other communities. There are five spiritual clan groupings: Wanam, Winchanam, Puch, Apalech, and Sara. About 768 people live here in 1978 including some in nine outstations.

The history of Aurukun is linked to the other Moravian missions established for the Presbyterian Church: Mapoon, the mother or first mission, Weipa and Mornington Island. Moravian Rev Arthur Richter established Aurukun Mission in 1904 with some Indigenous workers from Mapoon. It was originally called Archer River Mission Station and renamed Aurukun, the Wik name of the large lagoon at the back of the mission, in 1905. Missionaries Bill and Geraldine Mackenzie managed the mission from 1925 to 1965 and they supported the continuation of the people's culture through Bora initiations, traditional hunting and speaking the Wik languages. Despite such comparative liberalism, they were also authoritarian in some ways and their departure led to some instability. Strong supporters of education, they left a high level of literacy in Aurukun by the time of their departure.

Cape Keerweer, south of Aurukun, was the site of the first attempted European settlement in Australia by Dutch Captain Willem Janszoon in 1606 in his ship the *Duyfken.* Janszoon planned to build a city at the site. However, after the Dutch took some of the women on board, fighting broke out with the local men, several sailors were killed and the *Duyfken* turned back. Cape Keerweer actually means "turn back" in the local language. The *Dufyken* visit also links its history to Mapoon and Weipa.

People usually return to the township from their traditional homelands or outstations during the wet. Aurukun is at the junction of three pristine rivers: the Archer, the Watson and the Ward. Together with the Kirk and the Love Rivers, further south, they form the Aurukun Wetlands, one of Australia's largest wetland areas covering 1.1 million hectares. It has a wide variety of birdlife, plants and reptiles. Geese and lilies are abundant, including *paanja* or candlenut. Anglers enjoy tidal estuaries, white sandy beaches, near-shore reefs and rocky headlands.

The backdrop to the 1978 federal-state confrontation over Aboriginal affairs in Queensland has a number of elements to it. The Aurukun Aboriginal community, south of Weipa, is a particularly strong, outspoken people not easily intimidated. They still practice their tribal ways and speak their language but are willing to engage in the mainstream political process to avoid being railroaded and becoming a second Mapoon or second Weipa. They have seen the impact of mining on Aboriginal land and the impact of state government administration. This fear of becoming a second Mapoon or second Weipa is expressed a number of times at public meetings.

Another important player is the Uniting Church, who took over from the Presbyterian Church in 1977 when the Presbyterian, Methodist and Congregational churches united. However, it is still run by BOEMAR, the board of missions. The church has administered the community for over seventy years. BOEMAR also administered Weipa and Mapoon and the church is not going to be blindsided by the state government as it was at Weipa. Nor is it going to abandon the people as it had at Mapoon in 1963; both times for the sake of mining though the government gave other reasons. The church is embarrassed by *The Mapoon Story* that John Roberts and I have put out with the support of the Mapoon people and is not keen to repeat this experience. This time the church is going to go down fighting or will, hopefully, win the battle. The church is encouraging self-management and the outstation movement. It is also standing with the people in their opposition to mining. All three policies are anathema to the state government.

Under Premier Joh Bjelke-Petersen, the pro-development National Party Queensland government will not cooperate either with Labor or Liberal-National federal governments and invokes the ogre of southern stirrers and communists with all who disagree with them. Bjelke accuses the church and the North Queensland Land Council of being communists and the federal government of having stirrers on its payroll. Queensland is often referred to as "Banana Land" by those who don't agree with the Premier, the inference being that it is a social justice backwater.

Brisbane is the capital of Queensland and in World War 11, it was decided to sacrifice anything north of the Brisbane Line if need be, just over 2,000km, and defend the rest. A cartoon in *The Sun,* 8th April 1978, has Joh Bjelke-Petersen dressed in the uniform of southern USA in the Civil War with bayonet drawn, standing on the Brisbane Line facing opposite to the firing canons saying, "The guns are facing the wrong way – the threat is from the south." The headline reads, "Oh Joh, you're driving us bananas" by 7th Day Dunstan and reads, "Just like the great civil war of the United States, the battle will be over slavery and the blacks."

Steve Gray comments in the *Brisbane Times*, "By 1978, Queensland Premier Joh Bjelke-Petersen had hit his straps. After a shaky start, he'd been in power for a decade. He had honed his populist, authoritarian manner and he'd identified a coalition of enemies he could drag into the political stoush as required: Canberra, southerners, Labor, protesters, greenies, pinkos, even churches."[1]

The peanut farmer from Kingaroy, married to Flo, famous for her pumpkin scones, is one of our longest serving premiers in Queensland. He likes to raise his index finger to make a point, his halting voice, furrowed brow, graying hair and double chin adding to the effect. His disdain for the media led to him famously calling talking to them as "Feeding the chooks." He also said, "The greatest thing that could happen to the state and nation is when we get rid of all the media… then we could live in peace and tranquility and no one would know anything."

Lined up in the southern corner is the Fraser federal government. Prime Minister Malcolm Fraser passes a watered-down version of previous Prime Minister Gough Whitlam's land rights legislation for the Northern Territory and is making a name for himself in British Commonwealth circles as a fighter against apartheid. Yet, he has it on his own doorstep in Queensland. Somehow, he must assert himself as national leader against a recalcitrant state premier who believes Queensland can go it alone and won't toe the line with federal initiatives.

Stationed in the tropical tourist city of Cairns, a gateway to the far north Aboriginal communities, is the North Queensland Land Council with Chairman Mick Miller. An educated and politically aware Aboriginal leader; he was born on the Aboriginal community of Palm Island. He is closely related to the Aurukun community leaders and friends with parliamentarians and national Aboriginal leaders and support organizations. The North Queensland Land Council does not have legislative recognition and government funding but it has land rights committees and delegates on every reserve and town in North Queensland and is a powerful grassroots force.

I am good friends with many of the Aurukun leaders and we work closely through this time and beyond. This is partly through my close relationship with Mick, partly through my key role at the Land Council as editor of *NQ Messagestick* and research officer-come-campaigner, and partly because I have developed positive relationships and a good reputation after helping the Mapoon people move back to their land in 1974.

The stage is set for confrontation. One of the casualties of the fray is the first Aboriginal Liberal Senator Neville Bonner, a Queenslander who was appointed to a Senate vacancy in 1971 and re-elected. He is often called an "Uncle Tom" by Aboriginal leaders but he visits Aurukun and supports people who are criticizing state government legislation. He pays the price and is dropped from a winnable seat in the 1983 Senate election, resigns from the Liberal Party and runs as an independent, narrowly losing his seat.

In December 1975, the Qld government pushes through the Aurukun Associates Act 1975, granting a new mining consortium of Tipperary, Billiton and Pechiney, mining rights worth at least $14 billion. The Aurukun people have not been consulted and, with church funding, take them to the Supreme Court in 1976 and win. The matter is called Donald Peinkinna and others v. The Corporation of the Director of Aboriginal and Islanders Advancement and a writ is served in the Supreme Court of

Queensland on Patrick Killoran, alleging breach of fiduciary trust as a result of the passing of the Aurukun Associates Agreement Act, 1975. The court agrees it is an abuse of trust and rules that the Aurukun people have a right to challenge any mining on their land.

Premier Bjelke appeals to the judicial committee of the Privy Council in London which overturns the decision of the Supreme Court of Australia in January 1978. Because the church has supported them, Bjelke decides to get rid of the church and take over the reserve. In July 1974 the council, under Donald Peinkinna's leadership, made a submission to the Queensland government seeking freehold title to the Aurukun Reserve. Another thorny issue. Another spear in writing to challenge the government.

On 13th March 1978, the Queensland government announces it will take control of the Uniting Church missions of Aurukun on Cape York and Mornington Island in the Gulf of Carpentaria from 31st March. This begins a huge fight as the Aboriginal people concerned want the church to stay as it is promoting their self-management, whereas the Queensland government is an oppressive alternative. It is four years after the Mapoon people have moved back to their land and are struggling on as an illegal settlement in the Queensland government's eyes. Writing this memoir, I sense for the first time that getting rid of the church from Aurukun and Mornington Island is also payback for the church's support of the Mapoon people moving back.

Minister for Aboriginal and Islanders Advancement (DAIA), Charles Porter, briefed cabinet in February 1978 about the need for the takeover.

> "Over the years, the management of Mornington Island and Aurukun under the aegis of the church, and particularly the philosophies promoted by the Reverend John Brown, have been hostile to state government policies and programs." Reverend Brown was the general secretary of the Uniting Church Commission for World Mission.
>
> Mr Porter said much of the population of Aurukun was "dispersed" over the reserve "Living in the bush under

> primitive conditions and consequently presenting a major health hazard …"
>
> "It can also be expected, in view of known moves, that this island reserve (Mornington Island) will be the basis of a legal challenge to the state under the 'land rights' philosophies of the Uniting Church."[2]

Holding back a smirk, Porter triumphantly hands the takeover letter to Prof Roland Busch of the church on 13th March. Stunned, Busch takes a step back to take it in. Protests fall on deaf ears. Busch immediately sends a telegram to Donald Peinkinna, Chairman of Aurukun, informing him. Donald's eyes widen with surprise. Donald's charcoal face and piercing brown eyes are a contrast to his wavy white hair. He doesn't waste any time meeting with the people under the mango trees. The sun filters through the leafy trees, casting shadows over his yellow shirt. He scratches his head momentarily in consternation at the news and works out how to break the news to his people, other councillors at his side. Donald asks the people what they want to do. The response is resounding - stay with the church and protect their land.

Geraldine Kawangka, a former Council Chairperson, stands up, her face serious and voice assured. A dignified, respected leader she commands attention.

> "We want the church and the government to work together for the people of Aurukun. We need to put our heads together and stand side by side and speak up to them. You can't leave it to me and Gladys and others to speak up for you. You speak up."

His face furrowed with worry, Councillor Francis Yunkaporta says, "We don't want to be like Mapoon and Weipa."

"Policy conflict reason for mission takeover" screams the headline in *The Cairns Post* 15th March 1978:

> "Queensland Aboriginal and Islanders Advancement Minister, Mr Porter, has admitted 'conflict of policy' was the

> basic reason for the State Government's plan to take over management of two church-run Aboriginal missions, the Uniting Church Queensland Moderator, Rev Roland Busch said here (Brisbane) yesterday."

Part of that policy conflict is that the church is supporting the people who want to return to their tribal lands as a way of strengthening their culture and reducing inter-clan conflict. There is policy conflict over Aurukun but the inclusion of Mornington Island is a surprise to the church.

The story also covers the response of Mick on behalf of the North Queensland Land Council (NQLC). Mick has black wavy hair, mustache and side levers (sideburns), big brown eyes and a radio announcer voice. He was born on Palm Island, a former penal colony for Aboriginal people. The story says,

> "Mr Mick Miller, President of the North Queensland Land Council, yesterday called on the federal government to assume its responsibility for Aboriginal affairs in Queensland.
>
> Both Aurukun and Mornington Island," said Mr Miller, "have expressed the wish to be administered by the church rather than the Queensland government. Aurukun reaffirmed this decision as recently as last November.
>
> The North Queensland Land Council condemns the Queensland government for its blatant racism and hypocrisy in flagrantly disregarding the wishes of the Aboriginal people at these missions while pretending to be acting in their interests.
>
> The reason behind the takeover is threefold: to stop the Mornington Island land claim; to give easier access to mining companies in Aurukun; to stop the outstation or decentralization movement where six Aboriginal groups have moved out of Aurukun to their tribal lands.
>
> The mining subcommittee of the NQLC at a recent meeting at Weipa, unanimously passed a motion calling on the federal

government not to grant an export license to mining companies unless satisfactory terms are reached with the Aurukun people."

The Mornington Island Council sends the NQLC a letter thanking us for our support.

One month before the announcement, Bjelke-Petersen says, "White Australians would be converted to second-class citizens unless mineral rights were removed from aboriginal land rights legislation. Aboriginal control of a vital resource like uranium could lead eventually to an independent black state in the Northern Territory." (*The Age* 20th February 1978)

Porter and his director, Mr Paddy Killoran, are due to visit Aurukun. So the Chairman of Aurukun, Donald Peinkinna, sends the NQLC an invitation to come. Mick and Clarrie travel to Aurukun with a TV team to cover the meeting. Porter and Killoran bring a white policeman from Weipa with them.

Donald wears a suit when he travels south to plead his community's case but on home territory, his dress is casual. He is a humble man with great dignity and knows how to stand his ground. He is 53 years old, a strong Christian leader and astute political leader managing community alliances well. As the upper Love River is his clan estate, he is of the Apelech ritual group. Chairman of Aurukun since 1974, he launches the court case against Killoran over mining. In 1973, the church asks if the Aurukun Council would like to take over full self-management in 1974. The council, of which Donald is a member, restates its view that this is too soon but a transition process to self-management is put in place in 1974.

The waves lap gently on the shores of Aurukun and the trees whisper their secrets. The sea breeze cools the heat of the day. But this is no gentle meeting. Nor are there cool heads from the government. Killoran is master of all the Indigenous communities and rules with an iron hand. He is furious at this recalcitrant community. He thinks they are like rebellious children.

It is the 15th of March. The people look up at the light plane circling the community and coming in to land, the whirr of the engines ringing in their ears.

Porter and Killoran clamber off the plane; both in white shirt and tie, looking officious. They have a meeting with the people in the church rather than in the open under the mango trees where the people usually meet. They refuse to let the meeting be recorded on film. There is a resident film crew there who record many events of the two weeks in March 1978 and produce a documentary called *Takeover*[3], which I acknowledge as helping me to fill in some details of events. However, a community member uses a tape recorder to get some record of discussions. The church has a corrugated iron roof, red walls, and some of the walls are like layered slats. Fans spin inside as a light breeze stirs the fronds of nearby palm trees.

Porter fingers his mustache and raises his bushy eyebrows when he looks over the room at the expectant sea of black faces. He isn't really in the mood for a discussion but just wants to relay his intentions.

He says sternly,

> "The time has come, in your best interests, for us to take back the management of Aurukun. In a few months' time you'll be glad at the changes that have been made. The decision has been made. I didn't come here to mislead you. The decision has been made."

Geraldine is not cowered. She says forthrightly,

> "The state should not take over without our consent. Let us make up our minds."

Porter returns disparagingly,

> "This is the wisest and best way. If we had negotiated beforehand and made it public, there'd be a lot of discussion. Do you think we'd leave the decision for you to make?

In response to a question about the outstations, Porter takes a deep breath in exasperation.

> "The idea that people can go back to land which can no longer be effectively hunted on and lived on and pretend they are living some sort of hand down from the old days, I tell you that is a dream that will cost some people dearly. That's my view but we'll see how you go as time goes by. Try it. Try it and see what happens."

His voice seems to hold a challenge in it and the people react angrily. They have been speaking politely but now a few men shout at the same time. Women clap but some children start to cry. Porter closes down the meeting. He will not be challenged.

The women leave the church first, in their loose colorful cotton dresses, disappointed at the result. A bicycle is leaning against the church wall but most people are on foot. Porter and Killoran leave unceremoniously, as if glad to get out of there, getting in a green Land Rover to go back to the airport. The people are frightened. They are worried about their sacred land.

The same day, the federal Minister for Aboriginal Affairs, Ian Viner issues a press statement that he is committed to help the Aurukun and Mornington Island people with finance or legislation as required. This brings some hope at Aurukun and Mornington Island.

There is a reaction in the Australian Senate in Canberra to the proposed takeover. The following was tabled on 15th March in the Parliamentary Debates. "The letter is addressed to Mr J. C. Hooper, Division of World Missions, Uniting Church in Australia. It states:

> We, the undersigned members of the Aurukun Community Council, have, after extensive talks with the members of the Community of Aurukun, found that it is the people's wish to remain under the Administration of the Uniting Church of Australia.

> We would therefore appreciate it if you would pass this to the Synod of North Queensland, along with our thanks for their support. We look forward to working together in the future.
>
> The letter is signed by five members of the Aboriginal Council at Aurukun. They are Donald Peinkinna, Barry Ngakyunkwokka, Eric Kooila, Roy Landis and Fred Kerindun."

Also, "To Senator Bonner, Phone 726861, Canberra, ACT

> Council and community not consulted about government takeover. What is happening. Please help us.
>
> Larry Lanley, Prince Escort, Lawrence Dugong, Nelson Gavenor, Roger Kelly (Mornington Island Council)."

In that same debate on 15th March 1978 Senator Arthur Geitzelt, ALP NSW says,

> "On 25th January 1977, Mr Tomkins, the Queensland Minister for Lands, told the Queensland Parliament that he had vetoed the transfer of the Archer River lease, which had been purchased in the marketplace by the Aboriginal Land Fund Commission. The land was for the use of the traditional owners, who now reside in the Aurukun and Coen areas. It is ironic that such a blatant abuse of ministerial discretion should have been announced on Australia Day, and only two months after the land rights legislation had been passed. One can only say that it is perversity at its worst. We are confronted with an arbitrary, blatant and illegal decision by Mr Porter, the new Queensland Minister for Aboriginal and Islanders Advancement, who, as yet, has not even been sworn in before the Queensland Parliament. The Queensland Parliament met for only 38 days during the whole of last year. It has the worst parliamentary sitting record of all Australian parliaments. A man who has not yet been able to justify his position through parliamentary debate or decision, has made a determination

about these matters while the Parliament is in recess. It has been in recess for about six months. There has been no parliamentary debate on this matter."[4]

This was a relevant point to raise in this dispute as the Queensland government has the position that Aborigines should purchase land, not be given land rights. But then the government refuses to transfer the lease, preventing the sale going through.

Senator Jim Keeffe, ALP Qld says,

> "The real reason why this takeover, which will happen on 31st March, is being carried out is partly because of the co-operation between the State Government in Queensland and the mining developers. There is also intense animosity between the Premier and some Aboriginal people. One of the things that the Premier is trying to do, so he says, is prevent the development of a black State. He has made this statement publicly at least three times and it is one of the reasons why the Archer River Station deal did not go through. The Premier is now living in fear because the homelands movements are developing on Cape York. They are developing very satisfactorily. People are again able to bring back discipline into their families where there have been slight problems. The movements are fulfilling a very important role in the communities. I think there are some six or seven which have developed in this area.
>
> The case of Mornington Island is not greatly different. A considerable number of years ago, a decision was taken to improve the housing situation on Mornington Island. For three years the Department fought the Aboriginal population. The Department wanted the houses built in a certain area and the people who live on Mornington Island wanted them built in another area. For three years the timber lay rotting in the tropical weather and a lot of it was lost. Finally, the Queensland Department of Aboriginal and Islanders

> Advancement won and the houses were built where the Department wanted them."

Senator Bonner Qld Liberal is convinced bauxite is the reason for the takeover. He says,

> "…the Queensland Government rushed legislation through the Parliament in less than 50 hours. For the Queensland Parliament that was a lot of sitting hours. In view of the fact that it sits for only 30 days a year, the 50 hours must have been quite a strain on members. Because the Government wanted to get out the bauxite, it was prepared to sit for that length of time. It rushed through a piece of legislation giving the mining company the right to go ahead with its mining operations without proper consultation with the Aboriginal people or the Presbyterian Church, which at that time was responsible for the administration of Aurukun. I had the opportunity to accompany the Federal Minister for Aboriginal Affairs (Mr Viner) to Aurukun to talk with the Aboriginal people. We arrived there at about 1 p.m. on 21st January 1976. That afternoon we sat on the ground under the mango trees surrounded by 200 people of the Aboriginal community, together with their councillors, for six hours while the Minister for Aboriginal Affairs consulted with the Aboriginal people.
>
> The Minister and I, on our return to Canberra, consulted with the Prime Minister (Mr Malcolm Fraser). Just before our meeting concluded, I was feeling pretty low. I thought that we had tried but did not seem to have reached a satisfactory conclusion. The Prime Minister, with a broad grin on his face, said: 'Neville, I do not know what you are worrying about. There is a simple answer to the problem. I will report to Cabinet that the Queensland Government and the mining company will not be granted an export license until certain things (consultations) happen." [5]

It didn't stop Bjelke however.

Donald, Francis and another councillor went to Canberra to see Viner. The next day on the radio Viner said he'd received a telegram from Aurukun council saying that they didn't want the DAIA to take over from the church and asked for the Commonwealth to help and to visit. They and their legal advisor meet with Viner on 17th March in Canberra.

TV crews start to arrive in small planes, the first of many to come in the next three weeks. Hauling their cameras and sound gear, they interview Councillor Eric Kooila about the takeover. Eric, tall, slim and gray-haired, is a force to be reckoned with and says decisively:

> "No. I told them you are not getting permission from our law or your law to take over."

Gladys Tybingoompa, a dynamic younger leader with brown wavy hair, turns to the reporters and says,

> "So, I say all the government sees is the wealth on the land of poor Aboriginal people."

The reporter asks,

> "The Commonwealth will let you live on your tribal land but the state won't. Is that the case?"

Frowning, Gladys says,

> "The state won't let us have our freedom" while another leader says, "We want to develop on our own land."

On 16th March while some councillors are on their way to Canberra to see Viner, Gordon Coutts from the Uniting Church flies in from Mornington Island. It is the day after the visit of Porter and Killoran. Mick Miller and Clarrie Grogan from the North Qld Land Council are already at Aurukun and, joined by Eric and Gladys, meet him at the airstrip. Mick and Clarrie have already had extensive talks with the people. Clarrie is Mick's uncle, a former boxer of note and a key part of the Land Council team. Coutts is wearing a big brown felt hat and glasses. He is dressed casually with shorts and long socks. Mick is wearing a navy t-shirt with a red and white v-striped design on it and jeans. Gordon tells them that he has just come from meeting the people at Mornington Island and 158 adults told him they wanted the church to continue to administer the community with the help of the federal government. Eric meets Coutts barefoot, and tells him he strongly opposed Porter's plans to his face.

Gordon holds a hastily assembled public meeting of people sitting in small groups under the trees. He assures them that, in case they are hearing differently, "The moderator of the Uniting Church told Porter and Killoran straight away what the church had decided last October, that before any change, we want to know that the people agree. Yesterday, after the federal government met the House of Representatives and the Senate, they said they would not allow this to happen unless the people want it to."

Gordon excitedly elaborates,

> "Viner says if Porter says he is the crown, then Viner is the big crown. He will support the people if they want the church to stay."

Some of the Aboriginal men respond firmly. One man says,

> "They are liars. Killoran wants to send Ted Butler in as manager but we have a manager (Tony Morris) and council. This is our land and we say no."

Geraldine uses her hands to give emphasis to her statement,

> "We don't ask for money but we want our freedom and our traditional areas. Some greedy people in Qld want the minerals at Aurukun, Gordon. Three or four years ago we had visitors about this. But once we say no, it's no."

Another man said, "Tell them we say no." Others nod.

Gordon opens his arms wide and asks, "Do you want us to stay?"

There was a resounding yes. The Seven News TV was filming the meeting.

Gordon continued,

> "I hate to be formal but I need signatures" as he passes a petition around for people to sign. While it goes around, Gordon gets excited,
>
> "We're going to win. We've got Viner on our side." He laughs.

On 17th March, another plane comes in. On it is David Thompson, the federal MP for Leichhardt, their electorate. He asks for the people to be assembled again so he can speak to them. Dressed in white, he adjusts his hat and sunglasses and is happy to get a crowd. As the trees spread their shade, he offers,

> "Be sure that whatever you want, I'll help. I'm part of the federal government and it is the boss government. All the people of Australia in the 1967 referendum had a vote and 8 out of 10 of them in Qld said they wanted the federal government to be able to make laws for Aborigines. So, we have the right to do that and we are prepared to do that."

That evening, the news blares from the radio again. Viner says he has met with the Aurukun Council and is prepared to override the Qld government if he has to.

The next day, the Council return from Canberra and hold a meeting with the people to tell them the result of their meeting with Viner. Donald relays that Viner told him he had received his telegram and many others from around Australia expressing support for Aurukun and Mornington Island. While happy with the result, he seems to laugh a little nervously. It is a big responsibility on his shoulders.

A later photo of Chairman Donald Peinkinna, former Prime Minister Bob Hawke and Councillor Francis Yunkaporta photo Les O'Rourke/The Age

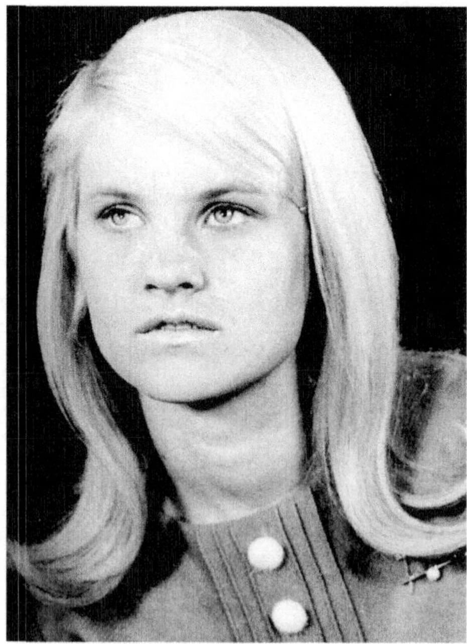

Author Barbara Russell Before Moving to Cairns

Mick Miller

Chapter 2

Battle With Bjelke Heats Up

Mick Miller, myself and the North Qld Land Council keep campaigning in support of the Aurukun and Mornington Island people. *The Cairns Post,* 22nd March 1978, reports Mick as saying,

> "The state government are treating the Aurukun Aboriginals as children and setting themselves up as 'The Great White Father' – the benevolent, or not-so-benevolent. dictator.
>
> Mr Porter is reported to have said to the Aurukun people the Queensland government is the father and the church is the mother – and the father is coming home to look after his family because the mother has not been able to do so. This is racism and paternalism of the worst kind."

It is ironic that Porter says to the people, "I come as a representative of the crown" to the Aurukun people, in all his pomposity. They know they are standing on the land of their forefathers. They also know the government calls it crown land and doesn't recognize their claim to it.

Porter accuses the church of brainwashing the Aboriginal people. The church informs Porter it will defy the eviction order and stay on after 1st April as long as the communities invite them to do so (*The Courier Mail,* 21st March 1978).

On 22nd March, Viner announces a game-changer - that the federal government plans to introduce self-management legislation for Aboriginal communities and he informs the Qld government.

On 23rd March the radio delivered its latest offering, with Aurukun and Mornington Island people hovering apprehensively to hear their fate. Porter announces he will ignore the federal government's threat of overriding it and press on with the takeover of Aurukun and Mornington Island at the end of the month. There is one week to go. Who will win?

As if to intimidate the people, a police plane circles over Aurukun a few days later. Watching it circle, some of the people have worried expressions while others are annoyed. When it lands, Sgt O'Rourke and a police inspector step off the plane with an air of authority and take a short walk around looking for anything suspicious. A few gruff remarks and they are gone again.

The next day, Greg Williams of the federal Department of Aboriginal Affairs (DAA) flies in. Tall and casually dressed, he strides along confidently and, in a collaborative tone, informs the council that the federal government will pass a law on 4th April to stop the Qld takeover. He then calls for a meeting with the people under the mango trees. He wants them to think about how they will handle the next few days,

> "What will happen in the 4-day gap between when the Qld government says they will take over and when the federal legislation is passed? Porter and Viner might get together and work something out. The federal government don't want to fight the state but we will support you."

Brow furrowing with worry, Eric asks,

> "What about the money as the state will cut off our funding on 31st March?"

Williams reassures them,

> "If the state does cut you off then Viner will put in the money to keep Aurukun and Mornington Island operating."

Eric smiles with relief but Gladys is troubled and says if Ted Butler comes in as DAIA manager, could they tell him there's no accommodation so go back. The question hangs unanswered.

Porter tells the federal government via a news announcement, "Not to interfere with the state doing its job and keep their noses out of it. We've had a degree of interference that is worse than the Whitlam government which was openly committed to centralization."

The tension is mounting. It's hard for the community to operate as normal with more news each day, more planes flying in each day, more officials calling for meetings nearly every day. How will it end? Williams confides to the council later,

> "Your solicitor in Brisbane can't ring you so I'm here in case something happens. There is some paperwork for the council to make it harder for the state to take over, if that's what you want."

A serious plan is put into action. It is for key Aurukun people to move into key locations and live there to prevent them being taken over. Donald and Barry Ngakyunkwokka start putting notices on the post office, police station, main office etc., that Aborigines live here and they can't enter these premises. Also, unless they have a permit, they will be sent back on the plane they arrive on. Donald erects a small green tent at the airport which he will live in. He puts up a sign that they can't go through the gate because it is private property. The bauxite-red dirt of the airstrip awaits those who step off the light planes but the sign "Welcome to Aurukun" is not for the state government. The welcome mat is now withdrawn.

On 27th March, a light plane arrives with Senator Neville Bonner and other federal parliamentarians: Senator Kathy Martin, Senator Knight, Mr Jull and Mr Hodges. Bonner has gray curly hair and is wearing cream trousers and a white shirt with a red tie. Qld Senator Kathy Martin's red dress stands out in the crowd. They sit on chairs while the people sit on the ground, as is their custom. Bonner stands and says he has talked Migaloo (white man's) way and now he'll talk Murri (Aboriginal) way and he talks in pidgin. This is a bit amusing, sincere as he is, because the Aurukun people don't speak in pidgin. He tells them "not to be *shamed*" but to speak up about what they want. He asks if they want federal intervention and, as a group, many say yes.

Another member of the federal team asks if anyone wants the state to take over and there is silence. Bonner encourages them not to wait to answer questions but to say what they want. However, they were asked if they wanted to keep their outstations. One Aurukun man, taking off his hat, replies "We Aborigines owned the land well before white man came." He says thank you and puts his hat back on again, his black hair glistening in the sun. The parliamentarians walk among the crowd to talk to them one on one to ascertain their views.

The following day, John Brown of BOEMAR arrives and goes down river in a small boat with the council and their advisors to get away from the TV crews. Their attention is not on the pristine scenery but on the serious matter at hand. Clambering off the punt, they sit on the ground in a semi-circle with John Brown in his city attire. They are receiving some legal advice from a young man when the rain comes beating down. As the wind stirs the trees, the group hurriedly retreats to a shelter which is little more than some corrugated iron on four poles. The rain beats noisily rattling on the roof as they continue to talk, seated on the sand with a briefcase incongruently part of the scene.

Peter White, from the Aboriginal Legal Service in Cairns, is at the meeting. A brown hat with chin cord to prevent it blowing away covers his ginger hair. He launches into his advice. He says the Council needs to meet anyone who comes into the community with questions such as "Do you have a permit? What are you doing here?" He said even if it's someone you know, you have to ask them these questions.

Eric emphasizes their concern,

> "It's up to the Council to remove staff not for the Qld government to be removing our manager for Ted Butler."

Later, Porter announces the state will still be taking over on Friday despite the passive resistance by the Aurukun people and their court action.

In *The Cairns Post,* 29th March 1978, Mick welcomes the Federal Government's decision to assume responsibility for Aboriginal Affairs in Queensland, saying it would help achieve self-determination. Mick says:

> "Queensland is the only State that has not handed this constitutionally given responsibility over to the Commonwealth Government. It is also the only State that controls Aboriginals under such racist legislation as the Queensland Aboriginals and Torres Strait Islanders Acts 1971."

Mick supports the call of the federal Opposition Leader, Mr Bill Hayden, in urging the Prime Minister, Mr Fraser, to recall Federal Parliament this week to pass emergency legislation to stop the Queensland Government's takeover of the two reserves. Mick also warns of a physical confrontation occurring at Aurukun if the Queensland government forces a takeover.

The paper reports that "Aurukun Aboriginals have already vowed to block State government access to key communication facilities – they have occupied the airstrip, police station, sawmill, post office, hospital and library."

Mick also answers Bjelke's criticisms re Aboriginal people owning land as apartheid and a black state. He says,

> "This is hypocritical because the Queensland Government has condoned apartheid since 1897 when the Queensland Aborigines Act was brought into being. Surely this is apartheid when a separate set of laws was instituted by the Government, not Aboriginal people, to govern Aboriginals on reserves separate from the rest of the community.
>
> If Aboriginal people prefer separate development, that should be up to them. It is only apartheid when it is forced on a minority group."

An article in the Melbourne *Telegraph* the following day reports Mick saying that half of the eighteen managers running the reserves in Queensland were recruited from white South Africans and Rhodesians by the Qld government. This was denied by DAIA Director Pat Killoran.

Mick and other NQLC delegates are on their way to Canberra to see the Minister for Aboriginal Affairs, Mr Viner, lobby other MPs and be in the gallery when the federal legislation goes through re Queensland communities. They stop over at a conference in Sydney.

The Sun, Melbourne on 30th March 1978, has a large photo of Mick as he travels the nation with an NQLC team raising media and financial support for the Aurukun and Mornington Island people's campaign. Mick also launches a petition to the House of Representatives in Canberra to take responsibility for Aurukun and Mornington Island.

However, shocking news came through the following day. The state government has done a deal with the federal government. Late on 29th March, Mr Nixon, the Minister for Transport, and Viner met with Bjelke-Petersen and his ministers in Brisbane and agreed for the state and the church to share responsibility for Aurukun and Mornington Island, again with no consultation with the Aboriginal people or the church on this proposal. Porter met with Professor Busch of the church and informed him.

The news report includes a statement by Mick Miller of the NQLC saying that the deal was a sellout to the Qld government by Viner. In *The Sydney Mornington Herald* article of 30th March 1978 "PM Rejects Deal on Aborigines" Mick says the deal is.

> "… disgraceful, shameful, deceitful, hypocritical and a sell-out."

The Aurukun community is devastated. Francis Yunkaporta says,

> "Viner dumped us in the dirt. The federal government should have talked to us first before making a compromise. We feel very sad."

But another shock! The next morning, the ABC national news announces that the federal government has reversed its compromise with the state government overnight. Viner instructs the government to press ahead with the legislation because of comments made by Bjelke last night which breach the agreement. Viner is to visit Aurukun and Mornington Island. Spirits start to lift again and hope rises. Maybe they will win the day after all.

Delegates from the Land Council go on a southern tour to coincide with the Federal Council for the Advancement of Aborigines and Torres Strait Islanders (FCAATSI) meeting in Canberra. Mick, Clarrie, Monty Pryor, Mark Noble, Joyce Hall and Ted Bowen travel to southern cities while I go to rallies in Brisbane with Rosena Toumese from Mapoon and Bob Holroyd from Aurukun. Marches in support of Aurukun and Mornington Island are held around the nation with 2,000 marching in Melbourne.

Mick is in Melbourne for a land rights meeting to raise support for the two communities and Laurie Oakes of *The Sun* interviews him on 30th March 1978 in an article entitled "Aurukun Deal Blocked, Viner: We will block Joh." He says he is skeptical of the way the federal government is handling the situation, adding further that the federal government had,

> "… to tackle Mr Bjelke-Petersen holus bolus, not just part time on the issue of two Aboriginal communities. The federal government has to tackle Bjelke-Petersen and take over administrative control of land councils (reserves) on all 18 or 19 Aboriginal communities in Queensland – just two reserves isn't good enough."

On the morning of 30th March, John Brown, Greg Williams and solicitors fly in from Weipa. They bring the newspaper with them, which has a photo of Donald by his tent. Williams informs Donald that Viner will be here just after lunch. Brown is quick to assure the people that the church has not agreed to the compromise. When Busch from the church learns of the decision, he and Senator Bonner go to the media that night and call it a sellout.

Brown tells them he is puzzled why Viner did it but says he must have been under a lot of pressure. He says that when Viner got back to Canberra, he met with Fraser. Bjelke was gloating he had another victory over the federal government. Porter notifies the media the state is going in on Saturday whether the people or the church like it or not. So, the federal government revoke the agreement. Williams says any agreement would have to be signed off by the people and the church anyway.

Viner Visit

Viner arrives in a fashionable short-sleeved blue safari suit, his gray sideburns contrasting with his brown hair. He meets with the council first inside a staff home, all sitting on chairs. Viner informs them any agreement will have to be authorized by the church and the Aboriginal people. Viner tells them,

> "The Premier said 'I couldn't care less what they (the federal government) said but I warned them of the consequences if they went ahead. There is no compromise. We just thew joint management into the ring to help the federal government and the church to get out of a spot.' So, I saw the PM. He agreed that because of what the Premier said there was no agreement. I'll recommend the government go ahead with the legislation."

Brown asks,

"What guarantee do we have that you won't do another deal with the state?"

Viner indicates that was not likely. Donald takes the occasional puff of a cigarette, as does Francis.

The same day, news came through that Bjelke is offering a 3-week cooling off period. They want the federal government to hold off on their legislation and Qld will hold off on the takeover. The people are getting weary of all the meetings, planes and TV crews and want their ordeal to end.

Viner meets the people sitting under the trees and declares there is no agreement unless they and the church agree to it. Dogs and cameramen wander around as people gather under the trees once more. The birds add their voices to the discussions. Viner, standing, says,

> "You are free Australian citizens with the right to manage your own affairs or be managed by who you pick." People clap. "Do you want to stay with the church?"

All say yes.

Gladys is still concerned. "Can Bjelke and Porter put who they want in here?"

Viner answers,

"Under the present law, yes."

Gladys winds up,

> "We speak strongly. If my grandfather was still here, he'd use a spear." We don't want to see another Mapoon."

Viner asks if they want joint management of the church and the DAIA and there are lots of voices saying no.

Geraldine points out why it would not work. She says,

> "The state government and church have different policies. It's impossible for us. We'd rather be with the church supported by the federal." Clapping breaks out.

Eric adds,

> "We don't want joint management. We have Tony Morris till he retires or gets sick." More clapping.

Viner is satisfied,

> "You've made it clear. Thanks, and God bless you.

On 31st March, Fraser makes a press statement that the federal government will provide direct support to Aurukun and Mornington Island and the church if necessary.

Viner holds a similar meeting in Mornington Island and has a similar response from the people.

At a news conference in Sydney on 3rd April, Mick is handed a telegram from the Prime Minister, Mr Fraser, saying that the federal government had prepared legislation and that in the event of the Qld government withdrawing funds from the reserves it controlled, the federal government would provide direct financial support. Asked by *The Canberra Times* in an article, "Bjelke-Petersen to use force" whether he thought the Premier would make a move before the federal legislation to block the threatened takeover, Mick replies,

> "Yes, knowing Bjelke-Petersen, he'll try anything. I'm certain that he'll move his staff in and that force will be used."
>
> In the same interview, Mick says "He's deliberately provoking a violent situation. Violence will be an excuse for him to say the church can't control the missions."

A news article on 4th April, "Government Accused of Sell-out on Land" reveals that the Commonwealth will go ahead with legislation to enable the Aboriginal communities in Qld to be self-managing but will not acquire the land. Mick, in his usual forthright manner, says it is still a sell-out,

> "No amount of talking will change the fact that as long as the Queensland government owns the reserves, people resident on them are going to be subject to the harassment of the Queensland police and the Department of Aboriginal and Islander Advancement.
>
> If the Federal Government was sincere, it would not need to legislate. It could simply acquire the reserves under the Land Acquisition Act and declare them Commonwealth land. That would stop the police from intimidating our people.
>
> In any case, Mr. Viner admitted at his press conference. the proposed legislation requires the consent and co-operation of

the Queensland Premier before it will accomplish anything. This is rather like Churchill asking Hitler's consent to abolish the Gestapo."

Commonwealth Passes Self-Management Act

The Commonwealth government passes self-management legislation on 7th April which enables reserves to manage themselves and come under federal government administration rather than the state government. It is called Aboriginal and Torres Strait Islanders (Queensland Reserves and Communities Self-Management) 1978. They expect this will solve the situation in Aurukun and Mornington Island and that other reserves will follow suit. Yarrabah and Mossman Gorge reserves both apply to come under the new federal legislation. Mr Alan Kynuna, a Yarrabah Councillor, telegrams the federal government advising them of a petition to this effect which is on its way.

Mick says the legislation will be useless unless it gives complete control of all the reserves and their administration to the federal government. He says if the NQLC doesn't agree with the bill, they will make a "ruckus" in parliament from the public gallery. He let the press know the Yarrabah people met to show their support of the Aurukun and Mornington Island people on the previous Friday and the police broke up the meeting.

Prompted by the dispute between the Queensland and federal government over Aurukun and Mornington Island, the Aboriginal legal service in Sydney appeals to the International Court of Justice for advice on the legal status of Aborigines on the ownership of Australia.

The NQLC and the National Aboriginal Conference (NAC) of which Mick is a part, spend four weeks lobbying Canberra MPs re the legislation. Mick watches the legislation go before both houses of parliament and urges amendments to the legislation to make it retrospective to 31st March. He is worried Bjelke-Petersen will outmaneuver the Commonwealth. At a rally in Melbourne, he predicts this will happen. Senator Geitzelt moves for amendments but the liberal senators say they are not in a confrontation situation with the Queensland government.

Bjelke Outwits The Commonwealth

Despite the valiant efforts of the Aurukun and Mornington Island people, the church, the North Qld Land Council and other supporters, Bjelke-Petersen outwits the Commonwealth government by abolishing these two reserves overnight on 7th April so that the Commonwealth legislation to give them self-management cannot apply as it depends on them being reserves. In the end, the commonwealth government caves in to the state and doesn't enforce its responsibilities given in the 1967 referendum to legislate for Indigenous people. It can amend its legislation in a counter move. However, it capitulates and lets the Aboriginal people down despite all its promises.

On 8th April 1978, a front-page news report titled *I told you so: Aboriginal leader* reports that Mick urged PM Fraser the previous night to, "Move right now tonight or tomorrow – by issuing a special Government Gazette to acquire the reserves under the Land Acquisition Act" but to no avail. In an interview with Arthur Gray, Mick says:

> "We knew exactly what he (Premier) would do, but the senators here (in Canberra) didn't listen. They ignored us. They ignored our advice. They didn't cross the floor, acting on the amendments and, as a result of this, it's the old case of 'I told you so' and that's what I have told them: 'I told you so.'
>
> We explained that this would happen, and we explained this particular point, that if they didn't make it retrospective from 31st March that Mr Bjelke-Petersen would move in and excise the reserves and say to the Commonwealth government 'Your definition of a reserve only covers up till the time when the Act was brought in' which could be next week."

Mick takes no joy in being able to say, 'I told you so.' He warns the repercussions are quite serious. The Aurukun and Mornington Island people are "Outlawed." He declares, "They now have no legal right to live in their own country. They are squatters …

> "Already the Queensland Government is starting to intimidate our people on the reserves. Mark Noble, the police sergeant from Yarrabah, was down here lobbying. He went back to Yarrabah this morning (Friday). He was fired. Mrs Rose Colless, one of the Commissioners of the Queensland Government's Commission of Inquiry into the Future of Reserves was also fired this morning.
>
> The managers on the reserves are threatening our people that if they elect to be administered by the commonwealth, they will lose the reserves and be thrown out of their homes and off the land.
>
> Basically, what happened is that the federal legislation was framed to deal with Aboriginal reserves. The Queensland Premier simply abolished the reserve status of Aurukun and Mornington Island so that the federal legislation could not apply to them. Bjelke-Petersen had snookered Fraser in a humiliating defeat with Aboriginal people as the losers. It could have amended its federal legislation but didn't."

Meanwhile a 180km an hour cyclone is roaring towards the Gulf of Carpentaria so there's not just a physical storm brewing but a possible natural disaster. Mick tells *The Sydney Morning Herald* in an article entitled "Qld Abolishes Reserves to Block Fraser" on 8th April:

> "My people at Aurukun and Mornington Island are taking a terrible beating. They are being bashed tonight by a political cyclone: and they will be bashed tomorrow by a real cyclone.
>
> The Qld action makes Vorster of South Africa and Smith of Rhodesia look like kindergarten teachers with regards to racial discrimination."

Another Compromise

Four days later, Bjelke, Hinze and Porter fly to Canberra for talks with Fraser and his ministers. Discussions are held late on Tuesday night 11th April and they come to an agreement that the state government would lease the land on the reserves to Aurukun and Mornington Island and give them shire council status. The Queensland Premier and the Prime Minister issue a joint statement. No Aboriginal people are involved in the behind closed doors discussions. Nor is the church involved, Rev Busch saying he is bitterly disappointed in the result and the Aurukun people are "Utterly devastated." Rev Brown said the agreement did not meet the aspirations of the people of Aurukun for land rights, self-management and decentralization. (*Aboriginal People 'Let Down'* 13th April 1978).

Bjelke tells the media when pressed that they are all winners, not wanting to jeopardize the agreement as before. Back at Aurukun, Francis Yunkaporta expresses his disappointment,

> "The federal government backed out and compromised with no consultation. We spoke for a long time but they don't listen. Not that they didn't understand. They understood but won't give us the right to own tribal land. But we won't lie down."

Senator Neville Bonner calls on the state government to at least give them a 99-year lease but the State grants a 50-year lease. I believe the uncertainty of these 50-year leases makes Aurukun a strong supporter of native title when the opportunity comes up later. They are later to run the famous Wik case as a follow up to Mabo.

The agreement between the governments is as follows:

> "Recognizing our mutual obligation with regard to the wishes and the welfare of the Aboriginal peoples at Aurukun and Mornington Island, the two Governments after long and earnest discussion, have reached the following agreement that in order to achieve self-management for Aurukun and Mornington Island communities:

> A local government authority for each to be created on the boundaries of the existing reserves.
>
> The local government council will consist of the existing councils until the next State Local Government council elections which will take place next April. These councils will be the managing authority.
>
> In order to support the communities, there will for each one be a coordinating and advisory committee to the Council consisting of people representative of authorities delivering services including one representative of the Commonwealth Department of Aboriginal Affairs.
>
> The Queensland Government has offered to consult with the Commonwealth Government on the terms of legislation required to provide for self-management through the operations of local government, in order to achieve mutual agreement between the relevant Ministers. In the context of that agreement, the Queensland Government plans to grant to each local government authority a special lease of the area, to secure the preservation of the people's traditional rights, use and occupancy of the land. The Premier of Queensland, after conferring with his Minister for Aboriginal and Island Affairs (Mr Porter) and his Minister for Local Government (Mr Hinze) believes that action in terms of this agreement could be introduced next week into the Queensland Parliament."

The Premier boasts to the media that he contacted the Prime Minister to ensure no more funding goes to the North Qld Land Council and he agreed. On 7th April Mick calls him out as "Mischief-making," saying that Bjelke had made a deal with Fraser from the outset that we would not be funded despite having elected delegates from every reserve and town from Townsville and Palm Island to the tip of Cape York. Mick says,

> "On 9th December 1976, the Premier wrote to the Prime Minister, Mr Fraser, seeking an assurance that the

Commonwealth would not fund the North Queensland Land Council. This he obtained."

Other Reserves Apply For Federal Legislation

Yarrabah and Mossman Gorge reserves both apply to come under the new federal legislation. The NQLC organizes a rally against the Commonwealth-State compromise on Aurukun and Mornington Island. It is held in Munro Martin Park on 13th April and Yarrabah holds its own rally. Mick releases a press statement saying carloads of police invade Yarrabah reserve to break up a peaceful demonstration of 200 Aborigines who are supporting their relatives at Mornington Island and Aurukun. He says there is nothing in Mr Viner's legislation that would prevent similar incidents on reserves all over Queensland. The Commonwealth does not take up the requests of these two communities so the legislation has never been used.

Cairns Rally

The following day, *The Cairns Post* carries a photo of me passionately addressing people at the Cairns rally. A large number of people are gathered in the park of this beautiful tropical city. Others who address the rally are Clarrie Grogan and Robert Smallwood from the NQLC, Commissioner Rose Colless, Len Watson from the Aboriginal legal service, John Grainer, Mareeba reserve and Evelyn Scott, Aboriginal hostels. Evelyn protests the sacking of Rose Colless from the Aboriginal and Islander Commission. She also calls for the other members of the Commission to be sacked as they are government appointed. Some people sit under shade trees, others stand, listening intently.

As I look out at the group of Indigenous people, it doesn't occur to me that it might be incongruous that I am the only non-Indigenous person making a speech, my blond hair and blue eyes irrelevant. The paper carries the story,

> "Ms Russell said she could not see how the Aboriginal people could be given self-management if the Queensland Act was still operating.
>
> "She said she saw trouble on the reserves until the land rights issue was resolved, because a tug-of-war would develop between the state and federal governments. The state government is planning to introduce legislation in Brisbane next week to tie up its agreement with the Commonwealth for control of the disputed Aurukun and Mornington Island communities."

Earlier, on 8th April, I spoke at a rally about the situation in Aurukun and Mornington Island in Cairns, re the gradual erosion of personal civil liberties in Qld. Over 100 people attended despite the rain. Rose Colless and members of parliament also spoke. *The Cairns Post* headlined it "Protest Rally a Great Success" on 10th April.

While I am speaking in Cairns on 13th April, Mick is in Brisbane raising support for Aurukun and Mornington Island. *The Courier Mail,* 15th April 1978, runs an article "The law takes a long look." Mick addresses a rally of over 1000 people at the Roma Street Forum, an open area near the largest railway station in Qld. Two police are photographed by the paper watching through binoculars from a high building nearby. No doubt there are paddy wagons just out of sight, waiting to arrest people if there is any sign of trouble.

Mick's teacher's voice is more like that of a media announcer as he addresses the rally. He never needs notes, being very good at off-the-cuff speaking, borne of many years in front of a classroom and his depth of knowledge of Aboriginal affairs. He has a way of cutting through and can be confronting or charming as the occasion demands. He tells the rally the Aurukun and Mornington Island people want self-management from the federal government and to be administered by the Uniting church. A group called Concerned Christians attends the rally and spokesman Father Dick Pascoe says that in Queensland, a concerned citizen is treated as if they are a communist. The Anglican and Catholic Bishops publicly support the Aurukun and Mornington Island people.

Mick and the NQLC threaten to take the matter of Aurukun and Mornington Island to the World Court. In "Aurukun Threatens Appeal to World Court," Mick tells *The Australian* on 13th April 1978 that was because the shire council status did not give them land rights,

> "We will fight the government in the World Court and take our case to Amnesty International. It's blatant racism."

On 17th April, the Aurukun Council sends a telegram to the North Queensland Land Council saying it is opposed to the leasehold agreement between the governments and is seeking our support to lobby against it. The Innisfail sub-committee of the Land Council organizes a meeting in Innisfail on Saturday night to discuss the issue and hear a report from Mick about his recent trip to Canberra, Melbourne, Sydney and Brisbane. Mick says the federal-state agreement,

> "puts Aurukun and Mornington Island squarely under state government control and gives the Uniting church the boot. The State Government will be nominating most of the members on the advisory body to the Aboriginal councils.
>
> Bjelke had Viner where he wanted him. The federal-state agreement reached in Canberra early last Wednesday morning was nothing but a sell-out by the Federal Government." ("Aurukun Aboriginals want freehold land" *The Cairns Post,* 18th April 1978)

What is in the press release and not in the newspaper article are a number of other important points made by Mick:

> "When the Premier degazetted Aurukun and Mornington Island as we predicted, the federal government men were like stunned mullets! The southern press reported me with the headline – 'I told you so!' So, then the federal legislation was useless for those two reserves.

> I am utterly opposed to Aurukun and Mornington Island being special leases. Self-management includes land rights in the eyes of the people. Mr Viner does not even know the length of the lease, whether it is 2 years or 99 years. That's how responsible he was when he made the agreement. Mr Viner maintains however, that he will intervene to acquire the land at Aurukun and Mornington Island under the Commonwealth Lands Acquisition Act if the people do not like the legislation the state government brings in next week. But I'm sick and tired of hearing him say he'll intervene when all he does is sell us out."

Innisfail delegate to the NQLC, Mr Alec Stevens, says that a marine biologist had found Mornington Island had the best potential of any reserve for a fishing industry and he believed the Premier wanted it for a tourist resort to please his multinational friends.

Joyce Hall, the Weipa delegate to the NQLC and who tours UK and Europe with Mick, says she is disappointed in the Aboriginal Advisory Council members who say the state government is a good master. "We, their servants, have been treated like slayed cattle," she says.

Joyce makes a moving speech,

> "Comalco are mining in my tribal land and made it like a desert place. They've made our oysters red with bauxite. Where is our royalty money? The Queensland government get it. Comalco and the Queensland government walked over us like a clean carpet making us dirty under their boots."

She talks about how, in 1963, the Mapoon people had been removed from their land by police, at gunpoint, to make way for mining. Labor Member for Cook, Mr Bob Scott, who is at the meeting with colleagues Bill Wood and Peter Moore comments on the Mapoon people who have been removed to Hidden Valley (New Mapoon) near Bamaga. He says,

> "New Mapoon is one long string of houses, falling down. They are the worst houses in my electorate. You can't get up

> the steps because the steps are missing. This is mismanagement, yet the state government wants to take over two more communities."

The Land Council is being so effective, the Liberal-National government in Queensland decides to attack it under parliamentary privilege as being communist. *The Cairns Post,* 22nd April 1978, carries the headline "Miller rejects 'communists' tag." Three MPs are involved in the attack – Dr Scott-Young (Liberal, Townsville), Mr Martin Tenni (NP, Barron River) and Aboriginal affairs Minister Charles Porter. Porter says the Land Council is not an Aboriginal organization and includes left-wing communists. Mick says the allegations have no foundation and all members of the Land Council are Aboriginal and all staff are Aboriginal, except one. That one, of course, is me. Clarrie was personally singled out by Mr Tenni as communist though he has never been a member of any political party.

Porter also claims in the above report, that communists are active in Aurukun and that many people have left their homes. Mick says,

> "The minister is deliberately misleading parliament. Six tribes moved back to their land at Aurukun in a movement that started two years ago. To assert that they moved out of Aurukun through fear of the Land Council is ridiculous and untrue."

We have a laugh when Porter says in the Queensland Parliament, "The Federal Department of Aboriginal Affairs is riddled with *left-wing communist activists* who have been put there in the Whitlam days." (*The Australian* 21st April 1978) He will bring a group from Aurukun to Brisbane on Monday to talk some sense into them.

Porter is furious that Clarrie is going around Aboriginal communities in north Queensland in a charter plane getting signatures on a petition asking for Commonwealth control. He asserts that Clarrie is waiting till people get drunk before getting them to sign it which I know is not true. Porter wants to know where the money is coming from. He says he suspects the World Council of Churches, but can't prove it. (*The Courier Mail,* 21st April 1978)

On 17th April, Viner meets with Queensland Ministers in Brisbane and on 18th April, he meets with council representatives in Mount Isa. Over the next two days, Viner again visits the Mornington Island and Aurukun Communities.

Porter does not fly the elected Aboriginal Council to Brisbane, or any of the clan elders for a press conference to say Aurukun supports the Queensland government's position. Instead, they approach an Aurukun Aboriginal living in Weipa to try to find people who support the government and offer them a free trip to Brisbane. However, Porter's plan is sprung when the person approached, Neil Peinkinna, shows the telegram from Killoran to Gladys Tybingoompa, a key Aurukun leader and NQLC delegate. Speaking to *The Cairns Post,* 27th April 1978, in an article headlined "Porter's claims refuted," she says that the delegates did not go to Brisbane of their own accord as Porter claims,

> "Mrs Tybingoompa claimed a telegram had been sent late last week to Mr Neil Peinkinna in Weipa asking him to go to Aurukun to persuade someone from Aurukun to go to Brisbane last Monday to talk to State Parliament. Mr Peinkinna is the brother of Mr Donald Peinkinna, the Chairman of the Aurukun Community Council. … Neil told me that if I was on the state side, I and others would get a free trip to Brisbane."

On the same day, Rev Gordon Coutts says, the delegates in Brisbane do not represent Aurukun but are Aboriginals from Weipa and Aboriginals from Aurukun who live at Weipa.

The state government are up to their old game of divide and rule.

Chairman Donald Peinkinna with his Tent at Aurukun Airstrip 18th March 1978 photo supplied

Mick Miller saying "I told you so." photo supplied

Barbara Russell Wearing FNQ Sports Foundation T Shirt Designed by Enoch Tranby. The FNQ Sports Foundation was an Indigenous organization founded by Mick Miller

Chapter 3

Getting Married in the Middle of the Political Conflict

State Government Debates Local Government Bill

On 27th April, the state government debates[6] the Local Government (Aboriginal Lands) Bill introduced the day before. It is instructive to see their real feelings about Indigenous people and their concerns: the creation of a black state, or Indigenous people owning and managing land as a group; affirmative action programs being seen as reverse discrimination; the old debate as to who is an Aborigine because of intermarriage; the belief they can't think for themselves and it must be communist stirrers like Mick, Clarrie and the federal government who are influencing them; land rights; mineral rights and state vs federal rights. The Member for Cook ALP, Mr Bob Scott, says,

> "I must say that there is no wind of change blowing in Queensland – none whatsoever – only a hot wind of racial discrimination." He makes the point that the Bill is simply the notorious Qld Aborigines Act with a new cover and that the coordinating and advisory committee to the councils will ensure the councils have no power. The committee of three representing Mr Hinze, Mr Porter and Mr Viner will see the

> federal government outnumbered. He continued that de-registering the reserves made the Aboriginal people worry if they were stateless. He was also concerned the Qld government had the power to decide who could reside on these communities."

Mr Martin Tenni, the Nationals MP for Barron River says,

> "… we have the Mick Millers and Clarrie Grogans going in and stirring them up, telling them all sorts of untruths, scaring the hell out of them with their *stand over* tactics. They are, unfortunately, accepting the advice of these stirrers."

He goes on to say, mentioning low housing rentals and mining royalties,

> "I say very definitely that in Australia today there is discrimination against whites … I am no more racist than anyone else. All I ask is that there be equal rights and privileges for all."

Dr Norman Scott-Young, Liberal MP for Townsville raises a key point in the State-Commonwealth fight, mentioning s106 and s107 of the constitution.

> "When this legislation was first proposed, I could not see that it was legal. Firstly, I could not see that the Commonwealth had any power to make a State within a State, because the States have maintained their sovereignty."

He continues that he wants to know who is an Aborigine and that this matter should be referred to the High Court "so we can find out where our money is going."

I thought we had gone past this point but our illustrious government is still fixated on it, with Scott-Young telling Parliament,

> "Anybody who claims to have Aboriginal blood automatically receives a handout. Previously a half-caste was not recognized by his race, he was not accepted and the women were not even listened to at all. A women's voice counted for nothing. Some

> of the most active radicals in the state are women who actually have no Aboriginal blood at all. They have Negro, Indian and Chinese blood and they classify themselves as Aborigines in this State."

Bob Scott replied, "You are a racist." Of course, he denied it.

Mr Bob Moore, Liberal MP Windsor, complains about special rights of Aboriginals and how the federal government discriminates against whites and he goes on to say,

> "People ask 'Whose country is it?' Some say it is the Aborigines' country. It is my country, too; I was born here. Which other country can I go to?"

Mr Hinze is surprised and says he thought Moore was born in Scotland. Mr Moore says his father was. Moore goes on to say,

> "If someone had burnt the history books the Aborigines would not be any the wiser. They do not read; someone else has to tell them that they have the right of ownership. They have no more right to this country than you or I, Mr Hewitt (Chairman of Committees). We all have equal rights."

Aboriginals can certainly read and, if they couldn't, they didn't need anyone to tell them they own the land. They know it was passed on from their forefathers through the generations before European settlement. Moore finally discusses the bill by his government that they are debating,

> "One of the sad things about the Bill now being introduced is that it is discriminatory. Even though it discriminates in favor of the Aborigines, it tends to create a division in the community that will not be of benefit to them in the long run. We should be seeking to integrate them in the community. That was Government policy; we are now departing from it.
>
> "... by giving one group self-government or self-determination we are sowing the seeds of apartheid or of a separate nation or a black State ... these areas (all the Aboriginal communities in the

> north) will never be viable. Someone asks, 'What are they producing there?' I will tell him what they are producing. They are producing black babies in vast numbers. Virtually the only product is children. Probably that is their own business, but the Australian taxpayer is paying all the bills."

Mr Jack Houston Labor MP Bulimba queries that this Bill is supposedly called model legislation. He is not happy that they used the Land Act to declare by Order in Council that Mornington Island and Aurukun Aboriginal reserves are abolished leaving the people with no community.

Mr Porter quickly interjects, "You would have let the Federal Government acquire our land, would you?"

Mr Hinze closes the discussion saying he would reply to comments at the second reading of the Bill.

Mapoon and Hopevale communities also ask for federal instead of state control and Weipa Council is discussing it. The Qld government fears it will lose "its" Aborigines to the commonwealth government.

Land Council And Concerned Christians Group

Joyce Hall does a national tour with Mick to support Aurukun and Mornington Island. He says he will be approaching the UN and the world court. Australia needs to be condemned for the same discrimination as South Africa and Rhodesia. He says the Land Council has had a huge impact since it was set up and it has a base on every reserve with two elected delegates and one delegate for each town in North Queensland. The full council meets twice a year and the 15-member committee meets four times a year. He is pleased that 10,000 signatures are now on a petition to rid the reserves of state government control and come under the Commonwealth after an NQLC meeting in Weipa decides that is the way to go. Frustrated, Mick says,

> "They (the commonwealth government) have got to come out and deliver to Bjelke now instead of softening him up with blows here and there. It's like a game of chess with Aborigines as the chess pieces."

The Concerned Christians group, one of whom is my friend the Rev Noel Preston, are holding prayer vigils in Brisbane re the situation at Aurukun and Mornington Island. They keep in touch with us re developments. In an extraordinary move, Queensland police arrest 13 of them, including three clergymen at Queens Park on Sunday towards the end of April. The arrests come after the Christian group hold a prayer meeting in King George Square. They are walking along the footpath to Parliament House to continue their vigil there. They are stopped three times in four blocks and told it is illegal to sing hymns while walking on the footpath. So, the Concerned Christians whistle the gospel songs only to be stopped again and told it was illegal to whistle Christian songs. They are not protest songs.

When the group arrives at Queens Parade, the site of Brisbane's first Anglican Church, they sit on the grass and sing hymns again. Police then tell them it is illegal to sing hymns on crown land. Police menacingly surround the group and order them to disperse from their "illegal assembly". Police push them onto the footpath and then tell them they are obstructing pedestrian traffic. Thirteen are then arrested for not obeying police instructions and resisting arrest with most spending the night in jail till they are bailed.

"So, it seems there was a new decree in Queensland," joked one commentator – "Thou shalt not sing on Crown land and no singing, humming or whistling of hymns on the streets of Brisbane. It is hard to believe that this is Australia."

The Anglican and Catholic Bishops come out in support of Aurukun and Mornington Island.

Local Government Bill Passes

The Queensland parliamentary debate that follows is a vicious attack on Aboriginal people generally, with Member for Barron River, Martin Tenni, saying that Aborigines in his electorate "love filth" and wreck their houses. He also thinks white people are being discriminated against by having to get permission from the Aboriginal council to visit Aurukun or Mornington Island. Mick replies in *The Cairns Post* the next day, 28th April 1978, "Black leaders blast claim as racist" saying that Mr Tenni's attitude is "Straight out racism." The recently sacked Rose Colless agrees.

Member for Cook, Bob Scott, is also concerned at the racist undertones of the debate. He says that the bill they were debating – the Local Government (Aboriginal Lands) Bill 1978 is virtually the old Queensland Aborigines Act under a new title. The Shire Clerk will be similar to the white managers they already have on state-run communities who hold all the power. Also, instead of the Council having their delegate on the Advisory Committee for these new shires, a position will be created for Mr Killoran or his nominee. He says the bill has "Absolutely nothing in common with the Local Government Act which effectively controlled activities of normal shire councils."

The state government's legislation passes despite representations from Aurukun and Mornington Island. Mick releases a press statement on 3rd May 1978 saying the Premier has "Pulled the wool over Fraser's eyes again," and that Fraser is a "Babe in the woods," when it comes to negotiating with Bjelke. He makes the point that the Queensland legislation is not a compromise with the federal government. He points out,

> "The Commonwealth has the constitutional power to override the State on Aboriginal matters. The Queensland strategy has been to shift the base of their control away from the Aboriginal Acts to the Local Government Acts, which is a safe area for Queensland because the Commonwealth has no power in local government matters."

He outlines a number of other concerns – that it removes the protection of the Qld Discriminatory Laws Act 1975 as it is based on the definition of a reserve in the Qld Act. It voids the Commonwealth's power to acquire reserves under s15 of its new self-management act for the same reason. It also creates a mechanism where all or part of the land can be resumed for mining or tourism etc. i.e., "Public purposes," without compensation or appeal. This would then maximize the compensation payable if the Commonwealth sought to acquire the land under the Land Acquisition Act as it will be more valuable than Aboriginal reserve. The implications are staggering.

On 4th May, Nixon and Viner visit Brisbane to talk to Hinze and Porter. A deputation from Mornington Island, including its legal adviser, Frank Purcell, also meets Fraser and Viner in Canberra. As a last-ditch effort, the Aurukun Council goes to Canberra and meets with Fraser and Viner on Thursday night. They are to come away very disappointed. An article headed "Disillusioned with Canberra, ANGERS AURUKUN, Ministers accused of siding with Qld" in *The Cairns Post,* 8th May 1978 Canberra (AAP) describes the scene,

> "Relations between the Federal Government and the Aurukun Aboriginal Council plummeted last night with the release of an open letter to the Prime Minister, Mr Fraser. In it the Council accused the Federal Government of siding with the Queensland Government over the State's legislation on the Aurukun and Mornington Island reserves.
>
> It was now apparent the Commonwealth would not acquire Aboriginal land in Queensland as it had at first threatened. According to the open letter, Mr Fraser told the Aboriginals that the amount of money involved in acquisition was not a consideration but that the Commonwealth did not want to have a political confrontation with Queensland. A spokesman for the Council said that the Commonwealth's position changed to where the Aboriginals were told they would have to 'live with' the legislation.

> The open letter (signed by their solicitor Frank Purcell) says, 'We came away totally disillusioned with you and your government as an ally.' Council members had time and again said they did not want to be under the Qld Local Government Act and a State Government. 'You heard and you did not respond,' the letter said."

Mornington Island Speaks

In a video called *Aurukun and Mornington Island 1978* by Jeune Pritchard and Luc Pelissier[7] of the Qld Solidarity Group, Chairman of Mornington Island, Larry Lanley, describes the hurt and frustration of the community. He says of the government, "They don't listen to us." Larry's curly black hair frames his smooth, fine-featured black face. The interviewer asks him what will the community do if the federal government doesn't help. He considers his reply and says,

> "Go bush … We don't trust the DAIA because we have homes destroyed by the cyclone two years ago not yet repaired."

This beautiful beachside community, with families using small boats to travel around, also has scenes of devastation with destroyed housing. The children nearby do a traditional dance – "Shake a leg."

Councillor Prince Ascot is with Larry. Some gray stubble frames Prince's slim face. Well-spoken and thoughtful like Larry, he says,

> "They should take notice of us or we're done."

The interviewer asks him,

> "Will you throw the DAIA off like Aurukun did?"
>
> "Yes" he replies without hesitation. "… this bill will be unworkable because the community don't like it."

Annie Chong, a vivacious young woman fears the takeover will, "Take our life, happiness, freedom, ways of hunting and camping. Leading our children to a European lifestyle."

DAA worker John Ormond explains the federal government already has a role at Mornington Island helping to set up a cattle business.

Porter speaks out determinedly,

> "If you believe self-government means Indigenous people can set up enclaves with a different type of government, I'm utterly opposed to it."

More Parliamentary Debate

On 10th May in the Senate, Senator Keeffe says,

> "There are people in the gallery today, I will put some of their names on record, who are sad and disillusioned. They have continued in this battle for their own land through their whole lifetime. I refer in particular to the Chairman of the Aurukun Council, Donald Peinkinna, to the former chairman, Francis Yunkaporta and to the others who are here: Barry Ngakyunkwokka, Roy Landis, Rowan Pootchemunka and Benjamin Kongotema. These people have been at the forefront of the struggle over a long period. Some time ago I wrote to the Secretary-General of the United Nations complaining of the lack of action by the Federal Government and of the drastic action that was taken in the then projected takeover of Aurukun and Mornington Island by the Queensland Government. I received a communication from the representative of the Secretary-General saying that the matter had been referred to the United Nations office at Geneva ..."[8]

Senator Keeffe continues,

> "The North Queensland Land Council set out its policy in a very succinct way, in half a dozen paragraphs. I propose to read only three or four of those paragraphs because I think they also ought to go into the record on this historic occasion

when the Government is repudiating the Aborigines of this country. The policy states:

1. Immediate ownership of tribal land by respective tribal groups.
2. That all Aboriginal reserves be handed over to the respective Aboriginal groups, and that the land be effectively controlled and owned by the Aboriginals in that area under their law and customs.
3. That Aboriginal lands include total rights to all natural resources, and that present mining and prospecting be suspended until negotiations are held with Aboriginals.

… The document of the North Queensland Land Council in a general paragraph states:

There are two different types of land claims; traditional claims and needs claims. Traditional claims are where there are strong tribal ties to the land e.g., Ti-Tree, Peret or Kendall River at Aurukun. Needs claims are where the Queensland Government has interfered so much that Murris from different areas have been brought in to confuse the picture: e.g., Palm Island and Mapoon would probably be considered needs claims.'

Ti-Tree, Peret and Kendall River, together with two or three other areas, are the homelands of the people from Aurukun and their tribal groups and it is to those areas that they have returned. This is the last thing that Mr Bjelke-Petersen wants to see happen. Four of those people whose names I read out a few moments ago wrote a letter to the Vice-President of the United States when he was in Canberra a few days ago. It is now history that he refused to accept the letter. The relevant information is set out in the last paragraph of that letter. It was to have been handed by the Vice-President to President Carter. It states:

> 'We ask for your help as President of the United States as one of the reasons we are losing control of our land and way of life is because the Queensland Government wants our land so that the Tipperary company - that is one of the three companies in the consortium, an American company - can mine the bauxite in the ground at Aurukun. We think that you would consider it wrong if Aborigines were to lose their land so that an American company can make money.'
>
> Another objectionable thing about this legislation is that it is referred to as an 'Aboriginal Lands' Bill. The only way that term is applicable is because through that legislation, the State Government, in collaboration with the Federal Government, is taking away land from the Aborigines in these two communities.
>
> That Bill gives the Queensland Government power to do the following: Set aside any part of the lease for unspecified public purposes, such as mining, tourism and national parks; under clause 16, to sack the Aboriginal council if it does not act in accordance with the wishes of the Queensland Government; under clause 27 (2), to determine who can enter into either shire; under clause 34, to approve or not approve the appointment by either shire council of a town clerk; under clause 18, to appoint an advisory committee consisting of two appointees who are Queensland Ministers and one appointee who is the Commonwealth Minister for Aboriginal Affairs. The Commonwealth Government will again be outnumbered by the State Government"

Discussion followed on recriminations over the Qld government making the federal government legislation re the two communities invalid on the same day it was triumphantly passed. Senator Cavanagh reminded them that Senator Gietzelt wanted to pass an amendment that would have prevented the state demolishing their initiative. He reminded them it was that:

> "Aboriginal Community' means a community of persons that, on 31st March 1978, was a community for Aborigines for the purposes of the Aborigines Act."

Senator Missen responds that it might have invalidated the legislation and that was the risk.

Senator Cavanagh replies with an issue that has still not been resolved,

> "No one really knows what power the Australian public gave to the Commonwealth in the referendum of 1967. It gave the Commonwealth power to make particular rules for the people of any race over whom it has power to make laws. Whether the courts will uphold the proposition that that gives the Commonwealth power to acquire land to establish settlements is something I do not know. That is a matter which I would be very hesitant to put to the High Court, if that were to be the end of the matter, in view of some recent judgments which have been given by it.
>
> One such decision was to the effect that the Commonwealth has power to acquire property, on just terms, from any State or person for any purpose in respect of which the Parliament has power to make laws. Let us put that decision to the test. Everyone realizes today that the problems of the Aurukun and Mornington Island reserves cannot be settled until we have acquired the land and have given it to the Aboriginals under conditions similar to those on which we have given land to the Aboriginals of the Northern Territory. Nothing else will satisfy the Aboriginal people. Nothing else will satisfy those people in Australia who believe in justice for Aboriginals.
>
> Let us acquire the land and see what happens. If we do not have the power to acquire land, we should tell that to the Aboriginals so that they do not build up false hopes. If we do not have the power to acquire land for the purpose of establishing settlements then we must make another appeal to the Australian people to give us that power."

Senator Cavanagh wants to confront the issue head-on. He was the minister who supported the Mapoon people with a grant, to re-establish their community which the state burnt down. When there is no response to this proposal, Senator Bonner adds another issue,

> "I believe also that clause 7 is not in the best interests of the people. It says that the grant is not to include improvements. Does it mean that the houses, the shops, the stores, the garage, the boats, the ramps, the tractors, the motor cars and the trucks will not belong to the people and that the Queensland Government will own them? If it is to own all the improvements, what are the people supposed to own? They will have nothing. I understand that the Bill has been taken before the Queensland Cabinet and that the Queensland Minister has stated that the Bill will be re-introduced next week. If I know anything about Queensland, the Government will want to rush that Bill through in one day and have it become law. The Federal Government has a responsibility and a duty to ensure that the Bill is not passed in its present form."

Senator Robertson, ALP Northern Territory, notes the cost of acquisition is minimal,

> "The Department of Aboriginal Affairs in a submission to the Minister estimated the acquisition costs of the reserves would be $211,964 for Aurukun and $63,469 for Mornington Island. Surely that is a small price to pay for the credibility of this Government. Surely it is a small price to pay for the welfare of the Aboriginal people. Yet did this happen?"

Local Government Bill Passes

Of course, the answer is no. Despite a public outcry, on 22nd May 1978 the Local Government (Aboriginal Lands) Act, constitutes the Aurukun Shire Council and grants to it Aboriginal Land Lease No.1.

On 24th May, the Land Council sends out a number of telegrams signed off by Mick in his expressive style. To Viner he says,

> "Your talk was big in promising to acquire the land if the legislation was unacceptable. But when the time came to put this into practice, you acted like a jelly fish and danced to the tune of the mad piper from Queensland."

On 28th June 1978, Clarrie makes a press statement that he has reports from Aurukun that the Department of Aboriginal and Islander Advancement (DAIA) is threatening to fire hospital staff if they do not become employees of the DAIA instead of the Uniting Church. "It is straight out blackmail," says Clarrie. "This move is typical of the state government's methods of riding roughshod over the people concerned." He continues:

> "The Aurukun Council has reluctantly agreed to run Aurukun with the assistance of an Advisory Committee consisting of a DAIA representative, Mr Ted Butler, Cairns, a Commonwealth Department of Aboriginal Affairs representative, Mr Don O'Rourke, Brisbane, and a representative for the Minister for Local Government.
>
> "The Aurukun people threw Mr Butler out on 16th May when he tried to set up a DAIA office on Aurukun without the Council's permission and without reference to the Advisory Committee. The Aurukun Council have informed Mr Butler that they will wait till 4th July, when the whole advisory Committee visits Aurukun, and they do not want him acting on his own beforehand."

The Queensland government try a public relations exercise patting themselves on the back for having two black shire councils in Queensland. However they have very different status and rules to other shire councils in Queensland.

First Meeting of Aurukun Shire Council

Local government minister Russ Hinze goes to Aurukun on 4th July for the first meeting of the Aurukun Shire Council. This is the same Aboriginal council but it now has Aboriginal shire status. Hinze threatens to sack them and put in a new council if they don't co-operate. Hinze's personal press officer attends so the people are concerned how the meeting might be portrayed to the press. So David Lee takes a video tape of the meeting. Bob Holroyd speaks up for land rights and is threatened with arrest. Hinze brings two police officers with him to the meeting.

Elder Francis Yunkaporta asks Hinze what rights the people have over the 1,000 acres of land excised from the Aurukun lease by the state and Hinze says no rights according to Lee's tape. Hinze is upset at all the questioning and walks off, closing the meeting. The NQLC makes this information available via a press release.

The Land Council launches an appeal for a fighting fund for a public awareness campaign re Aurukun and Mornington Island via an advertisement in *The National Times*. It is signed by:

Mick Miller, Chairman, North Queensland Land Council

Donald Peinkinna, Chairman, Aurukun Council

Lawrence Dugong, Mornington Island delegate, NQLC

Joyce Hall, Weipa delegate, NQLC

Monty Pryor, Townsville delegate, NQLC

Ted Bowen, Hopevale delegate, NQLC

Mark Noble, Yarrabah delegate, NQLC

Personal Matters

In 1978, I enroll in a Diploma of Education to become a teacher and fly to Brisbane in March to begin my course at Qld University. I've only been there a week or so when I receive a call from Clarrie, "Mick's had a car accident and is in hospital. He has to have surgery." I could hear the alarm in his voice.

"How bad is he?" I ask, shocked. "He'll be OK but it'll take a long time to recover," says Clarrie.

"I'll catch the first plane home. Tell him I'm coming. Thanks for ringing. I rush back to Cairns, packing everything.

Mick always seems so invincible. It's a shock to see him in a hospital bed. He smiles to see me. "Hello, beautiful."

"Hello maestro," I say, my nickname for him. I give him a hug carefully so as not to do any damage. He has a ruptured diaphragm; broken ribs, and they remove his spleen. "How did it happen?" I ask.

"I was on my way to pick up Marilyn (his daughter) at night and this car seemed to come out of nowhere," he says.

Once out of hospital, he needs to take some months off to convalesce. We have some idyllic time while he recovers without the normal demands of life and decide to get married. I don't go back to my course.

However, Mick doesn't get much rest as in March the Qld government decides to take over Aurukun and Mornington Island. In the middle of the Aurukun and Mornington Island conflict, Mick and I get married on 23rd July 1978 in Cairns.

"I'm not coming to your wedding," Mum tells me over the phone. It's as if I'm being hit with a cricket bat. And it's not the first blow.

My heart beats a bit faster. I clear my throat and ask, "Why, Mum?"

"Because Mick's Aboriginal. A Catholic as well. How could you do that?"

"I love him Mum and he loves me. I'm your daughter. You should come," I plead.

"Not on your life," she says, determined. I slowly hang up the phone, shoulders slumped a little.

After a few minutes, I straighten my shoulders. I need to do what I need to do. This won't stop me I decide.

Mick has been married before to Pat O'Shane who has become the first Aboriginal woman lawyer and magistrate in Australia after moving to Sydney to do university studies. Their marriage ends. This means he can't marry in the Catholic Church. I contact Noel Preston who is a Uniting Church minister in Brisbane and we decide to have an open-air ceremony in the Cairns Botanic Gardens. My father, though disapproving, decides he'd better do the right thing and come to Cairns to give me away. My brother Greg, who fits well into the family mould, thinks he'll have to give me away at first, and he comes too. My friends from Brisbane, Kat and Larry Silver, come with Kat being matron of honor.

I'm glad that Mick's uncle Clarrie and his daughter Gloria take Dad and Greg and show them around. Gloria even takes them to Kuranda. Dad starts to warm up to his new family. Traditional Aboriginal and Islander food is served at the reception. My Dad really enjoys the raw fish dish; "Numus." The fish is marinated in vinegar and coconut milk with some diced tomato and onion. Mick's family are very supportive of our marriage and have already made me feel part of the family.

Mick looks dashing in his blue suit with navy trim and, as usual, his sense of humor lightens what we know is a serious but joyful moment. I do have a bouquet but I hardly need flowers to be placed in vases because we are in the Flecker Botanic Gardens at Edge Hill Cairns. My bridesmaids are Mick's daughter Lydia, Glenys Grogan and Sandra Levers. Our flower girls are Barbara Willmett and Bridget Grogan. They are in blue with floral capes and the groomsmen; Clarrie Grogan, Peter Noble and Rod Small, a schoolteacher mate; match Mick's blue suit.

The afternoon sun filters through the rainforest. Flame of the forest and jade vine are two of the flowering vines that wind their way around the canopy. The Bowenia with glossy emerald leaves. Bright pink ginger flowers erupt from the middle of their leaves. Orchids, like a lady's slipper, peep through the foliage which is awash with color. Even the Heliconias seem dressed for the occasion as their brachts, or leafy structure at their base, cluster in reds, yellows, pinks and oranges. Fan shaped palms spread out their shade. Foliage plants provide shelter and food for many of the smaller animals that live within the gardens including butterflies, moths, bees, ants and lizards. We don't have an official photographer, so our wedding photos are poor quality and few in number.

As we say the wedding vows, the Bible on a lacy white cloth on a small coffee table, I have a few tears in my eyes. Noel wears his collar, the only indication he is a minister. He is slim and dresses casually, his short brown hair and shaven appearance a contrast to Mick's long black flowing hair, moustache and side leavers. Noel says to me afterwards, "I'm glad to see you cry because I was concerned if I was doing the right thing marrying you. This makes me feel it was right."

Surprised, I say, "Why did you have some doubts?"

"I usually spend some time with couples beforehand, making sure they are suited to each other and they understand the commitment they are making," he says. "I couldn't do that with you two."

We play Elvis Presley's *Hawaiian Wedding Song*, which we both love, at the reception. We have a quiet honeymoon staying with a friend of Mick's, Peter Gilligan, a federal department of Aboriginal Affairs official living in northern NSW. We find a snake one day, also sunning himself as we enjoy the garden. Mick goes with Peter on a few trips to visit Aboriginal communities. I go on some too and write a one-page article for *NQ Messagestick* on the alcohol rehabilitation center at Moree called MASH.

Mick finally tells me that Burnam Burnam hoped to play matchmaker for Mick and I by taking me to the meeting in Canberra where I first met Mick in late 1973. This comes as a surprise.

A new chapter in my life is beginning. Two weeks after our wedding we are back in the fray.

Barbara and Mick's wedding

Chapter 4

The Aurukun and Mornington Island Conflict Escalates

Bjelke Visits Aurukun and Mornington Island

In July 1978, Aurukun councillors attempt to oust the government-appointed administrators from their community. However, government representatives are able to remain in the community by living in the school building which is located on land gazetted for state purposes.

On 11th August 1978, the Land Council receives an urgent telegram from Mornington Island and I release it to the press. It says:

> "North Qld Land Council, Cairns
>
> The entire Mornington Island Council and Community refused to meet with and talk to the Queensland Premier today and his ministerial colleagues during their visit to Mornington. There is a deep feeling of resentment within the community at the continuous interference of the State Government in local affairs. There is bitterness resulting from the State Government's continuing refusal to abide by their agreements. We stand firm with Aurukun in

> rejecting any further co-operation with the Queensland Government.
>
> Signed Larry Lanley, Chairman for the Mornington Island Council"

The press release concludes, "Mr Mick Miller, North Qld Land Council Chairman, is expected to arrive in Cairns about 5pm today from Aurukun. He and his wife Barbara can be contacted on (070) 514008 or 514628."

When the Premier meets with Aurukun councillors, they demand that the Qld government let the federal government assume administrative control of the community. In a shock move, the Aurukun and Mornington Island Councils are dissolved by the Queensland Government August 1978. As they continue to resist the state government takeover and won't give up, the Premier decides to put in administrators. Mick predicted this would happen when he first opposed the state legislation. Mick sends a telegram to Prime Minister Malcolm Fraser and Bill Hayden, Leader of the Opposition on 15th August 1978. The one to Fraser reads:

> "Reports appearing in today's paper of your agreement with Mr Bjelke Petersen to put in administrators at Aurukun and Mornington Island take away all pretense of giving self-management to communities. It also contradicts your speeches to Commonwealth leaders re self-determination for Rhodesian and South African blacks. In Australia, your action re Aborigines belies your words. In March you stood up for Aurukun and Mornington Island and promised federal acquisition. In August you are being lied to about the situations of these two communities. Surely you don't believe them. I have video tapes of a public meeting at Aurukun and also cassette tapes of the secret meeting between Queensland Premier and Aurukun council. Premier's statements on Canberra government are not very complimentary. Communities hope you live up to your statements in London, or do you speak with forked tongue?"

Mick's telegram to Bill Hayden:

> "Please oppose Fraser's agreement with Bjelke Petersen to put administrators into the two communities. The Councils are determined to resist all attempts by the state government to enforce the legislation, shire clerk and administrator on them. I will bring to Canberra, transcripts of Council and public meetings with Premier at Aurukun on 11th August. The communities' only hope lies in federal acquisition of the land and true self-management. The only terror at Aurukun is what the people feel towards Bjelke's tactics of depriving them of their land, preventing outstation movements, preventing free enterprise and excising a thousand acres of land for special purposes, giving the go ahead for mining by Aurukun Associates, sending in the white police and threatening to sack the council."

I remember Mick standing under a building, tape recording a meeting of the Aurukun people with government. I wish I knew where the video and audio tapes are now. He said he actually had to crawl under the building to tape the meeting.

The Qld Premier claims in the press that there is a reign of terror at Aurukun and Mornington Island. Mick replies in a press release that it is the Premier himself instituting a reign of terror at the two communities. Mick says,

> "The Premier is using stand over tactics against the people. He is telling them they must accept state government legislation over which there was no consultation with the people; he has given eviction notices to Uniting Church staff against the wishes of the people; he has withheld money and then offered to provide it through an illegal DAIA office rejected by the people and he has now threatened to sack the two councils. Surely this is intimidation in the highest degree!
>
> It is time the federal government kept the promise it made on 11th April, that if the people of Aurukun and Mornington

> Island rejected the state local government legislation, then the federal government would intervene and take over the two reserves."

Mick returns from Aurukun on Friday where he is present at the meeting the Premier has with the people. He says,

> "Mr Fraser and Mr Viner might be interested to know that the Premier told the Aurukun people that Canberra's attitude to them would turn very cold soon and they would be dumped. The Premier said, however, the state government were their real friends.
>
> I believe that although the Premier would sack the two Councils, the people would re-elect the same councils unopposed. What impressed me was that the people of Aurukun were all of one voice."

The communities keep up their courageous stand and will not be bought. Mick tells *The Cairns Post* in "Back to Old Mission Days" on 16th August.

> "Mr Miller said three weeks ago, two Department of Aboriginal and Islander Advancement men went to the community bringing with them money for wages. The money was rejected 'because it had too many strings attached. The committee (council) rejected this interference by the DAIA as the communities were supposed to be under the local shire council, which has nothing to do with the DAIA,' Mr Miller said."

In a bold move, the Councils take the Queensland government to court for sacking them. As the agreement was that there be consultation between the state and federal governments and the state dissolved the councils without consultation, the Aborigines' solicitor, McMillan, was successful in getting an injunction. An interim injunction was granted from midnight Friday, 18th August. The Government is prevented from putting into effect the dissolution of the councils and the appointment of an administrator.

Senator Arthur Gietzelt raises this in the Senate on 16th August,

> "What else has to happen before the Australian Government will move? Does there have to be bloodshed? Does there have to be civil riots? Does there have to be turmoil or a legal challenge to resolve a matter which clearly is an area of responsibility for the Australian Government? I would go so far as to say there exists in these communities, and in some other Aboriginal communities in Queensland, an atmosphere which can only be described as being akin to partial slavery.
>
> I am sure that it will be conceded by this Senate that acquisition of the land by the Federal Government is the only way to meet the wishes of the Aurukun and Mornington Island Aboriginal communities."

Senator Keefe continues,

> "I suggest that if the Government had at that time, 6th April this year, taken notice of at least some of the amendments that were moved by the Opposition, this set of circumstances might not have arisen. In the last few hours, I have received the following telegram from Mick Miller, Chairman of the North Queensland Land Council." (He reads out the telegram Mick sent to Bill Haydon.)[9]

Mick and the Land Council fly to Canberra to raise support for the Aurukun and Mornington Island Fighting Fund Appeal. Clarrie arrives first and we release this statement on Sunday 20th August 1978 in his name:

> "Now that the question of the sacking of the two Community Councils is going to trial in the Queensland Supreme Court in the next 3-4 weeks, our appeal is even more urgent."

Press Coverage Re Health of Communities

As I am the press officer of the NQLC, on 31st August I put out a long press release, this time in my name. It hits the front page of *The Cairns Post* with three headlines "Land Rights Body Blames State Government," "Health Move Attacked," and "Issue and Excuse To Throw Church Out." The article reads,

> "The North Qld Land Rights Corporation said yesterday the State Government was to blame for the alleged declining health standards among Aboriginal families at Aurukun and Mornington Is.
>
> Research Officer for the North Qld Land Council, Mrs Barbara Miller was commenting on a report that Qld Health Minister Dr Edwards was going to Aurukun and Mornington Is next week to sort out health problems that precipitated the management struggle at the two former Aboriginal reserves.
>
> Mrs Miller said that health was only an excuse for the Qld government to force the Uniting Church out of the communities because of policy differences.
>
> It is absurd to say that Dr Edwards' health report precipitated the takeover as the Uniting Church was not responsible for health at the two communities, said Mrs Miller.
>
> The DAIA was responsible, and is still, the responsible authority on all Aboriginal communities in North Qld except at Aurukun and Mornington Island where it has recently passed control over to the State Health Department. So, the government has neatly transferred its health powers from one department to another and not without a fight from the DAIA."
>
> In one respect,' said Mrs Miller, "the state government is right. Health conditions are poor at Aurukun and Mornington Island but they are no worse in these communities than in any other Aboriginal reserve in north Queensland where malnutrition,

> underweight babies, infant mortality, running ears and nose, trachoma and VD are problem areas.
>
> Tremendous health and social problems are caused because double certificate sisters are not provided on reserves and mothers-to-be have to come to Cairns three months before time, where they are in a lonely environment separated from their husbands and other children. Their babies are often born underweight which causes a further period in Cairns. This causes some mothers to return home to families and leave their newborn babies in hospital to follow them later. A highly unsatisfactory situation.
>
> Alarming examples can be cited of neglect of government health officials on reserves e.g., an Aurukun baby died recently because it was kept at Aurukun two weeks (after becoming sick) before sending it to Cairns, she said.
>
> Also, I have received reports alleging that the nursing sister at Kowanyama is often drunk on duty. Recently a twelve-year-old girl was raped and bashed at Kowanyama and there was a delay before she was sent to Cairns. On arrival in Cairns, she was examined by a state government doctor who proclaimed her fit to return to Kowanyama. She died on arrival at Kowanyama.
>
> The state government is not doing anything about VD because sterilization is an after effect of VD and the state government want sterilization as a form of birth control."
>
> The state government does not care about Aboriginal health. Its real concern is politics, said Mrs Miller."

What is unused is that I call for a massive public campaign and appeal for funds to support the Aurukun and Mornington Island people to put pressure on the federal government to live up to their promises. I also point out that the Land Council is not funded by government and depends on donations to travel to the Aboriginal reserves to liaise; Canberra and southern cities to raise support; trunk calls; telegrams; welfare work; publishing our newspaper, *NQ Messagestick,* bi-monthly and a fortnightly 8-page newsletter. I outline a number of issues:

> "The Queensland Government has deliberately disregarded the wishes of the people on their reserves by:
>
> Throwing out Uniting Church management
>
> Not letting the people choose their own Shire Clerk
>
> Abolishing the reserve
>
> Excising 1,000 hectares of Aurukun land
>
> Letting the mining company into Aurukun without the permission of the people
>
> Keeping all royalties for themselves from any mining on Aurukun
>
> Not granting land rights
>
> Not granting true self-management, despite all promises
>
> Sacking the elected councils and imposing an outside administrator on the communities."

Councils Sacked and Security of Land Tenure

"Aurukun Council Seeks Land Tenure" blares the headline in *The Cairns Post,* 30th August, saying land is the central issue in its dispute with the Qld government. The article says,

> "The council in a special statement released yesterday through the Chairman of the North Qld Land Council Corporation. Mr Miller said:
>
> 'Unless there is security of tenure with freehold title, there is no basis for local government or any other legislation to work.'

> The Council said Mr Bjelke-Petersen's move of sacking the council seemed carefully aimed at destroying and utterly demoralizing the council and community, who, they said, were determined to fight on."

The Council is saying the administrator, Mr K. Brown, had arrived in the community the previous Thursday and told the former council that elections might he seven months off and he wanted to put in DAIA staff which they rejected. He said he would soon appoint a Shire Clerk.

Hinze says the administrator would strike off the electoral roll any "drop-outs, hangers on and agitators." The administrator will also control those who have right of entry to Aurukun and Mornington Island. The federal Opposition spokesman for Aboriginal Affairs, Dr Everingham, called it a complete disregard for human rights. (*The Canberra Times,* 31st August 1978)

On 12th September 1978, the Aurukun council writes a letter to British Commonwealth nations urging them to boycott the Commonwealth Games to be held in Brisbane in 1982. I have a copy of the letter with the original signatures of the Chairman, Donald Peinkinna, Rowan Pootchemunka, Eric Kooila, Roy Landis and Francis Yunkaporta:

> "We appeal to you as a member nation with Australia in the British Commonwealth, to boycott the Commonwealth Games scheduled for Brisbane, Queensland, Australia in 1982 because of the racist policy of the Queensland Government in oppressing the Australian Aborigines and restricting land rights in Queensland.
>
> "The Aboriginal people of Aurukun and Mornington Island in North Queensland Australia appeal to you. All we want is to have freehold title and manage our own affairs.
>
> The Queensland Government keep breaking their own Local Government Act by trying to set up their Aboriginal Affairs office in our communities and having their officers here

without permission. Also, they won't show us what the lease on our land is but we suspect it cuts out a lot of our former reserves. It is only a 50-year lease.

"So, we sacked the Shire Clerk appointed by the Queensland Local Government Minister and refused money from the Queensland Government because of the strings attached.

"The Queensland Premier himself visited us at Aurukun. We confronted him and told him we rejected his government and at Mornington Island we ignored him and went bush.

'The Queensland Premier sacked our two councils and gave an administrator the powers of the previous councils. He has also sent in white police. We have decided not to co-operate with the administrator.

"We appeal to you for support in this boycott and we offer you our support in the struggle of your people."

But Fraser is buying off the support of the African governments by appearing as their champion in Commonwealth circles.

Throughout this conflict, I continue to write articles for the *N. Q. Messagestick,* put out press releases and lobby support groups in the church, universities, aid groups and unions. Artist Enoch Tranby does the logo and drawings for *N. Q. Messagestick* and designs a t-shirt for the North Qld Land Council.

Snookered

Eventually we have to admit that Bjelke-Petersen has defeated all the efforts of the Aurukun and Mornington Island people to be self-managing and have the rights to their land. The State government has taken over and the church has been pushed out. The legislation the government puts in, the Local Government (Aboriginal Lands) Act 1978, is really a mockery of local government but the people have to adjust to it.

It takes another year before the first statutory meetings of the Mornington Island Council on Saturday 7th April 1979 and the Aurukun Council on Sunday 8th April. The meetings are attended by the Federal Minister for Aboriginal Affairs, Senator Chaney and the Queensland Minister for Local Government, Mr Hinze. With dignity, and perhaps a slap in the face to Hinze, the Aboriginal councillors on each community re-elect as Chairmen the ones who had been sacked by him the year before.

This uncertainty of land tenure makes Aurukun a forerunner community re native title with the Wik decision to come later assisted by the government funded Cape York Land Council when a decision is made to set it up in July 1990 at a Remote Communities Futures Conference in Townsville.

Michael Is Born

I have to go into hospital a few days before my son is born in 1979 because I have high blood pressure. I take the land council paperwork with me to do while I am there. However, as my blood pressure doesn't go down, I have to give Mick the paperwork to take back to the office for someone else to do. My ankles are also swollen. Nevertheless, a beautiful baby boy named Michael is born. He is given the name "Woonun" meaning "She-oak" in the Lardil language of Mornington Island by Lawrence Dugong. He is also given the Thaynakwith name "Gulapie" or "Tall dark one" by Joyce Hall from Weipa. Wanjuk Marika gives him the name of his sacred land - Bilirri. Wanjuk, one of the Yolngu people of NE Arnhem Land was a famous artist, actor and land rights activist. Wanjuk was on the Aboriginal Arts Board with Mick and would often stay at our home.

Lawrence Dugong, representing Mornington Is. Council, and Mick, attend a Land Rights Conference at Sydney University when Michael is two months old. Mick talks about how he is bringing international pressure on the Australian government over Aboriginal issues and enrolling Aborigines in Qld to vote. In an interview, journalist Graham Williams says,

> "Mick Miller is one of a new breed of Aboriginal reformers who is super-cool, relaxed and confident about the ultimate failure of racism and discrimination in Australia."[10]

The tropical heat of Cairns makes body contact a sweaty affair. I have just brought my son home from hospital. He is named after his father Mick and his father before him, Mick Miller Snr. I love him dearly and bond very closely to him so that he takes over my life. Mick is delighted. A son.

Michael is light at about 6½ pounds. He has plenty of dark brown hair, beautiful brown eyes and brown skin. Even today, I admire his thick, wavy hair, caring, thoughtful personality and ready smile. I enjoy his hugs.

Michael needs to feed, so I put a chair directly under the fan in the middle of the lounge room of our three-bedroom brick veneer home. I put him on my knee and start to breastfeed. He sucks softly at my breast. Even then, it is a sweaty though sweet moment. It is a profoundly personal moment, yet profoundly communal as well as family keep coming and going visiting the new addition to the family.

That day as I sit under the fan with my newborn son, there is a long procession of visitors coming to see the new heir of the revered Mick. He is 42. I am 29. Auntie Esme and Auntie Rose are among the many visitors. In fact, they drop in to visit most days. Both matronly figures, Auntie Esme starting to gray a little, they are very forthright with their points of view and involved on committees to bring positive changes for Aboriginal people. I love the brownie cake both aunts make. It is a big hit with everyone who visits.

> While I am pregnant, Auntie Ez says, "You're going to have a boy."
>
> "How can you tell?" I ask, amazed as the doctors have not said anything about the baby's sex.
>
> "You're carrying more on the behind than on the belly," she says. She was right.

As Mick's parents live in Innisfail we don't see as much of them as we see of Auntie Esme and Auntie Rose. Mick's Mum loves baking and asks me one day, "What's your favorite cake? I'll make some for you?"

> "My Nana used to make lamingtons and caramel tarts," I reply. "They've always been my favorites. They were treats for Christmas and birthdays."

I can always count on Mum Miller's tarts: caramel, condensed milk, pineapple and coconut etc. When I am going through a healthy period and eating wholemeal everything, she even makes me wholemeal lamingtons. For someone who all her life has not cooked with wholemeal flour, this is a big concession. It shows her love for me.

"The stork dropped me in the wrong house." It is the phrase I often say to Mick, much later realizing that I was repeating my mother's words to me as I didn't turn out how she expected. I feel such a sense of belonging in an Aboriginal family, even as a white woman. I can talk with Mick, his parents, Auntie Esme and Auntie Rose (my three Aboriginal Mums) in a way I can't talk to my own Mum and Dad because they share similar values and interests to me. I can only talk of superficial things to my parents as they can't agree to disagree. They just put my opinions down. I got to the point of not expressing them. Now I am heard. Now I am respected. Now I am loved. Now I belong. It means a lot to me.

My Mum comes up and visits us after Michael is born. Bringing a grandchild into the world softens Mum and she decides to make her peace with the situation. When she meets Mick, she decides she likes him after all. Mick could be very charming. The tide has turned. Mum stays in a hotel. Mick invites her to stay at our home but this is too much for her to cope with. We take her out for dinner a couple of times. Mum loves Chinese food especially curried prawns.

Visit To Palm Island With Michael

I come across a black and white photo of me nursing my son Michael in a sling. He is about six months old and we are both wearing cardigans. Even though it is the tropics on Palm Island Aboriginal community near

Townsville, it is winter. My hair is long and Michael has a slight frown from the sun. In the background is a wire fence and bushes obscure the building on the other side.

Mick was born on Palm Island in 1937. We enjoy time with Aunty Jean and Uncle Jack Sibley. Jack is a brother to Mick's mother, so this is where we stay.

It's not my first visit to Palm Island. A few years previously, Mick and I, Lydia and Marilyn and Aunty Esme came here for a holiday. We walk out to Butler Bay for a week to camp out in the open. We have no bedding. Mick just scoops out some holes in the sand. We sleep in our day clothes with no covers. I can't remember if we have a torch but the light of the moon and stars invades the pitch black of night. The sounds of the sea lull us to sleep. It is beautiful.

We take little food with us: some flour, salt, pepper, curry, tea, sugar and powdered milk. Aunty Esme makes damper, cooked on the coals, Mick catches some fish and shows us how to collect shellfish. Lydia and Marilyn are in their early teens. Lydia has great fun stabbing the clam shells to get them to open up to collect the creature inside. But it is so tough, even with much boiling in a billy can and curry added, it isn't an enjoyable meal. I love to collect the spider shells and other shells. Mick throws them on the fire for a tasty treat.

Midway through the week, Mick's cousin, Cecilia Barber, walks out to find us, bringing some sausages. "I was worried you'd be hungry," she says, "bringing children out here without food," a slightly scolding tone in her voice. Cecilia is the mother of famous runner Kathy Freeman and she grew up as a Sibley.

Mick laughs.

> "We're fine," he says. "You needn't have worried. "Sit down and have a cuppa and some damper. We'll put on the billy. But thanks for the sausages. The clam's pretty tough, but the fish is beautiful."

It is such an idyllic time. Yet this was the penal colony Mick and his family grew up on. Mick tells us of his boyhood growing up on Palm Island. He tells us how he and his brother Lennie and adopted brother Bill Apple used to ride horses around the island and go hunting and fishing. He tells us the stories his daughters grew up on like the one about the mythical *jiggibinna*. The *jiggibinn*a was a huge hairy creature with big pointy ears and liked to grab children. These stories were often told to keep children from straying too far away from the campfire or "The *jiggibinna* will get you."

Another story that Mick would sometimes tell me when we were home in Cairns was about the *Mulladumboon* Murri. He said that growing up on Palm Island there were a couple of these men and you could tell them by their red lips. They believed that by eating the kidney fat of other men, it would increase their strength. People feared them. He said they would make a hole in the ground and cover it with twigs etc. so that an unsuspecting passer-by would walk into the trap and stumble. Then the *Mulladumboon* Murri would make a neat incision in their back and take out the kidney. He would sew them up again and they might live for three days as if everything was okay but then they would die.

However, on this visit to Palm Island with our son, these stories don't come up. It's a very eventful occasion as it is Michael's first march. It is NAIDOC – National Aboriginal and Islander Week and we join the march with Aboriginal flags flying. Michael is in my arms, unaware of the momentous occasion.

Visit To Ipswich With Michael

Mick calls Michael "Possum" because he is so cute. He gradually changes it to "Poskums" and eventually "Posky" which sticks. I take Posky to Ipswich to visit my parents when he is about 18 months old. This is the first time my father has met Posky. After flying to Brisbane, I catch the train out to Ipswich, lugging a suitcase and with Michael on my hip.

It is a relaxed visit. Dad shocks me however by saying,

"I'm going to have to teach him to fire a gun because being Aboriginal he'll have to be able to defend himself."

"Dad! He doesn't need that," I say. Dad has a gun in the bottom of a clothes cupboard that I'd never seen him use. I think it was a rifle. Unloaded, no doubt. I'd never seen any ammunition.

"You never know," Dad says. "His life might be in danger one day."

I try to change the subject. This is my baby we're talking about. But I realize it's Dad's way of saying that he accepts Posky into the family and cares about him.

"He might need to protect himself," Dad says. "There's a lot of racism out there." I chuckle as I write this as Dad would be the last person who would use a gun against another person and I'd be the last person to encourage my son to do so. Of course, there is racism out there. I didn't need Dad to tell me that but it's interesting to know that he recognizes my son would experience it, which he does when he goes to school.

Dad is well-read and has a photographic memory. When I was a child, he encouraged me to learn the vocabulary list in *Readers Digest* and he liked to increase his own vocabulary. One of his favorite authors was Pearl Buck, who wrote about Chinese characters, and Dad liked to say I was "Number One daughter" and my brother was "Number One son" as a result of reading these books. However, there are no further numbers. I get my love of reading from my parents.

In later years, when Mick visits Brisbane and is a well-known figure working for Aboriginal rights and on TV etc., my Mum complains, "Why doesn't Mick ever visit us when he comes to Brisbane?" Mum's home in Ipswich is an hour's train ride from Brisbane. I don't say 'You not coming to our wedding doesn't help.' I just say, "He's busy Mum," which is true but also, there is little to encourage him to make the visit.

I remember growing up Dad was always at the Bowling Club over the weekend playing bowls, which he was very good at, or having a drink with mates. Greg was disappointed Dad never watched him play football. I was disappointed he didn't teach me how to swim as he had been a life saver, travelling an hour or two to the Gold Coast from Ipswich on the weekend to do so as a young man. I remember he did take me to a couple of swimming lessons at the baths in Ipswich but didn't get in the water. I couldn't get the breathing right. So I would take one deep breath and swim with my eyes closed. This resulted one day in me veering toward the deep end instead of swimming across the width in the shallow end. Dad was alarmed and didn't take me again. At school I was relegated to the shallow end with a few kids like me, who were ignored, while the teachers concentrated on those who could swim. This was humiliating and robbed me of my enjoyment of swimming.

Lydia And Marilyn

Despite this, I love to swim. One day, Mick takes his daughters, Lydia and Marilyn, and myself swimming to Crystal Cascades. A beautiful freshwater spot near Cairns where you walk a long way through the rainforest. Mick is watching us swim when suddenly I'm being carried away by a strong current over the rocks. It's dangerous. I'm scared and call out, "Help!" Mick lets out a hearty laugh. Lydia swims over to save me for which I'm very grateful. "Why didn't you help me?" I demand of Mick.

"You were OK," he said, still smiling.

"No, I wasn't. I could have drowned," I shot back, hands on hips, confronting him. I sit on a rock till I get over it, drying myself off as the sun beats down and I watch the foam on the water dance over the rocks.

One of my favorite memories was when I took Lydia and Marilyn to Green Island near Cairns for the day. On the boat back, they both fell asleep, one on each shoulder. I held them close.

While I am pregnant, Lydia and Marilyn move to Sydney at the request of their Mum to keep her company. Marilyn is about fifteen years old and Lydia is a year older. I miss them a lot but I know their mother needs them. They have been visiting her on holidays up till now. However, Lydia moved to Sydney before Marilyn.

Premier Joh Bjelke-Petersen and Aurukun Councillor Eric Kooila at Aurukun
photo News Ltd/Newspix

Prince Escort Larry Lanley Barry Ngakyunkwokka meet Mr Wilkes Victorian Opposition Leader in Melbourne photo *N. Q. Messagestick* Vol 4 No 1 Jan 1979. Over 2,000 attend their meeting at the Melbourne Town Hall. They also meet the Premier of Victoria and ministers in Tasmania and South Australia.

Mr Mick Miller Chairman of the North Queensland Land Council (left) and Mr Lawrence Dugong of the Mornington Island Council photo Paul Pearson/The Sydney Morning Herald

Michael Miller, 16 months old

Mick and Cissie Miller, Mick's Parents

Joyce and Mervyn Russell, My Parents

Lydia, Mick and Marilyn

Chapter 5

A Thorn In Bjelke's Side - North Qld Land Council

The tropical heat of Cairns is eased by a sea breeze that can lull you into complacency; beckoning you to take that siesta that some countries enjoy. Or, if you are more energetic, to stock your cupboard for the cyclones that come and go; sometimes with a lot of devastation. It is a time of late afternoon rains and sticky humidity. However, there is a large group of Aborigines and Torres Strait Islanders who are not complacent. They gather in Cairns, expectant that this time will be historic; that it will be life-changing.

They come from all over the north of Qld, from reserves and towns, to form the North Qld Land Council. As an organizer, I am looking after the logistics. It is January 1977 and I am 26. We meet at the Young Australia League (YAL), a non-descript building in a quiet suburban area but less than 10 minutes from the Cairns Esplanade. With a conference room, accommodation and catering facilities, it meets our low-cost budget. It has manicured lawns, bushes with splashes of red and yellow leaves, and palm trees that reach for the sky.

There is a big focus in my memoir on my time with the North Qld Land Council. Why? I was a key player in its formation and it was the main focus of my life, apart from family, for a number of formative years in my life. It was my vehicle to fulfil my passion for justice for Aboriginal people. Telling the story of the Land Council is part of the telling of my own story, even if I appear to be in the background when it is looked at through press clippings of Mick's work and the articles in *NQ Messagestick.*

I am working as a library assistant in the Cairns library when I am served with a notice to appear in court for trespassing on Weipa South Aboriginal reserve while helping the Mapoon people move back to their land. This is despite an invitation to be there.

I am also working in the library when, in the latter part of 1975, Mick and I, Clarrie and Peter set up the North Qld Land Rights Committee. Having no funding, I start the *NQ Messagestick* as an A4 newsletter printed on a Roneo machine at the library, with me paying for the paper and ink. It eventually took off from there to become a newspaper, though we still didn't have the finance to make sure it came out on a regular schedule.

We host a Land Rights conference in Cairns in November 1975 which is attended by many delegates and we support the movement of Aboriginals from Mapoon, Aurukun, Yarrabah (the latter moving to Buddabadoo) and Holroyd River, back to their tribal land. Our committee, consisting of: Mark Noble (Yarrabah), Eric Kooila (Aurukun), Bill Congoo (Palm Is) and Bob Holroyd (Edward River), attends a National Land Rights conference in Sydney in August 1976. In September 1976, we decide to form a Land Council even though we do not have the legislation or funding like the Northern Territory has. This will make us a lobby group but we will do all we can so Qld Aboriginals are given a voice and a pathway to recognition, self-determination and land rights.

Without money, this is a big ask. So Peter Noble, President of the land rights committee and his father, Mark Noble, who is the committee's Yarrabah delegate, travel to Melbourne, Canberra and Sydney to raise finance. Don Siemon of International Development Action (IDA) organizes their Melbourne meetings and Lester Bostock their Sydney meetings. Keith Smith of the Aboriginal Embassy in Canberra loans them his phone and car. IDA loans us the money for the airfares and Peter and Mark stay with friends they make along the way as there is no money for hotels. For three weeks, they walk, hitch rides and get lifts from supporters to meet with government, unions, students, churches and overseas aid organizations. Some funding comes through from Freedom From Hunger Campaign and Community Aid Abroad to open an office in Cairns in November and pay Peter full time to work there for about three months.

In December, Len Muller and Stuart McGill from the Northern Land Council in the Northern Territory meet with our committee to explain how their land council operates. Monty Pryor, our Townsville committee member and Tony Assan, the National Aboriginal Conference (NAC) representative for NW Qld attend and Tony agrees to advertise the proposed Land Council in his electorate.

Clarrie, Peter and Len Muller do a field trip to the reserves of Bamaga, New Mapoon, Cowal Creek, Umagico, Lockhart River, Weipa, Edward River, Kowanyama, Hopevale, Laura and Coen to hold public meetings to elect their delegates to automatically go on the Land Council at the Cairns conference in January. Mick and Clarrie do the same at Bloomfield and Yarrabah, Mick at Palm Island and Clarrie at Aurukun. The basis of representation is two delegates for every reserve and one for each town with some larger reserves having more delegates.

To bring in all the delegates and stage the formation conference of the NQLC is a big feat but we receive funding from the Australian Council of Churches, BOEMAR, Oxfam Canada, Christian Conference of Asia and trade unions. I put a submission into the federal government for finance and Viner approves it but PM Fraser bows to pressure from Bjelke and rejects it.

Some reserves and towns are setting up their own land rights committees to fund their delegates to come to future meetings e.g., Mornington Island, Charters Towers, Palm Island and Townsville.

I manage to persuade Gough Whitlam, the federal Opposition leader, to come and open the conference. He dresses casually in a patterned short-sleeved shirt with no tie. However, the federal and state ministers for Aboriginal Affairs do not attend. In fact, there was a ban on federal department of Aboriginal Affairs employees attending. This was lifted so they could report back. Ted Butler attends for the state and Don Egan (who took me to court re Mapoon) is busily spying for Comalco. Greg Roberts of the Qld Conservation Council is a speaker saying that Aboriginals and conservationists have common interests and need to work together.

It goes off like clockwork on 21-23 January 1977 and it is not all work. Eslyn Wargent, Jane O'Shane, her sister Marie and Frida Salaam organize a barbeque Friday night at which Tony Assan shows films of the cyclone that devastated Mornington Is. The Noble and Mundraby families do the daytime catering.

Who said Senators don't dance? Senator Jim Keeffe and Senator Jean Melzer wear out the dance floor Saturday night at a feast and dance organized by the social club. Barclay and Shirley Miller, Colleen and the Miller girls, Charlotte and Aslan Dean, Wayne and Pat Wilson, Jenny Martin and Ellen Lancaster receive much thanks for this. The Yarrabah band led by Vincent Schrieber encourages all to get up and dance while the highlight of the evening is the hula by Gwen Munn and her two daughters to the strains of "Pearly Shells." The film *Protected* about the 1956 Palm Island strike is shown on Sunday night by Bill Congoo, one of the strike leaders.

Peter Noble, Cairns delegate and President of the organizing committee, encourages all delegates to have confidence in themselves as members of the newly formed Land Council. So, what do the delegates say on such a historic occasion? Some of the highlights:-

Mark Noble fears the Mapoon story is a symbol of what may happen on other reserves in Qld. He forecasts the possibility of another Mapoon at Yarrabah and Palm Is. He says Yarrabah is being invaded by developers who want to build a deep-water port, an international airport and a tourist resort there. Facilities for these projects would require a town. Yarrabah is also being threatened by Colonial Sugar Refining Company (CSR) and timber interests. He says,

> "We've already lost False Cape from our reserve. There was also a rumor that people are looking for a site for a new reserve at Charters Towers and Cloncurry. The nearest reserve is Palm Island. Are there plans to move Palm Islanders off Palm Is to a new reserve so the tourists can have Palm Is?"

Geraldine Kawangka, chairperson of Aurukun, says she is also worried about a Mapoon situation developing at Aurukun. She speaks passionately,

> "Things are going on behind the back of the Aurukun people. Comalco just came in and we didn't know till Aurukun Associates told us. They're only three miles away in good fishing country. Aborigines should stand up and make a big song and a big dance over our tribal land. We have to stand up and fight, and one day we'll win."

Bill Congoo is troubled about a multi-million-dollar dam being built which is obviously not for the benefit of the Aboriginal people because its capacity is far greater than necessary. He slams the commission that the Qld government is setting up saying,

> "They're calling for applications, but they've already picked who they want and it won't be anyone here."

Agnes Wootten, also from Palm Is agrees and forthrightly declares,

> "Aboriginal people should live by black man's law which was given to us before white man's law."

Shorty O'Neill puts out *The Palm Islander* newspaper covering Indigenous issues and he points out,

> "When a black man does something bad, it's in big print, a front-page spread! But when he does something good, it's in small print if it gets in at all."

Ted Bowen from Hopevale says he's not sure if his people get any royalty from the sand mining at Cape Flattery on their land but he says if they do, it would probably be low at around 3%. Arthur Woosup,

Chairman of Weipa South is adamant that the royalty of 3% that the Aboriginals get from mining on their land is not enough. He says,

> "Ten thousand dollars come to Weipa from mining each year. Where is the rest of the money?"

Also, of Weipa, Joyce Hall says Comalco is not giving Aborigines enough jobs and Aboriginal people do not know the future plans of Comalco on their land.

Kenny Jimmy, Chairman of Kowanyama is annoyed at how it all started,

> "In the early days, my people were shot down like a mob of animals … Capt. Cook was a dirty varmint … Today, my people are like a mob of prisoners."

Roberta Felton from Mornington Is raises the issue of the early days of the mission when the Presbyterians took the children from the old people and put them in dormitories where they were locked up from 6pm to 6am and forbidden to speak their language. Despite this, the culture and language have been revived and they teach it in the school. With a rising defiance, she says,

> "The staff say to us you can't do anything, but the reason is, they won't let us. They hang on like leeches! We should legislate the Aboriginal Act out! … if we don't win, we'll challenge her Majesty the Queen of England," she says commenting on the Privy Council throwing out the case Aurukun had won in the Supreme Court of Australia to stop mining on their land.

Bamaga delegate Smith Lui shares he is on the Torres Strait Border Action Committee and is pleased now to support the Land Council. Mabel Bond from nearby New Mapoon complains the state government will not repair their rented houses. Steps are falling down; floors are broken and houses are leaking. These are the people the state removes from Mapoon to the tip of the Cape by police force. From nearby Umagico, a delegate complains the state won't let them build their own homes because they want them to pay rent.

Isaac Hobson, from Lockhart River, speaks encouragingly about the mapping of sites of significance occurring with the help of two anthropologists. However, Lawrence Foote of Edward River is disappointed that Aboriginal people are not permitted to run the store or do the bookwork.

Bob Holroyd, from Holroyd River, is particularly upset saying that he has been refused permission to live in his own community. He speaks intensely of not wanting to have a sick heart, sick mind and sick body from being kept away from his land. His own exile fresh in his mind, he recalls an earlier case of eviction and exile,

> "In 1936, Aborigines were chained by the neck and walked from Edward River to Coen and were shipped to Palm Is for standing up for their rights."

David Brookdale from Doomadgee is concerned uranium mining nearby has destroyed Aboriginal paintings and story places. Alec Stevens from Innisfail, Wompie Kepple from Coen and Alvina Ward from Charters Towers make moving comments.

Alanna Doolan from Townsville makes a stirring appeal for more young people and more women to be involved in the Land Council. She says women should not be the "little Mary" sitting in the corner anymore. Alanna is upset that history books show Aboriginals as savages and re-education of black and white is needed. She is proud to have been part of the Aboriginal embassy which has brought change. Re the Palm Is strike, it is still distressing for her,

> "It's the Qld Act that gives them the power to move blacks from mission to mission like a bunch of animals. The chains are not there today, but we are still prisoners in our country."

Clarrie Grogan, the Mareeba delegate, presents a detailed history of the NT and North Qld land rights struggles. He calls for the setting up of a Commission in Qld similar to the Woodward Commission to examine, not whether but how, land rights can be granted in Qld. He calls for the appointment of an Interim Commissioner to hear land claims. Re Mareeba, Clarrie says,

> "The commonwealth allocated money for housing for the Aboriginal people of Mareeba but because the state government would not allow Aboriginal people to own houses if they live on an Aboriginal reserve, the homes had to be built on a council reserve. This forced people off the state reserve to which they had spiritual ties. Both reserves are crown land, but the state would have taken over ownership of those houses built on their reserve."

Mick Miller, Cairns delegate and Vice President of the organizing committee sums up the points made by delegates. He warns them that every delegate's strength will be tested.

> "It will be plain sailing with the formation of the Land Council, but a ripple will develop, then a storm. How many strong ones will be left? There'll be little ways they'll get at you when you return, and big ways. Bjekle-Petersen doesn't want this Land Council formed.
>
> You are already losing parts of reserves like False Cape and Julgai Beach at Yarrabah. Orpheus and North Palm Islands have already been chopped off from the Palm Group and negotiations are underway for Phantom Is. Ansett has been named as an interested party. Palm Is will not share in the revenue of any development on Phantom Is. Aboriginals might be employed as yardmen or waitresses but would have no decision- making power."

Mick says he is also concerned at the government opposition to the outstation movement at Aurukun, Buddabadoo and Holroyd River and the settlement at Mapoon. Because of the restrictions of the Qld Aborigines Act, Aboriginal councils are "Paper tigers," who can make by-laws but no major decisions. So he challenges delegates:

> "When you go back to the reserves, try to tell the manager you want to keep the money from the store and canteen in your own reserve for projects and see how far you get!"

Mick continues that "The Qld Act enslaves a minority group". The Advisory Council to the Qld government is made up of the Chairperson of each reserve and is not representing the wishes of the people. He says,

> "It has never said we want to govern our own reserves or we want land rights. When we stand up for our rights, it's thrown back in our face that Bjelke-Petersen is advised by the Advisory Council. But who advises the Advisory Council? Paddy Killoran, the Director, just passes what motions he wants through onto his stooges in that body. I have sympathy with the councillors though, because it takes guts for a person to stand up and say I oppose that because he'll be victimized when he returns to his reserve."

Mick prepares them for what lies ahead and challenges them,

> "When the storm begins, where will we be? Bjelke will use the weak ones as a weapon to drive a wedge between us. He'll say the people in this town or that group on this reserve does not support the Land Council.
>
> If you are half-hearted, it's better you stay home, and don't come here and waste your time, our time, and the time of the people who sent you here. If you betray them, you shouldn't be here," he says forcefully.

He concludes by saying the Land Council will stand with the Torres Strait Islanders in their battle for land rights and self-determination. Joe McGuiness and Danny O'Shane give speeches in support of the Land Council as do Cecil Patten and Lyle Munro of the Sydney Aboriginal Legal Service. I remember Lyle from my days as part of the Aboriginal embassy demonstrations in Canberra in 1972 and Cecil from my visits to the Aboriginal Legal Service in Sydney in the early 70's. Cec is related to Jack Patten, the Yorta Yorta man famous for working with William Cooper and William Ferguson to launch the Day of Mourning in Sydney on the 150th anniversary of white settlement.

Cec tells the meeting that Paul Coe and himself invaded the shores of

England at Dover on 2nd November 1976 and planted the Aboriginal flag. Though it had been seen as foolish, it is no more ridiculous for Aborigines to claim England than it was for Captain Cook to claim Australia.

Lyle says the Sydney Legal Service sets precedents in European law to fight discrimination. They would be instigating a writ on Monday on behalf of Bob Holroyd against the Qld and Australian governments for depriving him of his right to live on his homeland. He says,

> "In Sydney, we work on a national basis: our culture has been destroyed, but we respect you, and we try to involve you with the precedents we set on your behalf."

Many resolutions are passed with the key ones being:

This conference agrees to the formation of a North Queensland Aboriginal Land Council and demands recognition of the council by the state and federal governments and funding by the federal government. Moved by Terry O'Shane, Seconded by Tony Assan.

This conference strongly recommends the abolition of the Queensland Aboriginal and Torres Strait Island Acts and their Regulations and By-laws. Moved Mervyn Akee, Seconded Alvina Ward

This conference strongly condemns the establishment of an Aboriginal and Islander Commission in Queensland and demands all responsibility for Aboriginal and Island affairs be transferred to the federal government in accordance with the 1967 referendum. Moved Mike Shegog Seconded Stan Connolly

This conference deplores the descent definition motion passed at the National Party conference July 76 proposing that anthropologists and genetic experts should decide 'Who is an Aborigine?" Moved Shorty O'Neill Seconded Alanna Doolan

The North Queensland Aboriginal Land Council urges the federal government to immediately appoint a commission of enquiry into how Aboriginal land rights could be granted in Qld. This commission should have powers similar to the commission set up under Mr Justice Woodward in the Northern Territory. Moved Stan Connolly Seconded Clarrie Grogan.

We the delegates for the North Queensland Aboriginal Land Council hereby demand that the federal and state governments honor and respect their international policies and propaganda in reference to racism, apartheid and genocide by completely and immediately abolishing the Queensland Act and granting land rights to the Aboriginal and Island peoples of Australia. This entails

a. the granting of all reserves and traditional lands to be controlled by the respective Aboriginal and Islander governing bodies.

b. The preservation of all sacred and traditional lands in accordance with (a)

c. The respective Aboriginal and Islander governing bodies be consulted by both the federal and state governments before any form of legislation is discussed and/or passed in reference to land rights for the Aboriginal and Islander people of Australia. Moved Alanna Doolan Seconded Roberta Felton.

A detailed list of objectives is passed, moved by Peter Creek and seconded by Monty Pryor. A committee is selected by secret ballot: Mick Miller, Peter Noble, Clarrie Grogan, Monty Pryor, Danny O'Shane, Roberta Felton, Agnes Wootten, Alanna Doolan and Tony Assan. Mick was voted in as chairman and Peter as vice-chairman of the Land Council. A decision is made not to incorporate in Qld but to seek federal incorporation and that the Land Council will meet three or four times a year depending on finance.

A thorn in the side for government is birthed. Also, North Qld Aboriginals unite in a genuine grass roots body to bring social change. I am part of this birthing process.

Peter Noble Raising Aboriginal Flag at James Cook University Townsville
where Mick was speaking 22.9.78

Gough Whitlam Opens the Formation Conference of the North Qld Land Council. Barbara Russell Sits at Table Left of Photo and Peter Noble and Mick Miller Sit at Right 21.1.1977. Photo *N. Q. Messagestick* Feb 1977

North Qld Land Council 2nd Annual Meeting. Top Photo Senator Neville Bonner Opens Meeting with Peter Noble at Head Table Far Left and Barbara Russell Far Right

Chapter 6

International Advocacy

Connections with First Nations People of Canada and USA

I'm not sure how we forged our connection with the Mohawk nation, who put out the newspaper *Akwesasane Notes*, but we start exchanging newspapers and letters in 1975. This leads to other contacts, such as *Alive Magazine*, Ontario, who we then exchange newsletters with. The White Roots of Peace group at *Akwesasane* write asking if 'the city-raised Aboriginal youth go to the people who still have the traditional ways to learn the old ways?' They wish us to be 'at peace and harmony with creation'. We start exchanging information with the Counsel for the Committee for Original People's Entitlement at the Berger Inquiry, based in Yellowknife Canada. The Long Island Safe Energy Commission also strikes up correspondence.

As editor of *NQ Messagestick*, I print a one-page article in our January 1977 newspaper that was from the *Indian News* September 1975 titled "What Do Land Claims (Non-Treaty Areas) Mean to Indian People?". The *Indian News* was put out by the National Indian Brotherhood in Ottawa.

On 20th August 1976, I send *NQ Messagestick* and a booklet by the Black Resource Centre in Brisbane on the Queensland Act to the Office of the Commissioner on Indian Claims in Ontario. I ask for information from them that may help with the claims process in Australia, though we do not yet have any relevant legislation. On 9th September, Stewart Raby sends us their publication, *Native Claims in Canada.* I write back on 8th December saying that we have loaned it to the Northern Land Council in Darwin, who are very impressed by it. I enclose a copy of the Aboriginal Land (Northern Territory) Bill before parliament and publications we have produced, including a pamphlet we have just sent out to our reserves in Queensland.

Responding to a request from John Bayly, the Counsel for the Committee for Original People's Entitlement, Yellowknife, Canada for more information on Aurukun, I reply on 20th August 1976:

'Enclosed are copies of our newsletter *NQ Messagestick* dealing with Aurukun and the book *The Mapoon Story* Vol 3, which has a chapter on Aurukun. The situation at present is that the Federal government has put a freeze on mining at Aurukun and the Queensland Government and mining company, Aurukun Associates, are trying to force the Aurukun community to accept mining but without success. I will give your address to the Aurukun community's solicitor, Frank Purcell, who can inform you of the present legal situation.'

On 20th December 1976, I receive a letter addressed to 'B J Russell' from Chief Greywolf, Spiritual Counsellor of the Indian Legal Service, Santa Barbara, California, wanting to hear from us. He writes, 'We are members of many other Indian groups across America. We are working for unity – for true unity is our key for liberation. We are not attorneys at law but a private Native American citizen group. We care. We are working for the children born and yet unborn. We want to keep our Indian identity and spiritual ways of the old ones, before reservation days. Numbers are support. Let us hear from you. We are not funded. We are all volunteers.'

On 7th June 1976, I receive a letter from John Bayly saying:

> 'As Counsel for the Committee for the Original People's Entitlement, one of the participants in the Mackenzie Valley Pipeline Inquiry in the Northwest Territories in Canada, I have

> had occasion to read the evidence to be presented by Theo T. Hills to which is appended a message from the Aurukun people. The Eskimos and Indians of the Northwest Territories in Canada face similar problems with oil and mining company development. Would you please give me some more detailed background information of the events that led to the 7th December statement and what has subsequently transpired?'

I continue to keep him up to date on developments. It's amazing to look back now and think I was able to help First Nations (Indian) groups a little with their claims process.

World Council Of Churches

Jose Chipenda of the Program to Combat Racism (PCR) of the World Council of Churches (WCC) visits Australia in June 1975 and amongst others, Mick and I are able to discuss the plight of Aborigines with him. At Helsinki in 1979, the World Council of Churches approves $37,000 in funds for Australian Aborigines to combat racism, split between the North Queensland Land Council, the Kimberley Land Council and the Aboriginal Community Organization Course in Melbourne.

In June-July 1981, the WCC PCR visits five Australian states to report on the situation of Aborigines. Mick and I have discussions with Vice-Moderator of the WCC Central Committee, Jean Skuse, and Information Officer of the Australian Council of Churches, Russell Rollason, in preparation for this. The WCC team put out a report called *Justice for Aboriginal Australians.*

It is the 25th June 1981 and the World Council of Churches arrive at Cairns airport, met by thirty Aboriginal people including Mick and Monty Pryor who had come up from Townsville. ABC Nationwide is also on the scene. There is a lot of excitement at exposing the situation of Aboriginals to the outside world. The WCC delegation is taken to the Land Council office for a briefing and are shocked at what they hear.

The Land Council team then takes them the 60km to Yarrabah, past pristine beaches and then up the steep mountain road. The WCC team, which includes Quince Duncan of Costa Rica and In Myung Jin of South Korea, are treated to traditional food, a talk on the history and legends of Yarrabah by elder Robert Patterson and then a fiery outline of current problems at Yarrabah and the need for land rights by chairman Percy Neal.

They are then given a tour of the community and see the dilapidated housing, unsealed roads and lack of drainage in the Aboriginal residential area. This is in sharp contrast to the European residential area with quality ventilated homes, lush gardens and Aboriginal yardmen to care for them.

They are shown the farming leases of the Yarrabah Co-operative whose crops languish for lack of irrigation and machinery. In comparison, the government-controlled farm boasts healthy irrigated crops with shiny new irrigation pipes and pumps. The shed is full of tractors and fertilizers. Despite paying 33% of their income towards the use of this equipment, it never seems to be available to the co-operative farmers.

However, the rainforest, beaches and the tranquility of the natural scenery captures their hearts and they can see why developers have their eyes on the beachfront community.

Up at 5am the next morning, the WCC team is off to Palm Is with Mick, keen to have the world spotlight on his home community. On the light plane from Cairns to Palm Is, Mick is asked if he had permission for them to come. Mick laughs. He never asks the DAIA for permission to visit a reserve, especially his home. However, the ABC Nationwide team gets there before them. There is a welcoming party at the airport of the Bwgcolman (Palm Is) community.

Meeting in the library, the WCC delegation stares in amazement at the by-laws pinned on the notice board: "Thou shalt not think for thyself. Tis a sin against The Department" and "If a policeman is hassling your mother, you shall assist him. Tis a sin to do otherwise." Someone was having a joke but if you read the actual by-laws, you'll see this is a good interpretation.

About 300 people gather in the canteen to meet the WCC team and the ALP Senators who fly in. Then it is a lunch of turtle, fish and possum and a tour to Butler Bay where Mick grew up. All the while, the WCC delegation is gathering information. E.g., the Palm Islanders would receive a $200 fine if they took one oyster from the oyster farm, the income from which goes to the Qld government. Also, there is a big contrast between European and Aboriginal housing and residential areas.

Back to Cairns for a public meeting and in the morning, Mick, Shorty and Bertie Button take the WCC delegation to Mantaka, Koah, Kuranda and Mossman Gorge so they can get an idea of what life is like for Aboriginals on the outskirts of small towns. Their visit comes to an end over an enjoyable kup-mari of traditional food, singing and exchanging of stories.

WCIP Sweden

Mick is in demand in Aboriginal politics and he is trying to fit this in with his job as a teacher. Peter Noble is manning the NQLC office with myself and other volunteers. The Education Department isn't impressed when Mick takes time off to attend the World Council of Indigenous People (WCIP) Second General Assembly at Kiruna in Samiland (Sweden). It is an important time for Australian Aborigines to connect with Indigenous people worldwide and share ideas and strategies. Mick goes in his role as Chairman of the North Queensland Land Council and represented the National Aboriginal Conference (NAC) as well. Other delegates are Charles Perkins, Kevin Cavanagh, Bobby Mellors and Ross Moore. It is September 1977 and is hosted by the Sami people previously known as Laplanders. Lapland is located above the Arctic Circle in Europe in the countries of Norway, Sweden, Finland and Russia and is a people with their own culture but is not a nation.

The World Council of Indigenous Peoples develops against a growing background of internationalism of the struggle of Indigenous people and the recognition of their common fate as colonized people. Since the late 1800's, Maoris and Canadian Indians independently made representations to the Queen or King of England with little success except that the Maoris managed to get 4 seats in Parliament. Aboriginal William Cooper in Australia gathered signatures in a petition to the King of England but the Australian government would not pass it on. Approaches were also made by the Maoris and Canadian First Nations people to the League of Nations and the United Nations. George Manuel, a Canadian First Nations leader, is the force behind the establishment of the World Council of Indigenous Peoples.

A definition of "Indigenous people" was developed at an international meeting in Guyana in 1974.

> "The term indigenous people refers to people living in countries which have a population of differing ethnic or racial groups who are descendants of the earliest populations living in the area and who do not, as a group, control the national government of the countries within which they live."[11]

Mick was asked to Chair the first session of the six-day conference at Kiruna along with a delegate from Mexico and Canada. Mick presented a submission to the conference on behalf of the North Qld Land Council which was accepted in full to be passed on to the United Nations. The WCIP is in the process of getting non-government status at the UN. Mick took the Qld Aborigines Act with him and a Canadian Indian delegate takes it home to study. Mick also tells them about the deficiencies of the Northern Territory land rights legislation and that there is none in Qld.

Delegates explain that the Meti, who have both Indian and white heritage, are not recognized as Indian and cannot own land. Mick explains the difference in Australia. Aborigines are Aborigines no matter what percentage of Aboriginal blood they have as long as they recognize themselves as Aboriginals and are accepted as such by the black community. They can own land corporately with the rest of the group. However, Australia as a whole is still waiting for land rights and compensation.

One of the most startling aspects of the conference is the stories of persecution, arrest and torture of some First Nations people from Peru, Chile and Argentina, some of whom are now in exile. Spanish, English, Swedish and Sami interpreters are on hand.

Mick is concerned that the biggest iron ore mine in the world is on Sami land. A huge mountain is being cut away but they get no royalties, jobs or job training. It is planned that the next WCIP conference be held in Cairns. However, Ross Jirra Moore organizes the 3rd General Assembly of the WCIP in Canberra May 1981 hosted by the NAC.

I meet Mick as he arrives at Cairns airport. I wait excitedly as the passengers come off the plane in ones and twos. He finally appears, "Hello, beautiful," he says smiling.

"I've missed you," I say. It's not like today where you can keep in touch with text, emails, Skype etc. I only had one phone call while he was away.

"I've got a present for you," says Mick. "It's a dress and you'll have to wear it for me tonight. I'll take you out to dinner to the Kowloon."

"Thanks," I reply, looking forward to it.

The restaurant is nearly full. It is his favorite and not far from our Land Council office which is 96A Lake Street, above Walkers Bookshop. As he asks for the chilli, he says, "I was surprised to find that there are white Indigenous people like the Samis. They dress very colorfully and love to eat reindeer. I tasted it for the first time. It was a great experience mixing with indigenous people from around the world and exchanging ideas."

"Reindeer meat! Wow! That would've been interesting. It must have been freezing. It would've been a great opportunity to let people know what's happening here," I exclaim.

Mick says,

> "Even though the conference was towards the end of summer, we still had two days of snow. The Land of the Midnight Sun

is a good name for the place," nods Mick. "The sun rises at 4am and sinks at 8pm but there was enough light for you to read on the lawn till midnight and start again at 3am," his eyes widening in amazement.

"How did you find Sweden?" I ask.

"They are surprisingly free and uninhibited compared to people I've met elsewhere. It's ironic that indigenous people are becoming recognized as the Fourth World. I think we are the First World as we were here first," he laughs.

I smile and nod.

The next day a letter arrives from the Education Department basically saying, "You're fired." He loses his job as a teacher because they decide he is too political and the government wants to remove his means of financial support.

"What are we going to do now?" I ask, worried and surprised.

"The bastards," he says. "I'll show them a thing or two. Don't worry, we'll just have to drum up some more finances from our supporters and I'll work full time for the land council."

We manage somehow but one day I notice the spare room is littered with unopened bills. The locks on our door are changed more than once by the bank because we are behind on house payments. Fortunately, we don't lose the house; always managing to get through. Mick is on a number of national committees and he gets travel allowance and sitting fees which help.

For most of my life with Mick, he is the public figure, the Aboriginal statesman, and I am his support. But for my first two years with him as I work on the Mapoon project, I am the frontrunner and he is my support. He is crucial to the project however, with his advice in the background and his contacts with key people. As I help the Mapoon people go back home to the place they lost, I find my home, the place I belong.

Harry Penrith, or Burnam Burnam, our matchmaker, says to me one day, "You might be white but you have a black heart. You understand how we feel and you think the way we think. "

"That's such a compliment," I reply, overwhelmed.

Jan Roberts

Jan Roberts of International Development Action, is the one who organized for me to move to Cairns to work on the White Colonialism in Australia project, which became the Mapoon project. The Mapoon people were moved off their land at gunpoint by police in 1963 at the order of the Queensland government to make way for mining. After we help the people move back to their land north of Weipa in 1974, and Jan publishes *The Mapoon Story Vols 1, 2 and 3* in 1975, she moves to England with her family.

It means that Jan is able to set up a base in England to promote Aboriginal causes and work with groups like Colonialism and Indigenous Minorities Research and Action (CIMRA) which she founds in London in 1976. Also, she works with Survival International. Jan develops worldwide connections and, with War on Want, CIMRA publishes Jan's 1978 book *From Massacres to Mining: the Colonisation of Aboriginal Australia.*

Jan also works with groups in Europe like Bread for the World. It describes itself as:

"Bread for the World – Protestant Development Service is the globally active development and relief agency of the Protestant Churches in Germany. In more than 90 countries all across the globe we empower the poor and marginalized to improve their living conditions. Key issues of our work are food security, the promotion of health and education, the access to water, the strengthening of democracy, respecting human rights, keeping peace and the integrity of creation."

Internationalization Of Australian Indigenous Cause

It appears the internationalization of the struggle for Australian Aboriginal rights takes off with Mick leading a NQLC delegation to UK and Europe. Jan organizes this trip and travels with them in November and December 1978. I am heavily pregnant.

Joyce Hall from Weipa, where Comalco is mining, and Jacob Wolmby from Aurukun, where mining is proposed, travel with Mick. The British press call Joyce and Jacob Chief and Mick the Paramount Chief though the term chief is not used by Aboriginal Australians. Harassed by immigration officials, having visa problems before leaving Australia and followed by special branch police to the Sydney airport, they travel to England, Scotland, the Netherlands, Germany and Switzerland.

The NQLC and Jan meet with the International Court of Jurists, the International Labor Organization and a number of Members of Parliament and embassies. In all they have 93 meetings in six weeks and speak also to mining companies, anti-uranium groups, churches and trade unions. It is very effective in raising awareness of the Aboriginal situation.

They meet with the British Energy Secretary, Mr Benn. AAP's report from London is covered in *The Cairns Post* 22nd November 1978. Mick tells them,

> He (Benn) said that though he had sympathy with the problems of the Aboriginals, the British Government needed uranium."

Mick is reported also as saying that the British people had "conveniently ignored" the Aboriginal people but they "haven't forgotten our mineral wealth."

Joyce, sister to the famous potter Thancoupie, and Mick chuckle at the pressure they put RTZ under when they go to the AGM and protest about mining at Weipa. Shareholders need to know the effect of their actions.

Secretary of the Netherlands Commission for Justice and Peace, Dr B. A. Meulenbroek, says interest in the Aboriginal cause, "is increasing in the Netherlands. We are very happy about this and we will help wherever we can." This comment was included in a report by Al Grassby, Commissioner for Community Relations, in his Paper No 2 *World Perceptions of Racism in Australia*, April 1981. The Dutch translation of *The Mapoon Story* contributes to this. Theology students help translate it.

The Nation Review, 12th April 1979, carries an article by Chris Forsyth "Globalizing Aboriginal land rights." It uses a photo of the front cover of *The Mapoon Story* Vol 1 in Dutch with a photo of Mrs Jimmy and Jerry Hudson. Comments by Dr H. C. Coombs and Mick Miller at a land rights teach-in at Sydney University 17-18 March are included with Coombs speaking of the genocide of Aborigines and that a treaty was never negotiated with a people who had a system of land tenure over the whole of Australia. Mick tells the 400 delegates that they have had to internationalize the fight for human rights and he has spoken to UN bodies and embassies who are supportive. The November to December visit by Mick and the N.Q. Land Council to England, Scotland, the Netherlands, Germany and Switzerland greatly assists this. The article says,

> "The members spoke at 93 meetings in six weeks; possibly nothing so power-packed has been undertaken by any Australians, black or white, since an Aboriginal cricket team toured England in 1868 and in 126 days played 47 matches.
>
> The NQLC delegates spoke to MPs, trade unions, mining companies, anti-uranium groups, churches, shop stewards, the International Court of Jurists, the UN Commission on Human Rights, the International Labor Organization and as well a number of embassies which will be sponsoring the Aborigines' fight for human rights in the UN.
>
> 'The fight for our rights must be taken up by other countries in the UN,' Miller said. 'The Australian government must be made to answer for allowing apartheid to operate in Queensland and

> for denying basic human rights to the Aboriginals of Australia, and for refusing to recognize that we, the Aboriginals, are the original owners of Australia and, as such, are entitled to compensation for the land being stolen from us'."

Through the work of Mick and other Aborigines who visit UK and Europe, support committees for Australian Aborigines are set up in Germany, Belgium, France, Denmark, Austria and Switzerland.

When Mick comes home, he is excited, "Billiton has agreed not to mine at Aurukun. What a victory. This'll mean so much to the Aurukun mob."

> "Wow. That's amazing," I say excitedly. "How did you manage that?"
>
> "We met with Billiton in the Netherlands. Though they have leases at Aurukun, Jacob and I told them the Aurukun people didn't want mining on their land."
>
> "It helps to hear from the horses' mouth," I reply, "to be confronted face to face with the effects of your policies."
>
> "Too right," says Mick.

However, one day shortly after his return he breaks out in gentle tears.

> "What is it?" I ask surprised.
>
> "There was this girl in Germany who cried when I told her the story about how Aboriginal people are treated. It broke her heart."
>
> "I'm glad that she has such compassion," I reply, giving him a hug. "You must have shared from your heart."

Joyce And Les Visit London Re RTZ

Joyce Hall makes another visit to London. This time with Les Russell of Victoria, who is chairman of the Aboriginal Mining Information Centre (AMIC). Co-ordinating and financing this are Jan Roberts of CIMRA,

Survival International, War on Want, the North Qld Land Council, the Kimberley Land Council and Victoria's South Eastern Land Council. This follows a CRA AGM in Melbourne. It is attended by Les, Shorty and Noel Preston of the Uniting Church Social Justice Department, to ask questions.

Les and Joyce have problems with immigration and are arrested at Gatwick in London. Sorting this out, their first task is a Tribunal hearing investigating RTZ. Evidence is heard from Canada, Namibia, Panama and NZ with Les and Joyce presenting last. The result is de-investment including the Greater London Council de-investing 375,000 shares.

Following this is the RTZ AGM. There are questions on Namibia, Panama and New Zealand and Joyce and Les ask questions on Australia. They raise issues of lack of consultation and desecration of sacred sites in Victoria, the Kimberleys and Weipa, with Joyce being very forceful.

Les pulls out a document which had been leaked to him from CRA which shows the company's PR plan is to publicly be in favor of Aboriginal interests but privately deny them royalties, compensation and land rights. It's called the Ashton Joint Venture Public Relations Programme 1981. It says the PR campaign will be more than paid for by saving money compensating Aborigines. Les says,

"Tuke (RTZ chairman) nearly fainted. He was speechless – and Carnegie (CRA Managing Director) – his jaw was bouncing on the floor … I can remember I ripped into Carnegie about his blatant lie in reply to the Victorian question earlier. I threw back at him facts and figures supplied by the mines department of Victoria. I then became very emotional as it involves a uranium deposit on sacred land of mine. I demanded consultation with all Aboriginal people and their land councils and finished by draping the flag over my shoulders and stormed out while pointing out that the laws protected white places of importance, but not sacred sites. And that the companies, such as RTZ, were complicit in this sacrilegious behavior. This was the cue for the meeting to break up, and it did. Tuke lost control of the meeting. I can remember looking at Carnegie as I walked out. He was in deep distress."[12]

The Australian delegation consider the trip to London a success because there is more de-investment in RTZ. Les and Joyce speak also to universities, support groups and community organizations.

Christian Conference Of Asia

Peter Noble is invited by the Australian Council of Churches to attend a conference in Auckland New Zealand in October 1978. Peter says all delegates found it educational.

> "Discussions centered on ways and means and how the oppressed and the minority groups of a country can best influence the government to see that justice is done for the oppressed minorities and how best peace and harmony can be achieved for the betterment of a country." (*NQ Messagestick* Jan 79 Vol 4 No 1)

NQLC Refused Visa to USA

A black American student organisation invites the NQLC to a human rights seminar in Washington DC in May 1979. Peter Noble and Cilla Pryor are refused visas to attend and miss the opportunity much to their disappointment.

Nuclear Free Pacific

Clarrie Grogan represents the North Qld Land Council in Ponape at a Pacific Action Front Meeting and Pacific Church Conference. Ponape (now Pohnpe) in Micronesia is one of the wettest places on earth and has lagoons with an amazing array of marine fauna. However, Clarrie doesn't have time for sightseeing. The conference supports a nuclear free Pacific and independence movements in the Pacific, including support for better conditions for Australian Aboriginals.

The Association for International Cooperation and Disarmament (AICD) organizes a Nuclear Free Pacific Forum in Sydney in September

1980. The 350 delegates end the conference on an emotional note with the singing of an Hawaiian peace song which came after a Maori song of struggle. Anti-war songs had also filled the air.

Delegates came from Japan, Vanuatu, West Papua, PNG, Fiji, Hawaii and Palau. Issues discussed are nuclear weapons, dumping and reactors in the Pacific, independence from France and the US and the struggle of minorities such as the Maoris and Aborigines.

Cliff Dolan from the Australian Council of Trade Unions (ACTU) speaks against the Ranger uranium mining agreement and Mick Miller speaks on Aboriginal rights issues. Hilda Lini from the newly independent Vanuatu, passionately outlines the need for recovery from a rebellion of 2,000 people on Espiritu Santo where infrastructure was destroyed.

On 15th January 1981, Mick receives a letter from Junkos Yamaka of the Asia-Pacific Resource Center in Tokyo. She asks if Mick remembers meeting her at the YMCA and says his short visit to the anti-nuclear movement was valuable. She finds it useful to watch the film *Dirt Cheap* he loaned her to watch. It is the first time for them to see the life of the Aboriginal people. A long interview with Mick is in the journal *Jishukoza,* and his photo is on the cover. She writes a short article on him in a Labor journal called *Labor Information.* Junkos says she will send him PQRC's newsletter, *New Asia News*, which carries a special issue on the no-nuke movement.

On 1st March they will be holding a nuclear-free Pacific Day in Japan and want him to come for it. Instead, Mick sends NQLC delegate Sandra Levers who attends peace meetings in Japan on the anniversary of the bombing of Hiroshima and Nagasaki, showing our support for the anti-nuclear movement. It is the 35th anniversary of the Japan Conference Against A and H Bombs, or *Gensuikin,* and Sandra has the opportunity to address the meeting in Nagasaki on 8th August 1980. She is disturbed to find that the Marshallese were displaced from their island for testing and there have been health effects from the testing. Even the death of children. Also, delegates from Guam and Palau tell their story of the dumping of nuclear waste in their waters.

Sandra addresses a similar conference the following day and urges the Japanese to stop the cycle where it begins: in the mining on Aboriginal and Indian land. Then it won't be dumped on the land of another indigenous group, the Pacific Islanders.

Sandra is also selected by church groups to attend a meeting of Pacific peoples in Tonga, where she is an able contributor.

The NQLC lobbies for the Pacific Islands to be nuclear free and is involved with the campaign against French tests in the Pacific e.g., against tests on Bikini Atoll. The daughter of the president of Vanuatu, Walter Lini, visits us in Cairns, cementing relationships and seeking support.

Japan is seeking to dump its nuclear waste in the Pacific and the anti-nuclear movement in Japan contacts us and others in New Zealand (NZ) to oppose a visit to Australia and NZ by the Director-General of Japan's Science and Technology Agency, Nakagawa Ichiro, in July 1981. The letter from Yamako Junko of Han-Genpatsu News says Japan is pushing Australia hard for its uranium development. Attached to it is information from a memo on 19th May 1981 to Lt. Governor Ada of Guam from Guam's Assistant Attorney General, Daniel Isaacson. Nakagawa is quoted as responding to Governor Camacho and Lt. Governor Ada:

> "I wish to welcome all of you. We want to apologize for any anguish that you have been caused. Your position is understood 100%. Japan has no intention of going ahead without the consent of all the Pacific nations. We will not proceed without an actual agreement. We will study your petition and get back to you later. I would point out that you can embrace, you can sleep in the same bed with these 55-gallon drums of concrete which contain the low-level nuclear waste. We have 280,000 drum-cans at 21 nuclear plants all in storage. Technicians move within these areas at no danger to themselves."[13]

He goes on to explain that they could not be stored in Japan because international standards say they needed to be at a depth of 4,000 metres with no volcanic activity. He is explaining to them and Japanese fishermen that they do not want to force the issue.

I look at this now and find the image laughable that one would feel safe or want to embrace and sleep with drums of nuclear waste made of concrete.

Strangers In Their Own Land Film

Mick is excited about a documentary on Aboriginal issues that will show on UK TV. "I had a call from Jan that Chris Curling will be interviewing me for a current affairs TV show in the UK. He's read Jan's book *From Massacres to Mining* and wants to interview me."

"Great," I reply. "We need to get the word out more internationally and raise support."

Mick also provides advice on this project which results in the groundbreaking film *Strangers in Their Own Land* directed by Chris Curling in 1979 for Granada Television in the UK.

On the film, shown in England in March, Mick provocatively says that South African and Rhodesian leaders could take a refresher course on racism from Bjelke-Petersen and compares Bielke's Queensland to Alabama.

I didn't remember till I was writing this memoir but Roger Moody, who works closely with Jan in CIMRA, writes that Joyce Hall, one of the most prominent members of the Weipa community and the NQLC, travels to Europe in 1981 to testify at an international tribunal on the degree to which her land has been rendered a dustbowl. Comalco mounts a defamation case against the Australian Broadcasting Commission (ABC) for similar allegations made by Joyce Hall in the Granada TV film *Strangers in their own Land.* It was shown on the 4 Corners program in Australia 19-20 May.

During the trial, Weipa people give moving testimony on how Comalco has failed to keep its promises. Gertrude Molton testifies that mining has destroyed the hunting, while their homes flood in the wet season. According to Andrew Miller, Comalco is not re-planting local varieties of plants, and animals will not return to their original habitat. Stanley Budbury says that he and his people have to walk twenty miles to catch pigs.

Joyce's testimony is the most riveting. For the first time in more than twenty years, she tells publicly what happened when bulldozers first moved onto her ancestral land at Weipa. Tongue- tied by emotion, she has to leave the court at one point. When she returns, she declares,

> "Since the mining come, a real sacred place was destroyed… that is where the bodies, the deads, were put on the trees. In our own traditional ways, the bodies are not buried. They are put up into the trees until the grease is down… left to dry before we could go back. This was destroyed when they burnt and knocked the trees down. They did not know it was there. Of course, whiteman should know better. Ask first."[14]

Couldn't Be Fairer Film

In 1984, Dennis O'Rourke is commissioned to make the documentary film *Couldn't Be Fairer* for the BBC program *Third Eye*, which is a series of programs focusing on the third world conflicts with western culture. O'Rourke tells *Tribune*, "North Queensland, for Aboriginal people, could be regarded as the third world. What exists there is basically a colonial situation, both on and off the reserves."

The title comes from a 1983 comment of Bjelke, "We treat them the same as everyone else: couldn't be fairer." However, I hear it a number of times from the Premier. *Tribune* says,

> "Mick Miller, time and time again, emphasizes the hypocrisy and racism which underlies such a statement. Unfortunately, *Couldn't Be Fairer* shows that Bjelke-Petersen's racism is shared by many whites in Northern Queensland. Hotel

> workers, white drinkers, police, mining companies, even workers in the tourist industry show, by their statements and actions, that Aborigines are not treated the same as everyone else in the Sunshine State."[15]

Mick is the writer and narrator while Dennis is the producer and director. Mick explains his reasons for making it,

> "A film had to be made to show that in the little outback towns, nothing has really changed. Blacks are still being bashed and arrested for minor offences and it's very difficult to lay charges against those responsible. We wanted to show that, in Queensland, Blacks are still being treated the way they were 30 years ago, and that in some of the pubs in the little towns there are still separate bars for Blacks and Whites. We Blacks still aren't allowed to drink with the local ringers and landowners."[16]

The film has confronting footage of Mick travelling through North Queensland as he talks to Aboriginal people on reserves and in country towns about the effect that mining and tourism have had on them. The racist pub talk of Australians is exposed as are the social problems on Aboriginal communities.

However, the BBC decide that parts of the film are "too shocking" for English TV audiences. Scenes dealing with drunkenness, the sexual oppression of Aboriginal women and the dire living conditions of Aborigines are cut from the English version.

Mick says,

> "They simply couldn't believe that a state in Australia could have laws or could subject its Black people the way Queensland does." Mick saw the BBC decision as symptomatic of the attitude of many whites when confronted with the facts about racism: they simply don't believe it exists or that it is as bad is you make out. "They say 'We're not all

> racist,' but lots of them still scream and oppose the little bit of help the Aboriginal people do get."
>
> ... The system is designed to pull us down and keep us in the muck, but we fought it. That's how we got to where we are today. Nothing would have changed through the goodwill of the government."[17]

Viewing it for this memoir, I love to see the footage of Old Mapoon and Weipa as it brings back memories of my time there and the people I know whose faces seem to look at me through the film. The flies and the dogs at Mapoon are an enduring image against its tropical beauty and the barest necessities of the early days of their return are depicted with log timber tables, chairs and beds etc.

Anchorage Conference Alaska

Shorty O'Neill is on loan from the North Qld Land Council to the Federation of Land Councils and so is based in Alice Springs. Along with Maureen Kelly from the Pilbara Land Council and Stanley Scrutton, chairman of the Central Land Council, he attends a conference in Anchorage in March 1984 to give advice to and learn from the people there. Discussions centered around the effectiveness of the Alaska Native Claims Settlement Act of 1971.

Mick Miller Address Australian Council of Churches Brisbane General Meeting July 1982

Mick Miller and Other Speakers at Kiruna photo supplied by Mick to *NQ Messagestick*

L to R Joyce Hall, Jacob Wolmby and Mick Miller in London photo supplied by Mick Miller

Nuclear Free Pacific Forum in Sydney, Mick is 2nd from left

Chapter 7

National Advocacy

Development Without Destruction

I must have a thing about organizing conferences. Not only did I do most of the organizing for the formation meeting of the NQLC and subsequent meetings, I also organize an alternative conference to the World Wilderness Congress in Cairns in Environment Week 9-13 June 1980. No Aboriginal communities on Cape York have been invited to attend, despite making up about three-quarters of the population. Also, the Queensland Premier has refused to transfer the lease to John Koowarta after his group has purchased a property on his traditional land near Aurukun. When asked later about his response to Bjelke declaring his tribal land a national park, John Koowarta tells *NQ Messagestick* Vol 5 No 2 September 1980:

> "I myself feel unhappy the way they are going to set up a national park around Archer River especially as we have never been told by someone about the arrangement. They are setting up the wild national park. Stop and think for a moment who are the first people of Australia, White or Aboriginal?"

In a plan hatched up between the North Queensland Land Council and the Cairns Environment Week committee, we hold our conference in the open air in Munro Martin Park across the road in full view of the World Wilderness Congress in their classy venue. I'm looking now at two photos in *Chain Reaction*, the Friends of the Earth magazine Vol 5 No 4 1980 by Barbara Hutton, where they carry an article on both conferences called "Black in Green" and include photos of the Mornington Island dancers delighting us at Munro Martin Park and Jean Jimmy from Mapoon speaking to us. I spoke on a Black State because it was a hot issue with the Premier. As well as Aboriginal speakers, we have conservationists and MP's who speak.

Some conservationists oppose the Congress, believing it has a development driven agenda. It started in South Africa and is funded by the government and big industry. There is an invitation to Congress visitors to hunt on magnificent ranches of private landowners. The one in Cairns received $80,000 from the mining industry and $90,000 from the Queensland and Commonwealth governments. Famous Aboriginal visual artist Dick Roughsey from Mornington Island, Percy Trezise, Wally O'Grady and Verne McLaren from Australia travelled to the South African congress and Dick was chased out of the whites only toilet in Cape Town because of being the wrong color.

I choose the name "Development Without Destruction" as the theme of our conference and it is at our conference that the idea is brought up of setting up a peak conservation group so all the conservation groups can work together to stop the logging of the rainforest. So, the following year, the Cairns and Far North Environment Centre (CAFNEC) is formed and I represent the North Queensland Land Council the on the committee. In 1988 a large section of the Wet Tropics Rainforests is declared a World Heritage Area. The world heritage value of the rainforest Bama, or Aboriginal people, is to follow with a cultural heritage listing.

The Development Without Destruction conference was so successful, we hold it again the following year and delegates from New Zealand and southern Africa attend as well as Aboriginals and others from around Australia.

Mornington Island Messagestick

Shorty O'Neill moves from Palm Island where he has been editing *The Palm Islander* newspaper to Cairns so he can take over from me and edit *N. Q. Messagestick* as I'm too involved with my son to do it. Later still, we form the Jaragun Publishing Company and Ted Maza becomes editor. Some of Mick's cousins work voluntary for the NQLC over the years.

In September 1981, Clarrie and Shorty of the NQLC make a field trip to the Cape York communities. They are joined by Bob Weatherall of the Foundation for Aboriginal and Islander Research Action (FAIRA) based in Brisbane, Bertie Button of the Cherbourg Concerned Citizens Committee and Alan Austin, a non-Aboriginal pilot and journalist from Melbourne who has links to the Victorian Baptist Social Justice Working group and the Division of Social Justice of the Uniting Church of Victoria. The latter groups help with funding.

Open meetings are held at Mornington Island, Aurukun, Normanton, Kowanyama, Coen and Laura and discussions with Aboriginals are held at Hopevale, Edward River Mission and Doomadgee. After meeting with the Weipa South Aboriginal chairman, the delegation is thrown off the reserve by white police at the instruction of the white manager. Sounds a bit like my experience in 1974 when I was banned from Weipa South reserve. When they arrive at the Lockhart River airstrip, they are refused permission to enter the reserve.

Some amazing quotes from Aboriginal community leaders are contained in the report of the trip by Alan Austin. Graphically, Harris Gregory, Chairman of Kowanyama says,

> "We saw our people taken away in chains when we were little, but we didn't understand. Then we realized. But the chains are still there today, only they're invisible."

Harry Daphney, a graying respected leader at Kowanyama, adds,

> "God gave us this land to look after. Then the white man came

to shoot us down. After they shoot the black man, they call it crown land. I don't see any crown land. I see land that God gave to us."

Tommy Creek, looking intently at them with his wizened face, complains to them at Coen,

> "All my children know my grandfather's secret place. We go there to see it. But now we got to get a permit or miner's right to go there. We can't light a fire or even walk over there without they get the police onto you … We own this place and now they want us to lease it. They got some hide, them fellows."

Jacob Wolmby of Aurukun who has been on a speaking tour with Mick to Europe, seems to reach deep within himself as he says,

> "Our great great grandfathers lived here many many years. My father was given this land by his father. My father gave it to me. Today this land has been stolen by the white man. He didn't pay nothing at all. We say this is our land. And we take responsibility for this land that belonged to our great great grandfathers."

The communities affirmed the right of Mick Miller as NQLC Chairman to speak for them and are outraged at the persistent attacks on NQLC staff by the Queensland government in the media and in parliament. Mr Austin describes what happened on Mornington Island,

> "In an eloquent and moving ceremony, the meeting of the Mornington Island *Muyinda,* or tribal elders, confirmed Mick Miller's authority with a messagestick of carved wood and brolga feathers.
>
> Tribal lawman Lindsay Roughsey painted the message on the timber. 'This will give Mick our feelings straight. This is for him to stand for the land, for our rights, for our people … This means words from our mouths, and from our stomachs."
>
> Accompanying the messagestick was a formal statement

> signed by the seven tribal elders. Roberta Felton says, 'If we just send feathers or messagestick the government might laugh at us. We must do it the European way too. Then they must take notice of us.'"[18]

As I research this memoir and find this report, I am touched by it and wonder where the messagestick is. Not long afterwards, I invite Marilyn, my son's sister, for dinner to celebrate her birthday. It is October 2016. Without planning to, I mention the messagestick. Michael surprises me by saying, "I have it in my unit. Uncle Timer passed it from Dad to me."

"I can't believe it," I say excitedly. "Can I see it please?" He lives in a granny flat attached to our house.

Marilyn and her partner Marcus are excited to see it too. Gray feathers adorn one end of the brown stick, carved out for the purpose of carrying a message. It is a special message of honor and tribute paid to Michael's father which he can now cherish even more, knowing the story behind it.

Noonkanbah, NLC and KLC

Mick, Clarrie and I, representing the North Queensland Land Council, meet with the Northern Land Council (NLC) and visit Kakadu. We are basically seeing how they run things and looking at how we can work together. We have talks with Galarrwuy Yunupingu, NLC Chairman, and also with the NLC solicitor Stuart McGill. We also visit Kulaluk to support the Aboriginal people there. We have talks with Bill Day, advisor to the Larrakia people, who is organizing a tourism boycott as part of the Kulaluk fight for land rights.

We continue on to Noonkanbah to support Western Australian Aboriginal people and to meet with the Kimberley Land Council (KLC) to see how we can support each other. Like the NQLC, the KLC is really a lobby group without government legislation or funding backing it. KLC Aborigines like Frank Chulong, Peter Yu and Jimmy Bieundurry are at the helm. It is in the same boat as our NQLC. It was formed in 1978, the year after the NQLC's formation in January 1977. Before that, we operate as the North Qld Land Rights Committee since 1975.

The Kimberly boasts rugged ranges, tidal rivers, waterfalls, rock pools and many gorges. We travel along the unsealed dusty roads to a beautiful landscape. As we sit around the campfire, we hear the crackling of the fire, the sounds of the birds and insects, and the animated chatter of the traditional Aboriginal owners.

Mick, I and our son Michael time our visit to camp out with a lot of Aboriginal people in a protest camp at Noonkanbah and meetings are occurring. Michael is about 18 months old and he likes to walk around asking the old men for a drink of tea out of their pannikins. I don't feed him tea myself so this must have been a treat for him. It is probably sweetened. I don't allow him cordial while he is growing up, only watered-down fruit juice. The old men think it's a great joke and are happy he has no fear of them though they are strangers and he is in an unfamiliar environment.

Why the protest camp? Under the leadership of Malaga Nipper Tabagee, the Yungngora people are fighting the exploration oil company Amax. In September 1967, the Commonwealth Conciliation and Arbitration Commission adds 'full blood Aboriginals' to the Pastoral Industry Award, resulting in equal pay but the sacking of many Aboriginal workers. They have to move off the stations to towns and Aboriginal reserves. In 1976 the Aboriginal Land Fund Commission purchases Noonkanbah for the Yungngora community and Tabagee and others return to the station.

However, the State government wants mining at Noonkanbah and the Aboriginal people oppose it with a blockade. In August 1980, the government sends a convoy of trucks, drilling equipment and many police to break the blockade. In the scuffle, Tabagee is one of fifty-five people arrested. They are released without charge. Drilling proceeds, but no oil is found.

As the sun sets, the baobab trees look black against the yellow hue that touches the black ground. Higher up in the sky, the pink hues fade away into the clouds. The baobab trees, also called bottle trees, have a massive girth. From their swollen trunks, their branches reach to the night sky looking as if they have many arms pulling the night sky down.

I look at some of the press clippings of the time, "Arrests in the North … but convoy pushes on" *The West Australian,* 11th August 1980. Eight unionists are arrested in the Pilbara in the first confrontations with the oil-rig company as it moves towards Noonkanbah all the way from Perth. Scenes are depicted on the front page of placard-carrying unionists, outnumbered and struggling with police. Bob Hawke is President of the Australian Council of Trade Unions and he declares drilling is unlikely.

The oil rig with its police escort arrive at Noonkanbah on 14th August and the Aboriginal people have closed the gate and gather in a big mob behind the gate forming a blockade. A confrontation follows as police scuffle with Aboriginal protestors and their supporters including clerics. Scores of people are arrested. Dickie Cox describes it:

> "They put us in the jail, me and Jimmy Bieundurry, in the police station for eight days. We'd marched along the flat; I came with the (Aboriginal) flag. I was at the homestead holding the flag and going out and shouting. We locked the gate. We pushed the police away and said, 'Nowhere on our property now'."

A Californian newspaper had an interesting take on the story with the headline, "Aborigines' lizard god to be defended at U.N." *Lodi News-Sentinel,* 27th August 1980. It reported that a group of Aborigines from the Noonkanbah area, aided by solicitor Philip Vincent, would be addressing the UN Sub commission on Human Rights in Geneva the following week asking for protection of their sacred site of Pea Hill under which the Great Goanna lives. It was said that if the Great Goanna was disturbed, the monitor lizards would not mate and it would cause a food shortage. The World Council of Indigenous People was providing the status for them to speak.

The forced exploration is all for nothing. No oil is found so it is a hollow victory for the mining company and the Western Australian government. It takes till 2007 for the Yungngora people to receive their native title. One of the outcomes though of the Noonkanbah protests is a greater solidarity between the Kimberley Land Council; the Northern Land Council, who are also at Noonkanbah supporting them; and the North Queensland Land Council. Mick persuades them to form the Federation of Land Councils which becomes an important national voice for the land rights movement. The Central Land Council joins and other land councils join as they are set up.

Australian Associated Press (AAP) reports from Perth that the chairman of the North Queensland Land Council, Mr Mick Miller, maintains that Aboriginal land councils throughout Australia plan to federate and that an Aboriginal land council for the Pilbara region is being formed. Mick reports (*The Cairns Post,* 6th September 1980) that the three-day meeting of six land councils decided to ban talks by Aboriginals with mining companies over access to Aboriginal land.

David Elias of *The Age* reports on the Noonkanbah meeting in "Quietly Flow the Words of Anguish,"

> "Occasionally, a delegate would get up and jump into the water to cool off on a hot steamy day. One was Mick Miller, chairman of the North Queensland Land Council, a big powerful man. He emerged from the shallows, his clothes dripping wet, to speak on how the first place to be affected by the Aborigines' decision to ban co-operation with mining companies would be the bauxite project at Aurukun on the west coast of the Cape York Peninsula.
>
> Mr Miller was the man who sent Galarrwuy Yunupingu, former star of the land rights movement, hurrying off home ahead of schedule. Mr Yunupingu, former chairman of the Northern Land Council in the Northern Territory, and the man who negotiated the Ranger agreement, called for moderation in a 15-minute speech. Mr Miller used his influence to prevent any support for Yunupingu."

Elias is entertained by Clarrie,

> "The court jester was Clarrie Grogan, a former professional boxer and now a member of the North Qld Land Council. He strummed a guitar and squeaked out a tune on a gumleaf. Occasionally he told jokes: "I come from the days when men were men and women liked it that way, ' for example. The man who used to weigh in at little more than 11 stone when he was fighting state and national titles, is now at least 15 stone. He fights now with words."

Mick was later interviewed by Martin Mulligan in Sydney while attending the Nuclear Free Pacific conference 26-28 September. Asked about the mood of people at Noonkanbah, he says,

> "The getting together of all the land council representatives was a terrific boost for the Noonkanbah people. It was a morale boost. It gave them just that little bit extra determination to fight on. All the old people told us this."

He continued,

> "Charles Court (West Australian Premier) is the main problem, because Amax was prepared to negotiate after their drillers had been called out on strike. But it was Charles Court, like a big school-bully who moved in a blitzkrieg fashion in order to smash any land rights campaign in WA.
>
> … at the moment, the breaking off of the negotiations (with mining companies) is growing. I'll give you a couple of examples. The Oombulgurri community (near Wyndham in the Kimberleys) has refused twice to let CRA prospect for diamonds.
>
> The Central Land Council (around Alice Springs) has told mining companies there will be no further negotiations until the Noonkanbah dispute is settled to the satisfaction of the Noonkanbah people."[19]

Federation Of Land Councils

The first meeting of the federation of land councils is held in Melbourne during the Commonwealth Heads of Government Meeting (CHOGM) and two subsequent meetings are held in Alice Springs. We have three people attend meetings from the NQLC. One from our working committee, one from the reserves and one from the rural/fringe dweller situation. The major issues the federation are working on are the Australian Mining Industry Council, the Northern Territory Land Rights Act, the Commonwealth Games, the Outstation movement, national uniform land rights legislation, self-determination policy, the international Charter of Indigenous People's Rights and the South Australia Heritage Act.

The Federation of Land Councils sends Shorty O'Neill of the NQLC to establish an embassy in London, publicizing Australian Indigenous issues to the United Nations and representatives of European nations. Survival International provides some support for him. Jimmy Biendurry of the Kimberley Land Council joins him for an RTZ AGM on 3rd June 1982. I believe RTZ was the parent company of Comalco at the time.

Chairman of RTZ, Sir Anthony Tuke, abruptly ends the meeting before they can speak. Shorty grabs the microphone but is evicted by police along with others in the uproar that ensues. This gets publicity however and the Aboriginal voice is heard. Shareholders start asking questions.

Growing Up Michael And Part Time Work

Clarrie likes to say, "You big wax. You're a drag on society," and "Good go." Mick's other nickname he calls himself is "The Phantom." He writes letters to our NQLC *NQ Messagestick* under the nickname "R U Ready."

I don't have an easy time with Posky. He is a very demanding colicky child. Sometimes he won't sleep long enough for me to have a shower. The only way I can do any reading is to read a little while I lay down feeding him. I breast feed him on demand and he seems to demand it every two hours for a long time. Sometimes I feel like I exist on the end of his mouth. But, I love him a lot and find that carrying him in a sling comforts him and is the only way I can get some housework done.

To get him to sleep at night, we take him for a drive in the car. When Mick is home, he nurses him to his favorite music, the Edinburgh Military Tattoo. Mick loves to watch this on New Year's Eve.

When Michael is a bit older, I do a little bit of freelance journalism for *The Australian* newspaper on, believe it or not, real estate features. I haven't done a journalism course but I like writing. Later I do a column for *The Cairns Post* on alternative health. I never gave up being a Christian but I explore New Age. For some reason I am in a time of searching and I'm not settled in a local church. Lydia and Marilyn have been confirmed in the Catholic Church. I try to take them there and then swimming for an outing but Pat and her family put a stop to that as they are anti-church. I don't find the Uniting church that inspiring.

I go so far as to do a yoga teachers course at the Satyananda Ashram in NSW, taking Michael with me and Rodney Molloy as a babysitter. Michael is used to him. Rod is a regular visitor to our home and likes to take Michael for a walk in his pram when he is younger. We stay overnight with Pat and Lydia and Marilyn in Sydney and Pat graciously gets us some Chinese take away for dinner and pastries for breakfast which are a treat. It is meant to be a month's course but I have to leave early as I am not getting enough time with Michael. The schedule is more demanding timewise than I have expected. Nevertheless, I do teach yoga for a while.

I haven't finished my university studies as I dropped out a couple of times to pursue my spiritual and political path. Now I enroll externally in English and finish my degree. I already have a history major and two years of psychology.

Aboriginal Land Fund Commission And The Koowarta Case

The Whitlam government sets up the Aboriginal Land Fund Commission (ALFC) in 1974 to help Indigenous people acquire land outside reserves. John Koowarta of Aurukun and the *Winychanam* group approaches the commission to buy their traditional land, part of the Archer River Pastoral Holding. In 1976, the Queensland government refuses to give consent to the sale, citing a Cabinet decision of 1972 that the government does not favor the acquisition of large areas of land by Aborigines "in isolation." (Qld Parliament 1976, Page 2008). Mick and I and the NQLC know John well and campaign on his behalf with the government and support groups. We meet with Charles Rowley (ALFC) a number of times in the process.

Mick had been involved in campaigning for the 1967 Referendum in his role as Vice President of FCAATSI. In fact, the Cairns Aborigines Advancement League, of which he is a part, are instrumental in having it passed as are other Aborigines Advancement Leagues from around the nation. I am in my last year of high school in 1967, so I am not involved. An important result of the successful 1967 Referendum is that Indigenous people can now be counted in the census and the federal government can now make laws for them. This means that the federal government is able to pass the immensely important Racial Discrimination Act of 1975 (RDA) which was to eventually help us get rid of the discriminatory Queensland Aborigines Act.

Also, importantly, it means that Koowarta's legal team can lodge a writ in the Supreme Court of Queensland claiming that the minister's decision contravenes the RDA. The case of Koowarta v. Bjelke-Petersen, Tomkins, Glasson, and the State of Queensland begins in 1981 and the High Court in May 1982 decides that the RDA is valid and that Koowarta is an aggrieved person under the Act. Though Koowarta has won his case, he would never occupy his land because in 1977 the Queensland government outmaneuvers us by gazetting it as a national park (later named Archer Bend National Park) and John passes away.

In 2012, a later Queensland government transfers it to Aboriginal ownership, partly as national park and partly as freehold. It was a landmark case setting a precedent. Prime Minister Paul Keating comments, "Without John Koowarta, there would have been no Mabo case, no native title legislation." Keating is quoted in "Aurukun Marks Land Win" *The Courier-Mail*, 10th November 1993. John Koowarta is known by some as the "Mabo of the Mainland." Neither John nor Eddie Mabo were to see the fruit of their labor, both dying beforehand.

50 Year Leases

After all the years of our campaigning against the Queensland Aborigines Act, Bjelke-Petersen announces on 19th March 1981, in Hansard, he is going abolish the Act before the Commonwealth Games in Brisbane because of intense criticism. Were we happy with this announcement? Were our goals finally achieved? Did all the international lobbying bring the pressure to bear on the Queensland government that we wanted?

No. Because there would be no security of land tenure and no local government or self-management. In July the Premier announces he will abolish the Aboriginal reserves in Queensland and replace them with 50-year leases on which rent will need to be paid and no militant activity will be allowed on the leases. This also raises the concern of the Anglican, Roman Catholic and Uniting Churches.

Leader of the federal Opposition, Mr Bill Hayden puts out a statement on 21st July 1981 that "The national government must, without prevarication, assert its constitutional authority to protect the Aboriginal population of Queensland from the latest attack on their rights by Mr Bjelke-Petersen."

The newsreader on ABC radio AM, 21st July 1981, starts off with a comment by Mick, probably from the print media as this isn't an interview, "A Queensland Aboriginal leader has said there'd be a lot of trouble on Aboriginal reserves if the State Government went ahead with its plan to convert the reserves to leasehold. A spokesman for the North Queensland Land Council, Mr Mick Miller, said the Aborigines wanted freehold title to land without any strings attached. He added that Aborigines knew they couldn't trust the Queensland Premier, Mr Bjelke-Petersen."

Fortunately, the Premier did not go ahead with this plan but we always seem to be in a battle.

Sundowner Or Saltwater Murri

We find out more about Mick's Waanyi Aboriginal heritage when we travel by car to the Nicholson River Land Claim for the Waanyi/Garawa people in 1982. It is held at Najabarra near Doomadgee in Queensland but it is under the Northern Territory legislation because there are Borroloola people involved. White state borders came long after Aboriginal tribal borders. Mick's grandmother is Ruby Carlton and his uncle is Morris Carlton. Anthropologist David Trigger prepares the claim for the Northern Land Council. The claim relates to unalienated crown land in the Northern Territory but most of the claimants live at Doomadgee in Queensland. Some come also from Mornington Island, Burketown, Gregory Downs, Floraville, Riversleigh, Camooweal and Mt. Isa.

On 5th October 1911, an old Chinese man called Samou Bau makes an entry in a book he keeps to record the births of Aboriginal children in the Bourketown district. Why he has such an interest, we don't know. Mick Snr's father, Arthur Miller, is Irish and is caretaker of Lawn Hill silver mine. However, Mick Snr is brought up by his full-blood stepfather Gajangga. Gajangga's nickname is Toby Emu because he is good at catching emus. He would hide in the bush and rush out and use a *dugle dugle* (musical instrument) to break the legs of the emus as they pass. Mick Snr is born at Lawn Hill station and later, they go walkabout to Riversleigh. Ted Scanlan, the head stockman on Riversleigh station knows the police are coming to take part Aboriginal children so he arranges for the schoolteacher, who is going to Carlton Hills station to take Mick Snr with him and Ruby and Toby join him three months later. At six years of age, he begins his working life doing stockwork; child labor. Mick Snr escaped the police as a child but as a young man he is forcibly removed from his country (land) to Palm Island ostensibly for cattle duffing (cattle rustling).

Now, he is accepted as a Bwgcolman which means, "many tribes – one people" or part of the local people in Palm Island where he spends most of his life. He is now used to a lifestyle by the sea. When he moves his family to Innisfail, he still loves to spearfish in the rivers or the sea. Driving through the dusty roads, the long trip to Doomadgee with Mick and me in our old car was an eye-opening experience for him. I don't think he'd been back since the police took him away as a young man. Now he is elderly.

"I'd always said I was a sundowner Murri," he says. "But now the dry dust and heat is a bit much for me. I'm a saltwater Murri now."

Mick chuckles. He loves nothing better than to go spear fishing himself or diving off the boat and wrestling with turtles or dugongs, traditional food for Aborigines. He won't use a harpoon or *wop* because he loves to dive and wrestle with the turtles. The Fisheries Department catch Mick with some cut up turtle in our fridge and they take him to court as it is a prohibited food unless you live in an Indigenous community. He has to pay a fine. We have a visitor from India visiting our home once. He is a vegetarian and is appalled at finding a turtle in our yard, lying on its back i.e., lying on its shell, waiting to be shared out amongst the families as a delicacy. I don't really like the green fat which is prized but I find the white flesh is similar to chicken breast and quite tasty.

I love to collect pipi shells off the beach, something Mick shows me to do and then curry them to eat with rice. Our Indian friend doesn't like that idea either. On my first visit to Yarrabah in 1974, Alf Neal lends us his net and Mick and I drag for prawns in the sea not far from the church and old council office. I love it, and then we go to Alf's home where the prawns are cooked and we have a lovely meal.

Mick and I go to Yarrabah regularly and often visit Back Beach. His friend Harrison Smith has a boat and they go out hunting at times. I want to swim but am told the rivers are crocodile infested which is disappointing. I get used to drinking tea from a pannikin, the tea made in a billy can with tinned sunshine milk added (powdered milk). A lot of the Yarrabah people have their beach or bush shacks with just the basics. It is such a beautiful environment by the seashore.

I can't swim in the rivers at Aurukun either, because of crocodiles. My first visit there is on my own on the Mapoon project but I go back with Mick a few times. I don't recall where we stay as there is no accommodation for visitors. There is a huge riot there on one of our visits and Mick tells me to stay out of the way.

We enjoy some home-cooked bread with John and Jeannie Adams, a white Uniting Church family who love the people and are loved by them. Rev John Adams works there as a community advisor. Mick wants Posky to be baptised by Rev Silas Wolmby, his relative who is a Uniting Church minister. Mick doesn't take Posky to Aurukun so it doesn't happen.

Maestro

One of my terms of endearment for Mick is 'Maestro.' It just comes out one day and it seems to fit. It usually refers to a conductor or director of music of an orchestra. It can be a term of respect for a teacher. To me, he is overseeing, directing and bringing together many elements of Indigenous affairs to improve the situation of Indigenous people. He is a master artist bringing harmony to a cacophony of sounds that haven't been playing along to a tune that benefits Indigenous people; sounds that are working against one another, pushing up against one another, grating against the ear. Out of this confusion, this stridency and bluster, out of this clamor, furor and discord, he is trying to bring a unity of perspective and strategy, a harmony of purpose and action. It doesn't always work. But often does, and it is a noble task. His nickname for me is 'Beautiful'.

Mick and Clarrie have a tactic they use. When Mick and Clarrie have a case for their people to take up with government, Clarrie fires first with bluster and complaint, and then Mick presents as the diplomat and they come to an agreement.

Bjekle Kicks Trachoma Team Out Of Qld

Trachoma or Sandy Blight is preventable and curable, but without treatment leads to blindness. It is an international scandal that Australian Aborigines have the highest rate of blindness in the world. Dr Fred Hollows and the National Trachoma and Eye Health Program (NTEHP) team visit more than 465 Indigenous communities across Australia between 1976 and 1979 screening about 100,000 people and restoring eyesight to 27,000 people. They perform about 1,000 surgeries in field clinics.

However, Bjelke sees red when he finds out Mick and Clarrie are being used as field officers in North Qld because of their knowledge of the people. Bjelke thinks he has the right to hire and fire people who don't even work for him. He personally contacts the federal Minister for Health, Mr Hunt, three times and Prime Minister Fraser once saying they are, "Unacceptable to the Qld government." Mr Hunt says he has "no hard evidence" to justify the sackings.

Bjelke insisted Mick and Clarrie were enrolling people to vote and telling them to vote ALP. Voting is compulsory in Australia but it was not compulsory for Aboriginals to vote in federal elections until 1984. They had enrolled some Aboriginals and white nursing sisters in their own time. Senator Bonner responded that is not illegal as he does it all the time. The interference by Bjelke shows that freedom to vote and freedom of speech is an issue in Qld. Mick indignantly responds that if someone asks him for political advice, he tells them how he'll vote and why but that it is up to them to make up their own mind.[20]

Registered nurse, Jilpia Nappaljari Jones, is part of the NTEHP in Queensland in November 1977 when they are "blind-sided" by Premier

Joh Bjelke-Petersen. Steve Gray covers her story as told in *Beyond Sandy Blight*:

> "On Thursday Island, our team encountered political discrimination and harassment against two Aboriginal liaison officers, Mick Miller, a Kalkadoon man, and Clarrie Grogan, a Kukuyalangi man.
>
> At this time, the Queensland government did not encourage the inclusion of Aboriginal and islander people on the electoral roll (a right they only gained after the 1967 referendum), and both incurred the government's wrath when it was alleged that they helped their people to sign on to the electoral roll."[21]

She further spoke of the effective espionage system the state had set up so that it was not long before the Premier knew of Mick and Clarrie's actions:

> "Joh Bjelke-Peterson came to hear any such news very quickly. Mr Killoran encouraged tip-offs from remote communities about which political dissidents intended to enter communities, or which disaffected Aborigines might need to be discredited by the government propaganda apparatus. Such trouble-makers could be shadowed by the police or be named in parliament."[22]

Dr Rodgers, the President of the Royal College of Ophthalmologists, flies from Hobart to Thursday Island to sack Mick and Clarrie despite Fred Hollows protests. The NTEHP in Queensland is prevented from operating. The federal health department does not challenge the Qld Premier. Of course, I remember the incident well from what Mick and Clarrie tell me when they return. Rodgers plans to take them back with him. Clarrie, with a grin, informs me Dr Rodgers tries to intimidate them so Clarrie stands in front of the doorway of the hotel room where the exchange occurs and bars it for a while to show he is not to be bounced around. An agreement is reached that Mick and Clarrie be suspended from the program, but a week later on 7th November, the whole program is thrown out of Qld.

Only six weeks before, on 22nd September, Mick is suspended from his job as schoolteacher after a 17-year successful teaching record. He has confirmation it is a political decision but the official reason given is that he would not take a transfer to Ingham. His application to stay in Cairns because he is still under medical treatment for a car crash, has two daughters at high school and owns his home is not accepted. Going to an international conference in Kiruna in the August school holidays did not help.

Two corrections on the news report, Mick is Waanyi and Kuku Yalanji, with Kalkadoon being a neighboring tribe to the Waanyi. Qld Premier Frank Nicklin introduced the Elections Act Amendment Bill 1965 on 3rd December to amend the Elections Act 1915 to give voting rights to Aboriginal and Torres Strait Islanders. They voted for the first time on 28th May 1966, Qld being the last state to allow Indigenous people to vote. However, it was not compulsory. Indigenous Australians had been able to vote in federal elections since 1949 on condition they had the state vote.

Lindsay Roughsey at Mornington Is Preparing Messagestick for Mick Miller and NQLC
photo *NQ Messagestick* Vo 6 No 4 Oct 1981

Noonkanbah, Aboriginals Close Gate to Mining Company Photo Supplied

Mick Michael and Barbara

Mick and Barbara Miller, Nicholson River Land Claim Hearing at Najabarra, 1982. Photo courtesy of David Trigger and Robert Blowes.

Clarrie Grogan and Mick Miller Speaking in Townsville After the Trachoma Incident. Clarrie Demonstrates His "pound of biffin" Photo Courtesy of Alex Trotter

Chapter 8

More National Advocacy

Commonwealth Games

I want to join Mick in drawing international attention to the plight of Indigenous Australians at the Commonwealth Games in Brisbane but our son is only three years old and Mick says I should stay home and look after him, which I do. I miss out on all the action and my old mates from the Aboriginal movement. Michael isn't a good sleeper, so I don't sleep well either. He is a colicky baby. It didn't dawn on me that there might have been too much happening in the house with people coming and going all the time. People like John Pilger the film maker and many others, whose names I don't remember now.

As I am looking through old press clippings, I see a photo of Mick, Steve Mam and Clarrie leading a march in Brisbane protesting for Indigenous rights during the Commonwealth Games of 1982. Steve is a great Torres Strait Islander leader like Eddie Mabo. He is flanked each side by Aboriginal leaders Mick and Clarrie; they have long been good mates. Mick and Clarrie have been good mates of Eddie (Koiki) also. In this photo, Mick, right arm punching the air, probably saying "Land rights now," is wearing a North Queensland Land Council t-shirt. The design is by Enoch Tranby. Steve is dressed in a short sleeved white suit coat and is waving a placard of Premier Joh Bjelke-Petersen. The photo on the placard shows two young Islander men carrying Bjelke to shore in the Torres Strait; so he wouldn't wet his shoes. The placard reads, "We've been carrying Joh long enough." Time to run our own lives. Clarrie, a former champion boxer, checked shirt, hat and glasses is ready to "Giv 'em a pound of biffin," if the police attack them. Behind them are lines of marchers with placards, the buildings of the capital city rise high on either side. By the way, I never saw Clarrie fight outside the boxing ring.

The Australian National University Press Library has an article on "Making Change Happen" and it has a photo of Mick addressing a rally at Musgrave Park South Brisbane re the Commonwealth Games. He is characteristically making a point with right hand outstretched pointing. Dressed in jeans and a check shirt, he makes an imposing sight as a young man in footy shorts pauses behind him to listen as Mick faces the crowd. I don't have a record of what he said. But the article says,

> "There were a series of major gatherings in the park, with high profile national figures lining up to talk. Senator Neville Bonner, a member of the conservative federal Liberal government, feared the marchers would be subject to police violence, but he was compromised by his party allegiances. Senator Susan Ryan received a better response. Then Labor Shadow Minister for Aboriginal Affairs, she pledged that the ALP, if it should win government under Bob Hawke in the coming elections, would ensure that Queensland joined all Australia in the new government's implementation of the firm Labor Party policy for national land rights. But the strongest applause was for the Aboriginal activists from Queensland, like Mick Miller, and those who had travelled such a long way to be there, like Gary Foley."

"Queensland Police Arrest 200 in Aboriginal Rights Protest" blares the headline in *The Guardian* 8th October 1982. Reporter Mathew Engel says,

> "About 200 people were arrested in Brisbane yesterday for trying to stage an illegal march for Aboriginal rights while, a

> few streets away, thousands watched the Queen tour the city center and a few miles further away, a capacity crowd watched the most important day of the Commonwealth Games athletics. This was the third batch of arrests since the games started. Those arrested included Ann Stephen, daughter of the Governor-General, Sir Ninian Stephen, for the second time this week, a television news crew and a nun."

I can't help but have a laugh over the absurdity of this. But that is Joh's Queensland.

Political Interference In Me Getting Work

I don't know if he is related to Don Egan, the policeman who arrested me for trespassing at Weipa, but Des Egan has a hand in the TAFE system that will not employ me in 1983. Rose Colless, who is running a shelter for homeless alcoholics at Douglas House, requests me as a casual adult literacy teacher with the residents on TAFE funding. She receives a letter from Keith Goodwin, Cairns TAFE, on 13th December 1982 that I will not be appointed. She believes it is politically motivated. Mick contacts Steve Mam who is the Chairman of the NAC for Queensland and he sends a telegram on 20th January 1983 to Mr RH Wallace, Queensland Director of TAFE alleging political interference in teaching appointments as I have the qualifications to do the job. I am employed.

Separation From Mick

Mick and I are having some difficulties in 1983. I can't remember what it is about but probably having so little personal time together doesn't help and he likes a few drinks with his mates. He isn't a problem drinker, however. When we first got together, he wasn't much interested in alcohol. Maybe the pressure of all his commitments is weighing on him.

I move out, taking four-year-old Michael with me and get a cheap little flat in West End Brisbane under an old couple's home. It's a bit dreary but I love catching up with a group of Christians at West End called the Waiters Union, led by Dave and Ange Andrews. They help those living in poverty and on the margins of society. Some are marginalized by mental or physical health problems or lack of education or coming from dysfunctional families. Some are Aborigines or refugees.

I join their Sunday night meetings in a hall of St Andrews Anglican Church South Brisbane. People sit in a circle and are encouraged to share with people taking turns to prepare a short message. There is a leadership group who are young, educated and who work part time so they have time for community work. Many of them live in community i.e., a number of shared houses that are connected and hold their finances in common. Most people bring along a plate of food to share at St Andrews, usually vegetarian. For me, the fellowship and food are attractions also, not just the spiritual sharing.

Some of these friends are Catholic and also attend St Mary's Catholic Church in West End with Fr Peter Kennedy who is to make headlines years later. Friends of mine, Noel Preston and Coralie Kingston, are not part of the Waiters Union but are friends of members. They attend St Mary's.

I receive flowers "From an Admirer" and wonder who has sent them. Then Mick turns up on my doorstep and says it was him. He asks me to come home. As I still love him, I agree. He asks to take Posky home with him, giving me a chance to pack more easily. I agree. I've only been away a few months and haven't had time to build up a new life in Brisbane. I have visited my parents in Ipswich however during this time.

Mick meets me off the plane and takes me straight to the beach. He knows how much I love the beach, so it is a good move on his part. Leaving the airport, I realize how much I have missed the coconut trees and the mountains of Cairns. It is a beautiful sunny day.

He has organized Bill and Lone White and Ron and Jette Stovell to come to our home that evening to spend time with us. Lone is from

Denmark and Jette from Sweden; they are both potters and have married Australian men who work for the department of Aboriginal Affairs in Cairns. They have become firm friends of Mick's, and so, of mine. There seems to be no separation of the political and personal. They are happy to see me and help ease in my return. Everything goes back to normal very quickly and Mick and I settle into a happy relationship.

Yarrabah Report

Mick decides to take me on a trip to Canberra with him in early 1984. I trail after him as he meets a list of important people including Charlie Perkins. I sit on desks and listen to some very interesting conversations. When we visit the Human Rights Commission, they discuss the Qld Aborigines Act which is finally going to be axed and replaced by the Community Services Act. Knowing of my research background and editorship of *NQ Messagestick*, the Human Rights Commission ask me to do some low budget research on Yarrabah as to how the legislation affects human rights. It is just to be a one-month project and they only expect a short report.

On reflection, I don't know if Mick encouraged them to do this so that he could keep me happily working on a project that would keep me interested and take my mind off any personal issues. If this was the case, it worked. He had the kind of pull to do that.

The Human Rights Commission get a lot more than they bargain for in putting me on the job. I spend a lot of time visiting Yarrabah. Talking with people, meeting with council and doing a lot of research. I produce a report of about 100 pages and go beyond my brief in looking at the human rights abuses of the new land legislation coming in, nicknamed DOGIT, because it is important to the people. My report is called *The Aspirations of Aborigines Living at Yarrabah in Relation to Local Management and Human Rights*. The report is so hot in terms of Commonwealth-State government relationships that it is not published for 2 years until 1986; just before the Human Rights Commission winds up, being replaced by the Human Rights and Equal Opportunity Commission.

On 29th March 1984, just as I am commencing my research work at Yarrabah for the Human Rights Commission, Mick receives a letter from the federal Minister for Aboriginal Affairs appointing him Deputy Chairman of the Aboriginal Development Commission (ADC). This is one of many hats he wears. He is also on the National Aboriginal Education Committee (NAEC).

While working on the Yarrabah project, I organize a workshop in Cairns regarding Aboriginal self-management to hear the views of Indigenous people. *The Cairns Post* covers it on 11th April 1984, revealing the workshop recommends an Aboriginal be appointed to the Cairns Hospital Board and two more Aboriginal liaison staff be appointed to the Commonwealth Department of Aboriginal Affairs. It reports,

> "Mrs Miller said some of the other recommendations passed at the workshop dealt with the Department of Aboriginal and Islander Advancement. 'These asked that all housing, accommodation and other facilities and assets under the control of the DAIA in urban areas be transferred to the ownership and control of local community-controlled Aboriginal organizations.'"

Mabo And Native Title

Eddie Koiko Mabo from Murray Island, or Mer in the Torres Strait, works closely with Mick and we lobby in support of his case. In 1981, Eddie speaks at a land rights conference in Townsville on the Torres Strait becoming an autonomous area within the Commonwealth and not being under state government control. Barbara Hocking, a Melbourne barrister, recommends Aboriginal people take up a test case for their tribal lands and Murray Island takes up the case. They have already refused to accept a DOGIT from the Queensland government as they don't want to be under their control. I'm not at the Townsville meeting as my son is only two years old.

The test case begins in 1982. Rev Dave Passi and James Rice from Mer join Eddie Mabo in the case. Greg McIntyre, our friend from Cairns, is the solicitor for Mabo and his barristers are Ron Castan and Dr Bryan Keon-Cohen with Barbara Hocking on the case for the first five years. The first hurdle is that Premier Joh Bjelke-Petersen tries to retrospectively extinguish native title rights in the Torres Strait. Mabo v Queensland (No 1) is decided in the High Court on 8th December 1988. It finds that the Queensland Coast Islands Declaratory Act, which attempts to retrospectively abolish native title rights, is not valid according to the Racial Discrimination Act 1975.

After a long battle, in June 1992, the decision of the High Court in Mabo v Queensland (no 2) is that "The Meriam people were entitled as against the whole of the world to the possession, occupation, use and enjoyment of (most of) the land of the Murray Islands in the Torres Strait."[23]

The High Court holds that the common law of Australia recognizes a form of native title to land so this can be applied to the mainland as well. This is a ground-breaking decision as it overturns the notion of "terra nullius" which is that Australia was a no man's land at the time of European settlement. This notion had been confirmed in Millirrpum v Nabalco 1971 or the Gove Land Rights Case, the first of its kind in Australia, where Justice Blackburn found against the Aboriginal people. The Mabo decision means that native title is held to exist where Aboriginal and Torres Strait Islander people have maintained their connection to their land and where government action has not extinguished their title.

The Commonwealth government enacts the Native Title Act in 1993 (Cwth) and a new Queensland government follow suit with the Native Title Act 1993 (Qld) putting a legislative framework around the Mabo decision and instituting a mechanism for hearing claims. I become very involved in advising the Aboriginal Coordinating Council (ACC) Aboriginal communities in Queensland re native title. This includes a research paper and a visit to a Horn Island ACC meeting to explain the implications of the Mabo decision.

Yarrabah Is Nearly Mabo – Two Test Cases

The Mabo court case and decision are a watershed moment for the nation of Australia. I am excited to discover on writing a book on Yarrabah in 2016 that it could so easily have been the Neal or Yarrabah case as well as Mabo. This is not well known and I had forgotten about this plan which the NQLC is privy to at the time. One of the barristers for the case, Bryan Keon-Cohen reveals this in an article he writes in 2000:

> "Initially, work proceeded on developing two cases: one for Mer, another for the Yarrabah community, located on an aboriginal reserve in Far North Queensland. Meetings and preliminary advices in mid-September 1981 raised these prospects and by March 1982, two draft statements of claim had been prepared. However, for reasons uncertain to me, but apparently associated with a death in the community in June 1982, and difficulties in obtaining instructions, the Yarrabah aboriginal action faded away. Alternatively, perhaps the complexity, and the expense, of running two such cases quickly became apparent, and all too much to contemplate. Some hard decisions were doubtless taken, somewhere, by somebody.
>
> Yet another explanation sometimes heard is that instructions from Yarrabah were coming mainly from one Mr Neal, who was 'entitled to be an agitator' *Neal v The Queen* [1982] HCA 55; (1982) 149 CLR 305, 317 (Murphy J), but who, during this period, was notoriously jailed by a local magistrate for spitting through a wire-screen door at a police officer."[24]

Our mate and NQLC supporter Percy Neal is Chairman of Yarrabah Council and is elected on a self-management platform but Yarrabah is still under the oppressive Queensland Act. His Council appeals to the Commonwealth government to take over control from the state using its powers gained in the 1967 referendum. There is no political will for this though the talk is there. Frustrated, Percy visits a number of homes of white staff one evening and asks them to vacate the community. When he goes to the home of store manager Daniel Collins (not a policeman), it is alleged Percy uses threatening language and spits at Collins through the screen door. In fact, it is not Percy who spits but his companion, who he protects by taking the blame. Percy is sentenced to two months jail in the Cairns Magistrates court. He appeals and instead of having his sentence reduced, it is increased to six months. Chesterman and Villaflor write,

> "This case became famous in September 1982 when the High Court upheld Neal's appeal against the Court of Criminal Appeal decision. (Justice) Murphy then made the following famous remarks: 'That Mr. Neal was an "agitator" or stirrer in the magistrate's view obviously contributed to the severe penalty. If he is an agitator, he is in good company. Many of the great religious and political figures of history have been agitators, and human progress owes much to the efforts of these and the many who are unknown'."[25]

Justice Murphy maintains Neal should not have been jailed but received a $130 fine. The court case and jail term did prevent Yarrabah being in the historic position that Mer was, re native title, and Percy Neal being in the historic position of Eddie Mabo, sharing that ground-breaking history with him.

Miller Report

In October 1984, the Hawke Labor government sets up a major review into Aboriginal employment and training programs called the National Inquiry into Aboriginal Employment and Education Programs and Mick, considered a prominent Aboriginal leader, is chosen to chair it. Seasoned government advisor, Dr HC Coombs is on the committee. This results in us moving to Melbourne for most of 1985 where the committee is headquartered while it travels the country. Mick, Michael and I travel first class on the plane which is the only time I've done this; it is a great treat. We stay in a hotel for about a week until we find a house to rent in Hawthorne.

We organize for our car to be shipped down but Mick doesn't really want to find his way around Melbourne. Clarrie decides to come down and help us settle in and he drives Michael to school with me in attendance to settle Michael in and learn the route. I am very grateful for this. Mick doesn't do the driving in Melbourne, I do. He has drivers for work purposes. I could have enrolled Michael in the nearest school but I decide on a school in Clifton Hill which is more working class but has a good reputation. It is his first year at school. As it turns out, my Dutch friends, Jeltje and Corny, live in Clifton Hill. So this gives me a chance to see them. Corny is an artist and they both work in the public service.

I found it frustrating that Cairns is not a University town at the time so I was looking forward to taking up studies in Melbourne. Before leaving Cairns, I greedily enroll in two courses at two different universities. I enroll in a Graduate Diploma of Sociology at Latrobe University and third year psychology at Melbourne University. They are in two different directions so I do a lot of driving. Mick sends for Rodney Molloy to come down from Cairns and live with us so that he can give me a hand with Michael as Mick is away travelling a lot with his work. Rodney is happy to do so. He is Aboriginal, short and slim and has long black bushy hair. He looks up to Mick. Rod doesn't smoke or drink but loves to spend time at the TAB (online betting shop) and he doesn't work. He stays for a few months till he finds a girlfriend then moves in with her.

I don't see much of Mick during this time. He comes back from his trips from time to time and tells me what he has experienced. He travels right round Australia and it is particularly moving for him when he visits Maralinga. This is where the British set off atomic tests. Mick met Yami Lester, a well-known Aboriginal man who was made blind by the tests but there are many other Aboriginal people who have suffered from the fallout. Mick sits in the dirt and talks to the people and really feels for their situation.

When Mick and the team are in Melbourne, we socialize together at restaurants etc. It helps Mick to have Dennis Ah Kee from Cairns working with him. Dennis is the brother of Mervyn who married Mick's sister

Margaret. I make friends at Latrobe but it is very much a year to focus on my studies. I can't recall Mick and I going out on our own except to visit Jeltje and Corny. Jan Roberts comes to visit us one day, having returned to Melbourne for a visit. Her daughter Katie comes with her.

The Review Committee finishes their report before I finish my university year so Mick returns to Cairns. Michael and I move in with Jeltje and Corny. I get up at 5am each morning to study and keep visualizing 4 A's for my sociology course which is basically a quantitative research degree. That's exactly what I get. I receive a credit for my third year Psychology. I basically turn my educational history around. I am 35 years old. My thesis is *Resource Competition, Authoritarianism and Contact as Determinants of Attitudes to Aborigines and Torres Strait Islanders*.

The Miller Report is a ground-breaking report and becomes the standard wisdom for many years to come in Aboriginal employment and training.

Mick has been home in Cairns a couple of weeks when I receive a phone call from him. "You better come straight home or I might do something I shouldn't." He must be getting lonely. I still have one piece of research work to hand in but I tell my lecturer I have to return. He says I can post it in. I pack quickly and return home. We enjoy time together and everything seems normal.

I go to the medical service as I contract a tropical ear infection not long after coming back from Melbourne. It is during the Wet Season, hot and humid. Sharon, the doctor, asks me why I come back from Melbourne early. She is a mutual friend of Mick's and mine and I tell her Mick asked me to return early. She doesn't comment.

Life goes on happily enough though Mick seems to be a bit jealous of me and is critical about what I wear though it is no different from usual. I am confused a few times over the next few months when I go to the airport to pick Mick up after he has been away on one of his many trips and he's not there. He tells me afterwards I'm too late. He comes home when he is ready. Who picks him up then or is he really on that plane?

I enroll in a Masters Degree at James Cook University Townsville and I can do some of it from Cairns and have to spend some time in Townsville. I have photos from Dutch couple Jules and Jeanine from Palm Island where they write on the back wishing us Merry Christmas 1986. They are students at James Cook University Townsville visiting from the Netherlands. They want to work on an Aboriginal research project so a university lecturer asks me if they can help me do interviews for my research in Cairns re attitudes to Aborigines. I agree and Mick agrees to them living with us for a couple of months in 1986. This is not unusual. We often have young people living with us who want to immerse themselves in the Aboriginal movement, some black but mostly white. Paul Gilding is one name I remember because he complained I put too much water in the porridge and didn't have enough chicken in the stir fry. I can't remember us ever charging anyone board. He was a good help at the Land Council office as a volunteer and we got on well. Mark Renwick was a good help also.

The research is a random sample so it is a lot of work and I am grateful for the help. Jules and Jeanine write their own paper as well. Jeanine is now going to work at the hospital and Jules at the canteen on Palm Island to get the feel of life on an Aboriginal community before returning home. I end up converting my MA to an honors degree in psychology because I want to work as a psychologist. My thesis is titled *Attitudes to Aborigines –A Social Comparison Theory Approach: Equity, Attribution and Contact in Relation to Affirmative Action and Prejudice*.

The results of the research work are disturbing, with a common attitude to Aborigines in Cairns being that they're "dirty" and "lazy." Seeing homeless Aborigines from remote communities stranded in Cairns parks and drinking alcohol influences this perception but does not justify it as this is a minority, however visible. They are stranded at times because they come to Cairns for hospital treatment, or court cases, and have no money to fly home. Sleeping rough and with poor nutrition and education, their physical and mental health is at risk and makes it hard for them to get work.

I've spent a lot of time lobbying for better legislation for Indigenous people but I know that changing legislation doesn't change attitudes. That is something I try to work on as well, through education and media.

Mick loves to hold court in his "downstairs office" as he calls it. Where he has coffee, chills out and if someone wants to meet him or ask for help, they can come there. Many do.

Mick and I are sitting on the lounge floor with opened Christmas presents around us. I'm in a long black nightie and Mick is wearing his land council T-shirt, shorts and thongs. He is sitting cross-legged with arms folded and looking a bit bored by the idea of a photo. Behind him is the closed door to the side patio and stuck to it is a decorative strip so we can measure Michael's height. The yellow and brown curtain that frames the window is pulled back to allow in some more light. In the corner is a decorated Christmas tree.

Dominating the lounge room is a mural by Aboriginal artist and friend Enoch Tranby. Taking up the whole wall, it features an Aboriginal man with a wooden sword standing beside a gunyah. Spears are leaning against the gunyah and boomerangs lay on the ground. Enoch's signature is the cassowary which also has pride of place in the painting. In the background are water, plains and mountains with a gum tree coming out of the foreground to the left. In front of the mural is the TV set with a photo of our son on top of it. He is already running around playing with his new toys.

Michael was never advantaged in any way by being Mick's son. Mick never had help from any Aboriginal funding program for his house and I paid for Michael's tutoring myself. When he grew up, Michael didn't take advantage of any subsidized job training program. If anything, he paid the price of Mick being away so much but Mick was a good father. The one perk Michael does have as a small child is being Santa's helper one Christmas on the farm. Mick organizes for one of the men who regularly comes to socialize on Warama farm to dress up as Santa and arrive in a helicopter with toys for the children of the families who come regularly. Michael is dressed up like an elf and is Santa's helper, arriving with him in the helicopter. He loves it.

L to R Mick Miller, Steve Mam and Clarrie Grogan Photo Supplied

Mick Connolly, Deputy Chairman of Yarrabah in 1984 When Barbara Did the Human Rights Commission Report photo Courtesy Yarrabah Aboriginal Shire Council

Former Mayor of Yarrabah Percy Neal on Yarrabah Beach
Photo by Brendan Francis 2000 Newspix 15 Dec 2001

Chapter 9

Divorce And Aboriginal Co-Ordinating Council

End Of Marriage To Mick

In early March 1987, my Dad asks me to go to China with him as my Mum has refused to go and he has booked for two. I'm happy for this opportunity. Sharon offers me a warm jumper to wear. I enjoy my time with Dad and love the visit to China though Dad has a bad habit of walking behind me and hitting me with his carry bag. A very annoying habit. His excuse is I should hurry up. Is this why Mum didn't travel with him? Her excuse is she doesn't like flying. I am away just over a week and when I get back, I receive a phone call from a woman whose voice I don't recognize. "Your husband's having an affair and your son knows who it is." I never did find out who rang me.

Shocked, I confront Mick. He clears his throat, turns away for a moment and then admits it is true.

"Who is it?" I demand to know.

"Sharon," he admits.

"I trusted you! You kept telling me you love me and wouldn't have an affair like other men. You lied!" I manage to get out, barely able to hold it together.

Maybe that's why he is critical of me lately when I feel I haven't done anything to warrant it. Is his guilt making him find fault with me? I am naïve, not suspecting an affair. Mick always makes a big thing about being faithful, as he knows a number of Aboriginal men who aren't.

Everyone in our circle seems to know except me. I need a medical check-up so I see Sharon.

"How can you do it?" I demand.

She sits back in her chair a little, her mid-length blonde hair tied back and stethoscope around her neck,

> "He said you have an understanding that he could have an affair," she replies in an even tone. "That it's OK and you know about it."

My voice rose and I say firmly,

> "We don't have an understanding and I didn't know and it's not OK." I storm out, Sharon rising and frowning.

What am I to do? Mick wants me to stay and share him with Sharon. I toss and turn some nights as I think about it. I cry a lot. "I can't do it," I say. It's her or me. Silence. "I'll move out then."

> "Why aren't you more like Fay?" Mick asks. "When Laurie had an affair, she fell apart and couldn't cope. You seem to be managing OK." (Laurie and Fay aren't their real names.)

I thought about Fay. When she challenged Laurie about his affair, he punched her and knocked most of her teeth out and the dental service had to repair the damage. This would have devastated her because they had been such a beautiful couple and worked in the Aboriginal movement together. Their marriage didn't survive too long after this. Mick is not a violent person but instead is mostly an affable, charming person.

> "I'm not Fay," I reply, surprised at the comparison. "I'm a strong person."

Does he need me to fall apart to prove my love for him? I don't think that is in doubt. Or my dependence on him? My identity is largely bound up in being Mick's wife and my work with the Aboriginal movement in which he is a key national leader. We work together. Most of my friends in Cairns I have met through Mick. No wonder he thinks I might fall apart. My whole world does change greatly. I still love him but it is no longer workable. My faith in God is not strong at this point but it still helps me so that my whole world doesn't have to pivot around Mick.

I move out with our son, staying in a caravan and then in emergency housing for three months till I can afford to rent a unit. What Mick doesn't know is that I weep for him for a long time and not just with visible tears. It is like I am crying inside, raining in my chest. I've never experienced that before and never have since. I couldn't get him out of my mind for a long time. But time heals. I get work at the Women's Information and Referral Centre as coordinator.

After I leave Mick because of his affair with Sharon, he tries a few times to get me to return but I am not prepared to as he will not be giving up Sharon and he has become difficult to live with as he would at times drink too much and he would be critical of me e.g., he says what I am wearing will attract other men. He would be argumentative at these times. When I find out about his affair, I feel that explains his behavior i.e., that he is feeling guilty and justifying himself and also that he is jealous that other men might find me attractive just as he finds other women attractive.

Before I find out about the affair and life with him is difficult, I decide to go on the pill as it will not be good to get pregnant while our relationship is difficult. I don't tell him that I'm going to the Family Planning place. Later that day, he says, "I know where you've been. I have my mates watching you."

It is a shock. I am under surveillance. Does he think I would have an affair and he wants to catch me out or does he just want to keep tabs on me? I certainly give him free reign with his time and don't require a blow-by-blow description of how he spends his day.

After we have been separated for a few months, Mick meets me and says, "Tell me if you still love me. If you don't, I won't bother you anymore."

I say, "I don't" because I want him to stop trying to get me back when all he wants is a threesome.

Not believing me, he says, "Take your sunglasses off and at look me and tell me that."

So, I take my sunglasses off and look him in the eye and lie, "I don't love you anymore."

It is rare that I would lie and this is a life-changing moment but I feel I have to close the door with Mick though I still love him greatly. Mick has mates that can have affairs, secret or otherwise, and stay married. He probably can't understand why I won't let him do the same. Life with him is not the kind of life I want to lead where he is having an affair and is jealous, argumentative when drinking, and suspicious.

Besides, I have learned not to trust what he says well before the affair. He regularly tells me and others he has done things when he hasn't e.g., paying bills or some Aboriginal rights matter that needs attending to. I think often he intends to do things and then thinks he has. Very often, I would pick up the pieces for him and follow through where it is needed. I know as a national Aboriginal leader he has a great weight of expectations on him and occasionally he will deal with it by just not turning up at meetings and disappearing to the farm or elsewhere.

I cry for a long time over the end of our marriage. Cairns is a small town and everything reminds me of him including our beautiful son Michael, same name and looking just like his Dad. I have to pray a prayer of releasing him to his higher self and forgiving him and blessing his relationship with Sharon. This is a test of being able to forgive someone if you can bless them and want the best for them.

After we separate, Michael occasionally spends time with Mick at the farm, on which Mick has built a stadium for a Living History Centre with government funding. When Mick's mates are there, they often light a fire and boil the billy or cook on it. Cans of beer are also regularly consumed. Unfortunately, Michael sees one of the men throw methylated spirits (denatured ethanol) on the fire to stoke it. He copies the man throwing metho on the fire and is burnt badly on the leg; having to go to the intensive care ward of the hospital. It is a long painful recovery for him with the burnt flesh having to be scraped from his leg daily. I don't blame Mick for it. I realize it was an accident but it is excruciatingly painful for Michael and my heart goes out to him. It is a difficult time. When he is allowed to come home, the doctor tells me he will have to only wear long pants to protect his leg from the sun. He has a big scar.

About a year or so later, his big sister Jenny visits from Townsville and gives him some shorts. He is coaxed out of the long pants and then has to cope with going to school scarred and the attention that draws. He has coped really well and now we don't even notice it.

I didn't mention Jenny, before did I? One day Jenny Pryor and her children arrive on our doorstep at Kevin Street and she announces to Mick that she is his daughter and these are his grandchildren. It is a big surprise. We welcome them into the family. Jenny looks like Mick and her mother is Ella Lymburner. When I first met Mick, he told me that Ella was his girlfriend on Palm Island. The nuns were concerned he would stay on Palm Island and not realize his potential, persuading him to go to teacher's college in Brisbane. This broke up their relationship. Mick didn't know she was pregnant.

Jenny says that she didn't find out till her father died that Mick is her real father. Her mother kept it secret till then. Mick's early story to me and Jenny's story match so I readily accept her. We don't see much of her as she doesn't visit Cairns often. I've just seen some information come through re the 60th anniversary of the Palm Island strike and find that the Lymburner family was among the ringleaders of the strike that was exiled so Jenny comes from a line of campaigners: the Lymburners and Sibleys.

Jenny is a key mover and shaker in Aboriginal organizations in

Townsville. For eight years she is Administrator of the Aboriginal and Islander Child Care Agency in Townsville being involved with the Secretariat of National Aboriginal and Islander Child Care (SNAICC) since it began in the early 1980s. She was a Commissioner with the Aboriginal and Torres Strait Islander Commission (ATSIC) for North Queensland with her portfolio being infrastructure, housing, land and natural resources.

I find it difficult to get work while I am married to Mick because I am seen as an activist and they think Mick or myself might cause trouble for them. An interviewer actually admits this privately to me afterwards. Even after Mick and I are no longer together, it is hard to get work as I am typecast as a stirrer in a small town. Also, by this time, all my experience is in Aboriginal affairs, even though mostly unpaid. I have to diversify. I find it hard to rent as a single mother. There are times when it looks like I have a tenancy and then they see a black child and it is suddenly unavailable. Things are tough financially. I work at the Women's Information Centre for a while and resume studies to complete my fourth year in Psychology.

When I become a newly registered psychologist, I manage to get a job with the Endeavour Foundation working with the intellectually and physically disabled. A new life, the fruit of all my studies.

Meeting Norman

I first meet Norman when Mick and I are invited to his 21st birthday party because Mick is friends with his parents Barclay and Shirley Miller. It is June 1984. The previous month I finish a six-week project and report on Yarrabah, the nearest Aboriginal community to Cairns, on local management, land rights and human rights for the Human Rights Commission. Our son Michael is 5 years old then. We probably took him with us, as we often did, and put him to sleep in a quiet spot. I really don't remember much about the event or Norman but he noticed me.

The next time we meet, years later, I am single. My friend Melinda persuades me to go to a night club with her. She is a single Mum like me at the time. Suddenly this good-looking young man is in front of me asking me to dance. He introduces himself and I am taken aback, aware he is a lot younger. Why would he want to dance with me? But he moves so beautifully, so gracefully. I accept cautiously. He stays at my side and by the end of the night is inviting me to lunch the next day. It will be a Saturday and he will be working till lunch in a store selling men's clothes and wants to meet me him at the Redlynch railway station. Here we would have lunch on the train converted to a restaurant.

I check with Melinda. "Say yes," she says. I ring her again in the morning. "You sure I should go? He's too young for me."

"Go and find out if the age difference matters," she urges. "Just go and enjoy yourself."

I go along, still uncertain. Working in a men's store, Norman dresses well. He particularly favors shiny silver long pants and dressy shirts and ties. His smile and easy laugh are engaging and the railway carriage is a picturesque place to have lunch. He talks a lot, mostly about his family. It is easy to see how much he loves them and I decide this is a good quality. Norman's parents and brother and sisters are in Brisbane for the weekend at the wedding of his sister Joanne. It is 26th September 1987. Norman and I click and continue to see each other.

Aboriginal Co-ordinating Council And Deaths In Custody Report

After about a year at Endeavour Foundation, I am approached by the Aboriginal Co-ordinating Council (ACC) to do research work for them in a Criminology Research Council project as they know I have been involved with the remote Aboriginal communities. I am 39 years old, my son is 10 years old, and I begin an exciting period in my life as a figure in Aboriginal affairs in my own right, not in the shadow of Mick. I publish a number of papers in the *Aboriginal Law Bulletin* and the *Aboriginal*

Health Worker and write a number of reports and submissions for the ACC. I also speak at some conferences organized by the Criminology Research Council on crime prevention and social control on Aboriginal communities.

I eventually become the Secretariat Director, or CEO, of the ACC. The ACC is a local government body representing land-based Aboriginal communities in Queensland (the ex-reserves). It is a statutory body advising government and is a peak body for Aboriginal elected councils. During my time as Secretariat Director, we manage to get grants from different organizations and expand our support, doing service delivery as well as advocacy, the latter being our main role. We work on local government legislation, by-laws, policing, the court system, a mediation project, customary law, land rights, resource management, fishing and mining rights, child welfare, domestic violence, health, AIDS education, housing, education, employment, ranger training etc. It is a busy, fruitful time.

I sometimes describe working in Aboriginal Affairs as being "like a cat on a hot tin roof" because of the sensitivity of the work. However, I am able to second guess the Chairman of the ACC, Merv Gibson of Hopevale, an Aboriginal community near Cooktown. I know what decisions I can make on my own and what I need to consult him about. I prepare press releases for him and I am also interviewed myself, speak at conferences and am involved in high level advocacy to State and Federal governments.

I organize for Mick Dodson, a lawyer working for the Northern Land Council in Darwin, to come to our meeting in Cairns of our working group of Mayors on by-laws for the communities. These had not really been overhauled properly since the discriminatory Queensland Aborigines Act was replaced with the Community Services Act.

Royal Commission Into Aboriginal Deaths in Custody

I am asked by Commissioner Lou Wyvill to do a report on Deaths in Custody. I cry many nights over this as I read the cases of the young men who have died in custody. I produce a 107-page report for the Royal Commission into Aboriginal Deaths in Custody which is launched with much press interest. Many of its recommendations are incorporated into the Commission's Final Report.

I certainly give the press plenty to talk about when I give evidence to the Human Rights and Equal Opportunity Enquiry into medical services provided to Aboriginals in the Cooktown area. They quote me in three separate articles by Elizabeth Hinshaw in *The Cairns Post*, 8th August 1990. One article 'Inquiry told of Aboriginal deaths out of custody,' says I raised the issue of the high rate of deaths out of custody:

> "Ms Miller told the inquiry's Cairns hearing the peri-natal mortality rate for Aboriginals was three times the national average (includes still births and deaths within the first month) and the birth weight of Aboriginal children born on communities was three to five times lower than the national average. She said this led to the stunting and wasting of children, some brain damage and was connected to heart disease in adults."

The article continues to quote my comments on adult Aboriginal life expectancy statistics, homicide, suicide, self-injury, inter-family fighting, alcohol, mental health and environmental health issues such as unfit water supply. My testimony includes a devastating occurrence:

> "There are sewerage problems in the communities … two children drowned in pools of sewerage at Doomadgee."

In another article, "Birthing centers needed," I am quoted as telling the enquiry that birthing centers are needed for Aboriginal communities because Aboriginal women have to come to Cairns at least two months before their babies' birth and this can result in family breakdown and in women leaving sick babies behind in the Cairns hospital to return to their other children, they are worried about.

In the third article, "Woman tells of body in car," I say the ACC has made a submission to the Parliamentary Select Committee of inquiry into ambulance services asking for QATB centers to be set up on Cape York Peninsula. I am quoted:

> "I believe a lot of communities are discriminated against because they don't have essential services such as ambulances."

The ACC believes that rather than just handing my submission over to Commissioner Lou Wyvil, we should have a launch at the Pacific International Hotel on 27th September and invite government departments, Indigenous organizations and the press. Chairman Merv Gibson was not available so Eric Deeral, a Hopevale Councillor and former National Party member for Cook, chairs the meeting. He is the first Aboriginal to hold a seat in the Queensland parliament. The meeting is well attended. I wear a suit made from Norman's red ochre batik fish design with a necklace to match. A photo of Eric and I is in *The Cairns Post* the next day, Eric's jet-black face contrasts with his white shirt. We are not smiling for the camera. It is too serious a matter.

The article's headline blares out "Aboriginals Triple State Death Rate." The Member for Leichhardt, John Gayler, says he supports most of the recommendations. One of these is for a permanent body to be set up to oversee the implementation of the recommendations. Unfortunately, Aboriginal Deaths in Custody are still occurring today because not all the recommendations of the RCIADIC Final Report have been implemented.

The Sydney Morning Herald article by Greg Roberts, an old friend from my university days, also comments on 28th September on my submission. The statistics I release are so staggeringly bad I can't even type them now. I think the headline says it only too well "What do Aborigines do more than most? Die." There is a flurry of other press. This includes an interview with Karen Dorante, ABC Cairns on 5th October 1990. When the final report of the RCADIC comes out, the ABC interviews me again, commenting that many of my or ACC's recommendations were included.

The ACC executive ask me to use a numeric code for communities so particular communities will not be embarrassed by the statistics. Today I don't remember what the code was. Nevertheless, the ACC supports my releasing very troubling information. I am probably one of the first to call out domestic violence and child abuse on Aboriginal communities in Cape York and identify how serious the problem is of self-injury, suicide and homicide. My submission is not just the result of researching the statistics though that is there. It is really about talking to people on the ground in communities and finding out their issues, their needs and what they think should be done about them.

Steve Rous writes "Hinze OK 'to bar in park'" in *The Courier Mail* September 1990 covering the release of my ACC submission with its 211 recommendations. However, its focus is on my complaint of a beer canteen being built in the middle of a children's playground in Aurukun despite the wishes of the people. Local government minister Russ Hinze insisted it be built saying it was discriminatory for them not to have one. It also focuses on my calls for a special Aboriginal police unit in the Queensland police service with Aboriginals recruited for it. Also, watchhouses on communities being torn down and rebuilt as they are not presently in reasonable condition.

Desmond Zwar writes for *The Sunday Mail* 14th October with the headline "The blonde who dropped a bombshell … 70's rebel is stirring for justice." He writes:

> "She is white. She has intense blue eyes, cascading blonde curls and a beautiful face. The people she has devoted her life to are black."

I am photographed with my 11-year-old son Michael who is wearing a T-shirt with an emu on it, his tousled black hair and brown eyes a contrast to me. Zwar takes me to lunch at the Cairns Hilton; contrasting its sunny environment with the shock report I have just written where I say, "Aboriginals on communities, as a powerless group, have turned their rage in on themselves."

He follows it up on 2nd December with an article for *The Sunday Age* headlined, "White Woman Black Heart". I'm pictured wearing a maroon summer dress with a flower pattern and hugging my son wearing his school uniform and shyly smiling. Zwar writes, this time in an interview at the ACC office, a hive of activity with people in from the communities for meetings:

> "What she found, she says, is that when anger and frustration at 'seeing no light at the end of the tunnel becomes too much, an Aborigine often smashes glass louvres in his house (which can be home for up to 20 people), deliberately cutting his wrists and his body. It is rage turned inward. Black crime in Australia is … generally against the Aborigine's own family, his wife, girlfriend or de facto are the most likely victims. Men are fighting their brothers, fathers and uncles and bashing their mothers, she says. Women are running away from sons-in-law."

Norman regularly found me crying when I was writing this 107-page submission because of the sheer pain I was seeing. In the same interview, Zwar quotes me as saying:

> "One woman said, 'When I am angry, I reach the point where I can't get rid of the anger any other way besides smashing things or getting stuck into somebody.'
>
> "When an Aboriginal woman finds her home is not a safe place from assault and psychological violence, where does she go? Women's shelters do not exist on most of the communities. There's nowhere to go except hide in the bush overnight, seek refuge with friends or relatives (where she is sure to be found), or spend the night in the watchhouse or hospital."

I go on to talk about the appalling incidence of child abuse, sexual and physical, and child neglect and the pornographic videos fueling some of the problems. Cases of sexually transmitted disease are all too common and in very young children.

Zwar's article is followed up by a similar one in a Bangkok

newspaper, which I can't put my hands on now, but they were fascinated regarding a comment by Alison Woolla, Chairperson of Aurukun council, who told Zwar,

> "They say that maybe you were a child somewhere else, a black child, and your spirit died, and you were born into another world from us and you have come again to us …"

At the time Alison said this, she was looking at me and I did get emotional as it reflected my great affinity with Aboriginal people. However, as a Christian, I don't believe in reincarnation.

But I am relieved to say that although these issues continue, great improvements have been made on these social issues and measures to deal with them, including improved facilities and services. The ACC Executive and the Mayors on communities who make up the ACC are visionary and dedicated. We take the ACC from being a local government body to a service provider and advocate on a whole range of issues affecting Aboriginal communities in Queensland. I look for extra funding from a range of bodies to do this and we employ a male domestic violence officer to work with men, a women's officer, a children's worker, an AIDS education officer, a mediator and a community justice worker. They all spend most of their time out on the communities, supporting people in their actual environment, lobbying for facilities like women's shelters to be set up and staff to be trained. I give talks to white police and hospital staff and lobby for cross-cultural training of those in regular contact with Indigenous people.

The Foundation for Aboriginal and Islander Research Action (FAIRA) based in Brisbane holds a "Two Laws" conference in Brisbane with talks by experts on legal, cultural and spiritual issues and the conflicts of Aboriginal customary law with western law. Mary Graham and Bob Weatherall from FAIRA spoke, plus Irene Moss the Race Discrimination Commissioner. Ms Moss said federal law was the only recourse for Queensland Aborigines as Queensland was the only state without its own law protecting human rights.

I was a speaker too and the press focuses more on what I have to say, maybe because it's more challenging. The headline reads "Need to weed racist police out of force" 6th December 1990 with no by-line. The press clipping I have only has a handwritten "T/B" on it, so I assume it's *The Townsville Bulletin*. I am quoted as saying:

> "There should be a screening process to weed out racist police who cannot be retrained so that they do not work in areas of high Aboriginal population." Ms Miller told the conference on Aboriginal law and spirituality ....
>
> Ms Miller said the ACC welcomed moves by the Queensland Police department to involve Aboriginal councillors on the interview panel to select police applying to work in Aboriginal communities."

I also have the opportunity to speak to a couple of conferences of the Australian Institute of Criminology. Judy Atkinson is also a leading light in the area of family violence and crime prevention and it was great to work with her at the ACC.

ACC And Federation Of Land Councils

ACC supports the proposed formation of the Cape York Land Council in July 1990. ACC also attends an early meeting of the Federation of Land Councils in Brisbane in 1991 and works with FAIRA, the North Qld Land Council and the Federation of Land Councils in lobbying for land rights legislation. We organize a workshop on the Aboriginal Land Act 1991 in Cairns in June 1991, at which I explain the legislation to Councils and Council clerks. Feedback from this workshop assists the Legislative Review Committee into Aboriginal local government legislation, with their work. The ACC requests me to attend their full meeting at Horn Island in the Torres Strait after the Mabo decision to explain the ramifications to them. Jesuit lawyer Fr Frank Brennan is also providing advice to the ACC, as he has done for years.

A photo of ACC Chairman Jeffrey McLean, who took on the role in

March 1991, is in *The Cairns Post* 13th April 1991. He holds a copy of the ACC Land Rights Policy document under the headline "Aboriginals Launch Policy." The policy document is written by me in consultation with the communities. The 40 plus delegates from 22 communities endorse ACC's policy at their four-day quarterly conference in Cairns. The policy is wide-ranging but the newspaper article focuses on Aboriginal aspirations to own national parks:

> "He said until the land rights issues were resolved, no new national parks should be declared, and agreement should first be reached with the appropriate Aboriginal group.
>
> If an Aboriginal group agreed to a national park, they should be given inalienable freehold title and then lease the land back to national parks,' Mr McLean said."

In writing this memoir, I am stunned to read the opening paragraph of this policy 30 years later as there is so much talk now of sovereignty and treaty during the constitutional recognition of Indigenous people debate. It reads:

> "ACC recognizes the sovereign rights of Aboriginal people to Australia and does not cede or give up these rights. The Federal Government should immediately negotiate a treaty with the Aboriginal people of Australia."

Council Of Australian Governments (COAG)

As the ACC is providing top level advice and advocacy to federal and state governments, we are invited to the Council of Australian Governments (COAG) meeting at the Hobart Wrest Point Hotel and Casino during my term with the ACC, probably 1990. I go too. The meeting is at Sandy Bay minutes from the Hobart CBD and has a tower with stunning views of the Derwent River. I am surprised to see a lot of colonial architecture in Hobart, the capital of Tasmania, the apple isle as it is sometimes called, over the water from the base of mainland Australia.

It is an incredibly large oval table and around it are many comfortable brown leather chairs. Attending are the Prime Minister, Bob Hawke, federal government ministers, the premiers of all the states and chief ministers of the territories with their state ministers. Merv Gibson, ACC chairman has a seat at the table of this peak Australian inter-governmental forum. Advisors like myself are sitting on less comfortable seats behind them, near the walls. An Australian flag is duly positioned on a stand.

COAG is established to replace the Premier's Conference and expand the state/commonwealth engagement beyond fights over money to a reform agenda to improve the federation, reduce duplication and grow the economy. The different levels of government have agreements across a range of areas including healthcare, education, disability, water, transport, infrastructure and housing. Performance is assessed against benchmarks for a number of national agreements including Overcoming Indigenous Disadvantage.

I take it in my stride to offer our ACC chairman advice at such a high level, whispering in his ear occasionally when he turns around to ask for advice. I feel so privileged to be in this position.

Opposition

Even though I had been headhunted to work at the ACC, a young Torres Strait Islander man working for the ACC decides I am getting too much limelight and that he should have my job. A white woman shouldn't be doing it. While I have some time off on my honeymoon (more on that soon), he falsely accuses me of embezzling money. A government audit proves him wrong and he resigns but not at my request. The audit finds I have worked a large number of hours above what was required with no overtime payment. I am not only exonerated but commended.

Though this time is difficult, I'm glad it happens because it has strengthened me. I know before God that I am in the right so even though the accusations against me had hit the local newspapers, I decide God's view of me carries more weight. I don't defend myself in the media and I don't take it out on my accuser. Even though the story of me being cleared isn't published and I don't receive an apology, I let my reputation go and my need to be justified before people. This gives me an incredible freedom. Sensitive to criticism before, I now see it as, "Water off a duck's back." Knowing who I am in God's eyes is more important. This lesson stays with me.

However, I decide that I need to move out of key roles in Aboriginal affairs and make room for Indigenous leaders and I phase myself out over the next six months. Again, I'm going to have to diversify.

QLD Centre For Training And Research

I do this by setting up the Qld Centre for Training and Research and for the next few years write research reports for the ACC on local government, land and resource management and crime prevention on Aboriginal communities. I also do research for other organizations and run training courses. I prepare a training manual for Aboriginal community police for the Qld Police Service after consultations in Weipa and Cherbourg. Sgt Trevour Adcock is a valuable support in doing this. He has previously organized for me to do cross-cultural training with white police while I am at the ACC.

Barbara and Norman

Barbara Miller and Eric Deeral at launch

Barbara with son Michael in article 'White Woman Black Heart'
The Sunday Age 2nd December 1990
photo Russell Francis

Chapter 10

Marrying Norman and Losing My Dad

Marrying Norman

Norman and I plan to marry 12th January 1991. Again, Mum tells me over the phone, "I'm not coming to your wedding."

"Not again Mum," I plead. "Why?"

Her voice hardens, "Because he's Aboriginal". I have never accused her of being racist but I thought it.

"You haven't even met him," I say, frustration building. "We love each other and he's a wonderful person."

"I'm not changing my mind," she says firmly. "I'll never be able to stay under the roof of an Aboriginal person."

Exasperated, I hang up thinking here we go again. My Dad doesn't come to my wedding either but my brother comes and gives me away. I can't remember Dad objecting to the marriage, however. We have a wonderful service in the Assembly of God church we are attending and a reception at the Workers Club afterwards. At the service, Norman sings to me in a beautiful voice, "You are the Wind Beneath My Wings" by Bette Midler, bringing tears to my eyes.

I look up now at the wedding photos on the bookcase. In one photo are Norman and I with his parents and my brother. In the other, are

Norman and I with his brother Tom and my son Michael as groomsmen and Norman's sister Lillian as my bridesmaid. Lillian is dressed in red, my favorite color and also hers. Norman, Michael and Tom have red cummerbunds and red bowties and Norman is wearing a white coat. I'm wearing a hugging white dress. I wish I was that slim now.

Norman is hurt that my Mum doesn't come but he spends time praying for the Lord to take his hurt away and to have no resentment to my Mum. I don't hold it against her either but there is a distance between us because we aren't on the same wavelength. We visit Mum in Ipswich a year later. Mum is not expecting us and when she opens the door, Norman says, "I love you Mum" and offers her a hug. She hesitates but invites us in. The ice is broken.

Later she comes to visit us in Cairns and stays in our home. Norman puts fresh flowers in a vase. "Barbara will like these," says Mum.

"But they're for you," says Norman. Mum is shocked. I can't remember if Mum ever received flowers.

Mum looks a bit confused, "Thanks," she stammers. Norman puts fresh flowers in her room every day and waits on her hand and foot making her cups of tea and anticipating her needs. After two weeks, when it is time to go, she asks me plaintively, "Can I take him home with me?" The tide has turned. Dad hasn't treated her like this. She visits us occasionally over the years and we visit her.

My Dad and his mate Jess, a kindly graying Scotsman with a rather bulbous nose, visit us in Cairns and stay in our granny flat where our son Michael now lives. As Norman and I don't drink alcohol, Dad needs his drinking mate to enjoy the trip. We enjoy Dad's pumpkin soup and he plants some vegetables in our garden. He and Mum have always loved to garden and have a huge garden at their Ipswich home. The heat and humidity are really getting to Dad. As they have come up by train, Dad travelling free as an ex-railway worker, Norman and I pay for them to fly home and buy return tickets. The following year they use the tickets to fly up to visit us and enjoy their time including a day we spend at Port

Douglas. Unfortunately, Dad suddenly gets sick on the long train ride home. I regret I didn't foresee that. He recovers after resting.

Norman's Parents

Norman's father Barclay Miller, is close to his family, warm and friendly. He easily strikes up conversations with people as he walks around town, even strangers. He likes to buy eggs in bulk from a farm and give them to neighbors in Cairns. He is moved by the plight of homeless people and often drops food to them and, when it is cold, blankets where they are camping. The Mayor of Cairns enlists Dad to help them liaise with homeless people when there are problems between them and local businesses. Dad works voluntarily with agencies to find shelter for them. He has a heart for stray cats too and takes them in.

The Queensland government would not allow Aboriginal people of his generation to be educated past Grade 4, the age of nine-year-olds. So, he is self-taught. Norman grew up at Wondecla near Herberton in north Queensland. The family used kerosene lamps, gathered around the campfire, drinking billy tea and eating damper. Norman and his brother Tom and sisters swam in Nigger Creek, named after a massacre in the early days, and played on the rocks. It has recently been renamed Wondecla Creek. Barclay works as a wardsmen in the Herberton hospital.

Norman's family eventually move to South Johnstone near Innisfail where Norman's parents cut sugar cane to put food on the table and his father also works as a wardsmen in the Innisfail hospital. They then move to Cairns where Norman's mother Shirley works as a cleaner in a nursing home for many years and is well loved for having such a happy, kind personality and being a hard worker. Norman's father gets work as a hospital orderly and later works in various government departments, teaching himself how to use a computer. He works for the Commonwealth Employment Service and the state Aboriginal affairs department. During his time working for government departments, he helps Indigenous people get housing rentals, jobs and put in claims to have some of their stolen wages returned. The government withheld the wages of Indigenous people as a matter of policy for many years, putting it in the Aborigines Welfare Fund. It was used for general expenditure.

Once, Dad was not given a permit to visit Napranum (Weipa South) Aboriginal community because they thought it was me. We had the same initials: B. Miller. He later stands for Aboriginal and Torres Strait Islander Commission (ATSIC) elections and is successful. Norman had planned to stand for this but when he found his Dad was standing, he withdrew.

Norman's mother is part of the 1950's revival at Bethel AOG Church, Pinnacle Pocket in the Atherton Tableland when she is a child. She remembers the Aboriginal and other members of the congregation meeting every night for hours of prayer and worship. The move of the Holy Spirit is so strong and exciting they can't stay away. There is no leader but different members of the church share as they feel led to by the Holy Spirit. Seeing the miracles of healing and the answers to prayer gives her a strong unshakeable faith. She remembers having to be carried home from church because she is so filled with the Holy Spirit that she can't walk. She also remembers that other children and herself were talking in tongues at school and it took them a while to get back to talking English again.

My son Michael is welcomed as a grandson to Norman's parents along with Darryl and Scott Miller, Norman's sister Colleen's sons. The three are great mates. Norman and I take the three of them fishing and swimming when they are young. We have a particularly wonderful time one Christmas after we buy Darryl and Scott an inflatable boat, then we paddle down Freshwater Creek in it. It's great fun. When Norman and I move into our Manunda home, Michael walks home from school to Norman's parents' home for the first couple of months until he gets used to our new home. He is loved into Norman's family.

Shirley is a tower of strength for the family and is the one who prays for them to become Christians and eventually sees them all make a commitment. Dad, Tom, Col and Debbii all give their heart to the Lord after Norman and I pioneer a church as pastors in 1996. Lillian and Joanne are very committed already and have studied some Bible College in Townsville. One day I feel the Lord calling Dad a songbird and when I tell Mum her eyes light up and she says, "He's always singing." Dad plays guitar and loves to sing Christian songs.

Norman and I do not have children together but he is a wonderful second father to my son. We nearly don't marry as we break up at one point because of his drinking and I have to get him out of a pub once because he wanted to fight someone. As much as I love him, this is not the life I want. I miss his wonderful family as much as I miss him because they have become part of my life and I want my son to have that family life too. I move and don't let Norman know where I am but he knows where I work and brings flowers into the Aboriginal Co-ordinating Council office and tries to see me.

Norman's mother and grandmother are strong Christians and Norman has been brought up in Sunday school with his cousins and with aunties who teach Sunday school. He has a praying mother. Breaking up with me brings a crisis in his life and he goes to his local pastor who prays for him. Norman gives his heart to the Lord and gives up alcohol. He persuades me to attend church with him and his family. I can see he has changed so we start going out together again. I won't marry him though till I can see he has been off alcohol for a year. He has a genuine faith in God and he has never touched a drop of alcohol since. I like the occasional drink of Tia Maria or Galliano and orange but Norman asks me to give it up to make it easier for him. I do. We never look back.

He stops going to nightclubs or anywhere he might be tempted and he gives up dancing, though he is a beautiful dancer, because of the association with alcohol in those places. He has been a DJ, doing 21st birthday parties and weddings etc. As much as he loves music, he gives his huge record collection away. He has never been a grumpy ex-drinker. He also gives up gambling though it was mainly once a year on the Melbourne Cup.

One of the things I really appreciate about Norman is his honesty though I find his confrontational style a little difficult at first. If there looks like being a disagreement between us, I would be inclined not to mention it when we first get together. But Norman surfaces it and tackles it and we sort it out before it festers and escalates. I grew to really appreciate this. He rarely needs to do it after all these years but if he senses the need, he will.

Recommitment To God

I drift from my Christian commitment over the years through my focus on Aboriginal affairs crowding out my time for prayer, reading the Bible, worship and fellowshipping with other Christians. I'm still a believer but I don't have the close relationship with the Lord I once had and I need to get it back again. It's hard to find my way back to the place where I would hear God's voice clearly. He is silent. Yet I don't want to make a recommitment just because it will fit in with Norman and his family.

I am ready and spiritually open. The ACC sends Horace Neal, from Yarrabah, and I to the north island of New Zealand to attend a Commonwealth Law Conference, which Indigenous people would be attending, and a Hui Manu Fenua or Maori gathering. It is really interesting listening to Maori, Canadian and American First Nations people speak about land and government issues. I am also interested in the youth justice conferencing that is occurring in NZ where young people who have broken the law meet with their victims and elders who guide a reconciliation and reparations process. I bring back a lot of recommendations to the ACC from what I learn there.

But first we enjoy a visit to the hot springs at Rotorua on the weekend. My first impression is of the strong sulfur smell, reminding me of rotten eggs. Steam rises from the geothermal activity and we see food lowered into the hot springs being prepared for a *hangi* or feast. We visit a living Maori village and enjoy cultural performances of song and dance. We see traditional wood carving and weaving and the distinct reddish-brown color of the A-shaped maraes or carved meeting houses. I love the red, black and white beading on the headbands the women wear and get one to bring home. I also get a green kiwi for my mother.

I'm surprised Horace agrees to come with me to a church service. We meet a couple who offer to take us sightseeing after the service. It is an Apostolic church and I make a recommitment to God at the service. This is a significant turning point for me and I never look back from this full-on commitment which sees me become a pastor in a few years' time after completing Bible College with Norman. Horace is probably surprised but doesn't say anything. Our hosts make sure they do take us on an enjoyable time sightseeing.

Bulletin Article

Greg Roberts writes a general interest story on my work for Aboriginal justice in "White Light for Black Days" *The Bulletin* January 1995. There is a photo of me at home working on the dining room table, paperwork scattered around me and a plant in a black and white vase with an ethnic design in the middle of the table. I'm dressed smartly in a red, black and white dress, looking up from my work with a very matter-of-fact expression, my hair permed and curly. Behind me is a warm scene into the kitchen through a red brick archway with family photos and a clock on the wall and cane hanging baskets with greenery. The article also has a photo of Norman, fresh-faced with a kind expression learning forward to talk to Myrna Shortjoe, a gray-haired Aboriginal woman, enquiring if she is okay. They are in the park where homeless Aborigines tend to camp. Norman's wearing a blue patterned shirt and the palm tree seems to lean forward also to listen to their conversation. The article begins:

> "For the past 25 years, Barbara Miller has labored tirelessly to improve the lot of Aborigines in remote north Queensland communities. She has been a key figure in moves by displaced Aborigines to return to tribal lands and has been instrumental in highlighting domestic violence and other social problems in Aboriginal society.

> "The Cairns based psychologist and social researcher has twice married Aborigines and has an Aboriginal child.
>
> "Few white activists have achieved the level of respect and affection that Miller, 44, enjoys in Indigenous communities across the state. For several years, she was director of the state's peak Aboriginal body: the Aboriginal Coordinating Council (ACC). Successive governments have regarded her as one of the most articulate, if least public, exponents of Aboriginal and Islander causes."

It describes Mick and I being a "formidable combination" while together and that now I'm married to Norman who is working as a counsellor at the Bama Healing Centre helping homeless alcoholics.

Bob Katter was the Queensland Minister for Aboriginal Affairs when I wrote the ACC Deaths in Custody report. He represented the National Party government of Premier Joh Bjelke-Petersen which had been so destructive to Aboriginal people in Queensland for so many years. However, he was trying to change the entrenched culture of this portfolio. The press asked him for comment on my report and I was surprised it was positive. A few years later in White Light for Black Days in *The Bulletin* 24-31 January 1995, Greg Roberts writes:

> "In an indication of the respect she commands on both sides of politics, Katter said he greatly admires Miller despite their differences. 'She was one of the few people in Aboriginal Affairs who was really sincere and really cared,' Katter says. "She wasn't in the do-gooder class. She stood out like a neon light in everything she was involved in'."

Other Press Articles About Me

Later I remember some of the other press articles about me at the time. I have a few tears as I type what Gladys Tybingoompa said about me. She became famous as a Wik elder for doing the shake-a-leg, a traditional dance, spontaneously outside the High Court in Canberra to celebrate the Wik decision on 23rd December 1996. This held that statutory pastoral leases do not automatically extinguish native title rights. Gladys famously repeated her dance, this time bare breasted with grass skirt and body paint, on the lawns outside Parliament House in Canberra during the Senate debate on the controversial Wik legislation over native title issues. Senator Brian Harradine and other Wik dancers with body paint and spears joined her.

In her excitement after the case, Gladys says, "My name is Gladys. I'm the hot one. The fire. Bushfire is my totem. And I'm a proud woman of Cape York today. It is for me, here today, a historic moment as a Wik woman. I am not afraid of anything."[26]

Gladys told reporter Desmond Zwar,

> "Her outside appearance is white. But she has a black heart and black mind. Even though Aunty Barbara and Uncle Mick are not together now, she never put her back on us. She is loyal. We trust her and she trusts us. Some of the things Aunty Barbara has done are personal and I would not speak to people outside the clan about them. Within the clan, yes. But not to you. It would be an embarrassment.
>
> "When she brings Michael, her son, to Aurukun, they give him gifts and take him fishing and hunting. They wait for him now. When she arrives, it's like a queen arriving. A tribal leader."[27]

I take Norman and Michael to Aurukun for a visit and the people are very happy to see Michael, with Gladys Tybingoompa taking him fishing. He cut his finger on some fishing line and Gladys thinks I'll be annoyed but I realize it is an accident. The people still call me "aunty" though I'm no longer with Mick, and now call Norman "uncle" as we are married.

Yarrabah is the nearest Aboriginal community to Cairns and I have had a lot to do with it over the years. I am reminded of comments to Zwar by Mick Connolly re my ACC Report into Aboriginal Deaths in Custody, a number of deaths having occurred at Yarrabah:

> "Mick Connolly, 38, community councillor at Yarrabah (population 900) community on the opposite side of the bay to Cairns, said when he read her report: 'It isn't just because she was married to an Aborigine that Barbara has an understanding of Aborigines. Her attitude is such that even if she hadn't married Mick Miller, she still would have been accepted.
>
> "She not only understands Aboriginal ways, but when she puts it on paper, it is the skill of her research coming out. Her report is spot on.
>
> "She is one of those white people who almost has more knowledge of us than we do ourselves."[28]

However, from 1995 onwards, I scale back my activism in Indigenous affairs, believing that this role is better served by Indigenous people. Still, my commitment and passion never wane. Norman and I pioneer a church in 1996 and a lot of our energy and time is spent spreading the Christian message and working on reconciliation locally, in Australia and overseas.

Pioneering A Church

As our faith deepens, Norman and I go to Bible College at nights at Cairns Christian Centre for a couple of years and are on the ministry team. Norman is also doing youth work and Aboriginal ministry and I'm counselling at the church one-two days a week. We pray for people on the prayer lines on Sunday and visit those in hospital. In 1994, Teen Challenge ask me to work for them in Brisbane as a psychologist starting in the New Year and Norman and I pray about it. It's hard to leave Cairns as we are happy in our family, our church, our city and our work. Norman is working as an alcohol counsellor at the Bama Healing Centre. Working with Indigenous people, mainly from remote communities. More than once I get a phone call at night from Norman to come over and talk someone out of committing suicide.

We believe the Lord has given us a scripture that is confirmation we should go to Brisbane. It is Jeremiah 29:11 "'For I know the plans I have for you,' declares the LORD, 'plans to prosper you and not to harm you, plans to give you hope and a future'." We rent our house out for a year and move to Brisbane, renting a house in Carina and settling Michael into school there. It is 1995 and he is 16 years old, in his second last year at high school.

But after making this expensive and time-consuming move with furniture etc., Teen challenge tells me they don't have a job for me after all. It is a big blow. Why didn't they tell me before we left? We have to stay. We can't afford to move back. Finances are tough but Teen Challenge finds another job for me as manager of an after-school care program which isn't what I want to do but we need the finance. Norman is then able to get a six-month contract supervising unemployed Indigenous youth working on public art projects.

We ask ourselves if we heard from the Lord about moving to Brisbane or are we mistaken? As I continue to pray about this situation, I receive the same scripture but this time I sense that the emphasis is on "I." In other words, God knows the plans He has for us and we don't. We don't have to know what those plans are but trust Him that He does. Also, I have the sense that it was hard enough for the Lord to get us to move to Brisbane and He has used the Teen Challenge job as a way to get us there for His other purposes.

Two very key changes occur in our lives in Brisbane which bears this understanding out. Because of our interest in reconciliation, we go to a reconciliation meeting in South Brisbane. It is run by an Anglican priest in a Uniting Church. As soon as we walk in the door, the priest, Jim Nightingale, stops his talk and prophecies over us. He says that we don't even have to do anything about reconciliation but that we live reconciliation. At the end of the meeting, he says if you want to work on racial reconciliation, you need to work on healing the original division between Jew and Gentile. This is what has created a spiritual platform for other divisions to build on. The division between Jew and Gentile has opened a door spiritually for division. This resonates with us and we realize we don't know many Jews. We ask God to download a love for the Jewish people and it is almost instantaneous for both of us.

The other significant development was becoming involved with the ministry of Chris Gaborit and Christian International so that we are mentored in moving in prophetic ministry and develop our knowledge of apostolic ministry.

Michael's sister Marilyn lives near us, Norman has two sisters living in Brisbane, Joanne and Debbii, and we are able to spend some time with my parents in Ipswich. So, we are able to enjoy family still. Norman and I love to visit West End and spend time with our Waiters Union friends and to go swimming at Southbank.

We believe that it is time to move back to Cairns after about a year. We return to our old church but the pastors have moved out of town to be with family. We feel led to set up our own church which we do in September 1996. We call it the Pentecostal Church of Reconciliation and we work across churches as much as possible. In 2000, we change the name to Tabernacle of David because of our emphasis on praise and worship and prayer. We set up the Centre for International Reconciliation and Peace in 1998 after attending a reconciliation conference in England which inspires us.

We are very active nationally. One example is through conferences which we have held in most capital cities and four times in Parliament House Canberra over the years, bringing reconciliation, healing and a Christian influence on government.

Losing Dad

In 2001 I'm working as a teacher at the Tropical North Queensland Institute of TAFE. I'm teaching and writing courses in the Aboriginal Health Worker Education Program after doing courses to be a TAFE teacher. It's ironic I work here as it is a program Mick set up but one of the few, I didn't help him with. Sharon did. But he had a good team of workers and government funding. Mick and Sharon didn't have anything to do with recruiting.

Dad is sick and Mum is concerned enough to pay my airfare to visit him. I help look after him at home for a few days but the doctor decides to hospitalize him. He seems to be recovering so I return to Cairns not wanting to lose my job and not realizing Dad was going to pass away. It is a big regret. My brother delays to tell me how serious he is as does my mother. I get the call too late. I don't have the money to fly down but Norman and I leave straight away and drive the long distance to Ipswich, driving through the night, desperately trying to make it. I don't. At least I talk to him on the phone and Greg tells me his face lights up. I'm devastated to miss seeing him and hugging him again, talking to him face to face.

Mum and Greg have trouble holding it together and ask me to do the funeral as I'm a pastor. It's very hard to do this for your own father. But I do. Mum decides to cremate him and his ashes are at Goodna cemetery. For me as a Christian, the worst thing is to think that my father has gone to a godless eternity. Yet as Norman and I are driving to Ipswich, I feel a strange comfort that he is with the Lord. Am I kidding myself? I have no evidence of this. All I know is that I have this assurance in my heart. I remember when he sent me a book about the Dead Sea scrolls and another book about Judas. I feel he was searching and trying to reach out. I hope, even believe, that he made his peace with God before it was too late.

We are grateful that Norman's father, Barclay Miller, flies down for the funeral and helps Norman drive back to Cairns.

Wedding Photo L-R Barclay Miller, Norman, Barbara, Shirley Miller and Greg Russell

Gladys Tybingoompa, Senator Brian Harradine and other Wik dancers, Wik Decision 1996
Photo Andrew Meares/The Sydney Morning Herald

Chapter 11

Finding the Right Road Ahead

Woyan Min Uwamp Aak Ngulakana

One of the unfortunate effects of the imposition of local government on Aurukun is that their state minister, Mr Hinze, forces them to open a canteen serving alcohol on the community saying that it was their human rights to be able to drink. There is no tradition of social control within Aurukun of how to deal with alcohol and it leads to a lot of social problems in the community. Due to community unrest and high levels of juvenile offending, the council closes its canteen in April 1991. However, the sly grog trade increases and so does unrest. The government informs the school's thirteen teachers they can leave if they feel unsafe and eight do, never to return.

After a riot at Aurukun, the council and government decide to send in a task force or support group to recommend how to deal with the issues. I am asked to do a quick review, along with John Adams, former Uniting Church worker at Aurukun and Phil Venables of the Department of Family Services and Aboriginal and Islander Affairs (the department Mr Porter was previously minister for but which had a name change under the Goss Labor government.)

While Aurukun and Mornington Island do not come officially under the ACC as they are now under different legislation from the rest of the

Aboriginal communities in Queensland, they still come to our ACC meetings and we service them despite not being funded to do so. This is great for me as I am able to continue my contacts with them. This is probably why the Aurukun people reject an Aboriginal woman the government proposes to put on the task force and asks for me.

Between September and December 1991, we go house to house talking to people, as well as having small group and community meetings, and our report is called Woyan Min Uwamp Aak Ngulakana or Finding the Right Road Ahead (1991).[29] The people want to gain greater control over their lives and the way government institutions work in their community, e.g., the school, hospital and police. Also, we report that agencies need to treat the people the way they see themselves, i.e., not as one single community but the way they identify as family, clan and regional ceremonial groups.

Our report points out that divisions in the community are often viewed by outsiders as a breakdown of law and order and social cohesion but they are actually part of the social organization at Aurukun. Conflict between some groups existed before that mission was established at Aurukun and is basic to their relationship. In a later paper where I comment on the work we did at Aurukun, I say,

> "The clan or land-owning group is the primary focus of spiritual and social identity at Aurukun and there are over thirty clans. Added to this artificial community is a situation of overcrowding, lack of community amenities and alcohol. It is no wonder that long-standing hostilities between family and clan groups are played out in ways outsiders see as a crime, involving community breakdown or law and order crises."[30]

A more basic social division is between "top-end" and "bottom-end" or between inland and coastal or eastern and western peoples respectively.

The high truancy rate is partly a result of children not being able to sit in the same classroom because of inter-clan differences. Also, there is no schooling available in the homelands or outstations. We recommend that parents be more involved in the school and that schooling be reorganized to be more culturally compatible.

As the Aurukun people want greater control of health services, the Finding the Right Road Ahead report recommends the setting up of a local Aurukun Health Authority and for it to be placed within the new Regional Health Authority structure.

The people request a community development worker to work with clan and family groups around alcohol issues and the council requests legislative changes to give greater community control over alcohol including a permit system for people bringing alcohol into Aurukun for better policing of sly grog. The Council also want to be able to declare alcohol free areas within the township.

As a result of our consultations and report, the Aurukun people immediately form the Woyan Min group, the Women's Group and Manth Thayan with some modest funding. The Woyan Min group are clan leaders who are Uniting Church members and have a focus on helping youth and Manth Thayan do community development focused on art and culture. As our report recommends community development planning, the North Australia Research Unit (NARU) was engaged to investigate the capacity for community control and facilitate community-controlled planning with funding from ATSIC.

I make the point that,

> "The Aurukun people have the cultural strength to find "the right road ahead" and need to be supported to do so by government agencies who treat them as equals, as partners, not part of the white man's burden. A community development approach to crime prevention means that the people themselves create their vision for the future based on their strengths and continuing traditions."[31]

Mornington Island

Race Discrimination Commissioner, Irene Moss, receives a petition in November 1990 signed by 163 Aboriginal residents of Mornington Island requesting her to investigate an incident they had with the police. A report finds that there are broader systemic issues in the community, not just in the criminal justice system but in all aspects of the life of the community. Following visits by Nerida Blair, Chris Cuneen and others, a comprehensive report is put out in 1993 in which my work is quoted with regard to crime prevention, youth offending and mediation generally on communities within the sphere of the Aboriginal Coordinating Council. My recommendations regarding mediation as an important ingredient in establishing community justice mechanisms that align with customary law is referenced as well as other reports I did for the ACC.

> "Barbara Miller has noted that Aboriginal and Torres Strait Islander communities in northern Queensland 'want mediation centers with trained local Aboriginal people as mediators. Aboriginal JPs, community police and women's groups have all expressed interest in mediation training to improve their personal and work skills.' (Miller 1991, P11)"[32]

I work with the Community Justice Program to help set up mediation in Aboriginal communities and travel with their staff to Aurukun and Yarrabah, for example, to introduce them to these communities. I also help organize the first Aboriginal mediators to be trained in Cairns.

Chapter 12

Losing Mick and Norman's Dad

Mick Passes Away

It is 5th April 1998. Mick phones me this Sunday morning and after the pleasantries asks, "How are you?"

"Fine thanks, how are you?" I reply.

"Very very tired," he says. He doesn't say he isn't well. There is nothing in his tone of voice or words to suggest this will be the last time I will speak to him. Whether he knows it is or not, I don't know. Probably not or he would get to a doctor sooner.

"I'd like to borrow Posky's car."

"Sure, we'll drop it around on the way to church," I reply.

I don't ask what has happened to his own car. Norman and I are about to leave for church. I drive our car and Norman drives Michael's car to Mick's brother Lennie's home. Michael doesn't have his license yet so he can't drive the car and Mick hasn't asked to see Michael or talk to him on the phone. We don't have much time to spare before we start our service. Norman says to me, "Wait in the car. I'll take the keys in." He doesn't notice anything unusual about Mick. I wish now I had gone in to see him.

Late that evening, I get a phone call. I don't even remember who it is from. I am only told there has been an accident involving Mick. I think he must have had a car accident.

"Is he all right? I ask alarmed.

But then I'm told he had a heart attack; the ambulance was called and he didn't make it to hospital. I don't try to find out what happened. I'm too shocked. I'm told he was wearing his blue sulu at the time. Michael's car sits there unused.

The funeral is probably the biggest Cairns has ever seen – over 2,000 people crowd into an overflowing St Monica's Catholic cathedral. His old mates who were with him when I first met him are there: Gordon Briscoe, John Moriarty and Charlie Perkins. Bob Katter was among the Members of Parliament. Jenny Pryor and her children come to the funeral and change at our home.

His mate Percy Neal brings in a dance group from Yarrabah as a guard of honor. Even now it is a tearful moment for me to remember it though much is blurred. It is almost like a state funeral. There are a number of priests officiating, including his Uncle Monty Pryor, a deacon from Townsville. Gracelyn Smallwood sings over his grave. Sandra Levers, another cousin, has written the eulogy, probably with others contributing. I'm left out of any arrangements. After all, I have remarried. Norman comes to the funeral with me. The wake is held at the Idinji centre afterwards. Sharon is nowhere to be seen. Someone tells me she has just married and could be away. Mick's first wife Pat flies up from Sydney to pay respects and comfort her daughters. Michael is whisked away to sit with them. When Norman and I and Michael earlier attended Mick's mother's funeral in Innisfail, Michael was whisked away also, to sit with Lydia, Marilyn and Pat.

In looking at Mick's awesome legacy, I start to wonder if I was left out of things after I have Michael. Mick and I did everything together in the North Queensland Land Council and the North Queensland Land Rights Committee that predated it. I edited *NQ Messagestick* and wrote many of the articles in it and did a lot of organizing and administration.

But Mick was travelling Australia and the world. He was on all these committees where only his airfare was paid. I don't recall feeling lonely. I certainly wasn't resentful as I was very supportive of his work which I saw not as a job but as an important calling. He often said to me that he was glad I didn't complain like other wives did who were in the same situation. He liked the freedom I gave him. I had members of Mick's family, who still regarded me as part of the family, say to me that Sharon wouldn't let him have open house like I did and they didn't feel welcome at Sharon's after he moved in with her.

It was a surprise after the funeral to find out via Mick's brother Lennie that Mick had a son called Manfred in Germany. This was probably the son of the woman he had a few tears over when he returned from Germany in late 1978. He never spoke of her again but they must have been in touch. I would have been pregnant with Michael when Manfred was conceived. I was disappointed to think I was pregnant when he had this affair. However, I keep Manfred in my prayers daily.

I look back at my time with Mick. My life has been forever shaped by my time with him. His TV announcer voice echoes through the decades. His smile lit up many a room. He had a presence that others were acutely aware of, a dignity of bearing, a wit that could be engaging and at times cutting when criticizing Aboriginal affairs policy. He was well educated and informed and could comment on anything off the cuff. He was a charming dinner guest and made more friends than enemies.

Just about every area of Indigenous affairs received valuable, life-changing, advocacy and policy development expertise from him: health, land rights, self-determination, governance, employment and training, education, economic development, arts, culture and sports. Yet his particular passion was to see his people not treated as second-class citizens but to rise out of third world health conditions and crippling intergenerational poverty. He achieved so much for his people. But his focus was not on himself and he died early at 61 years, of a heart seizure while living at his brother Lennie's one bedroom flat in Cairns, sleeping on a couch in the lounge. It was a humble end to the life of a great man.

However, he was a thorn in the side of the Bjelke-Petersen government and its Indigenous affairs henchman Paddy Killoran. Mick didn't mind a fight with the Queensland government though he didn't pick fights for the sake of picking them – real issues were involved. He made mates of federal government Indigenous affairs staff but would criticize them if they started to work against Indigenous interests. He wielded great political clout in Canberra and knew most of the government ministers by first name and was friends with them. He stayed on top of the action and was an influencer. No wonder the Foundation for Aboriginal Research Action (FAIRA) described him as an Aboriginal statesman.

Though he is never elected to Parliament he is recognized by his people as an elder statesman. He helps set up what is the first approximation of an Aboriginal parliament, the elected National Aboriginal Consultative Committee (NACC) which then became the National Aboriginal Conference (NAC). Later it was replaced by ATSIC and he was an elected delegate for the Cairns region.

Even without this, he strode the national stage as a pioneer of many national Indigenous organizations and the international stage as a spokesman for Indigenous rights. When he passes away, speeches are made in his honor in both parliaments. The federal government MP, Martin Ferguson, the Member for Batman, compared Mick to social justice pioneers Paul Robeson and Martin Luther King. Ferguson said on 7th April and recorded in Hansard,

> "... The night before the march, Martin Luther King gave a prophetic speech in a local black church where he told his people that, just like Moses, he had climbed the mountain and seen The Promised Land. He said: I have seen The Promised Land. I may not get there with you but I want you to know tonight that we, as a people, will get to The Promised Land. Moses did not reach the Promised land and Martin Luther King did not reach it either. He was assassinated the next day. Mick Miller, a great Australian leader of the Aboriginal community, also did not live to see the Promised Land. He died this week. I

> only wish that the Prime Minister (Mr Howard) had sufficient dignity to enable Mr Miller to pass away this week in the knowledge that the Prime Minister had given the Australian people an apology for the stolen generation …"[33]

The Member for Mulgrave, Naomi Wilson, read out his eulogy in the Queensland Parliament on 21st April and paid tribute to him. It is amazing that he had tributes from both sides of politics, the ALP nationally and a National party parliamentarian in Queensland. The speech is recorded in *Hansard* including the comment from the eulogy,

> "Mick passed away on the 30th anniversary of the death of Martin Luther King, a great leader in the struggle for social justice and black rights in the USA. Similarly, to Dr King, Mick Miller had a dream – a dream that a person would not be judged by the color of his/her skin, a dream that Aboriginal people would again be recognized as the original owners of this land Australia, and that Aboriginal people would gain economic independence and an equal standard of health, education, housing etc. to other Australians.
>
> He lived his life to fulfil that dream. He worked tirelessly, often without pay, without asking favors for himself …. It was what he lived for and what he died for …."

Church, Israel, Elections and Dad Barclay

In the same year Mick passes away, Norman and I organize an international conference on reconciliation in Cairns with speakers from England like Brian Mills and from New Zealand, Linda Ohia, a Maori Christian leader. We actually start our international ministry in 1996 when we share at the first World Conference of Indigenous Christians in NZ. In 1997, we travel to England to a reconciliation conference at Coventry Cathedral. Also, to Canada, to a reconciliation conference at the First Nations reserve of the Ojibway people at Sagkeeng, Manitoba. We get an opportunity to share at both, though not on the official program. At Sagkeeng, we are delighted to taste traditional food including buffalo meat and have blueberry pancakes for breakfast each morning, staying at the home of a local First Nations family.

We travel to the All Nations Convocation Jerusalem, hosted by Ps Tom Hess in October 1998 with Ps Noel and Dianne Mann as leaders. We are very touched by seeing people from about 200 different nations dressed in their national costumes and worshipping God in their language. Where there were tensions or hurts between nations, they stood in the gap and said sorry. We are deeply impacted by it.

We host ten conferences in Australian capital cities on 24th July each year on the theme of Psalm 24:7 Opening the Gates to the King of Glory. In 2004, we host it in Parliament House Canberra and invite Noel Mann, Apostle David Swan from Malaysia and Ps Michael Maeliau from the Solomon Islands to speak. Michael is the leader of the All Pacific Prayer Assembly (APPA) and Noel is the leader of Australia and the Bethany Gate. Ps Tom Hess has a revelation to divide the world into 12 prayer gates and Australia is in the Bethany Gate with part of Asia Pacific and the Arab Gulf States.

In 2005, we are invited to attend the APPA in NZ and in Brisbane just after it, Noel passes the baton on to us to lead Australia for the ANCJ. The APPA and ANCJ want to co-host a conference in Cairns in 2006 with the Centre for International Reconciliation and Peace. In fact, Norman and I are to be the main organizers. It is to be held in May to coincide with the 400th anniversary of a prophetic declaration of Portuguese explorer Ferdinand de Quiros that Australia and the Pacific are the South Lands of the Holy Spirit. This is considered by many Christians to be a very significant event so we have over 3,000 people attend, mostly from the Pacific Islands with some from Asia, Australia and the Middle East. Ps Tom Hess decides that our conference is so anointed and effective that he makes Norman and I the leaders for the whole Bethany Gate.

Tom also asks us to be the inaugural leaders of the Indigenous Track and we sit on the International Council of Elders, have meetings with MKs at the Knesset etc. We continue in this ministry till 2012. We go to Israel ten times over the years including for its 50th, 60th and 70th birthdays as a modern state although it is an ancient kingdom.

Our ministry at home and abroad is a key area of my life and Norman's and it doesn't deserve to be glossed over but I leave it mostly for another time. Briefly, we set up the Centre for International Reconciliation and Peace in 1998 with the aim of bringing reconciliation and healing between races, between Jew and Gentile, between nations, between male and female, rich and poor, old and young and church and community. We travel to many nations bringing this message: Zimbabwe, UK, Canada, USA, Israel, Turkey, Jordan, Malaysia, Thailand, Singapore, Papua New Guinea, Solomon Islands, Vanuatu, New Zealand and Guatemala.

In 2010, we take a team of Australians and New Zealanders (ANZACS) to visit the Holy sites and the battle sites of World War 1 and 2 and are there for the 31st October anniversary of the charge of the Australian light horse in 1917. This was part of the third Battle of Gaza. The British drove the Turks from the west and south of Beersheba and it took the NZ Mounted Rifles a hard day's fighting but they took the eastern flank of Tel el Saba. However, the wells of Beersheba were still in Turkish hands and the Allied horses had been without water in the desert for a few days. They needed to take the wells by dark. Australian Lieutenant-General Harry Chauvel and Australian Brigadier General William Grant ordered the 4th and 12th Light horsemen to charge cavalry style in a surprise sunset attack straight into the Turkish canons while German planes were firing on them. The light horsemen were mounted infantrymen not cavalry. What appeared to be a foolhardy charge had shock value. The Turkish trenches were overrun and the Australians stopped the Germans from blowing up the wells. This victory enabled the Allied forces, under British General Sir Edmund Allenby, to continue on to enter Jerusalem victoriously in December 1917.

The Balfour Declaration passed by the British Parliament on 31st

October meant that, along with the military victory, a Jewish homeland was able to be set up in Palestine under the British Mandate with international support. This was a stepping stone to the formation of the modern state of Israel. We take an international team of fifty people to Israel for the centenary commemorations in October 2017. We are not glorifying war but the fulfilment of Biblical prophecy that the Jewish people would return to their land, never again to be uprooted from the land God had given them e.g., Amos 9:11-15.

One of the early struggles I face as a Christian is to reconcile my anti-war values with the wars written about in the Bible where the battles of ancient Israel and Judah are described. The Catholic Church talks about just wars and unjust wars and I've not looked into that. All loss of life is sad. While I work for peace and reconciliation, Bible prophecy tells us that there are more wars to come and that most nations of the world will join together to fight Israel. My earnest prayer is that Australia will not be one of them.

We have also been working for some time on reconciliation of Jews and Arabs and host a Sons of Abraham conference in Jerusalem in 2017 as a follow up to one we host in Sydney in 2015. This is as a result of a dream of mine to go into Israel through the brothers: Jew and Arab.

Norman and I are in Israel in 2007 taking a team of Christians from Australia to the ANCJ. While we are away, Prime Minister John Howard calls a federal election. Even though Norman only has 5 weeks' time to campaign on our return, he stands for election for the federal seat of Leichhardt as an Independent.

Sadly, we unexpectedly lose Dad during the campaign. He has been sick at home for a while but one night he is taken to hospital. All the family except those living in Brisbane are able to spend the whole night with him. It is a real high point as Dad is happy to have us all around him and very talkative. We probably should have let him rest but we chat animatedly all night. He makes me feel so loved. No doubt he makes all of us feel that way and feels our love for him. I have no idea it will be his last night with us. We just want to be with him because we all love him so much. In the morning, we all go home to shower and eat and let Dad rest.

Tom and his wife Judy stay a bit longer and are asked to leave the room for a moment by the nurses so they can attend to him. Suddenly Dad is gone. Mum, Norman, Norman's sisters and I have only just got home and we need to turn around and go back to the hospital again. It's a shock. I mourn for him very much. The family takes it hard but we know he is in heaven. He is still very much in our hearts and Norman talks of him often. Norman's sisters make a key ring with a photo of Dad on one side and a photo of the family on the other side. I still carry it with me today.

Bob Katter

It is the federal election campaign May 2016 and Norman and I are having coffee at our favorite place on the Cairns Esplanade. In walks Senator Bob Katter, Brad Tassell, the Katter Party candidate for Leichhardt and half a dozen others from their party. Norman and I say hello to Bob and Brad who join us. Brad used to play for Kangaroos Football Club with Norman and they have a good chat. Casual clothes cover Brad's still fit frame, his brown hair contrasting with Bob's shock of white hair. Bob, with his signature hat, sits beside me and becomes animated. He had a bit to do with me as Mick's wife and Norman and I have bumped into him a few times over the years. Bob went to school with Mick at Mt Carmel Catholic boarding school Charters Towers and, a few years younger, looked up to Mick.

> "Mick Cossins and Mick Miller were rugby players and good friends, big fellows, over 6ft," Bob says "and no one at Mt Carmel got bullied because they would stand between them and the bullies and protect them. After Mick got into Aboriginal politics, Mick Cossins got really upset with him and he asked me one day, how do you take Mick when you are on the opposite side of politics? I said I see him as still standing between the bullies and other people protecting

them. Mick wasn't convinced but somehow, they got together about 6 months before they passed away and became good friends again. They died within a few months of each other."

"I didn't know that story," I say.

Bob moves closer to get a better look and says, "You haven't changed. You know, I couldn't get over Mick taking up with that doctor and losing you." Bob gets that twang in his voice that makes him sound so sincere. I have noted this tone of voice over the years when he has been talking about Aboriginal people or issues and he has just oozed concern even when we've had disagreements over policy. However, I hadn't expected him to comment on something so personal to me.

My eyes open with surprise, not knowing he knew about Sharon. "She didn't stick with him when he needed her though," I said and changed the topic.

Chapter 13

Community Transformation – Building Spiritual Capital at Aurukun

I have an opportunity in 2005 to develop an innovative approach to youth offending at Aurukun by looking at broader community dynamics rather than a single-issue approach. It is hoped to move the community towards transformation and build the spiritual capital of the people i.e., work with them at the level of meaning, values and fundamental purpose to build the well-being and resources these generate and to tap into people's spiritual intelligence not just intellectual or emotional intelligence (IQ or EQ).

The term spiritual capital is described by Zohar and Marshall:

> "We need a sense of meaning and values and a sense of fundamental purpose (spiritual intelligence) in order to build the wealth that these can generate (spiritual capital)." This leads to a sustainable society. They make the point that spiritual capital is "wealth we gain through drawing upon our deepest meanings, deepest values, most fundamental purposes, and highest motivations, and by finding a way to embed these in our lives and work" [34]

How do we define spiritual breakthrough and what would we be looking for at a place like Aurukun to know when we had it? I believe we'd be seeing the following indicators:

- The raising of the spiritual capital of individuals and the community
- A greater sense of empowerment in the community and less hopelessness
- Individuals and the community having a vision of where they want to head
- Individuals and the community having a path, direction or strategy to get where they want
- Those in the community with a passion to make a difference feeling that they have some support
- Happier families, with less conflict between parents and their partners and less conflict between children and their parents
- Little or no inter-clan conflict
- People being appreciated for who they are rather than what they do or achieve
- A healthier, safer, prosperous community

I know of a number of examples of community transformation and one first-hand – Almolonga, Guatemala, South America where Norman and I visited in 1998.

About 20 years ago, they went from being in poverty, having huge problems with alcohol, crime, family violence, child neglect, poor health, a depressed community etc. to the opposite and have maintained it. Many now own businesses. What were the ingredients of this change?

- There was a small group of people (one or two families) who had the vision and desire for change who were persevering leaders and acted as catalysts.

- The small group prayed and fasted on a regular basis and asked for transformation of their communities and they maintained this after their communities were transformed.
- Research was done re social injustices in the history of the community that caused wounding of groups so that people knew what healing was needed.
- Representatives of groups said sorry for events where their group had caused group wounding or offence to another group.
- Paying the price - the commitment of putting one's life on the line if necessary, as well as time, energy and perseverance
- Commitment to territory or loving the people and place you are living and working in. Then you are more likely to receive insights into keys for bringing change.
- The church engaged the community and shifted its focus more to community change

I have identified four steps to personal and community transformation:

1. Having a vision or dream
2. Having a pathway to achieve your vision or dream
3. Having hope of achieving your vision or dream
4. Passion or motivation to follow your vision or dream

There needs to be a paradigm shift from:

- Blurred vision to clear vision
- Lost pathway to found pathway
- Hopelessness to hope and
- Apathy to passion

I asked natural groupings and individuals at Aurukun what their vision or dream was for the community, how they thought the community could get there and what would give them hope and motivate them to move towards their vision or dream. The project ran part time from May to December and a community workshop was held in August to feedback results. Further feedback was given to the Council in September. Neville Pootchemunka, the Mayor of Aurukun was my community mentor and Arnold Wallis was my Youth Justice mentor.

It is evident that there are caring, committed people in the community and that the community is well resourced. However, some resources are not being used or not being allocated to some of the community's needs raised during this project. There are finances available for preventative youth strategies, for example, that are not being used. Training and mentoring of local staff are required and outside staff may need to be bought in for a time so that local people are trained on the job. The strategies and recommendations that follow need not necessarily involve a lot of extra money coming into Aurukun but a reallocation of resources that are available. Much funding for Aurukun goes back into consolidated revenue each year and has done so for some years. Also, some of these strategies involve other government departments so an inter-departmental response is required.

It was easier for people at Aurukun to focus on issues rather than how they would like Aurukun to be. While a number of issues were identified, the main categories were – parental responsibility, school attendance, offending and addictive behaviors. After a community workshop on 24th August at which I gave feedback on what I'd been receiving during the course of my consultations, there was consensus that of greater concern than petrol sniffing was cannabis use, alcohol abuse (despite the Alcohol Management Plans having made a big difference) and gambling. So, I had changed my heading of petrol sniffing to addictive behaviors by the time I met with the Council again to give feedback.

This is the feedback I gave to the Aurukun Shire Council (all Aboriginal) on 6th September after months of consultation with the community. While Aurukun is a community facing a number of difficult issues, it is also a community that has a number of positives: caring, committed people, financial resources and, from the community consultations that I have done, corporately has a handle on what its problems are and the strategies that need to be put into place to deal with these problems.

What is lacking is, firstly, to have the financial resources that are available directed to the strategies that the community people are recommending. Resources are either unused or need reallocating to the area of most need. Secondly, there are underlying attitudes in the community that won't be solved by running programs. Attitudes such as lack of responsibility and lack of discipline. However, the welfare reform can provide some inroads to this. Also, traditional culture placed a high value on both responsibility and discipline and had ways to pass this on, a major one being initiation. Now that initiation is no longer carried out, ways need to be found for this to happen; such as men and boys' camps.

Caring, Committed People

The Council, particularly the Mayor and the Aboriginal Community Justice Group, of which Donovan Walmbeng is the Chairman, are caring and committed and are a force for good progress in the community, though I would be concerned about them being overwhelmed by the magnitude of the task. The health clinic, police, school, childcare and Home And Community Care for elderly and disabled (HACC) staff, both from outside the community and local, are also caring and committed to the good of the community. This is a big positive. Again, we need to be concerned they don't burn out. I've consulted with all these groups a number of times during the project and also Woyan-Min Wik elders group, youth, Community Development Employment Program (CDEP) work for the dole work gangs, rangers etc.

Resources

I have had a number of people in key positions tell me that resources are not a problem for this community. Between government grants, monies raised by council, income from Comalco etc., there is considerable finance available to the community.

Strategies

During my consultations, I had small focus group meetings and I asked people what their vision was for Aurukun, what was the pathway for getting there, what would give them hope of achieving it and motivation to achieve it. Basically, many people found it difficult to envision the community they wanted. It was easier for people to talk about the problems and what could be done about them. I was careful just to listen and not put forward what I thought might be solutions. Some groups provided little information because they hadn't thought about these issues much and others provided a lot of information. Basically, the feedback and strategies could be grouped around the four main headings:

- School attendance
- Parental responsibility
- Addictive behaviors and
- Youth offending

School Attendance

A recent innovation by the school is rewards for the best attendee and most improved attendee on a weekly basis. The school has a weekly parade outside the council office under the mango tree meeting place where certificates are presented with some parents attending. Photographs are taken and the child's name and photo are put in a new school newsletter and posters are put around the community displaying the attendance rate of each class for each week and the names of those receiving awards. This has been happening for about six weeks with excellent results in increasing attendance, which had been the worst in the Cape.

The school has employed an Attendance Officer with experience in international education. As part of its carrot and stick strategy, the school is introducing consequences for parents of children who don't attend school regularly. This involves a progressive strategy of home visits by the new school attendance officer, letters, going before the Aboriginal Community Justice Group to explain and then referral to court for fines. This strategy was developed about two years ago during meetings between the Justice Group, police and school but is only now being implemented. So, it is at the home visiting stage with about 160 families visited. Also, the school has developed a re-entry strategy for children who are returning to school after months, or years, of heavy truancy and the teachers have been trained to deal with it. There are also now rewards for the Aboriginal teacher aides with the best class attendance.

While the reward and consequences strategies are necessary, strategies need to go much deeper. Parents don't seem to place much value on education. Children know there are only CDEP or work for the dole jobs to look forward to. Parents give children, even preschool children, the choice whether to go to school or not. A choice they are too young to make. If the children don't want to go, their parents will not force them. A non-CDEP workforce and economy needs to be created and parents need to be educated about the age at which children can make decisions.

Children are fed two meals a day at the school to encourage them to come so they are able to receive teaching. Culturally appropriate life skills classes at school, including budgeting and relationships education, are needed. Also, boarding school is promoted. Culture camps are held by the HACC program and the school, where elders can pass on culture in a bush setting to the children. The old women will teach the girls how to collect pandanus for basket weaving and the old men would be teaching the boys how to cut boomerangs.

It is good that a guidance officer from Western Cape College Weipa attends Aurukun campus every Wednesday and teaches protective behaviors to the children e.g., dealing with bullying.

Other strategies raised during this project were that:

- A non-CDEP workforce and economy needs to be created. (This is not to recommend the demise of CDEP)
- Parents need to be educated about the age at which children can make decisions, about parental responsibility and laws re school attendance
- Life skills classes at school, including budgeting, are needed
- Relationships and parenting education at the school would be beneficial
- A culturally appropriate behavior management workshop for teachers would be useful
- Engaging Aboriginal teacher aides in teaching safe behaviors to the children
- Culturally appropriate assistance with children's learning difficulties needs to be available
- A careers event at the school needs to be held so students will broaden their career choices e.g., not just truck driver positions but manager positions. Comalco and other agencies could attend
- Aboriginal teacher aides have suggested a video be made of successful Aurukun students attending boarding school, recommending its advantages to other Aurukun students

Parental Responsibility

There are said to be about 60 families with responsible parents. However, this leaves a lot of parents where there is concern about their lack of responsibility. The Mayor says there is a reversal of roles where children look after parents instead of parents looking after children. Council said they were concerned about grandparents looking after children and being tired, worn out, stressed and worried and there is general community agreement on this. Children often say, "give me, give me." They said mothers are gambling, fathers work and then bypass the children for the tavern. An Aboriginal health worker said she has a mental health problem because of looking after her grandchildren.

The preschool bus can sometimes take two hours dropping children home in the afternoon because parents will not be at home to receive them. They are in gambling rings or fishing or go to the tavern when it opens at 3pm. The bus driver goes house to house until someone is found who will take the child.

Koolkan Child Care has developed a proposal to teach parenting skills. This will need to be culturally appropriate e.g., recognizing the roles of mother's uncle in discipline, include carers who are not the parents, use local role models and take into account top and bottom end when selecting role models or mentors. This is because there are historically divisions between people living in what is called the top end and bottom end of the community though this has lessened with intermarriage.

A video could be made that shows good parenting role models and once BRACS is up and running again, this could be beamed into homes via people's TV sets. The Mayor seemed interested in the video proposal. The Broadcasting for Remote Aboriginal Communities Scheme (BRACS), was introduced by the Federal government in 1987 after the launch of the Australian satellite, Aussat. The dishes on communities enabled the broadcast of locally produced radio and video material, along with the reception of mainstream radio and television programs. However, it has fallen into disuse.

The community identified the need for relationship education for couples. There has not been a marriage in Aurukun for many years and people go from relationship to relationship. Jealousy is a major cause of fights and this causes problems for children who are often put aside when parents move on to another relationship. There also needs to be alternative recreation to the tavern and gambling for parents.

The school is planning to undertake values education. This will include choosing a different value each week and promoting it in the school and the community e.g., persistence or not teasing. This will not be undertaken until a Parents and Citizens Committee (P & C) has been set up so that culturally appropriate values can be chosen and it is hoped that the P & C would drive the process. It would be good if this was a whole-of-community process.

I asked Council if they wanted parenting skills taught and if the Child Care agency was the appropriate agency to do it and they wholeheartedly agreed. They asked that fathers be included also, not just mothers. A major barrier to overcome will be that Aurukun people, including children, often resist advice and help by saying to white and black alike, "You not boss belong me."

The need for a family worker to support families and sex education, including birth control education, was identified as a need. One of the key elders said a birthing center is needed at Aurukun so that women can have their babies in the community, bringing closer family and cultural ties. This has been a long-standing issue for Aurukun and other communities with mothers to be having to travel to Cairns a few months before birth, separating them from their family.

Youth Offending

There seemed to be agreement that the Aurukun Youth Strategy and the Aurukun Youth Orbit are not working and these projects need to be reassessed. Four youths take part in a one-month successful pilot project for the Aurukun Youth Orbit in April 2005. However, it was not continued.

The church, with community support, runs an excellent Kids Club for young children Monday night and older children Wednesday night, but there needs to be a Youth Club. Since the project commenced, the older Kids Club on Wednesday night has been replaced by a Youth Club on Thursday nights. It started in October.

A full time Youth Justice Caseworker, or Youth Worker, is needed on the ground full time at Aurukun. The youth worker is now in place but adequate funding is needed to support this position and support the training of local youth workers so that the community can take responsibility for this area. An exit strategy needs to be developed for the departmental youth worker. Local youth workers need to be trained. Since this project commenced that is now happening informally on site with a Department of Communities youth worker and others providing the training. Train the trainer programs are needed for departmental youth workers to train community youth workers. This training also needs to be evaluated.

Sport and recreation programs that help prevent youth boredom are in place and need to be expanded. The Council Sport and Recreation Officer, the school, police, clinic and the Department of Communities youth worker all contribute with sport and recreation activities. Aurukun has its own football oval, pool and indoor sports complex that is floodlit. Suggestions for improving recreational programs are: monthly movie nights at the Sport and Recreation Centre, fishing competitions, culture camps and a BMX track. Building of the BMX track has commenced. Youth football teams could play against other communities, just as adults do.

Youths who are well behaved need to be rewarded. Also, successful youth role models need to be enlisted to encourage the youth. At the moment, youth offenders are role models.

Anger management, conflict resolution and domestic violence programs are needed for youth and families. Domestic violence programs are provided by an outside agency. The Department of Communities has the following programs available to run on communities: education, self-esteem, goal setting, parenting skills, culture/lore, Vocational Partnership Group, Choice and a new behavior management program based on

Neurolinguistic Programming (NLP). These will all be linked to an intervention strategy.

A program for sexual abuse perpetrators and a program for victims of sexual abuse are needed.

Trauma counselling for those who've witnessed murders is needed, e.g., for children who've witnessed their parents murdered.

Wathanin outstation needs facilities geared to young people and other outstations could be developed for this purpose as well.

A mechanics course should be held for youth so that they can handle cars in a controlled environment as they regularly steal cars. The AYS was providing this through the school but it has stopped through lack of numbers in AYS.

A safe house for youth needs to be provided for youths who are hungry and who are not being fed by parents as, sometimes, they break in for food, or money to buy food, because they are hungry. One suggestion was for a soup kitchen to feed those in need with the community contributing to it.

Addictive Behaviors

Values clarification is needed as people need to be asked what is and is not acceptable behavior. This is a concern for a number of leaders and could be achieved through the school's proposal to have values education that would involve the community as well, and be overseen by a local P&C.

A night patrol and safe house are needed for petrol sniffers. At the moment no money is allocated for this but there is a night patrol bus that is not in use. Apparently, it has been vandalized and there is no program around its use. The empty house where the sniffers congregate could be converted into a safe house if this was deemed suitable by Council and the funding and staffing was available.

Opal gas needs to be introduced for use in boats and lawn mowers so that petrol is not available for sniffers. As my project was completed, the first opal gas arrived and will soon be in use. Access to paint that could be sniffed needs to be curtailed. Alcoholics Anonymous and Al Anon are needed for sniffers, drug users, alcoholics, gamblers and their families. There are some qualified persons at the clinic but they are not really staffed to work with the sniffers.

At the moment, there is no real intervention for sniffers except an occasional brief one-to-one drug and alcohol education program if they are referred to the Alcohol Tobacco and Other Drugs Service (ATODS) by the court or a youth justice caseworker. The ATODS worker told me he is not prepared to do counselling when there is no support structure in the community to back up his intervention. There are only general preventative sport and recreation programs. The library is used every afternoon and sometimes a worker reads to the children or youth and sometimes there is karaoke. There are also regular discos and sporting events.

The Community Justice Group has recommended a detoxification facility in the community and payment of the Justice Group. They are considering incorporating so they can receive money directly rather than through Council.

After school programs are needed and the Department of Communities youth worker has organized training for three youths, who did a short course with a Brisbane trainer in August, with the plan of them working at the Sport and Recreation Centre. The clinic said that they could work one-on-one with youth if there was an after-school program available that could become part of their program. These linkages need to be made.

There should be support for the Health Action Committee that Apunipima Cape York Health Council is organizing. As local people take responsibility for health, this may mean Federal government money is attracted to Aurukun to expand services into the area of prevention.

Discussions could be opened between Aurukun and Apunipuma Cape York Health Agency re their assistance in meeting the needs re addictive behaviors in Aurukun.

Grief and loss workshops and counseling are needed because of the intergenerational effects of loss of authority to govern, loss of rights to land (even though this has been restored), loss of culture, loss of economic independence etc. Added to this are current issues such as loss of health, loss of relationships and loss of loved ones through the high number of deaths that occur.

More than one community leader said some of the issues they saw in Aurukun were a lack of love and care by families and the low expectations the youth have of themselves and other people have of them. Plus a lack of discipline.

Some community comment has been that if the clinic reallocated some of its money to preventative work, then, over a period of time, the amount of money needed for treatment would decrease and the amount dedicated to prevention could increase without an overall increase in spending.

Matching Resources To Strategies

What is needed is to match resources to the strategies and use unutilized and underutilized resources by reallocating them or dealing with the issues that are causing underspending. At the end of the financial year, Aurukun regularly loses money from its allocation because it is not spending it. One reason is that the Council prefers to employ local people and then local people don't apply for positions advertised as they don't think they are capable of getting or performing in these positions. An example is that there was funding for a Community and Family Services (CAFS) worker and it took a long time to fill due to lack of applications. Finally, a woman was moved from her role assisting the Justice Group Coordinator to the CAFS worker position (after interviews) and then given on-the-job training.

I did some negotiating with government departments re getting two youth worker positions filled with locals with ongoing training. Regarding reallocation of monies already earmarked for Aurukun, I recommended, after consulting with Council, that this go to Kookan Child Care Agency for their proposed parenting course.

Training Local Community Members

A skills audit and training needs analysis would need to be done. Training local community members could be done by bringing in trainers e.g., Apunipima Cape York Health Council, an Aboriginal organization, or by people doing short courses in Cairns e.g., at TAFE. This would help address the concern of Council to recruit locally and the low response re applications.

Ongoing Mentoring And Support

It is not sufficient to train local people and put them in positions in Aurukun that may be stressful. They need to be adequately resourced and to have a support structure and ongoing mentoring. They could possibly have a mentor in Aurukun and one outside the community. They need to be able also to talk to peers or workers doing similar work to them in other communities, both on the phone and face-to-face through workshops etc. They also need some professional development. When I raised this with Council, they were very supportive of it.

Dealing With Underlying Attitudes Or Unhelpful Mindsets

There is only so much that can be achieved by programs, as good as they may be, and by workers, black or white, as dedicated as they may be. Underlying attitudes need to be changed and there are people in the community who realize this is one of the main issues. However, this is also the hardest area to change.

It is not impossible however. One example is the photo that went around the world of the Vietnamese girl who was burned by napalm and was running away from the fire, face marked by terror, naked as her clothes had been burned off her. This one photo of the human face of the war turned the tide of public opinion against the Vietnam war, particularly in Australia and the USA.

What is the one thing or what is the picture that could turn the tide in Aurukun away from the self-destructiveness that occurs there? This is particularly pertinent considering that Aurukun people agree that they don't like to listen to what other people say, be they black or white. It is understandable that people say "You not boss belong me" but there is a closing of the ears even when there is no bossiness involved.

Some of the underlying attitudes or unhelpful mindsets that people have identified are: lack of responsibility; lack of discipline, including self-discipline; lack of voluntarism.

It is not difficult to see where some of these attitudes have come from when the government and church mission took away the control people had over their own lives. Although records show that the Aurukun people voluntarily moved into Aurukun over a long period of time rather than being rounded up and herded into the village. Once it happened, the missionary ruled in an authoritarian manner. Also, although records show that families voluntarily left their children in dormitories for schooling while they went out hunting, gradually the mission took over responsibility for child rearing. This meant, over time, that traditional parenting skills were not passed on to the same extent they would have been without the mission. Interestingly, those who are middle aged today came out of the dormitory and point back to the mission times positively as a time when there was discipline and lack of social problems in the community.

Traditionally, Aboriginal culture placed a high value on responsibility, which was reciprocal and very clear as to the expectations on all parties. Not meeting these responsibilities had very severe consequences and discipline was unfailingly metered out for breaches of the law/lore. The mainstream legal system in Australia has not really come to terms with customary law and this has led to the breakdown of Aboriginal methods of enforcing responsibility, discipline and social order.

There have been no initiations held at Aurukun for some time. Since responsibility and discipline is such a big issue, I raised this with Council whether there could be some substitute for initiation through men and boys' camps for example. The Council members were very supportive of this. Derek Walpole agreed and Neville spoke of the need for discipline. He said that young people don't go out hunting. Instead of the spear, they buy a steak. Instead of gathering yam, they buy store food. He said parents need to take more responsibility. Councillors Doug Ahlers agreed as did Denny Bowenda and Janine Chevathun.

Inter-clan or inter-tribal fighting however appears to have been an issue before the mission days even when clans were living in their own lands and before they were brought into the village. Today, there are often rolling family disputes that will last for days. It may begin with an argument over a CD or some other apparently insignificant event and then others will take sides until there is major fighting occurring. This tends to break out a number of times each year. People I've talked to about the top end – bottom end division either regard it as real or don't. Those who regard it as real don't seem to know how it started or what keeps it going except that that's just how things are. It was originally partly a geographical thing. This division has been broken down somewhat by intermarriage and by a new housing division near the airport.

The introduction of a money economy has meant that it is difficult now to get people to do things for free. For example, if the school wants elders to take the youth out for the weekend for culture camps, the elders apparently don't want to go unless they are paid. Children expect to be paid to do things and even to be paid first, not afterwards. One reason the Kids Club is so successful is probably because the children get lollies on arrival and for good behavior, prizes for their coloring in and cake and cordial at the end. Also, the worker, Linda Sivyer, has a good relationship with children and parents she has built up over a long time.

Teachers at the school put in a lot of hours outside their work hours as do staff from other agencies but I'm told getting Aboriginal teacher aides to do things outside their work hours for the community is difficult. This may be because they are not involved in the decision making on outside school hours activities or it may be because they consider they should be paid for everything they do. Until recently, even the church elders got sitting fees for their meetings.

However, the Community Justice Group work voluntarily and they are in high demand doing a very necessary job in the community, liaising with the court, Department of Communities, Department of Corrections, mediating family disputes, and meeting with the school and families re truancy etc.

Noel Pearson a few years ago identified passive welfare or welfare dependency as a major issue facing Aboriginal communities. Through Cape York Partnerships and the Cape York Institute, he has been working to address this. One of their initiatives is the Family Income Management scheme, which has been introduced to Aurukun and a few other Cape York communities.

One of the issues raised at a workshop I organized to get feedback for this project is that it is a false economy at Aurukun with people depending on CDEP income, sometimes with a top up to make it into a "real job" and income from gambling and sly grog. There are attempts by Council to generate income for the community through enterprises and attempts by Cape York Partnerships to introduce real jobs into the community. These are issues that need to be grappled with.

Chapter 14

Which Way? Wik Way, Community Transformation

Strategies To Deal With Underlying Attitudes And Mindsets

Further to my 2005 work on Aurukun, a number of underlying factors or unhelpful mindsets and associated issues were identified and discussed: lack of responsibility, lack of discipline, responsibility and causality, loss of authority to administer punishment, welfare reform and mutual obligation, vicious cycles and inter-clan fighting.

Men's and boy's camps, and women's and girl's camps, to pass on traditional knowledge deemed appropriate today, would help. The school, HACC, the church elders and the Council recreation officer are willing to assist with this. Recently the Department of Communities youth workers organized one of these men's and boy's camps with the help of other agencies using programs developed by the Indigenous program team in Cairns. It was very successful, covering personal development and effective strategies for living and learning.

Getting BRACS satellite communication repaired and someone trained to operate it and seeing if the new P&C from the school is interested in working with the community to prepare a video on traditional and modern understandings of responsibility, discipline, self-discipline, voluntarism and passive welfare would be useful. These understandings could be workshopped or discussed in small groups, both before and after the video is made.

While the Community Justice Group has been doing an excellent job in mediating disputes, there needs to be some analysis of the most common sources of the disputes so that strategies may be devised to help prevent or at least minimize these fights. Justice Groups would benefit from mediation and facilitation training by the Attorney Generals Department Dispute Resolution Centre.

The Community Justice Group would like to visit other communities to see what works and doesn't work there. There needs to be exposure of community members to the level of voluntarism happening in other communities, whether by visits of key people to these organizations or via videos.

The government needs to continue to support the Cape York Partnerships and Cape York Institute as key Aboriginal leaders have raised the issue of welfare dependency and passive welfare as an issue that needs to be dealt with by moving to the concept of partnerships between the community and government.

There is a need to identify vicious cycles and plan interventions to break out of the cycles. A gamechanger i.e., saying sorry, would bring a healing between the government and Aurukun, and the church and Aurukun, re some of the wounding that occurred in its history. This could be done by state government representatives and church representatives.

My recommendations revolved around the implementation of the above strategies and having a workshop in Aurukun to establish implementation priorities, possible staging of implementation, looking at who would be responsible for implementation, resourcing etc. A second stage of the project I recommended was to train key leaders in the community in leadership and personal development skills to build leadership capacity. General and community-specific cross-cultural training for government workers is recommended as are cultural mentors in the community.

Healing The People, Healing The Land

There has been transformation of a number of villages in Fiji as a result of a government initiative of funding a Healing the Land team of Fijian Christians who spend two weeks in a village doing workshops and counselling. They work on healing tribal conflicts and then husband-wife conflicts and parent-children conflicts. It often involves bringing healing from historical events that have wounded the whole community. This has then resulted in the land flourishing.

One example is a village where 40 plus years ago, the water in a creek became bitter and poisonous. When the leader of the Healing the Land team visited the village, he asked what had happened around the time the water became poisonous. He was told that there had been inter-tribal fighting and that blood had been shed. He asked the living representatives of that tribe who had the authority to speak for it if they were willing to say sorry. They were, and the land miraculously responded by the water becoming drinkable and fruit and vegetables, which had not been able to grow near it during this time, were now able to grow and were edible.

In other villages, similar things happened. For example, after a healing ceremony, lightning struck the coral reef, which then started to regenerate, and the fish that had left the area came back in large numbers. Crabs, fruit and vegetables are now large and plentiful.

I showed a video about what happened in Fiji, *Let the Sea Resound* and there is sufficient interest in it that the Mayor and the church have approved the Healing the Land team coming to Aurukun.

I suggested to Council that it would be good for the Mayor plus one representative from the church go to Fiji to see for themselves the changes that have occurred in villages and how the Healing the Land team works.

They could then make an informed decision about having the Healing the Land team come to Aurukun and maybe the Fijian government could be approached about contributing to such a team coming to Aurukun. As well as working with Aurukun, they could train a trainer with Aurukun learning how to take this Healing the Land concept to other Aboriginal communities who may be interested.

The Council was supportive of this and the Mayor suggested that maybe Denny Bowenda go with him as he is on Council as well as the church board. I know Rev Silas Wolmby and Ralph Peinkinna are interested. I said that I would look for government and non-government sources of income for this.

The Mayor thanked me for my time on the project and said that a letter would be written from the Aurukun Council to the Department of Communities who had funded my time there commending me for my work.

On another occasion, I took Vuniani Nakauyaca to Aurukun for a visit. He spoke to the people about the Healing the Land concept and they were very interested. Norman and I met Vuniani in Almolonga, Guatemala, where an amazing transformation took place and he said he wanted to see it happen in Fiji and he did. Vuniani had a team ready to come to Aurukun but unfortunately, I couldn't raise the finances.

So, what example did Almolonga provide for Fiji? In 1974, in this village of about 18,000 Indigenous people, poverty, alcoholism and violence were rife and jails were full. However, Almolonga experienced a spiritual, social and economic transformation which Norman and I, along with Vuniani, saw firsthand in 1998 when we attended a conference there. Through prayer, miracles of healing and social reconciliation, their society was gradually transformed so that alcohol abuse and violence greatly decreased and the jails closed for lack of use. The people used greater initiative in farming and the land seemed to respond to a more healthy society by an increase in the size and amount of vegetables. I saw carrots e.g. as big as a person's arm. Instead of exporting four truckloads of produce a month, it increased to forty truckloads a week. The people became very well off. This transformation continues today.[35]

Yarrabah

Norman and I also took Vuniani to Yarrabah and the people there were excited about the healing of the land in Fiji and took up some of Vuniani's suggestions. Fr Les Baird from Yarrabah said the people were excited when certain bird life came back to Yarrabah.

Dutch The First Europeans To Set Foot On Australia

March 2006 is the 400th anniversary of the first European contact with Australian Aboriginals with the *Duyfken*, a Dutch ship coming to the Pennefather River and sailing down to Cape Keerweer or, translated to English, Cape Turn Again. Here, a skirmish occurred and there was loss of life on both sides causing the Dutch to turn again and go. Leaving it for Captain Cook to come later and say that he "discovered" Australia, even though Aboriginals had been living here for thousands of years. I recommended that a Healing and Commemoration Ceremony be held at Cape Keerweer, Aurukun March 2006 or Weipa April 2006 during the Dutch Prime Minister's visit on the 400th anniversary of the Dutch landing in the *Duyfken*.

The Queensland Government and the church need to have a healing ceremony with the Aurukun people to heal history also, as unresolved issues often obstruct progress in the present. The Queensland Government was very involved with a reconciliation ceremony when the *Duyfken* replica visited Weipa in 2002 after retracing its 1606 voyage. Commonwealth and State Governments and the Dutch Embassy in Canberra are busy gearing up for 2006 commemoration events and Norman and I visited the Dutch Embassy in Canberra to talk to them about it when we were there for other reasons.

This would deal with the hurts or wounds of the history of European-Aboriginal relationships the community has carried from generation to generation and which affects today's youth. This includes issues of grief and loss in relation to land, governance, culture, economic self-sufficiency, identity and child rearing.

Another recommendation was that a Healing Ceremony be held between the church (Presbyterian and Uniting) and the Aurukun Community re their past relationship.

All The Way To Holland

Aurukun receives no formal apology from the Dutch at the 400th anniversary of the *Duyfken's* visit to Cape York, so the Aurukun people later decide that they will go to the Netherlands and release forgiveness. All the attention to their turn-back story has brought them to realize it is time to let go of their grief and anger and have a new story. I believe my time at Aurukun in 2005 talking to them about this issue has helped bring this about. However, it was their own initiative.

The Aurukun people decide to give 12 Wik Ceremonial Law Poles by sculptors Ron Yunkaporta and Joel Ngallametta as a permanent expression of the wish to reconcile with the Dutch. They will be formally handed over to the Netherlands government in the course of a ceremonial installation in dance and song.

Queensland government Minister of Trade, John Mickel, puts out a press release on 12th October 2007 with the headline 'Indigenous People Reconcile with the Dutch after 400 Years'. It becomes a government-to-government reconciliation. Interestingly, the press release mentions the later Dutch voyage by Carstenz. 'More Dutch explorers later arrived at the Cape [Carstenz, 1623], again resulting in bloodshed and the incident is remembered, through song and ceremony, of the Wik language-speaking peoples of West Cape York and has been handed down the generations as the "turn back" story.'

The Australian government is represented. Chairwoman of the First Chamber of the Dutch Parliament, Yvonne E. M. A. Timmerman-Buck, accepts the law poles for the Netherlands government:

> 'It is with great joy that on behalf of the Dutch people I accept these law poles as a sign of peace and reconciliation. The Aurukun Wik Law Poles will remain a lasting remembrance of the first contact between Dutch sailors and the Aboriginal population of Australia in 1606 and of the very special year of commemoration that Australia and the Netherlands celebrated in 2006.[36]

The Dutch Reconciliation Coalition releases a statement saying they are deeply humbled that Aboriginal peoples of Australia have come to their nation to extend forgiveness, without waiting for the Dutch to say sorry first.

Trouw newspaper reports that mayor of Aurukun, Neville Pootchemunka, who leads the Aurukun delegation, says,

> 'For us, it is important to reconcile with the Netherlands. With this gift, we want to see to it that history will be commemorated in both countries.
>
> 'The Law Poles carry decorations and symbolism of two clans of the Wik.' Pootchemunka explains that: "The red dots represent the air bubbles in the surf. So, they symbolize water. The red color is the sign of the setting sun." White feathers represent the Wik warriors; and also, the *Duyfken*.'[37]

The old turn-back story ended in the Aboriginal Art Museum in Utrecht, the Netherlands, on 19th October 2007 and a new story of reconciliation began. This is really what reconciliation is about, being able to move on from the old story of pain and anger to a new story of healing and hope.

Passive Resistance And Cultural Differences

Unfortunately, I was not able to do follow up myself on the time I had in

Aurukun having taken up other responsibilities. At the end of the project, I identified other factors like passive resistance, linguistic differences and cultural differences re child rearing that impact on Aurukun. Linguistic differences are too complicated to discuss here but involve Wik preferences for concrete over abstract thinking and contextualized learning which can affect schooling and adult education programs. While Aboriginal culture has had to adapt to western society and has shown great resilience in doing so, it basically values stability not change, conformity not innovation. There is a basic orientation of looking backward not forward Backward to the good traditions of the past, not forward to an unknown future.

There is a western concept that change is inherently good and desirable. I don't think this is the Wik way. For Wik people, stability is desirable, knowing how everybody fits in, what their rights and responsibilities are to each other, how they are expected to act. Constant change challenges the Wik worldview and is liable to be resisted. This resistance to change can even become passive resistance so that government programs can fail because people don't value change. Maybe even feel threatened by change, or are not really engaged in the process. Instead of saying we don't agree with this, people vote with their feet and act in subtle ways to not support initiatives, maybe even undermine the process. Also, it appears that there are some vicious cycles that are operating. One is that the people don't engage well or get enthusiastic because of the high turnover of non-local staff. Staff then give up because of local response.

This is not surprising for two reasons. Aboriginal lore/law didn't change, not like white law can with Acts of Parliament, so there was no expectation of or value placed on change but on stability and security. Also, passive resistance was probably a good coping mechanism for white colonialism and living under the notorious Qld Aborigines Act. Not to say there were no battles fought. There were. But spears could not match guns. This may be a learned strategy that continues through habit or it may still be useful to cope with government policy. Passive resistance is a tool of those who aren't empowered, so empowering people to decide if they want to do something and how they want to do it is key. It would be useful to get people to look back to their values from their culture and lore and see how these can be adapted to the present situation.

Regarding child rearing. Barbara Sayers, who spent many years in Aurukun with the Summer Institute of Linguistics translating the Bible into Wik and later assisting in developing bi-lingual materials for the school, makes some useful observations. She says a child's behavior is usually managed by teaching them to be aggressive from infancy. Shaming them, frightening them with stories of ghosts or police, shouting and verbal abuse.[38]

Childcare agency staff said aggression is valued and trained into children from babies. This could affect family violence, which is not traditional but is common today.

According to Sayers, children are allowed a lot of freedom so become independent at an early age. Not being told what to do but deciding for themselves, including whether to go to school. They are unrestricted in what they do and say. This can affect truancy. The child is not usually considered naughty or disobedient, even when destroying something of value, and is not likely to be punished. This may explain why destruction of property is a youth crime issue at Aurukun.

Responsibility is mostly defined in terms of meeting kinship obligations and these kinship obligations are more important than many other values. Like: responsibility to an employer, getting an education, caring for possessions, paying bills etc. So, in the sense that is most important to them, the people are carrying out their responsibilities. What we have is a clash of worldviews. In fact, so important is it that kinship responsibilities are met, that a person is basically denying their own identity if they do not meet them.

Families Responsibilities Commission

Noel Pearson, a national Aboriginal leader and lawyer from Hopevale in Cape York, was instrumental in the formation of the Families Responsibilities Commission (FRC) in 2008. It was given authority by an

Act of Parliament to oversee welfare reform in Aboriginal communities in the Cape who signed onto it. Five communities did and one of these was Aurukun. This meant that anyone on welfare whose child was absent from school without reason for three days, or whose child's safety was at risk, or who had committed a crime or was involved in domestic violence or was behind in rent would come to the notice of the FRC.

The Commissioner and two local Aboriginal Commissioners would hold a conference with that person to get them back on track of taking responsibility for their lives. This could involve a number of responses - no action being taken, issuing the person with a warning, encouraging the client to enter into a Family Responsibilities Agreement (FRA), referring them to support services or, as a last resort, putting them on a Conditional Income Management (CIM) Order for a period of 12 months. Some community members decide to go on a voluntary income management order.

Noel Pearson stated in the FRC's 2019-2020 Annual Report, "The beneficial impact of this early intervention on our Indigenous children cannot be overstated and should continue to be supported and recognized by all stakeholders. The FRC is also a powerful example of local Indigenous empowerment. This year, Local Commissioners held over 90 percent of conferences alone, applying their skills and knowledge of their own people to effect behavioral change in hundreds of community members."

New Leaders Speak Out

However, there is still pain in Aurukun. The Four Corners TV program travel back to Aurukun in 2011 and interview the daughters and niece of key women they had interviewed in 1991 like Alison Woolla and Peggy Kalinda. Alison is a former Chairperson of the Aurukun Council who campaigns for the canteen (tavern) to be shut down. Alison tells them in 1991,

"A lot of things that gone wrong, and we ladies not happy

> about it. Kids run away, they hungry, they frightened because their father, brother, uncle, they are violent when they're drinking. They get really angry."[39]

Alison's daughter, Keri Tamwoy is vocal like her mother. She is a successful businesswoman and later to become Mayor of Aurukun. Twenty years on, she says,

> "It's not the millions of dollars government is spending on putting up centers in this community or the programs they set up for people to follow, that's not the solution. The solution is the individual itself, a change of heart, you know. A change, you know, I don't want to do alcohol anymore. You know, a change for the better. That's the only way Aurukun will ever become a better place."[40]

Alison was the first female mayor of Aurukun from 1983–1985 and also 1991–1994. Part of her legacy is the setting up a women's shelter in Aurukun. She was honored by having an award named after her in 2020: the Local Government Association of Queensland's Alison Woolla Memorial Award which "acknowledges those individuals who are making a significant, local contribution to awareness and prevention of domestic and family violence." The inaugural award was presented to Pormpuraaw women Myrtle Foote and May Ballie by Alison's daughter Keri Tamwoy, Mayor of Aurukun.

Phyllis Yunkaporta, Peggy Kalinda's niece, is the Deputy Mayor of Aurukun in 2011 and one of the main forces behind welfare and educational reform. She says they want to see a better future for their children.

Interviewer Matthew Carney ends on a positive note,

> "Eventually, the strong women of 1991 succeeded. After a long battle, the booze was banned and the tavern was finally closed in 2008. Aurukun Mayor Neville Pootchemunka says it will stay that way."[41]

However, the cycle continues. The ABC who had covered the 1978 takeover drama at Aurukun decided to go back and find out why the entire teaching staff of the school was evacuated to Cairns for safety reasons in 2016. In *Return to Aurukun: Material from the Four Corners archives, 'Our cultural leadership is being taken from us'*, they say it is hard to understand without taking the 1970s as a reference point as today's violence in Aurukun had no mirror in the 1970s before the state government takeover. Robinson refers to this in her article,[42]

> "It was a decade when the men and women of the town that had a sawmill, a butchery and thriving market gardens sought not only freedom but responsibility.
>
> Power, as it turned out, was not so easily gained.
>
> The imposition of state power at Aurukun by Joh Bjelke-Petersen's government in the late 1970s is referred to by locals simply as The Takeover.
>
> Worse was to come. In 1985, the Queensland government forced the imposition of a wet canteen at Aurukun against the vehement objection of elders.
>
> Within a decade, homicides, non-existent at Aurukun during much of the mission era, had risen exponentially, and suicides were not far behind."

Herbert Yunkaporta, grandson of Francis Yunkaporta, who is a pastor and trained counsellor who works with the men's group, told the ABC's Natasha Robinson,

> "This is where I believe that Aurukun started nosediving down. That next decade alone was the darkest decade in the history of Aurukun."[43]

Robinson says,

> "As some have pointed out this week, the small group of uncontrollable children that have forced the closure of the

town's school for the next five weeks, the school principal was threatened with an axe and machetes, are themselves the children of Aurukun's grog generation.

Blanket alcohol restrictions were introduced to Aurukun in 2005, and there's been a corresponding drop in murders and assaults, but social breakdown and generational trauma is widespread and deep."[44]

Silas and Rebecca Wolmby, Aurukun photo by Leigh Harris

Mayor of Aurukun Aboriginal Shire Council Neville Putchemunka. Photo by Brian Cassey

Norman With Local Child at Almolonga, Guatemala

Chapter 15

Darnley Island (Erub)

Ps Aiden Pensio invites us to Darnley Island (*Erub*) as speakers 6-13 November 2006 as the churches combine to host a conference. We help him choose this date to be there on 9th November 2006, because of the scripture Amos 9:11 about the Tabernacle of David. About 300 people come from the Torres Strait Islands, PNG and Sydney. A lot of healing occurs. The PNG people mainly come from Daru in banana boats. These are 6-7 metres long, are motorized and have a horizontal stern forming to a curve or point at the bow.

A few of us travel by banana boat to *Kemus* (Treacherous Bay) where the London Missionary Society (LMS) landed on 1st July 1871. It is an exhilarating experience, feeling the sea spray and being out on the open sea. Darnley Island is the east gate of the Torres Strait and the gospel went from here to each Island in the Torres Strait and on to PNG. Indigenous missionaries and their wives from the islands of Lifu, Mare and Fiji were with the LMS missionaries Rev Samuel McFarlane and Rev Archibald Murray. The Erub chief, Dabad, was the first to become a Christian and he introduced Amano, the Paramount Chief to the missionaries. The Coming of the Light (Christianity) is celebrated on 1st July each year in the Torres Strait and by Torres Strait Islanders living on the mainland.

Thursday 9th November is the main day and the whole conference goes out in banana boats to pray on site at *Bika*r (Massacre Bay). I really get a sense of being among a sea-faring people whose livelihood comes from the sea and the love of the sea is so much a part of their lives. Aiden thinks that the Duke of Edinburgh landed here at *Bikar* on 9th November 1954. We carefully climb the cliff to where the monument is and read the plaque. We are excited to discover it was 1956, exactly 50 years to the day that we are here. So, I proclaim a jubilee: release of the captives, freedom for the land. We could have been one day too early or one day too late or 10 years too late. The opportunity to be there on the 50th anniversary was amazing. So, the elders and leaders step into their jubilee.

You may ask why the fuss about the Duke of Edinburgh landing at Darnley Is? The Queen of England never visits Darnley Is, though requested, and the Duke, on the Royal Yacht *Britannia*, stops off for a swim on his way to PNG. So, it is partly a need for recognition on the island that the monument is built. A ceremony has not been held there, however, since the monument was erected. Ps Aiden says the kingdom of God visited Darnley in 1871 and the kingdom of man visited in 1956. I declare that *Britannia* does not rule the waves and that God's sovereignty and the sovereignty of the Torres Strait Islands (Zenadh Kes) would be recognized.

We then go to the well a bit further inland. Six men from a whaleboat party were killed in July 1793 (Ian Nicholson "Via Torres Strait"). They went ashore on 1st July, the same day of the year the LMS landed in the next bay. Eight men went ashore on 3rd July and disappeared. On 10th July, a party of 44 men went ashore under the command of Mr Dell. Their first action was to hoist the Union Jack. This was the 3rd time in 23 years the island had been claimed for the British crown, Captain Bremer having done so in 1838. This was illegal as they were on a commercial vessel, not a navy vessel.

This was the first commercial passage through the Torres Strait by two British vessels: *Shah Hormuzear* commanded by M. W. Brampton and *Chesterfield* commanded by M.B. Alt. They found a dead body and, believing the rest of the party dead, they burned and destroyed 135 huts and 16 canoes and the sugar plantations. They killed a number of people.

This is known as the Chesterfield massacre. It was a planned punitive expedition because of the murder of the sailors on their friendly visit ashore.

The local people told missionaries in 1888 of a massacre dated around 1840 where the crew of a vessel were killed for washing in the well of Erub with soap and fouling the water supply. They had been given permission by the Erubians to drink the water but they washed on the edge of the well and some soap went in. When asked to stop (by sign language) they didn't. Many Erubians lost their lives as a result. Huts were burned and gardens destroyed. The village was never lived in again. As there is no evidence of another boat being here around at this time, both of these incidents may be the same incident.

Ps Annie Pensio asks one person from each of the 12 villages to bring a stone with the name of their village on it to put in the center of the well. Carole Koroknay, born in England, says sorry and gives them water and soap as a symbolic gesture to come in the opposite spirit of what had occurred at the well. The sorry is received and Annie stands in the gap for Erub to say sorry for the English who were killed. This is also received. Ps Kenny Jobi from Bamaga sees a light come down and hit the well. We found out later that *Bikar* means "light shines" so this seems to be a sign that God has restored the well. It was as if there had been an invisible line dividing the east and west sides of the island. After our time at the well, this division seems to disappear.

George Mye is the elder statesman for the whole Torres Strait and he spends Friday night giving us the history of the island and information on its traditions. Afterwards, Norman washes his feet and says sorry to him for the lack of prayer of the church to government figures, Indigenous and non-indigenous and for teaching that the church should not get involved in politics. I think this broke a barrier between the church and the community and between Aboriginal and Torres Strait Islander.

There is much more to tell but this gives us a taste of what happened. In 2014, I write and publish a book which includes the journey of the Spaniard Torres through the Pacific in 1606. He is the first European to realize there is a separation between PNG and what came to be known as Australia. His name is given to the Torres Strait that he sails through. My book is called *The European Quest to Find Terra Australis Incognita: Quiros Torres and Janszoon.*

Norman Prays Over the 12 Stones at Darnley Island. Photo Barbara Miller

Chapter 16

Yorta Yorta Country Visit

Visit To Cummeragunja On The Murray River 2011

I am fascinated by the story of William Cooper, a Christian Aboriginal activist of the Yorta Yorta tribe who was one of the early founders of the Aboriginal movement. He founded the first national Aboriginal organization, the Australian Aborigines' League (AAL) in 1932 after he moved to Melbourne from the Murray River area being born at Echuca in 1860. It still exists under a slightly different name. His mother Kitty saw the first white settlers move into her homeland.

As well as being a prolific letter writer to politicians and newspapers, William Cooper gathered nearly 2,000 signatures on a petition to the King of England for the rights of his people but the Australian government would not deliver it. He led a strike of his people at Cummergunja reserve because his people were dying from poverty, harsh treatment, lack of sanitation and food. With NSW leaders like Bill Ferguson and Jack Patten, he and others from the AAL led a Day of Mourning in Sydney for the 150th anniversary of white settlement. He initiated Aboriginal Sunday which eventually became National Aborigines and Islanders Day Observance Committee (NAIDOC).

He has been embraced by the Jewish community in Australia and in Israel for leading the AAL in one of the few private protests worldwide against Kristallnacht, the start of the Holocaust even though he was not a citizen in his own land. Norman and I were privileged to be at Yad Vashem in Jerusalem when an Academic Chair of Resistance to the Holocaust was named after him in December 2010. I was privileged to help organize a re-enactment of the 1938 protest walk to the German Consulate on 6th December 1938 when I launched my first book about him 6th December 2012. The German Consul, Michael Pearce, apologized for the Holocaust to the many Holocaust survivors and children of survivors who walked with us. It was an emotional and healing moment.

I decide to write William's story about May 2011, and I feel I need to visit the place where he was born, where he lived and where he was buried. I want to see the beautiful Murray River where the paddle steamers plied their way up river with bales of wool in William's time and see the beautiful forests. In particular, I want to get to know the people of the land more. I write about his activism for Aboriginal people in my book *William Cooper Gentle Warrior* in 2012 and White *Australia Has A Black History* in 2019. I write about his activism for Jewish people in *Shattered Lives Broken Dreams* in 2020 as well as the earlier gentle warrior book.

We attend a Gala Dinner in honor of William Cooper in Melbourne. Alf Turner, otherwise known as Uncle Boydie, his grandson, is at the gala dinner and gives me permission to write the biography of William Cooper. He can't meet us when we visit his country, however, as he will be at a meeting. Slim and wiry, the white-haired Uncle Boydie is a gentleman like his grandfather, exuding a quiet dignity. A local Aboriginal pastor, Joe Day who ministers at Cummeragunja says it would be fine to visit but he is taking a group to a football match. David Jack offers to drive us there. Beautiful forests open up before us. It is Victorian country scenery. The land is grassy and hilly, and a heavy fog hangs over it.

We start to see dead trees, stripped of their leaves as a result of the deadly fires that occurred about two years previously. The area is still recovering. David says the fire raged along the road we are travelling on.

About two hours into our trip, we come to Tatura where David and his son Andrew worked on a large mural in three pieces that showcases the town's history and natural features. As we drive on to Echuca, we pass through Nagambi, known as the rowing capital of Victoria where many schools would bring their children to compete in rowing contests on Lake Nagambi near the Goulbourn River.

We finally reach Echuca port and the Murray River. Norman spots a statue of Ned Kelly in the town. We go to the river bank and see the place where William was born. The bridge over the Murray River into NSW is above us on the right. The ground beside the river is cracked and mossy. There are large stately gum trees near the river bank. A few paddle steamers are moored at the jetty. The paddle steamer has several large bales of wool on it to make it look like the cargo of days gone by. Echuca was the largest port outside the capital of Melbourne in the early days, buzzing as it was with paddle steamers carrying wool to market.

A little further down, there is a bend in the river, and we can see downstream. There is a huge wharf area on the left where many paddle steamers are anchored. They are very picturesque, ready to be hired out to take passengers for a ride or even accommodate them for an overnight stay on board.

We then make our way over the bridge and into NSW, driving into the beautiful little town of Moama just inside the border. It is exciting to follow the road through forested land on the way to Barmah forest where William lived for a time. We are keeping an eye out for the Aboriginal community of Cummeragunja (Cummera). We drive past a turn off to the right and notice some houses in the distance. Thinking it might be Cummera, we turn around and look closer at the open, wooden gates. On each side is a tiny Aboriginal flag. There is one notice with the name Cummeragunja on it. We find it and drive in.

It is a small community of well-kept brick houses. Quiet, as most people are at football. We stop at a house where there is some activity, and the eldest *Koori* (Aboriginal) comes out to greet us. He is from Swan Hill but married to a Yorta Yorta woman. We tell him who we are, where we are from, and why we are there. We ask him if it was okay to visit William's grave. He says yes and gives us directions.

We drive around the corner and along to the graveyard which has a high arched entrance to it. As we enter on foot, there are clumps of cow dung and patches of an unusual green leafy plant. William's grave is further away; near the fence with towering pine trees providing shelter on the other side of the fence. On the way to it, I see the graves of other famous Yorta Yorta people like Selwyn and Geraldine Briggs and Hyllus Maris. However, there are not a large number of graves here.

William's grave has a branch with fresh eucalyptus leaves on it. It seems a new headstone might have been built in 1995. Around the grave is a gray granite edge with a black basalt headstone. The top of the grave is covered with white quartz gravel and moss. A small angel adorns it and a teddy bear with a football.

It is a blessing to pay tribute to this man of God, this pioneer for the uplift of his Aboriginal people who also had heart for the Jews. As I pray a blessing over him, his family and the Yorta Yorta people, I feel to compare him to another William: William Wilberforce and his long struggle to rid the British Empire of slavery.

We then drive into the small village of Barmah, which is very close and which has a caravan park. As we have to catch a plane, it is time then to make the journey back. About a two-and-a-half-hour trip. We pass through Shepparton on the way back. Uncle Boydie would still be at Echuca at his meeting with the Yorta Yorta people, so we bless him as we drive through the town. He lives in nearby Mooroopna, about four km from Shepparton. It was at Mooroopna hospital that William passed away, after which he was taken to his beloved Cummera to rest.

Visit To Uncle Boydie, Mooroopna 2012

I need to talk to Uncle Boydie some more and see Shepparton and Mooroopna where many of William's descendants live. Also, I want to make another visit to Barmah, Cummera and the Murray River. This time, Uncle Boydie is able to be our guide for the three-day visit.

Norman comes with me, and we time our visit so that we are in Shepparton for the fourth anniversary of the Apology to the Stolen Children generation on Monday 13th February. Also, we particularly time it to be in Melbourne for Friday night's dinner on 17th February where the Victorian Government will honor Aborigines; William Cooper among them.

We arrive at Queens Gardens Shepparton at 8.15am for the Apology breakfast. It is out in the open with finger food. It is hard to hear the speeches outside, but we are able to meet a few people. Uncle Boydie meets us there and hosts us for the rest of our trip.

We meet Leon Saunders at the breakfast, he says he is a descendant of Thomas James who married William Cooper's sister Ada. He says Thomas had a vision before he left Mauritius to come to Australia and work with Aborigines. Thomas had planned to be a doctor but went to a meeting missionary Daniel Mathews had and offered his services to teach Aborigines.

At the Friary Coffee Shop, we chat to Uncle Boydie who says William was a big man, heavily built. He continues,

> "Mum told me he was a hard man on them, but the grandchildren could get away with a lot more. I was the youngest who lived with him in Melbourne. He was in his seventies, but he walked twelve km to the CBD. It took us two hours to do the (commemoration) walk in 2011.
>
> We walked over the bridge they named after him. The woman who bought the house we lived in named it after grandfather. We walked to Federation Square and Friday night's event is at Federation Square."

It was heartwarming but also sad to hear Uncle Boydie talk of his first-hand knowledge of such a towering figure in the history of our nation. Uncle continues,

> "He died when I was thirteen years old at Mooroopna hospital. He got sick in Melbourne, and they brought him up here because Mum was here and he got worse and went into the hospital. When I asked what he died from, the doctor said he was just worn out. He was 80 years old and real bright and just after we left, he passed away. It was a big funeral. Many knew him.
>
> When I look back now, he was a father figure to me. I was only a baby when I went to live with him. My family broke up. We lived on the Murray River before moving to Melbourne. I'm probably the only person alive who knew him."

Uncle remembers his Mum was living on the riverbank and working in the fruit cannery and his step-dad was picking fruit. He'd go to school at Mooroopna.

He looks back at the people who came to meetings at William's place in Melbourne: "While with grandfather, I'd open the door for people attending meetings: Doug Nicholls, Lynch Cooper, Marg Tucker and Bill and Eric Onus and people who lived in Fitzroy, about 15-20 people. A couple of white people came too. Arthur Burdeau who worked in the railways and Helen Baille."

Uncle talks a little about the family. He says William's second wife was Agnes Hamilton. William remarried after the death of his first wife. Agnes and William Cooper had Amy whose first husband was Alfred George Turner, and they had Boydie, also called Alf Turner. After they broke up, she married Henry Charles.

Uncle Boydie remembers his grandfather writing letters. Some days he could not get out of bed; he was so sick. He would put a red blanket around his shoulders, and he would still write letters. William had been writing for years before moving to Melbourne, but they went in the wastepaper basket because no one would listen. It was a lonely struggle for the rights of his people until he moved to Melbourne and founded the AAL.

Much earlier, William left the mission because of the regulations and went to a little place and ran a fish and chip shop for several years because he had to feed seven children. This was about 1906 at a place called Mulwala. He was about 45 years old.

William's first wife and he had two children, but one died. The other was a daughter called Emma, who married Tom Donolly. Emma's son and grandson are buried with William at Cummera.

Dan was the eldest child of William's second marriage, and he died in action in the First World War. Another son, Gillison, spent all his working life in the Victorian railways and became the station master at Mooroopna. He also was the "Man in gray" in a cubicle at Spencer St station who you could go to and ask questions. William's son Lynch won the Stawell Gift run in 1928, the year Uncle Boydie was born, and in 1929, he was the world sprint champion. He married Eva Christian.

Amy, Uncle's mother, ran a hostel in Melbourne and another relative, Sally, ran a safe house in Melbourne for young Aboriginal girls. She married Mick Russell, a New Zealander. She had one son, Kevin who is Kevin Russell's father. Kevin has been very active in promoting William's legacy.

William and Sarah looked after three other grandchildren. Cyril who played for Carlton, Esme and Bruce. Bruce's mother Jessie had died in childbirth. Cyril and Bruce both fought in Papua New Guinea (PNG) and were not the same when they came back.

Uncle remembers one of William's contemporaries who worked for Aboriginal rights, Jack Patten. He says, "He was a funny man, jolly to be around. He was a nice fella, and everybody liked him."

After this time of talking about family history, we go to a BBQ lunch down by the river which is part of the Apology Day celebrations. One of Thomas James' descendants is very busy cooking, even though he is an elder. A couple of young girls help him.

Yorta Yorta Nation Aboriginal Corporation

Uncle Boydie takes us to the Yorta Yorta Nation offices in Shepparton, which are very impressive looking. One of their most important totems is the long neck turtle, more commonly called the broad shell turtle. It is on the Yorta Yorta Nation logo.

Yorta Yorta Nation Aboriginal Corporation (YYNAC) was incorporated in 1998 and represents the clans speaking the Yorta Yorta language, including the Kaitheban, Wollithiga, Moira, Ulupna, Bangerang, Kwat Kwat, Yalaba Yalaba and Ngurai-illiam-wurrung. Yorta Yorta country is within an area currently known as the central Murray Goulburn region in northern Victoria and southern NSW.

Yorta Yorta Nation has had a climate change working group since 2008 and when we visit are working with the universities who are offering them assistance to train youth to interview elders who have the cultural knowledge. They have already done a cultural mapping exercise looking at current harvesting activities on Yorta Yorta country and found a large number of sites of significance. Other research planned will cover sustainability of flora and what water need requirements there are. They are planning an Indigenous Knowledge Survey.

Though they lost the Yorta Yorta native title claim, which is a great disappointment, their joint management arrangement with national parks enables them to maintain their cultural identity with the landscape.

They are continuing the work of William Cooper, lobbying the government for water allocations, for land, and for self-management. There have been many petitions since 1874.

A valuable lobby group is the Murray Darling River Indigenous Nations which consists of thirteen Indigenous nations in four states: Queensland, NSW, Victoria and SA. Working together to preserve Aboriginal cultural and environmental knowledge and land management of the Murray Darling river area.

Bangerang Cultural Centre

The plan for Tuesday 14th February is to visit Barmah forest, the Murray River, Echuca and Cummeragunja. We stop at the Bangerang Cultural Centre in Shepparton on the road out to Barmah forest. Marlene Atkinson shows us around.

Opened in 1982, it is the first Aboriginal cultural 'keeping place, or museum' to be developed and managed by the Aboriginal community in Australia. Artefacts and artworks from Aboriginal communities across Australia are housed here, though it concentrates on local communities of the Murray and Goulburn Valleys. In Victoria, the largest number of Aboriginal people, about 7000, live in the Murray Goulburn region.

It is an amazing place. They have a very large possum skin cloak in a case that has a map of tribal land on the back of it. Life-like scenes of traditional living of the Aboriginals are displayed in dioramas designed by George Browning. The titles of the dioramas, beginning in a clockwise direction from the entrance, are: Bogong Moth Feast, Riverina Economy, Mount William Technology and Corroboree. I especially like the scene of the family on the Murray River.

What is very interesting is they have a section on the photos of elders and the Bangerang and Yorta Yorta enjoy the same elders, many of whom are famous. William Cooper and Doug Nicholls, for example, are there. It seems that that the Bangerang are part of the Yorta Yorta and some people call the Yorta Yorta land claim the Yorta Yorta/Bangerang land claim.

The Banks Of The Murray River

Uncle Boydie takes us to the banks of the Murray River near Barmah, where he lived with his grandfather William. There are no houses here now. They had their house a bit back from the water's edge because of flooding. William lived here after he left Cummera and his home was a very basic one made of hessian which he painted white. It had a corrugated iron roof and a fire for warmth. There were other houses here too at the time. It is a beautiful spot.

It is wonderful to be able to see the place alongside the Murray River, where Uncle Boydie lived with William. Uncle shows us the exact spot where they lived. We are on the Victoria side of the Murray River and, as we look across the river, Uncle shows us where Cummera is located on the NSW side. He shows us the land where the house of Thomas and Ada James and their son Shadrach had been. Families were living all along the river and all along a path to the river in the days of the 1939 strike. Being here is a very special moment!

He is disappointed to see, in the place he used to live, a fence with padlocks on it which cuts off access to the river. He says it should be public access all along the river bank. Uncle Boydie explains this camp was a refuge when the black cars came to Cummera looking for children to remove from families. The people would scatter and cross the river. He remembers the names of the families based on their children as he was young then. There were some missionaries and a church in the camp as well. William and Sarah Cooper's dwelling was to the left of the vertical fence.

Yorta Yorta Nation Centre At Barmah Forest

Our next stop is the small town of Barmah and we visit the Yorta Yorta Nation headquarters, which is linked to the Yorta Yorta Nation office in Shepparton. This is where the Yorta Yorta Nation store their archives. They are kept in a special room which they hope to make into a library. A lot of information from the native title case is stored here, and some volunteers and Yorta Yorta people have indexed it.

We speak to Kellie Jones, currently Manager of Yenbena Training Centre who says they have a rangers program with Parks Victoria. They have five rangers on secondment to Parks Victoria to get skills and then they'll come back to Yorta Yorta as their own employees. Part of their work will be doing traditional burn-offs of protected areas.

Yenbena Training Centre runs Cert 1, Cert 11 and Cert 111 courses in Conservation and Land Management and delivers other accredited training and lifestyle courses to Yorta Yorta, Indigenous and mainstream students. They have a partnership arrangement with Greening Australia who will teach the students. Yenbena will own the accreditation. The students will stay in Shepparton, Echuca and Nathalia.

After a re-registration and compliance process, Yenbena is now an Indigenous-owned and operated registered training organization (RTO). "We've got no special funding. We apply like others" says Kellie. "We're just more likely to take Indigenous students and utilize elders in all cultural aspects. We plan to provide Gr 11 and Gr 12 students with a pathway to university in the future."

Kellie says that by July 2011 they hope to open their doors officially. NSW Health would put on a two-day course for Aboriginal and Torres Strait Islanders in Mental Health First Aid that starts in March.

She says,

> "Yelima used to be a cattle property, but now it is Yorta Yorta Nation property (since the 1990s). We hope to establish tourism and outback accommodation there eventually. Colin Walker, Uncle Max and Aunty Rachelle camp there and look after the place."

They plan to collect seeds in conjunction with Parks Victoria to develop a nursery to restart the native plants. The young people doing the training will develop it.

Kellie says,

> "I'm passionate about my work. Seeing the DVD *Lousy Little Sixpence* about the stolen children changed my life".

Colin Walker, Yorta Yorta Elder

We meet Colin Walker who has written books titled *Mission Voices* and *The Living History of Colin Walker.* Col and Uncle Boydie's grandmothers were sisters. Col's mother was Florence Johnston and was a sister to Agnes, William's second wife. Florence was the first Aboriginal nurse. She worked as a nurse on the steamers on the Murray River.

Barmah Forest And Lakes

We venture down the Moira Lakes Rd. There is a Barmah Café and Park. Uncle used to milk cows for a farmer before school. During the war, he made charcoal here and would ride his bicycle the three-hour trip from Mooroopna on Sunday afternoon for work, going back Friday afternoon.

As we drive along in Uncle's car, we pass cattle yards on the right where they used to do a muster and branding once a year. They don't do these days because all that's here now are only a few brumbies (free-roaming feral horses). We come to a place called the Dharnya Centre. The visitors center is closed because of white ants. Before, schools would come and see Aboriginal exhibits, and there was accommodation here. The Yorta Yorta would run programs on location. The place is now deserted except for a caretaker. There are a lot of tiger snakes who now have free rein. Uncle is very fit and has a lot of energy as we are to do a lot of walking in the hot sun. It doesn't bother him at all.

There's a fenced-off Aboriginal site of significance and Uncle Boydie came here during the Yorta Yorta land claim. We see four wild emus. We go deeper and deeper into the Barmah forest. There are sand ridges and box trees and many gum trees. This is the biggest red gum forest in the world and an amazingly beautiful place. We see some stunning lakes.

We come to Snake Is and see two egrets. Suddenly, 30-40 birds flock across the lake. The Barmah Lakes fill from the Murray River. When Uncle was small, they used to take a horse and buggy across the lake when they could. We travel a long way into the forest before heading back.

Before leaving, we see a national parks' sign that declared that Barmah is Yorta Yorta country.

Cummeragunja Visit

We make a visit to Cummera where William lived for a time after the people were moved from Maloga Mission by the government. The NSW Land Council runs it as it is on the NSW side of the border. A rice farm is nearby. Uncle doesn't seem to know people living here or want to spend much time here apart from going to the cemetery. He says people from other places have moved in here. Uncle never lived at Cummera though he went to school there. The church sometimes holds services at the school and we visit it before we leave.

We go straight to the cemetery where William is buried. Norman and I have been here before with David Jack. There are a lot of bindis (lawn weeds). Uncle is disappointed at the lack of upkeep. There are three graves with William's, all from the Dunolly family.

It is very moving again to see William's grave. A plaque was put on it in 1995 by a great-granddaughter. Uncle Boydie's wife's parents are buried here: Sophie Amy Briggs, died 16th November 1982 and William Briggs died 6th February 1964. Lady Gladys Nicholls (1906-1981) and Sir Doug Nicholls (1906-1988) are buried here side by side. It says, "We pressed toward the mark for the prize of the high calling of God in Christ Jesus." Their son, Ralph Doug Nicholls is buried there too (1949-1996).

Visit To Rumbalara Aboriginal Cooperative

The following day, we visit Rumbalara Aboriginal Cooperative Ltd in Mooroopna with Uncle Boydie, who lives at Mooroopna near Shepparton. It has offices in Shepparton, but its biggest operation is in Mooroopna. Rumbalara has a Community Justice Panel, a Women's Family Violence service, Men's Offender Mentoring and Support, Men's Family Violence, Youth Justice and Women's Offender Mentoring and Support and other services.

Uncle Boydie tells us there are 4-5,000 Aboriginal people on Rumbalara's books and it is the biggest Aboriginal organization outside

Melbourne. It has three-four acres on the riverbank at Mooroopna. They can't build too close to the riverbank because of flooding.

We see the new medical Center, which has three doctors, and we visit the Harmony Centre, where there are family violence classes for men and women on different days. A teacher arrives for a class while we are outside. They also have a dentist here.

We spend most of our time talking to Lance James, the Bringing Them Home worker. His grandmother was William Cooper's sister Ada who was married to Grandpa (Thomas) James. Lance lives at Barmah across the road from Yenbena and drives to Mooroopna for work. The police took Lance's mother away from her family at 14 years of age and she was trained as a domestic at Cootamundra Girls Home. She had to work for two years to get her freedom. This is another incredible story of survival against the odds.

Rumbalara preserved some old houses to show tourists and schools what people used to live in before they moved them off the river bank into new housing because of the flooding. Lance tells us the Council of Elders is meeting at Yenbena on Friday which means he can't go to Melbourne for the Honour Board dinner. They are expecting sixteen to come because there are sixteen family groups.

Seated in his kitchen, Lance tells us about the Drug, Alcohol, Mental Health and Emotional Wellbeing programs. He says the kindy (kindergarten) used to be here but moved to Shepparton. We see the aged care area which isn't residential (that is in Shepparton) but they can have indoor meals or an outdoor BBQ here. There are thirty-five aged care beds. That is stage I and they'll expand to seventy. There are thirty-five self-contained units. I was surprised that Shepparton and Mooroopna have the highest Indigenous population in country Victoria.

Rumbalara employs about 150 people and is the biggest service provider in Victoria. There are lots of trees around and different buildings for different purposes. They have boys doing apprenticeships on building projects and getting their licenses. Eighty per cent of the staff are women because of the caring role.

Lance says Rumbalara leads in Aboriginal health and aged care. Lena Morris, the manager of Home And Community Care (HACC) has taken them on holidays on house boats on the Murray River and other places. Norman and I remember Lena from when she brought a group of fifty-four Victorian Aboriginal elders, including Uncle Boydie, to Cairns the previous November and we hosted them with a BBQ at Wu Chopperen Health Service.

They have a Woongi Mental Health program because too many young men commit suicide. They are going to build a healing center which will be part therapy and part counselling.

Rumbalara have community-based programs for offenders. Lance says,

> "They can clean up and do their hours here. It fits in with the Koori Court. Col Walker is on it. We need to retrain elders what to do. Not just to say I know your mother or father. We'll soon start to refer them to Domestic Violence programs at the Harmony Centre. There they'll learn to communicate not just with their hands."

On 26th May, Lance said they'll have a march and BBQ making the point the constitution should acknowledge the first people. Lance is cochair of the local Reconciliation Committee. He says he'd like to revitalize Maloga Mission. There are over sixty graves there but the landowners have put a shed over it.

It is impressive to see Rumbalara and meet the people who work there, especially Lance. William, Ada and Grandpa James have left behind very capable family who are working hard for the good of their community and doing a wonderful job.

Uncle drives us back to Shepparton where our car is parked. However, he is not ready to say goodbye after three full days of spending time with us, so he invites us back to Mooroopna again, this time to his home. We happily follow him in our car.

Uncle Boydie's Home

Uncle invites us in for a cuppa. I think he's grown quite fond of us as family and we feel that way about him too. We really don't want to say goodbye either. He has many family photos of his beautiful wife and children. Amy died 18 years earlier of cancer, so Uncle has lived alone a long time. However, he lives a very full life with regular meetings of Rumbalara to attend and his daughter and her family close by.

On Uncle Boydie's mantelpiece lies an old certificate where William Cooper was honored by Maribyrnong City Council in Reconciliation Week Ceremony 29th May 1998, long before his fame spread.

It was an honor to return to Rumbalara Aboriginal Cooperative who host the first launch of my book on William Cooper on country on 5th December 2012 to a room full of his descendants and supporters.

Millers at Echuca on banks of Murray River 2011 Photo David Jack

William Cooper's headstone Photo David Jack

Bangerang Cultural Centre, Uncle Boydie beside photo of William Cooper and other elders 2012
Photo Norman Miller

Uncle Boydie showing author his country where he lived with William and Sarah Photo Norman Miller

Rumbalara, Mooroopna L-R Lance James, Norman and Barbara Miller and Uncle Boydie

Chapter 17

Life With Norman

Fathers Day 2016

It is 25 years since we have married. We have been away for a Father's Day weekend, really Sunday to Tuesday as we have church on Saturday, and no, we're not Seventh Day Adventists. We do, however, believe Saturday is the Sabbath so that's when we worship. I think of what a good father Norman is and what a good son Michael is and how blessed I am to have a harmonious relationship between them. Michael sells his old car and buys a computer tablet for his daughter Jaydah and pays for an upmarket dinner for Norman and I during our weekend away.

Driving back to Cairns from Port Douglas, the right-hand side of the road rises high with a rock wall at times. At other times we see a hill covered with green shrubs and trees and some dry grass. On the left side of the road, it drops down to the sea and a fence hugs the roadside preventing cars running off the edge. The beautiful beaches below are mostly deserted and inviting, the road winding with the coastline has green shrubs and dry grass covering the slopes. I say to Norman, "It's such a beautiful drive, isn't it darl?"

He replies, "Yes sweetheart," and, while it is a reply I hear often, it caresses me. Norman's words so often caress me, rarely critical, always affirming and encouraging; waves of gentleness. It's as if he knows intuitively that I was raised on criticism and he needs to make up for it. Yet it's so natural. It's just him being himself. I almost don't register it sometimes because it is so frequent, so much a part of our lives. I live in a sea of gentle words and gentle touch. Almost every morning, he tells me how beautiful I am. Sometimes he tells me in the car as well, when we go out. He is looking at me and smiling and his voice sounds so genuine. I know I don't look as young as I used to. I don't think he's saying it however to bolster my confidence. It's what he truly sees. He will very occasionally, late in the day, tell me I look tired and need to rest. I usually, however, press on.

We drive on and the coolness of the air conditioner is refreshing on my face. It is the first week of spring and it is warm outside. We approach Hartley's Creek and the terrain changes so that both sides of the road are similar, no hill on the right and no drop to the sea on the left but a tree-studded flat terrain on each side of the road and an occasional anthill. Our three-day break is nearly over and I'm feeling refreshed. I reach out and touch his left hand as he drives with his right. It is cold from the aircon. I caress the back of his neck.

Norman has never been threatened by my higher education and he is very supportive of the time I spend researching and writing as he wants me to be happy, do well and achieve my goals. There's never been any competition between us and we support each other. In fact, Norman is always saying to me, "Do something for yourself," as he sees me as always helping others and spending a lot of time helping him achieve his goals re his book, his paintings and our ministry.

But for some reason he says, "I left school at grade 10. I stayed on at the holiday job I had at Cook and Piccones selling fruit and veggies." I reply, "You may not be well educated but you are wise." And he is.

He doesn't reply. Maybe he is weighing it up, letting it sink in. He drives on while I relax and look out the window at the trees as we pass by. We come to Ellis beach with an eatery and life-saving club on the right and caravans and huts on the left, nestled and half hidden amongst the trees with the beach in the background, the light starting to fade towards the end of the day.

When we first got together, I was finishing off my psychology degree and I wondered if the difference in our education would be a barrier, a gap too wide to cross. But I could sense the depth of understanding of interpersonal relationships Norman has. His sensitivity to my facial expressions and tone of voice and his ability to size up situations and where others are coming from is amazing. He makes wise, mature decisions and acts honorably. My son has said to me at times, "Don't use any of your psychology training on me," and I have assured him I don't and that is true as far as I am consciously aware. I don't use it on Norman either.

Norman and I are so happy together that I often wish I could package what we have and serve it up on a silver platter and give to others. This is especially because I have counselled a lot of couples over the years for marriage or relationship problems. I can say it's because we love one another and it just works without effort. But there are so many couples that love one another, or say they do, and it doesn't work. Some of them don't like their mate or they are nasty to them. But that's another story.

We have God in our marriage and that transforms it but I counsel Christians whose marriages are on the rocks. Sometimes they have misunderstood Christian teaching about men being the head of the household and those men are controlling. Yet the Christian message is that men should be prepared to lay down their lives for their wives; as Jesus laid down His life for the church.

Norman is very protective of me but also very releasing of me at the same time. As I get older, I have put on weight and I'm not fit. I need help sometimes getting into or out of the pool etc. or getting out of a chair that is too reclining. Norman likes to know where I am and what I'm doing but doesn't stop me doing what I need to do. He is not controlling. He does more than his fair share of the housework to enable me to do what I need to do, whether ministry, counselling, mediation or writing.

Norman and I have not been big earners but we have done what we have chosen to do, putting money further down our list of values. I remember one time we led a team from Australia to Jerusalem for a Christian conference and left our bathroom unfixed for many months. The tiles on the floor had broken up, come apart and made a big mess. It wasn't our first priority but eventually we got it fixed. Nevertheless, Norman has always been good with the money he has, managing it well and being responsible about paying bills.

We settle back into routine with Norman painting and me writing. I do have some mediation and counselling appointments and we have a pastor from New Caledonia we met in Israel who is in Cairns and wants to meet up with us. The Lutheran sisters from Sydney also want to meet with us. I wake up about 3.30am and can't get back to sleep. It doesn't happen often. Norman is also awake and rolls over and caresses my forehead and massages my back and shoulders to help me back to sleep. It usually works and he has a routine of massaging me to sleep at nights. We love to go to sleep in each other's arms. I love the warmth of his body, the fullness of his embrace and the feel of his skin as he often doesn't wear a shirt. I love his tenderness. Now as he reaches out in the early hours of the morning, he says, "I'm here for you." This is a new refrain which I'm hearing a lot of lately. I know it's true. He's here for me emotionally, physically and spiritually.

I reply, "Thanks. I'm here for you too."

"I know." I can almost see his smile in the darkness of the early morning. There is never grumpiness, an impatience, a complaint, "You're keeping me awake." If Norman wakes up before me in the morning, he'll go and lie in the lounge a while, not wanting to come back to bed in case he wakes me.

On rare occasions, I think of the movie "Ghost" where the two lovers can't touch or hold each other because one has died in an accident. I'm so blessed I can touch, embrace and hold my lover.

In the evenings, I usually give him a foot massage early and delay receiving my neck and shoulders massage from Norman as long as I can because he relaxes me that much, I can no longer return to the computer to write. I need to write my memoir. I have put it off so many times because of other demands but it seems as if this is the time of my life where I must finish it. This is the season I am in, wanting to leave a legacy.

One of the things that people comment on about us is that we are people who don't just talk about things. We do it. I have often said to people, "Norman has the vision. I add to it and put legs on it." This is particularly true of our ministry and the national and international conferences we've hosted. It has also been a huge step of faith to organize conferences on very little finances, especially when much has to be paid up front. But in the end, it has paid for itself and been a huge blessing for many people, healing them physically and emotionally, creating life-changing moments.

For all Norman's gentleness, there is an incredible strength about him. His is a shoulder I can lean on to get support. He is not someone who can be tempted away from the morality he believes in and lives. Some of the frequent words I hear him say when giving talks to groups are "integrity and accountability" and he lives this. I can depend on his word. I can depend on him doing the right thing and it comes from a deep sense of who he is, not from a sense of "this is how I should be." I believe I am like that too.

He has been called "Stormin Norman" by a number of people over the years because he can have a fierceness of conviction about his Christian beliefs in the face of a world whose standards are shifting, almost rootless and confused. Yet he has compassion with it for those who've lost their way. Like his father Barclay did, he often reaches out to help the homeless.

Neither Norman nor I have been great earners though I have the potential to because of my education. However, I didn't follow a career path. Norman was working as the Indigenous Liaison Officer at a Catholic school for the last two years and the children, parents and teachers loved him as he is so engaging, outgoing and helpful. Some children came into his room at lunch time so they could color in coloring books and he provided them with materials. Now, however, he is working from home in his home art gallery.

Nearly time for me to go back to bed for a little while as I'll be too tired to face the day. Yet my mind goes back to our weekend away. Norman is concerned to find me crying over Stan Grant's book *Talking to My Country*. "What's upsetting you?" he asks with a frown on his face. "You're supposed to be having a holiday." The only time I read for relaxation is when we go away for a few days. I read a lot but it's mainly internet research or hard copy research.

I look up from the comfortable lounge overlooking the pool. The words won't come out. If I try to speak, I will only cry more. I try to get the words out, wait a bit and try again. They come out in a wail, my face screwed up, tears flowing.

> "When the children in Stan's class turned 15 years old, the headmaster called them to his office and said they were not legally required to go to school anymore. Better go fruit picking or get a job on the council. It was rejection again. It shattered their self-confidence, their hopes for the future. Some drifted. Some died." I haltingly got the words out.

Norman comforts me. My heart goes out to these children. I also think of my own son who went as far as Grade 12 and was glad he was safe at home, living in our granny flat. In fact, he rings three times in the three days we are away. Very unusual as we are lucky to hear from him when we travel but he is happy to sell his old car and wants to pay for us to have the best dinner we can find in a restaurant.

Norman comforts me.

A couple of days back home and it is "R U OK Day?" Meant to remind us to check on people and prevent suicide, a worthy thing to do. However, I can't help thinking that this is a regular question Norman asks me. Occasionally he notices a look, or a tone of voice I have, that alerts him to inquire but mostly it is a habit he has acquired from his father who was always concerned to see how his children were going. My response at first is that this question is uncalled for but I grow to appreciate it and my usual response is something like, "I'm very OK. What about you?" This will usually draw a smile. Sometimes he asks, "Are you alright?" instead.

Aboriginal Art

When I meet Norman, he loves to draw cartoon characters like Mickey Mouse and Donald Duck. Recognizing his talent, I encourage him to complete an Associate Diploma of Art at Cairns TAFE and he is one of the early ones to be part of an exciting course under Anna Eglitis that produces a number of notable Indigenous print makers. He also loves to do acrylic on canvas and batik dress materials and scarves. Norman sets up a home gallery in our granny flat in 1996 and then moves it into rented premises in the Cairns CBD where he has an artist-owned gallery for about 25 years in various locations. He enters a number of exhibitions, wins the Oceania Art Prize in 2006, and has his work in four coffee table art books. While tourists and art collectors are more familiar with the desert dot paintings, rainforest Aboriginal art is coming to the fore. Norman paints under the name of Munganbana which means Mountain Water in Jirrbal. He comes from three rainforest tribes, Jirrbal, Bar-Barrum and Tableland Yidinji.

Mediation Business

I have been mediating for over 25 years as a casual member of the Queensland government's Dispute Resolution Centre (previously Community Justice Program.) I mediate neighborhood disputes, family and workplace disputes and facilitate large scale community disputes. I work full time for a few years for Relationships Australia mediating family disputes. In 2010, I start my own small business mediating family and workplace disputes: Mediation Works Qld. People say about me over the years that my calmness and gentleness help them. Yet I exert my authority also to keep conflicts from escalating. I think mediating fits in well with my ministry of reconciliation. I also counsel as a psychologist.

Jaydah

I'm having Sunday lunch with my only granddaughter Jaydah, from my son Michael and her Mum Erica. It is her last year of high school. It's a busy spot, the food court of Cairns Central Shopping Centre. Norman and I take her shopping afterwards. Noisy, bustling crowds. She has long brown straight hair, is slim, beautiful and has an easy-going, pleasant personality. Sometimes Jaydah wears thick black glasses which hide her beauty. She goes to Trinity Bay High School and she tells me that she walked into a room to the shock of seeing Mick's image on the wall. "That's my grandfather," she said amazed. She had never met him as he died the year before she was born.

"Is it an etching burnt onto wood?" I ask. Receiving a yes and a nod, I say,

> "There are three in the set, your grandfather, his uncle Clarrie Grogan and Eddie Mabo. It was done to honor their contribution to Indigenous affairs and I have seen it over the years when I've visited Wu Chopperen Medical Service which your grandfather founded."

Jaydah has Torres Strait Islander as well as Aboriginal heritage on her mother's side. I tell her more about her grandfather and his parents.

> "He comes from a family that stood up for their rights. Your Dad now has a copy of the image you saw, which he was given after his Uncle Timer (Lennie) passed away earlier this year."

The beautiful Jaydah. She has her whole life ahead of her. One minute she is a model, the next she is playing football or volunteering at the Police Citizens Youth Centre (PCYC) to occupy children in healthy ways during school holidays. Then she is working at a pizza shop and completing her final year of studies at school. She says she still finds time to relax with family and friends despite this daunting pace. What a pity she didn't meet her grandfather and what a pity he didn't get to hold her in his arms. She hopes to become a primary school teacher, which would mean she would follow in his footsteps.

Later, I check out online the etching Jaydah spoke about, not knowing quite how to describe it and find that the three images are in the National Museum of Australia's collection of Aboriginal and Torres Strait Islander Affairs Art. I have never been keen on the image of Mick because the ones of Eddie and Clarrie are smiling and Mick is not, yet he had a wonderful sense of humor. I was later to find this same image in a number of places on Palm Island, including at the school. I also find photos of my sons' grandparents Mick Miller and Cissie Sibley and their parents at the school on Palm Island. They are part of an old collection by a visiting anthropologist from Adelaide.

Coffee And Aboriginal Health

Norman and I are having coffee at the Coffee Club in September 2016 and he is reading something in the paper about Aboriginal people being in the high-risk category for diabetes and other diseases. He knows he has a family history of it as well. He rarely gets angry but he says,

> "I'm angry when I read that Aboriginal people are at high risk of diabetes. It sounds like a death sentence spoken over us. I don't want to receive it. I know of the power of the spoken word. Besides, it's so unfair."

Tears come to my eyes. Not a convenient place for it but I can't help it. I feel my face screwing up. "What's wrong?" asks Norman, a little surprised though he has seen me tear up while reading the newspaper many times, usually about Indigenous issues.

I can hardly get the words out. I stop myself knowing that if I can get the words out it will release a torrent of loud sobs. I wait till I can compose myself a bit.

> "It's the intergenerational poverty that has led to intergenerational bad health. Because of stolen wages and below award wages, many Aboriginal people were living on damper and syrup over the years. They bore the results in their bodies of the discriminatory treatment they received and their children and grandchildren are paying for it with their health."

Norman looks startled.

> "Yes, sometimes that was all we could afford as I was growing up. But my parents worked so hard to put food on the table for us. They cut cane, back-breaking work. And they walked miles to get work. I used to sometimes eat sugar cane stalks. Now we are told to avoid sugar."

By now I have regained my composure.

> "Yes, I remember eating sugar cane too," I say. "We lived beside a sugar cane farm in Bundaberg. I remember we had to close the door and windows when they burnt off."

We return to reading our papers but I can't help thinking about the injustice of it all. Not only has white settlement removed Aboriginals from the land and their healthy hunter-gatherer lifestyle eating natural foods, but then it denies them the wages for their labor which would enable them to feed their families healthy food.

Norman and I discover, to our surprise, that inflammation causes most disease. So we start eating food that is anti-inflammatory, low sugar and low fat. I need to do this because I have degeneration of my lower spine and osteo-arthritis in my hips and knees which affect me mainly while I lie in bed at night. Long hours at the computer writing books and doing administration for the church, Norman's art and my mediations doesn't help.

Munganbana Norman Miller and Barbara with his Paintings at the Pullman Hotel Cairns

Michael and his daughter Jaydah

Chapter 18

Losing My Mum And Friends

Norman's Massages And Visits To Mum

The big marlin is an icon on top of Earlville Shopping Centre. Cairns is the giant black marlin capital of the world, says one fishing company, as they come to spawn each year on the Great Barrier Reef. Here it rides the sky instead of the waves. We drive past the shopping center to visit my Mum in a nursing home at Woree. However, sometimes we stop to do some shopping for her on the way: biscuits, cashews, mint lollies or prawns. The order is doughnuts and chocolates till she starts getting too heavy for the nurses and they ask her to stop eating them. However, Mum is not obese.

As we pull up at the nursing home in our blue Holden Astra, Norman drops me at the door. While he drives to the parking lot, I sign the visitors' book. Mum shares a room with another woman who is rarely awake and has the sides up on her bed to stop her falling out. She rarely has visitors. Mum can't actually see her because of a divider cupboard between them.

I'm really glad Mum's bed is beside the window which takes up most of the outside wall, and she has a glass door. She can see the sun, trees, grass and rain and hear the birds. An empty swimming pool is nearby, not used anymore. A mother and baby curlew are often outside her door and

Mum enjoys them. The curtain is pulled at night or if the sun is too strong in the day. Mum really appreciates the air conditioning though she wears a jumper all the time to keep her warm. On the end of her bed she has a colorful rug that she crocheted in better days. She has the bed sheets at the end of her bed raised so they won't drag on her feet which are swollen.

Mum has to use a wheelchair now and she greatly regrets that she didn't keep walking as she got older but used the taxi in Ipswich just to go two-three blocks to the chemist. I remember when I was small, she was a fast walker and I had trouble keeping up with her. Now it's my turn to walk slowly while wheeling her around shopping centers so Norman and I don't whizz past things she wants to look at.

Her pink-rimmed glasses frame her brown eyes. Mum's gray wavy hair used to be dark brown and as she grayed, she called her hair "salt and pepper." I look at the photo of her on the shelf. It's my favorite. She's so beautiful with her dark brown hair nearly to her shoulders, and swept back off her face in a roll as was the custom in the 1940's. She is wearing a stylish black crepe suit with white V neck and large white leaves on each side of the V. Mum has few wrinkles on her face even now, though the folds in her neck betray her age. She is annoyed at a scar on her forehead from a fall she had in Ipswich while feeding the birds outside her unit. She is also irritated by a large mole on her forehead that has suddenly appeared. The nurses often tell her how smooth her skin is. Mum has red blotches on her arms and legs though from bumping them or being held too tightly by the nurses as she bruises easily having thin skin. Mostly these blotches are hidden under the bed clothes.

"Hello Mum. How are you feeling today?" I ask brightly.

"Hello. I'm OK." She smiles and then she frowns, "You're fat," she says as her eyes look me over. I don't like that dress very much. Is that a new one? You've got too many clothes."

"I like it Mum. Norman got me this dress for my birthday".

Undeterred, she continues,

"I've got some mail for you to read and bills to pay. Telephone and chemist. And Denise (her niece) sent me some photos of her grandchildren. Can you find some blue tack and put them up on the wall? And straighten up those photos while you're at it. They seem to be slipping. And move that one over there. No to the right a bit more. Down a bit so it's under that one. No that's not it. Move it over a bit more. That's better."

"Phew. That's over," I think and sit down. Norman starts to massage my shoulders. I'm not sitting for long when Mum says,

"Check to see if I have enough powder. I think I'm getting low." I check.

"You will need some more soon, Mum." Mum pulls out the list of jobs she has for me and adds the powder to it.

"Your memory's pretty good Mum," I venture.

"It's getting harder to remember things. I have to write them down."

Mum's always loved to make lists. Norman starts to massage my neck and shoulders again.

"Look in my cupboard to see if my black cardigan is there. I haven't seen it lately. It mightn't have come back from the laundry. They're always losing things."

I get up again. I think it's hard to enjoy my massage. Norman shifts around in his chair thinking here we go again. He patiently waits for me and talks to Mum about what's on the TV. I start to feel like a yo-yo. The next time she wants something, Norman says,

"Stay there. I'll do it."

Mum's battery-run furry cat in its bed has pride of place on her shelf, heaving up and down as if breathing. She brought it with her to Cairns. Beside it is a small white bear with red heart saying, "I love you" and red flowers I gave her once. Mum loves cats and especially dogs. Photos of Greg's Weimaraner dogs adorn the wall plus many family photos, some of Norman's paintings and a William Cooper postcard I put there. Amongst the pressure stockings, and nebulizer mask is the Ulysses butterfly jewelry my son gave her. She loves these butterflies so much the nurses put a photo of one beside her name at the entrance to her room.

Every time Norman and I visit her in the nursing home, Norman sits behind me and massages my neck and shoulders. Visits to Mum when she is well can be prickly at times as she can be critical. Norman makes these visits more enjoyable. Mum is intensely interested to watch him massage me. In the last few months of her life, when she is drifting in and out of consciousness, she would watch him closely. Her eyes which were drifting would suddenly become alive and attentive to Norman massaging me. Was it the black hands on the white shoulders that fascinates her or the loving kindness he shows me, something that has been missing for her? Over the years, whenever I offer to massage her, she always resists me doing it.

In her last few months when she is declining in health, I caress Mum on the forehead or the arm and tell her a lot, "I love you Mum." Telling Mum, I love her was a daily thing on my visits or by phone for years but Mum would get annoyed at my touch or if I said it too much. Mum doesn't ask me any personal things about my life. Is it an emotional distance she wants to keep? We only talk about surface things, practicalities. Though she does share some of her regrets, like marrying Dad when she had a number of suitors. Some of them didn't come back from the war though.

Occasionally, Mum talks about her mother. My brother Greg and I know as children that Mum is very nervous about visiting Grandma every Friday. Mum takes the long train ride and then has to change trains and it takes over an hour from Ipswich to South Brisbane. We look forward to her coming back as she brings us a chocolate éclair each with mousse, not cream, in the middle. You can't get them today. Mum says,

> "Mum would play us children off against each other, even as adults. When I would arrive there, I would look to see which photos had prominence on the mantel piece and I would know

who was in and who was out. I dreaded these visits."

Grandma was a short stout woman and had short dark brown wavy hair when she was younger. She wore glasses. I have flashes of the commode and the walking stick she used as she got older. I didn't get to know my Grandfather as he died when I was two years old. In the photo I have, he looks kindly, graying and wears glasses. He is dressed in a double-breasted suit and tie. Mum told me in the past that he was an accountant but when I ask her again, she says he was a clerk in Roma where she grew up.

"I remember being fed junket and stale foods when Greg and I went to visit Grandma in Brisbane," I tell her. "We didn't like it much either. Greg said he always seemed to get into trouble from her. She didn't seem to like him."

I reflect that I didn't have much to do with my parent's families growing up. This is so much different from my experience with Aboriginal families who stay in so much closer contact. Having just looked briefly at ancestry.com at what I could find out about Mum's family, I ask Mum,

"I was surprised to find that Grandma had brothers and sisters. How come we never met them and you didn't even mention them except for Lilly?"

Mum tries to get more comfortable in bed. I help her rearrange her pillows.

"Oh, I did know about them," says Mum "but we didn't have much to do with them. Mum and Aunty Lilly had a falling out and didn't talk. They accidentally came face to face in Brisbane shopping one day and took one look at each other and turned on their heels and took off. They hadn't spoken for years and never did before they passed away."

"Do you know why they avoided one another?" I ask.

"No," Mum shook her head as best she could.

On another occasion Mum tells me how when her father is dying in Roma hospital, she makes the trip from Bundaberg, where they are living, to Roma and visits him every day.

> "I'm pregnant with Greg and have to walk uphill to the hospital every day. I stay with your Grandma but she doesn't feed me much. I'm starving and that's why Greg is born underweight. I think she expected me to buy food but I didn't have any money."
>
> "You would think your own mother would treat you better," I say, astounded at this treatment.

Mum sounds very hurt about how she was treated and she tells me this story a few times over the years. On one occasion I ask her, "Didn't Dad send you any money?"

> "No," she says, disappointment in her voice.
>
> "Didn't you have any money in a bank account of your own?" I ask.
>
> "Mum looks surprised. "Yes, I did," the realization seemingly only now coming upon her.
>
> "Why didn't you use it Mum? Did you have your bank book with you?" I ask, not trying to put the blame on her but looking at what other options she might have had in what was obviously a traumatic situation.
>
> "I don't know," says Mum.

In the last six months of Mum's life, her excellent memory is deteriorating, particularly her short-term memory so that she can't remember what she's had for breakfast at times. A urinary tract infection has even caused some hallucinations at times with Mum saying,

> "Greg's here."
>
> "What makes you say that?" I ask.
>
> "Because his dog is under the bed and it's restless. It needs a

feed."

I reassure her she is dreaming as she falls asleep often during the day.

She never seems to dream of Dad. I occasionally ask her over the years if she wants me to put a photo on the wall of them together.

"No, I don't need it," she would say.

I remember my Nana, Dad's mother, very fondly. She would cook us lamingtons and caramel tarts and was always welcoming when we visited. She seemed to worry whether we had enough food and would bring plenty with her when she visited us. Mum was really grateful for it and appreciated her. She was a wonderful part of our lives.

We have been visiting Mum twice a week for a few years. Mum now complains the nurses have become "lovey-dovey." She had some mean nurses in the beginning but now they all seem caring. Mum resists my caresses less and less as time goes on. I can only think she didn't have much physical affection growing up or in her marriage. I don't remember Mum and Dad hugging but then I don't have a lot of memories of growing up. I don't remember getting much hugging from her as a child. I remember her wrestling with Greg when he was little so touch was experienced by him that way.

On my visits or in my phone calls Mum would say, "I love you too." She never said it first. Mum's last words to me were, "I love you too. Bye" as we finished our visit. The next day, she couldn't talk. I'm sure she could hear Norman and me however, and feel our caressing touch.

A Call

Norman and I do an interview with Channel 7 TV about a bronze medal he wins for his coffee table art book: *Reef and Rainforest: An Aboriginal Voice Through Art and Story*. It is an International Independent Publishers (IPPI) Award in the Multicultural Nonfiction category and will be presented in Chicago soon. We are excited. The interview takes place around a table in our beautiful rainforest back yard. It will be on the TV news the next evening, Tuesday 18th April 2016, and Norman plans to tape it.

But I get a call from the nursing home at 3.30pm. It's just under a month since Mum's 92nd birthday. "Joyce is declining," the voice says. "I think you should come." I ring Norman and we drop everything and rush to Mum's side. Mum is not awake and her breathing is labored. It looks like a long night. Is it the end? Norman's moment of triumph is overshadowed by a life-or-death situation for my Mum. We turn Mum's TV off. Hazel, my mentor for my second book, rings to congratulate Norman and he tells her we are at Mum's bedside and can't watch the news item.

The nurses move Mum to a private room called Galilee Room 22. It has a bathroom if we need it and beds if we need to sleep, no adornment, just practical. Norman and I sing Christian songs for a long time. We pray for Mum and caress her. Norman reads the Bible to me in the half-light as his eyesight is better than mine. Norman is watching Mum closely, praying. At about 12 minutes to midnight, he has a vision of Jesus walking on the Sea of Galilee and then walking into Mum's room. He sees a light. Then Mum is gone. He calls out, "Barbara!" I move closer. Mum has stopped her breathing which was labored even with the oxygen. She is white and looks very peaceful.

"No!" I call out". I spend a few minutes with her telling her I love her and stroking her while Norman tells the nurse. She comes and looks at Mum, uses her stethoscope and confirms there is no heartbeat. Mum is gone. I continue to cry. Norman comforts me. I ring my brother and let him know. The nurse asks, "What funeral parlor is doing the funeral?"

"I haven't booked one," I sigh.

"You'd better hurry," she says, "because we have no refrigeration here."

Norman is here for me and here for my mother.

My Family, Greg And Steve Russell

Greg and his son Steve arrive for the funeral on Friday and keep me up late. No sooner do we enjoy the Chinese take away Greg buys, then an animated discussion occurs around our kitchen table. Greg and Steve have loud voices and drown out the TV news. Michael and Norman retire to their rooms, Norman to check emails. I draw the maroon and cream curtains so we have some privacy from the street as the night darkens. I love the curtains. Their design reminds me of an Arabian tent and I have purchased a maroon Persian carpet to match. I have matching pillows as well, placed around our brown suede lounge.

I am surprised though. Instead of talking about memories of Mum they show me Monty Python skits on their phones or iPad. Skits from *The Life of Brian* which they love and I don't follow. At least I have a couple of laughs but I don't get the jokes as much as they do. I suppose they are also testing me because of the anti-religious nature of the skits. They mention the outrage of the church over Monty Python at the time. They probably also want to prevent the evening getting too sad.

Greg's relationship with Mum was so different to mine. I would go softly softly and he would yell at her, criticize her and "tell her off," and he said she liked it that way. And she did seem to. She could give him a good serve back. She missed him when she came to Cairns and I just had to accept he was the favorite as she talked about him and worried about him a lot.

Greg insists, "You were Dad's favorite." I look at him perplexed, though I've heard him say it before.

"I didn't see it." I ask, "What makes you say that?"

"Mum told me you were Dad's favorite," he says. "and you used to get out of work at home while I had to do my chores."

"I was only let off housework leading up to my senior exams so I could study, not all the time," I reply.

"He took you to China," says Greg. "He didn't ask me."

I forgot to tell Greg that Mum told me Dad had bought air-conditioning for Greg and his wife Lea's home to make up for taking me to China. We left the discussion there, any differences in perception not ruining our relationship.

Almost non-stop Greg and Steve have a friendly argument over history for the whole time they stay with Norman and I. Greg is a history buff from watching the history channel and remembers shows well. Steve is doing his doctorate in chemistry but seems to have a great interest in, and knowledge of, history as well. One of the arguments they have is over the Australian Light horse charge at Beersheba. Greg says it was the last great cavalry charge in history. Steve says they weren't cavalry. They were mounted infantry.

> "You're both right," I interject. "They were mounted infantry but they surprised the Turks by charging their trenches and I read somewhere it became the last great cavalry charge in history."

They also argue over where the Ark of the Covenant is hidden. Steve says it's in Ethiopia because the son of the Queen of Sheba and King Solomon of Israel took it there. Greg maintains it is hidden under the Temple Mount. I agree with Greg on this one. After the funeral service, Greg says to me jokingly,

> "Now I know where the Ark of the Covenant is. It's in your church."

We do have a replica of it in our Tabernacle of David as it is an important representation of the presence of God.

> "I won't be mentioning in the eulogy that Mum didn't come to either of my weddings," I tell Greg.

He surprises me by saying,

> "Pop was Catholic and was disowned by the family for marrying Nan, a Protestant." These are my father's parents. "Our family was Catholic," my brother says, "but when I sent

> Stevie to a Catholic high school there were eruptions in the family who were anti-Catholic. Even Auntie Eva couldn't marry Pop's brother because she was Catholic. She was a teacher in Ipswich and they were engaged for 25 years before they finally married and it was too late to have children."
>
> "I knew about Auntie Eva," I say, "but not about Pop." I think about it later and suppose that Pop's brother must not have been Catholic. It's disappointing to see people's religious beliefs divide families like this.

Later I think this might explain the animosity towards Catholics but it doesn't deal with the race issue.

Burial Of My Mother

It is Martyn Street Cemetery Cairns around midday 26th April 2016. The sky is overcast and there is no one around except our little party. Plastic flowers adorn the rows of graves. We come to a spot where a tent and chairs have been assembled near a freshly dug grave. As the coffin is removed from the hearse, we hear the strains of *Don't Cry for Me* by Libby Allen. But it is hard not to. The song goes, first verse and then chorus:

"Don't cry for me
Don't shed a tear
I've been set free
No need to fear
God spoke to me
My time had come
He made a way to bring me home

Don't cry for me
My pain is gone forever
Don't cry for me

My body's been made whole
Don't cry for me
We'll soon be back together
Don't cry for me
It's well within my soul."

I bury my mother with a Bible in each hand: a black pocket-sized New Testament she had been given in 1937 by the British and Foreign Bible Society; the other a red-covered complete Bible I gave her when she came to live with me in Cairns. She had returned it to me for lack of use and when mine wore out. I have been using it for about a year. My mascara is smudged and stinging my eyes. I have to go to the bathroom to remove it. As I type the words, I cry just as I cried when I first heard the song and chose it for the graveside. Why did I choose it? But then, I cried at every song I chose.

I led her in a prayer of commitment to God in Ipswich Hospital in 2008. She was living in a retirement village in Ipswich after my Dad died in 2001 and had lost her balance and fell, lying on the floor of her unit for 23 hours before she was found. She had a minor heart attack while lying there. When she came out of hospital, I brought her to Cairns to live with me. However, after a short period, she was hospitalized in Cairns with a urinary tract infection and they insisted she go to a nursing home because of mobility issues. It was taking both Norman and I to take her to the toilet a number of times during the night.

I wrote out the Lord's Prayer for her in a card I gave her in Ipswich hospital and she surprised me years later saying that she had said it every day since. In fact, one day when Norman and I visit her at the Cairns nursing home, she cries because she has lost it so I write it out again for her. Only after she passes away, I discover the nurses have pasted it into a scrapbook of memories for Mum they give to family afterwards e.g., cards and letters she has received and a few photos.

I'm a pastor of a church with a strong faith. Yes, Heaven is a better place and I can't overestimate the comfort to me that she is now there. Yes, at 92 years of age she lived a long life. Yes, I know she is now relieved of any pain and the limitations of a body that wasn't working for her anymore. And she left this earthly life loved and cared for. But I am still grieving.

Mum didn't want me to be part of an Aboriginal family. In the end, it is Mum's Aboriginal family who help me bury her. Norman's family. They visit her, pray for her, give her hugs and gifts and are my support. Mum was uncomfortable to come to big family occasions with Norman's family and she experienced pain if she sat in the wheelchair too long. But Norman's Mum Shirley and sisters Debbii, Lillian and Colleen would visit Mum when we brought her to our home or took her out to celebrate her birthdays or Christmases. I can't help but see the irony of her being surrounded by loving black faces as she is buried.

Mum missed my brother Greg. He had not moved away from Ipswich where my parents lived while I had as soon as I was old enough. Her final moments were spent with the black sheep of the family, the child who'd sometimes repeated her mother's words, "The stork dropped me in the wrong home".

My son Michael and my nephew Steven are shoveling dirt into her grave. Lonely figures, just the two of them, as the rain softly falls. My tears break out again. My Mum has only two grandsons to fill her grave. She has no granddaughters. Just one great-granddaughter. The sky is bleak. The rain starts to blow even though we are under a tent. Michael is tall, slim and athletic looking with dark brown hair and brown eyes, wearing black trousers and white shirt like Norman. He's bracing for the physical pain of his osteo-arthritis as well as the emotional pain of burying his grandmother. He has been keen to research the genealogy of my mother's side, the Dorsetts, and he's even called himself an Aboriginal Dorsett. He knew the pain she had suffered with her rheumatoid arthritis.

One black grandson and one white grandson. Steven is large and bald. He is wearing brown trousers and maroon shirt; matching his father Greg, my brother, who is large as well and graying. Steven is studying for his PhD in Science at the University of Queensland, majoring in Chemistry. My brother brings to Cairns his DNA results revealing about 20%

Scandinavian so Steven has a keen interest in the Vikings, dressing up and taking part in historical games. But today is a time for grieving. After he sits down, his head slumps and the sobbing wells up.

Before Mum's coffin is lowered into the grave, Norman gives an inspirational message. "We gather together today to commit Muriel Joyce Russell to her final resting place. We gather to comfort each other in our grief and to honor the life Joyce led. A life that was full of hope, happiness, laughter, and love … through good times as well as in bad.

> We pray the Lord will be able to say to Joyce, 'Well done, good and faithful servant! You have been faithful with a few things; I will put you in charge of many things. Come and share your master's happiness!' Matthew 25:21
>
> Joyce, as we honor your memory and the love you leave behind, we offer your spirit the blessings for obedience from Deuteronomy 28:6:
>
> 6 You will be blessed when you come in and blessed when you go out.
>
> 12 The LORD will open the heavens, the storehouse of his bounty, to send rain on your land in season and to bless all the work of your hands …
>
> In sure and certain hope of the resurrection to eternal life through our Lord Jesus Christ, we commend to Almighty God: Muriel Joyce Russell. We commit her body to the ground; earth to earth; ashes to ashes, dust to dust. The Lord bless her and keep her, the Lord maketh his face to shine upon her and be gracious unto her and give her peace. Amen.
>
> As we hold Joyce in our hearts and memories from this day forward, we commit ourselves to honor her memory. We release you now to the next part of your spiritual journey as you walk hand in hand with your Creator. All those who have gone before you light your way."

> I sit in silence. Michael and Steven are shoveling. I wear a black lace suit with small embroidered white designs. I bought it to wear in Israel when William Cooper was honored at Yad Vashem Holocaust Museum in 2010. I have new clothes that are black and white but the fashions are too short for a funeral so I put on my old faithful. Behind me are many graves. Line upon line of them, row upon row, they remind us of the departed.

Mum only had one great-grandchild, Jaydah, who sits beside me and gives me a hug. I put my arm around her as she softly weeps too, in tune with the rain. Her long brown hair in a ponytail. At 17 years old, she has already made an impact modelling at the Cairns Indigenous Art Fair and playing on the football field. Her mother Erica is with her. My husband Norman comes over and gives me a gentle hug, "Are you OK?" he asks, clearing his throat.

"Yes," I reply. He massages my neck and shoulders briefly.

He has just officiated the graveside service but he can't escape the tears now that he has finished the last blessing and prayer. My brother Greg ambles over and gives me a big bear hug. Little is said. Words are hard at the moment. We all lovingly cast in the rose petals, fragrance and beauty, for her journey to the next life.

At the funerals of Aboriginal families there are huge crowds. At least a half a dozen men have spades to fill the grave. Two weeks ago, Norman and I were with Michael at his uncle's funeral. He helped fill in the grave of his Uncle Timer, Lennie Miller, his father Mick's only brother. It was a big family occasion. Tears and hugs and a time for reunion. I had hoped for some of these family to come but they didn't. Mum hadn't really been part of the lives of my son's father's family.

Apart from Norman's wonderfully supportive family who all give me a hug, I only have Greg and his son who flew up from Ipswich and my son, his daughter and her Mum Erica, her brown hair tied back neatly as she hovers protectively around Jaydah. Over seventy years old herself,

Mum's niece Jan finds the church service brings up too much emotion and doesn't come to the cemetery. She doesn't even say goodbye. Just leaves a note. She lost her own mother a long time ago and has been visiting my Mum regularly. My Mum was the last of her siblings to go. There are plenty of empty chairs. I asked for 50 to be set out. The empty white plastic chairs stand out starkly on the green grass.

My mother's death was not a headliner, nor would I expect it to be. But I shared at the funeral service at our church earlier,

> "The angels are rejoicing to have her now as one of the saints in heaven. You might say, Joyce wasn't a saint like Mother Theresa but that's what we call believers - a saint. We don't get into heaven by good deeds. We get into heaven by being sorry for our sins and accepting Jesus as our Savior and Lord, and Mum did that. The good deeds follow because of our love of the Lord. I would find today a lot more difficult if I didn't believe she was with her Maker. Jesus (Hebrew name Yeshua) said that in His Father's house are many mansions and He goes to prepare a place for us. He has prepared a place for Joyce."

The tent flaps in the wind. The sound of the shovels ceases as the funeral director tells us we can leave as the men who work here will finish filling in the grave. The service ends to the refrain of the Christian song "You Raise Me Up" by Josh Groban. It might seem ironic to choose this song of being raised up when Mum's coffin has gone down into the earth. But the song is about being spiritually uplifted and Mum will be raised up with Christ (Messiah). We get into the few cars on standby and return to the church for the reception. There is a sense of finality but Mum is really beginning the next part of her journey.

Norman and I go for a coffee before heading home, knowing that I need a break from the emotion and some head space before spending a couple of hours going through Mum's things with my brother before he flies back in the morning with Steven.

It's late afternoon now and everything at our favorite coffee shop looks the same, as if nothing of note just happened. Some patrons are animatedly talking while others have heads buried in newspapers or are busy checking their mobile phones. Bob Marley music is piped over the sound system. As I look over to the Esplanade across the road, I see some people taking a leisurely stroll, looking at the tide which has gone out, exposing the mudflats. Others, determined to get fit, are doing their daily run. Norman can't help himself but cut to the chase,

> "Mum didn't really know you," he says. "She didn't know all the things you can do, how you spend your time or about your books."

I sigh and say,

> "I know. She showed so little interest in my book on William Cooper that I didn't even show her my second book. She didn't know I'm writing my memoir about Mapoon or *The Faces of Eve* books about the experiences of Jewish and Arab women.
>
> What's worse? Feeling I can't show it to her as she won't appreciate it while she has a dozen books on her shelf she is avidly devouring? Or showing it to her and seeing her lack of interest? But that's my life with Mum, not sharing what is important to me as it misses the mark with her. I hold back because it disappoints too much to be spurned. She didn't really want to hear what my faith means to me. We could talk about the news though. She liked to keep up with that. I've just had to accept the limitations of our relationship; overcome the disappointment."

He reaches out and takes my hand. "I'm here for you."

"I know," I say, "thanks. And I'm here for you too."

Clarrie Grogan And Fred Hollows Pass Away

It's early in the morning. Norman and Michael are asleep. The house is quiet, and I am crying for Clarrie as I just checked out on the internet when he passed away. 1993 at 60 years of age. I wasn't sure of the date. I can't help crying as I remember him, full of life. He was always at Mick's side. Which means he was always near me too, for the many years Mick and I were together. A few months ago, when I was looking for information on the North Queensland Land Council, I was surprised there was so little but it was before the days of computers and people videoing and taking photos on their phones. The local paper records about 2,000 people attend his funeral. He was a likeable character.

But now I find something that really touches me. It is the story of Clarrie being at the side of Fred Hollows and his wife Gabi and their children when Fred died. He is there giving support in the days leading up to it. Hovering, so caring, so supportive, sleeping in the corner. I cry from a deep place within me as I knew Fred as well and am touched that Clarrie is there for him. Norman and I had been together for a few years by then so I didn't know Clarrie had done this. I'm even more touched now to find that, after holding Fred's hand as his life slips away, Clarrie's life is to slip away a few months later. Fred is an atheist but Clarrie believes in God from his upbringing on Mona Mona, a Seventh Day Adventist Mission near Kuranda.

Marge Overs writes of this scene in her book *In Fred's Footsteps: 20 Years of Restoring Sight*. She was visiting Fred who requests a drink of scotch despite the four tubes coming out of his "sunken body." His wife Gabi puts a straw in his scotch which he flings to the corner of the room muttering,

> "'You don't put bluddy straws in scotch, Gabi.'
>
> Now, as it happened, sleeping in a corner armchair in the dark, directly where the scotch-soaked straw finished up, was Clarrie Grogan.

> Clarrie was a former light heavyweight boxing champ. A polite, non-swearing, Christian blackfella from north Queensland who loved Fred to death. Clarrrie had stood back-to-back with Fred in a couple of country pub brawls in Joh's Queensland, when some clown had made a racist remark and Hollows had objected. Now Clarrie had come down to watch over his mate, the Professor, in his final days.
>
> The catapulting straw hit the champion pug in the face and woke him up. He bounced out of the chair, primed for action again. It was a funny moment.
>
> 'Settle down Clarrie. There's no bluddy problem, ol' fella. Take it easy,' said Fred with a sweet smile in his voice.
>
> He died a couple of days later with Gabi and the kids (and Clarrie) by his bedside."

Marge recalls her last interview with Fred,

> "What if you get to the other side, Fred, and find that there is a heaven after all?' I asked him in his last TV interview for *60 Minutes*.
>
> "'Well, I'll just have to renegotiate!' I hope that's what he did."[45]

Peter Noble Passes Away

Peter Noble also touches my life. Mick, Clarrie and Peter are a trio and make the North Queensland Land Council what it is, Peter manning the office while Mick is teaching. With his father Mark Noble of Yarrabah, Peter travels to Canberra at the height of the Aurukun and Mornington Island dispute to raise support for them. At the North Qld Land Council, we are concerned about Indigenous health so we do a survey to look into the need for an Aboriginal medical center. Peter and his wife Evelyn, Auntie Esme's daughter Eslyn, Les Collins and others, help do a land council survey into Indigenous health which leads to the formation of the Wu Chopperen Medical Centre. Peter also helps Mick set up and run the Woompera Muralug Housing Society. Peter and Clarrie are with me in September 1974 when we support the Mapoon people to return and rebuild their community. Peter was also chairman of the council of the large Aboriginal community of Yarrabah. I saw more of Clarrie than Peter because Clarrie lived a few minutes away by car whereas Peter lived an hour away.

Tragically, Peter was killed in a car accident on Roberts Road near Edmonton in 1989. He was only 47 years old. His son Rico has followed in his footsteps, being a key person on the government funded North Queensland Land Council that replaced the one Peter worked for. Mostly voluntarily, as did I. I was working at Endeavour Foundation when Peter passed.

Peter suggested that I attend Business College which I did in the late 1970's. I think he may have been one of a number of leaders that recommended the ACC approach me re being their research officer in the late 1980's. I think Thomas Hudson, then on Kowanyama Council, may have had a hand in it too. I never asked. I only know I came well recommended.

Friends Pass Away

We all need to make our peace with our Creator, hopefully long before we are called home. 2016 seems to be a year for me to cry for those who have touched my life and their time in this world has come to an end. In April, Tiga Bayles, Maureen Watson's son who is an Aboriginal radio broadcaster and activist, dies two days before my mother. Soon after Torres Strait Islander leader Steve Mam passes away.

Mick's brother Lennie Miller also passes away. He is a key person running Woompera Muralug Housing Society for many years and supporting Mick not only to set up the housing society but in many other ways; despite a limp, as he had polio as a child. He lives with Mick and I till he gets his own flat and he loves to cook. I especially remember he liked to cook fish soup from the heads, tails and bones of fish. As the year goes on, we lose Pastor Bill Hollingsworth's wife Ruth and Pastor Noel Mann. Noel values intimacy with the Lord more than anything else and is a man of prayer. Our first visit to Israel is with Noel and his devoted wife Dianne who both love Israel with a passion.

Jan Roberts Passes Away

The first person to pass from this world in 2016 that I am connected with, however, is Jan Roberts who I work with to help the people move back to Mapoon. Jan transitions from being John, a former priest who had married and had children, to Jan. It is for this reason she moves to England with her family after the Mapoon books are published. She eventually has a sex change operation and separates from her wife who takes the children back to Australia. Jan writes a book about her transformation.

I had been trying to find Jan for well over a year, having lost contact with her a long time ago. Then I find her younger daughter Katie via Facebook and am excited about this, especially as I find out just before Norman and I are due to visit Melbourne, where Katie lives. We are in Melbourne for the launch of the 40 Stories Project where 40 Indigenous Christians speak of what their faith means to them on video. Our good friends David and Carol Jack take us to visit Katie, who makes scones and tea for us. She is an artist and Norman and Katie discuss art. David is also a videographer for this project and a videographer for most of the conferences we host.

I find out to my shock that Jan had a massive stroke about six years ago and is in a nursing home in England. I knew she had been living on a boat on the river Thames, doing journalism and film making. Katie went over to visit Jan. I ask about photos and files, hoping to find some photos of Mapoon people and information but Katie says that there was mildew on Jan's photos and they couldn't be saved. Whether there were Mapoon photos there, Katie doesn't know. Jan left a lot of paperwork and other property in a friend's shed in Melbourne hoping to retrieve them sometime. Unfortunately, they had been ruined and destroyed as well. This is very disappointing. If only they had been given to an organization that knew how to look after them e.g., the Institute of Aboriginal and Islander Studies in Canberra or even better, the Mapoon community itself.

Katie lets Jan know that I have been to see her and is happy to hear that. But before I can establish contact with her, she passes away. Katie lets me know. I cry for her. I haven't seen her for a long time but she was once a good friend. Katie had loaned me a book of Jan's which she now needs returned to help her write a eulogy. I grieve not just for Jan's passing but because she got involved with wicca (pagan witchcraft). As an ex Catholic priest who had a sex change operation to become a woman, she explores female priesthood and pagan religion. I am concerned for her eternal soul. She does not have a Christian burial. Her cremation and ceremony are held 9th March 2016.

Jan has been living on her boat for 18 years working as a freelance journalist, TV documentary maker and author. In 2001, she takes on *Leonid*, a boat of teak and oak. She writes on her Facebook in January 2010 that it is: 7 degrees outside and she can't get off the boat because of a sliding door that is frozen and wouldn't open, even with a hammer. She is sick and has trouble breathing. She writes,

> "try to walk dog - essential she says … door frozen cannot get off boat … trying to breathe, wretched asthma-like. … bash bash bash the door … got to be able to escape … why cannot breathe … oh that is better … door moves … slides now easily on the ice … carefully walk, grab railings … dog stumbles over ice floe."

She tries to cook but the gas cylinder is frozen. No gas, no oven, no kettle, sink blocked, the winter is closing in. She worries the boat is a death trap. Her friends try to get her into social housing. At least she can pursue her passion for a little longer - writing.

Joyce Dorsett Before Marriage to My Father Mervyn Russell

My Parents' Home in Ipswich Back Row Barbara, Shirley Miller, Joyce Russell, Barclay Miller
Front Row Jess Barratt and Mervyn Russell photo Norman Miller

Reception at Tabernacle of David After Funeral. L-R Back Row Greg Russell, Barbara, Erica Savage. Front Row Jaydah Savage and Shirley Miller. Photo Norman Miller

Chapter 19

Chicago Visit and Norman's Book Award

Norman's Book Wins International Award

It's Monday 11th April 2016. The afternoon sun casts shadows through the shrubs in the nature strip outside our window. From where I sit, I see the splash of color from the flowers, but it's the greenery I love. I'm in my usual spot at the dining room table working on my red laptop which is at the far end of the table. Norman and Michael can walk past the table without squeezing past me and I can pile up my paperwork and my printer on the pine dressing table in the corner. There are papers overflowing everywhere.

The dressing table has a pine chair to match, with the same leaf design as on the drawers. The chair has a cushion boasting a rainbow swirl of color and the hint of a butterfly design. I don't sit on it though as it's not comfortable. Instead, I use a practical office chair. Not content with three large bookcases of books in the lounge to my right, I have a small bookcase nudged under the counter to my left. It leads through a space in our feature brick wall into the kitchen. Instead of the counter being used to eat at, there are more papers untidily placed there.

I typically work at home Mondays. On my writing or whatever else needs doing for the church or my mediation work but I don't take appointments. Norman persuades me to do this, to reduce my heavy workload. I'm continually grateful to him for it as it makes an easy start to the week, having, as I often do, some difficult mediation cases to handle. Sometimes it is fathers wanting access to their children with the mothers denying this or limiting it. Sometimes it is mothers having difficult times with their ex. I help them negotiate a parenting plan which can be lodged at the Family Court. At times, separated parents need a mediator to help them negotiate a property settlement which is more complicated if they own a business. Of course, they need to get legal advice.

I look over to the lounge room and Norman is looking for lino prints in his art folders. Just as well we have more than one lounge suite. One is taken up with folders of Norman's small prints and some of his files and we never sit on it. It's almost impossible to get to see what's in two of the bookcases because boxes of Norman's art book are stored in front of them. Some of his large canvas paintings also find their home in our lounge room. Our creative space has always crowded out our living space but we are happy with each other's creative mess.

Our beliefs are also apparent in our house. There is Jewish prayer shawl or *tallit* in the lounge which I sometimes use when I pray, the lounge room being my favorite place to pray. I prefer to kneel as I pray for about an hour in the morning. This is also Norman's favorite spot to pray. He tends to get up in the middle of the night, pray, then come back to bed. When he prays during the day, he prefers to sit reading his Bible and prays at the same time. A menorah, a seven-branched candle holder, sits on top of the shelf to my left. It is a replica of the one used in the days of the temple in Jerusalem. A number of books on Israel sit on our coffee table. Over the years, we have visited Israel ten times.

My mobile phone rings. It's Norman's publisher, Bronwyn Simpson of Renbro Publishing. She is based in Perth but the head office is in Adelaide.

"I've got some great news!" she says excitedly.

"What is it?" I ask, putting my phone on speaker and telling Norman it's Bronwyn.

"Norman's book has just won an international award. I just received an email about it."

Norman's eyes open wide with surprise.

"We didn't know you'd put it in for an international award," I say. "What award is it?"

Norman comes closer to the phone beaming.

"There were about 5,000 entries from around the world. It's the International Independent Publishers Award and Norman's book won a bronze medal in the Multicultural Non-Fiction Adult category. Congratulations. The awards will be presented in Chicago on 10 May. I'm thinking of going. Would Norman like to go?"

I handed the phone to Norman. "That's wonderful," he says "but hard to believe. I'd love to go if I could. Can you email through the information?"

"Yes, I'll email it through and I'll try to get some funding for you to go. I'd better go. There's a lot to do but find out how much the airfare is from Cairns."

"Bye Bronwyn and congratulations. Thanks for entering Norman's book for the award," I say.

"Yes," Norman says, "You and Renato (the graphic designer) did a great job and Barbara too."

Ending the phone call, Norman gives me a big hug.

"Thanks for everything," he says. "This is your book too because you did the editing."

"Thanks. An award for your first book is pretty good," I reply. "Praise the Lord. Now a lot more people will see your beautiful paintings: all 200 of them and the stories to go with them that showcase your growing up, your culture, your spirituality and some history of your people."

"Would you write a press release?" asks Norman "So I can get the word out."

"Sure. What do you want to say?'

"I guess we should wait for the email from Bronwyn first."

Travelling To Chicago

It's 9th May. Only three weeks since I lost Mum. I'm still not sleeping well at night as I keep thinking about her. Yesterday we had a seafood subway at Earlville Shopping Town. Norman reminds me that a few months ago we bought Mum a seafood subway here on an outing to get her some new glasses. She took forever to eat it but enjoyed it so much. I've not been able to eat a seafood subway since, as I think of Mum. My tears well up again. Norman comforts me and I can't help sobbing. By the time we pick up the glasses we have ordered, Mum is no longer reading but she does watch TV with them a bit and is so pleased to have them. I think of the handbag I bought her that day for her birthday even though it is not till March and this is only January. She is never to use it as she isn't well enough to go out again. But she is pleased knowing that she has it.

We stop travelling because of Mum's health, having cancelled two trips this year. But now Mum is gone, we can go without worrying about not being there for her when she needs us. Bronwyn can't raise the finance so I use my credit card to pay for the trip. We pack some warm clothes as when I google Chicago, I see it's called "Windy City." It's much colder than Cairns.

As Norman and I get off the plane in Brisbane en-route to Chicago, Lydia, my son's sister, meets us off the plane. "Lydia, I didn't expect to see you," I exclaim and give her a hug. Norman hugs her also.

Lydia is dressed warmly as she has just flown in from Sydney. Her long black hair is tied back in a ponytail. Her face lights up and she says,

"I can't believe it. I'm here to meet Marilyn off the plane from

> Cairns. We're going to a funeral. Seeing as you came in on Virgin, she must be on Jetstar."

"Is it David Page's funeral?" I ask. He died unexpectedly on 29th April, aged only 55. He was for a long time the composer and music director for the award-winning Bangarra Dance Theatre, composing scores for 27 of the company's 35 major works. He also contributed many musical scores to Aboriginal movies. His brother Stephen Page is the artistic director and choreographer of Bangarra. The other brother in the trio, Russell Page, had been the lead dancer, one of the best in Australia.

"Yes," says Lydia, her smile fading for a moment. She asks how I'm coping with losing Mum and I thank her for phoning me before the funeral. She also asks how Michael is. We chat a little while and then I say,

> "We'd better let you find Marilyn before you miss her and we'd better get over to the international terminal."

Marilyn in particular is very close to the Page family through her long relationship with Lawrence Page and through her time dancing for Bangarra. Marilyn is now the Artistic Associate of the Cairns Indigenous Art Fair. Lydia has long been Executive Director at the Aboriginal and Torres Strait Islander Arts at the Australia Council. They have both spent some time acting. When they were little, they would always be making up plays and performing them for their Dad and me at our Kevin Street home in Cairns. I ring Marilyn with my condolences as we arrive at the international terminal.

Lydia and Marilyn have just featured on National Indigenous Television (NITV) with their mother Pat for Mother's Day. Pat O'Shane was the first female Aboriginal teacher in Queensland, Australia's first Aboriginal barrister, the first woman and Aboriginal person to head a Government department in Australia, and the country's first Aboriginal magistrate. Lydia shares a house in Sydney with Pat who is a pioneer and trailblazer. Lydia and Marilyn's father, Mick Miller, along with Phil Stewart, were the first Aboriginal teachers in Queensland, both qualifying in 1959 and both from Palm Island.

We board the long flight to Los Angeles (LA) the first port of call for flights from Australia to the USA. I've brought a book to read but I get as much sleep as I can because we've had such a busy time the last few weeks. We have three seats to ourselves so I stretch out with my feet on Norman's lap. Later, I put my head on his lap instead. "You take a turn stretching out," I plead. "You need some sleep too."

"No," he insists. "I want to help you sleep". He massages my head as I rest on his lap."

Arriving In Chicago

We finally arrive after an 18 hour plus flight from Brisbane to LA. It's a large, noisy, busy terminal. We have to collect our luggage, clear customs and fly to Chicago. I am surprised how expensive the food is and not impressed that we have to pay tax on top of it.

We arrive in Chicago, the same city where Obama, the President, lives. Our taxi driver happens to be from Kenya, the land of Obama's father. We strike up a conversation. Our son is a fan of Michael Jordan, the basketball player and wants a guernsey with his signature if possible.

> "Michael's a millionaire and doesn't live here anymore. He's in New York," our driver says, depositing us at our hotel.

We decide it wasn't great advice from our travel agent to tell us to take a cab because they are cheap in the USA as it is a long trip and tips are expected on everything. I am furious and flabbergasted to find our travel agent didn't book us in for the first night. We left Australia on 9th May and arrived in the USA on 9th May because of the time difference and we are booked from 10 May. Fortunately, they have a spare room but now we have to pay a much higher rate. It is an unexpected blow.

The entrance to the hotel is from a busy street. A red curtain-like sign with scalloped fringe announces the name of the hotel in gold print: the Congress Plaza. Across the road is Millennium Park with lots of attractions that we would explore on our last afternoon.

The hotel is aging but ornate with the lobby featuring a high ceiling with gold chandeliers and gold wrought iron features. The ballroom is similar with gold arched entrances and gold curtains on the second floor and carved images of children or nymphs above each archway. The rooms are modest however and we realize how spoiled we are in Australian hotels which provide a fridge and tea and coffee making facilities. There is a coffee making machine but, as we like our tea as well, it tastes terrible when we boil water in the coffee machine. No one in America, it seems, drinks tea.

We are excited however that Norman is to receive his medal tomorrow and amazed that our Jewish friends Irene and Alex Shaland will be driving about seven hours from Cleveland to join us while Norman receives his award and then driving back the next day for a half day of work. We only recently met them at our home in Cairns through a mutual friend. They arrive at our hotel early, about 5pm, so we can travel to the award ceremony together. Irene gives us a big hug saying,

> "I'm so honored to be able to be with you Norman as you receive your award."

Irene is a travel writer and sought-after speaker about Jewish communities around the world. She is slim and lively with short red hair and is wearing a stunning jacket in gold and earthy tones. Alex gives us a big hug as well. He does photography and offers to take photos of Norman receiving his award. Alex is dressed fashionably but casually in brown coat and slacks, his gray hair betraying his age.

"We're the ones who are honored by your travelling all that way," says Norman.

We sit down on the red leather lounge chairs in a waiting area and chat for a while till Norman's publisher, Bronwyn from Perth, and an editor who worked on his book, Eliza Cavanagh from Melbourne, arrive. We travel to the event in a cab. Norman and Eliza are dressed smartly in black and white, Norman wearing a white coat. Bronwyn's organza red ochre dress is more in tune with Indigenous tones than my pink coat but I decide I want to wear pink for a change. I wear long black pants thinking we may be exposed to the wind on the sky deck but it is closed in.

Receiving The Award

We arrive at the Willis Tower, craning our heads up to look at how high we will soon travel. The IPPY event is to be held on the sky deck of this 108-story skyscraper. When it was completed in 1973, it surpassed the World Trade Center towers in New York to become the tallest building in the world, a title it held for 25 years. In 2016 it is the second highest building in the USA and more than one million people each year visit its observation desk. We have to take two lifts to get there. The sky deck has glass windows all around it and we are amazed to look out at the Chicago city lights.

Bronwyn sheds her coat. Our host for the evening, Mr Jerrold Jenkins, is greeting people there so Bronwyn energetically engages him in conversation. We find he wants to run a similar event in Sydney and is asking about venues. How opportune was this meeting? Bronwyn and Eliza move around making what connections they can.

Waiters ply us with delightful treats. As Norman and I don't drink alcohol, we opt for orange juice at the bar and are pleased to mingle and meet people including a few black American authors. "Come on everybody," a voice calls out. "Time to take your seats." Some people have already put bags on seats in preparation. There is a huge amount of excitement in the room. Authors put a huge amount of work into their books and Norman is no exception. For publishers also, it is a big effort. Writers don't always make money from their efforts so to get recognition from your peers and industry experts is a big thing.

Norman is excited, expectant. One by one the categories are called out and the recipients of the awards came forward to receive their medals. There are no acceptance speeches. Just receiving the medals and a few minutes for photos. The MC says a little about each book as the award winners come up:

"Now we have the Multicultural Non-Fiction Adult Award and the bronze medal goes to (pause) Norman Miller and Renbro Publishing for the book *Reef and Rainforest: an Indigenous Voice Through Art and Story*. It even has a song written and sung by the author and an audio-visual presentation that goes with the book."

Norman, Bronwyn, Eliza and I go up and the medal is put around Norman's neck and he receives a certificate. Cameras flicker, hands clap and it is all over. "Congratulations darl," I say as we're back in our seats.

"I'm trying to let it sink in," says Norman. "It's still hard to believe."

The place is still buzzing after all the medals are given out and people are doing last minute connecting over drinks. We say farewell our friends the Shalands and head back to the hotel.

Attending Book Expo America

We are up early for the next three days to attend Book Expo America (BEA) which is the largest gathering of booksellers, librarians, retailers, publishers, licensing, and book industry professionals in North America. The BEA is held at McCormick Place on the shore of Lake Michigan and is only minutes from downtown Chicago and about 10-15 minutes from our hotel. A line of fountains presides over the manicured lawns of the impressive multi-stored building which houses a hotel, shopping center and offices.

"It's huge," I remark as we make our way in and have a coffee at Gloria Jeans. I hope I can find where my Blogging Conference is so I can be there on time."

Norman finds his book in the New Title Bookcase but my book on William Cooper hasn't arrived in time before the organizers left New York. We bring a spare copy in for them the next day. Norman is meant to do a book signing event but there is a mix up and it's too late to re-organize. Bronwyn and Eliza arrive after us because Bronwyn has been redesigning and printing a flier for Norman's book.

The Expo is a great place to discover new titles and authors, conduct business and network, and learn the latest trends. There are many meetings going on all over the place, many books being launched and book signings with free giveaways taking place. Workshops on the publishing industry continue at various venues and times and we fit in what we can. Bronwyn has other books to promote besides Norman's.

We meet a black American author who is a pastor and who invites us to his church. We exchange books with me giving him my William Cooper book. We want to attend his church but we have already organized a church to go to Sunday morning.

We attend the book signing of Jewish rabbi Evan Moffic who has a Christian publisher. He is giving away his book and I give him my William Cooper book as well. Intrigued with the title of his book, *What Every Christian Needs to Know About the Jewishness of Jesus*, I ask him if we can go to his service and when and where they meet. He invites us to go to the Torah study Saturday morning. The Torah is the first five books of the Bible.

Solel Synagogue, Highland Park

We rise early on Saturday morning and take a cab to the Solel synagogue in Highland Park, Illinois. Just under an hour's cab ride from our hotel. We didn't realize it would take so long to get there and are praying that someone will take us back. We arrive a little early for the 9.15am Torah study and wait at the door for someone to open it. Established in 1957, congregation Solel is a Reform Jewish congregation which describes itself as pathfinders committed to sacred worship, social justice, and lifelong learning embracing interfaith families and all who seek a spiritual home in their synagogue.

It is a spacious modern building which also houses a school and is surrounded by trees. Situated by a lake, it is a very peaceful atmosphere away from the bustle of daily life.

We are welcomed into a room where about 30 people, mostly elderly men and women, gather around tables arranged to make a square. We are pointed to the tea and coffee to help ourselves. Rabbi Evan Moffic is slim with brown hair. At 40 years of age, he is one of the youngest senior rabbis in Reform Judaism and has written a number of scholarly articles and speaks at interfaith meetings. He arrives, dressed casually, and is surprised but happy to see us. "I'm glad you came and I must get your William Cooper book Barbara to show our people. Please, Norman and Barbara, introduce yourselves. I met them at BookExpo America and invited them today." He passes my book around for people to look at. Norman and I introduce ourselves.

Rabbi Evan then turns to Leviticus 19:5-14 and says;

> "Holiness is about separation. The 'Mitzvot' (commandments) are ways of separation. Judaism is about expressing faith through action. It is a practical religion that limits greed. We don't want to take every penny we can. The obligation of 'tzedaka' is a law in the Talmud that you have to give a poor person enough so he can give to others. It is good for your soul."

The Talmud is Oral law, or a legal commentary on the Torah. We enjoy what is basically a question-and-answer session with the rabbi asking questions and people thoughtfully and enthusiastically discussing various issues.

I Google 'tzedaka' after getting back to Australia as it is the first time I've heard the word and discover that it literally means justice, righteousness or fairness but is commonly used to signify charity. It is different from charity though as it is an obligation and charity is more spontaneous and voluntary generosity.

Rabbi Evan continues,

> "The principle is that it is God's, not ours, anyway. The land is not ours. We are stewards so don't glean to the edges of your field. Leave some for the poor".

I think of the Gentile widow Ruth in the Bible who gleaned in the fields of Boaz and he instructed his workers to leave extra for her as she was looking after her Jewish mother-in-law.

"What is the meaning of poor?" the rabbi asks. I think of the answer before he says it but I stay quiet out of respect not to change the flow of their meeting. "The widow, orphan and stranger or foreigner were the three legal categories because the latter were not protected by the tribe," he says, answering his own question. We felt so privileged to attend this lively discussion in which there was high participation.

A few weeks later, I am delivering the Shavuot (Pentecost) message to our Tabernacle of David congregation in Cairns and read Leviticus 23. I am aware of v22 from before but had not put it in the context of Shavuot and so am delighted to put the two together. The verse reads:

> "When you reap the harvest of your land, do not reap to the very edges of your field or gather the gleanings of your harvest. Leave them for the poor and alien. I am the Lord your God."

Shavuot commemorates the giving of the Torah, or law, to Moses and the people of Israel after they have come out of captivity in Egypt and are on their way to the Promised Land. It is the birth of Judaism about 3,300 years ago. About 2,000 years ago, Jesus, a Jewish rabbi, told his followers to wait in the Upper Room of the Temple in Jerusalem and pray. On Shavuot, a rushing mighty wind from heaven and tongues of fire came on them, a sign of the Holy Spirit, and the Christian church was born as they excitedly told others what had happened.

Intrigued with the social justice orientation of congregation Solel, I find on the internet later that Martin Luther King was invited to speak at Solel in June 1966, and police and state troopers attended in case there was trouble. Over 1,000 people attended his speech which coincided with the Chicago Freedom Movement, lobbying for fair open housing in Chicago. Each year since 2009, Solel has held a commemorative Sabbath service as a memorial to Dr. King's legacy. In January 2016, the 50th anniversary of Dr. King's visit to the synagogue, a service is held which also recognized the significant role of Jewish clergy and lay leaders in the Civil Rights movement. In April 2015, Rabbi Moffic and Cantor Vicky Glikin joined a symbolic march from Montgomery, Alabama to Washington DC, to call America to remember the principles Dr. King stood for. A plaque adjacent to the sanctuary commemorates Rev King's visit with the quote, "Now is the time to rise from the dark valley of segregation to the sunlit path of racial justice."

Rabbi Evan leaves after the Torah study. We decide to stay for the Cantor Service in the auditorium as the congregants come and go. We are then invited to a special lunch with smoked salmon, feta cheese, salad and hummingbird cake, as it is Cantor Vicki's last time with them and they are sad to see her go.

Visit To Illinois Holocaust Museum

One of the women, Diane Gordon, offers to take us back to downtown Chicago as we are nearly an hour away. We are very grateful. She has just become a guide for the Illinois Holocaust Museum and Education Center in Skokie.

"Would you like to stop there on the way back and have a look?" She asks.

"Yes," we both say, unaware it existed. "We've been to Yad Vashem for the honoring of William Cooper in 2010 and I launched my book on him at the Jewish Holocaust Centre in Melbourne and the Sydney Jewish Museum in 2012," I add.

"Who's William Cooper?" Diane asks.

"He was an Aboriginal Christian and led one of the few known protests worldwide against Kristallnacht in 1938," I reply.

"He did this at a time when Aborigines were not citizens in their own country of Australia."

"That's amazing," says Diane.

We did not really expect to find a holocaust museum in a Midwestern state in the USA. As if hearing my thoughts, Diane says:

"The museum in Skokie opened in 2009 and was partly as a response to the neo-Nazi's announcing they were going to march through Skokie, a mostly Jewish community. One in six residents was a Holocaust survivor or was directly related to one. This was about thirty years ago."

"That's very intimidating," I say, stunned and appalled.

"Yes, they had stayed silent and quiet but now they could do so no longer and had to stand up for themselves. They were prepared to defend themselves with baseball bats if necessary."

In the end, a deal was worked out and the Nazis agreed to march in Chicago rather than in Skokie. The survivors formed a committee in 1981 and opened a storefront museum in 1984 dedicating themselves to combating hate with education. They decided to educate about all kinds of genocide and discrimination of different groups from around the world; the Rwandan massacre, being one example.

It is always difficult to go through a museum of this nature. Diane proudly ushers us into a small lecture room and there is a man on the stage answering questions. He is Pinchas Gutter, a holocaust survivor who lives in Toronto, Canada yet here he is sitting in front of us answering questions with appropriate facial expressions and body movements. But this is a holograph and is programmed to answer 2,000 questions which he has recorded. It is like being in the room with him and can be used after he dies. This is an innovation which is being trialed because there are now so few Holocaust survivors left. It is a very impacting visit.

Visit To Stone Church, Orland Park

Before coming to the USA, Norman says,

> "The two places I would like to go are Azusa Street where the Pentecostal movement started and Martin Luther King's museum."
>
> "I'd love to do both too," I say.

I find King's museum, called the National Civil Rights Museum, is in Memphis, and incorporates the Lorraine Motel where King was assassinated.

> "We don't have the money to get to Memphis but there is the DuSable Museum of African American History in Chicago we could go to."
>
> "That would still be good," says Norman. "What about Azusa St?"

A friend in Sydney, Diane Taylor, not knowing we were going to Chicago, sent us an email saying the Azusa Street revival of 1906 moved to Chicago and from there to Canada and around the world and that there were prophecies about a bigger revival in one hundred years' time. I check the internet and find that the revival came to the Stone Church in Orland Park near Chicago. We are not only excited to visit it but that also we are here on Pentecost Sunday 2016. The Azusa St revival brought the restoration of the power of the Holy Spirit and tongues to the church after nearly 2000 years of not experiencing it. We are here 110 years after the 1906 Chicago revival. It has to be God's timing for our visit. We pray to come back with a revival anointing.

We run out of time to go to DuSable Museum of African American History in Chicago as the Stone Church is so far away and in an isolated area. However, we have a wonderful meeting at the church and we fly home early the following morning.

Receiving the Award L-R Bronwyn Simpson, Barbara, Norman, Eliza Cavanagh and Host

Chapter 20

Award Wages and Deaths in Custody, Yarrabah and Palm Island Visits

Yarrabah 2016

While working on my memoir *White Woman Black Heart Journey Home to Old Mapoon, A Memoir*, I take time out to update some previous research work I did on Yarrabah, reframe it and retitle it as The *Dying Days of Segregation in Australia: Case Study Yarrabah*. I reconnect with the 1984 Chairman and Deputy Chairman Roy Gray and Mick Connolly for their comments on the update as well as Fr Les Baird, a key Yarrabah community member. I also meet with former Mayor Percy Neal for comments and the current Yarrabah Aboriginal Shire Council on 14th September to run the draft by them.

I feel it's appropriate to launch the book at Yarrabah and the Mayor, Ross Andrews, recommends 31st October 2016 as it is Deed of Grant in Trust (DOGIT) Day. "Perfect," I say excitedly, "that fits in with the topic of the book."

Michael Sands, Deputy Mayor, chuckles,

> "I remember the day. Katter came in by helicopter to hand us the deeds and he gave lollies to the children."
>
> I smile, "That's what Paddy Killoran used to do."

I'm even more excited later when I realize that it will be 30 years to the day Yarrabah received their deeds of grant in trust. These deeds were granted to all Aboriginal and Torres Strait Islander government managed ex-reserves in Queensland and were the first time that crown land was transferred to Indigenous land. The newly independent Indigenous councils were to be trustees and hold it in trust for the whole community.

Norman is excited and says at the council meeting,

"31st October is the anniversary of the Australian Light horse charge at Be'er-Sheva. It'll be great to have the launch on that date. We took teams of Australians and New Zealanders to Be'er-Sheva during the three-day prayer tour of Israel at the end of our conferences in Israel nearly every year from 2007 to 2011. Yarrabah had people in the light horse and we've taken them and shown them the cemetery there."

The Mayor replies,

"We've asked Geoff Wharton to do some research on Yarrabah's servicemen for us."

"That's good," I say. "I can put you in touch with Gary Oakley from the Australian War Memorial in Canberra. Norman and I met with him re Indigenous servicemen including William Cooper's son and we had him deliver a talk to a Christian conference we organized at Parliament House Canberra in 2011."

Michael says, "I have family buried in the Middle East, didn't come back from war. I'd like to know where he's buried. I think I need to go to the War Memorial in Canberra."

"You might think about coming to Israel with us next year for the 100th anniversary of the Light horse charge at Be'er-Sheva on 31st October" I say. "Norman and I took a team of 14 Australians and 7 New Zealanders around all the battle sites of World War 1 and World War 2 and the holy sites in 2010.

I designed the tour myself and we timed it to be in Be'er-Sheva for the 31st October anniversary."

Their eyes light up at the prospect.

"People talk about Gallipoli," I say "but they are finally finding out about Be'er-Sheva. Hundreds of Australians will be there next year."

Councillor Ian Patterson says,

"Beersheba's in the Bible isn't it?"

Ian is the younger brother of Robert Patterson who was Chairman of the Aboriginal Coordinating Council for part of the time I was the CEO there.

"Yes," I reply. "Abraham's well is there and it is a place of treaty and reconciliation. It is a very important place."

Michael says,

"I remember my uncle coming back from war and going to a pub in Brisbane with his mates, all dressed in their uniforms. They refused to serve him because he was black and his mates smashed the place up and walked out with a drink." He laughed thinking about it. "White soldiers got given land when they came back from war but Aboriginal soldiers didn't," he says in a heavier tone.

"I know," I say. "What's worse is that Aboriginal land was taken from them so that it could be given to the white soldiers returning from war. I found this had happened in William Cooper country for example, around the Murray River."

Bringing us back on topic, the Mayor says,

"Your book will be really important for young people to know the history of Yarrabah. They need to know what the elders have done. I'm glad you've recognized their contribution in this book."

"Yes," says Councillor Cannon who has been following everything with interest but not saying much.

"Thanks. I was conscious of that," I reply. "I still remember when I came back from Mapoon after helping them move back to their land in September 1974, and some of the Yidinji from Yarrabah came to Mick's home to find out how they had done it. They wanted to move back to Buddabadoo and did so a few days later. Mark Noble, Fred Mundraby and Stan Connolly were among them. Alf Neal was often at meetings we had at Yarrabah in those days."

Michael says, "Probably Alan Kynuna too."

"Yes," I nod.

"They were the early ones to get blocks of land for hobby farming," he says. "What about Arnold Murgha?" Lowering his voice, he adds "He's not with us anymore."

"Yes, I've mentioned in my book his work for award wages. Actually, Mick and I and the North Queensland Land Council gave him a lot of support too, as well as the AWU (Australian Workers Union)."

"I remember going to Brisbane with him too on his campaign," says Michael.

"Now I come to think of it, I wrote a short paper on award wages for the Human Rights Commission. I can provide you with a copy of it if you like," I offer.

In 1979, Arnold, a laborer, supported by the AWU took a test case to the Industrial Commission re the lack of award wages paid to Aborigines. The government maintained it was paying a training wage (about 57% of the award). Arnold won his case. The government increased wages but promptly sacked 25% of Aboriginal staff on all communities so that its budget would not change. It still didn't bring wages up to award level even though it was saving millions of dollars. It was in clear breach of the Racial Discrimination Act 1975.

In 1986, when Councils became the employers of workers on their communities rather than the government, the government did not fund them sufficiently to pay award wages without further retrenchments. This was deliberate.

> Michael says, “I was sacked because they didn’t want to pay award wages but I was a union member and I went to the AWU and they took up my case and I was reinstated.”
>
> I didn’t ask him what year that was. “I see Hans Pearson is taking up a case now regarding stolen wages. It’ll be a class action. It needs doing because those who got $7,000 or $4,000 from the Beattie government in compensation received a pittance,” I add (He was later successful.).
>
> “Yes,” says Norman. “The government got out of it cheap. My Dad Barclay helped people fill out their claims for compensation.”

For nearly 100 years, wages of Indigenous people on and off reserves in Queensland were paid not directly to the Indigenous worker but to the manager or police officer in charge who held their bank accounts. He would only dole out a small amount to them and their families to live on and the rest went into the Aborigines Welfare Fund which built hospitals etc. for the non-Indigenous community. Some was probably used in funding Aboriginal communities to save using government coffers. Many of the people who have had their wages stolen from them have died now but it has resulted in inter-generational poverty for Aboriginal families in Queensland.

Norman gave a giant cheque to Queensland treasurer Andrew Fraser a few years ago as a symbolic protest re the stolen wages. He was virtually saying this is what my people have given you but not voluntarily, you stole it. Now you need to return it. Norman makes a giant cheque again in 2019 and stands outside the office of the Member for Cairns with the cheque protesting stolen wages. I join him.

There have been many allegations of fraud against police who managed Aboriginal wages, but it is not possible to verify this as

Aboriginal workers were never shown or given records. The Coen police station was mysteriously burnt down in my time with the NQLC and I remember we thought it was a cover up for stolen wages. That was one of the reasons we started the Trade Union Education Project.

The 1957 strike on Palm Island is about under award wages and repressive working and living conditions. The government is sued by two Cherbourg nurses in 1981 and seven Palm Island workers lodge a complaint to the Human Rights Commission in 1986 for wages stolen since the Racial Discrimination Act 1975. They lose. They try again ten years later with the Human Rights and Equal Opportunity Commission supported with research on government decisions by Dr Ros Kidd. She says:

> "The Commissioner concluded the government had 'intentionally, deliberately and knowingly' underpaid the claimants during the period 1975–1986. He suggested damages for loss of income of $7000 per person. The Borbidge National–Liberal Party coalition government said it would ignore the decision and the claimants lodged their case in the Federal Court. In April 1997, the Borbidge government sent the minister to Palm Island to apologize to the claimants and hand over the $7000 cheques. Payment was conditional on workers indemnifying the government against any legal actions relating to the 'protection' regime. At that time, the records show the Palm Island claimants were owed between $8500 and $21,000."[46]

The Queensland government finally freezes the Aborigines Welfare Fund as late as 1993. Dr Ros Kidd says that Premier Beattie said about $500 million could be missing. She outlines the Beattie Labor government's response in the same article:

> "In May 2002 Premier Beattie made an offer of $2000 for people under the age of fifty, and $4000 for those older, as 'reparations for the decades of control by former Queensland administrations of the wages and savings of indigenous

> people.' The government estimated there were 11,400 surviving potential claimants in the first group, and 5000 in the second, giving a total projected payout of over $55 million. The premier said the payment would 'deliver some overdue justice to ageing people' rather than forcing them to endure protracted court cases and the risk of dying in the interim.
>
> Yet this 'generous' offer (his words) was closed to descendants of those who had died before May 2002; the government had no intention of compensating or repaying monies lost across generations prior to that date. To get the payment people had to sign an indemnity against taking legal action on any aspect of the 'protection' regime; and the government is well aware that very few people have any idea of what might be missing or owed, having never seen any documentation. This, it seems, is justice Queensland style."

The issue has never been satisfactorily resolved. Imagine the interest on that fund. Today some of it is being used to support Indigenous students in their schooling, students who, for the most part, see it as some government largesse and don't realize it comes from the back-breaking labor of their elders. The issue of under payment of award wages all those years, advantaging government coffers, is a separate issue to the stolen wages that went into the Aborigines Welfare Fund. No wonder there is a high level of intergenerational poverty amongst Indigenous people.

But I digress from our Council meeting. Back to the Mayor's table. We were talking about some of Yarrabah's pioneers and Arnold Murgha's name came up.

> "The Knowledge Centre will be the place for your launch," says the Mayor "and Janelle, our CEO, can help you work on a program."
>
> "Could we have some dancers?" asks Norman.
>
> "Yes, the school can provide some dancers," says Mayor Ross.

"Thanks," I say. "I can provide some food and donate a copy of my book to Council and the school."

After further pleasantries, we go to the Knowledge Centre which has been newly set up. When I did my initial research for the Yarrabah book, I was visiting the old council office by the sea. It was on the opposite side of the road to the church where we have preached a number of times over the years and seen people healed. Even now, we meet someone having a difficult time and asking for prayer, which we do. The old council building has been pulled down and replaced by one which houses Yarrichino, a take-away, an arts and crafts center and the Knowledge Centre.

We are greeted by a bubbly staff member who knows us, Pamela Mundraby. She actually went to a Christian conference we hosted in Uluru in 2005. We are greeted with a hug. A glass wall allows us to look out to the beach and the sea. All I want to do is drink in the sight. "What a place to work," I say.

It houses a basic library, a long desk with computers, a large table and chairs and a comfortable lounge arrangement. Pam says the Wontulp Bi-Buya Bible College students come in here and work at the computers. In one corner is a radio station that has been partially set up. It is a welcoming space. This is where we'll launch my book. There is plenty of room.

We meet Desmond Fourmile outside and Tennyson Singleton and others. We ask for Elverina Johnson but she's on lunch. Desmond went to a Christian conference in Israel with us a few years ago. We were regularly taking teams from Yarrabah with us to Israel with the help of Fr Les Baird. Now Les takes them himself as he continues to go every year. "Are you going again this year?" asks Norman.

"Yes," Des smiles. "Fr Les and I and two others."

"Are you taking your didjeridoo?" Norman asks.

"No," he looks surprised. "I might borrow one to take."

Norman and I have to go but the pressure is on for me now to have the book in time for the 31st October launch. It is very successful and is covered on the TV news that night. Mayor Ross launches my book and former Mayor of the Council, Percy Neal, delivers a stirring message.

Palm Island 60th Anniversary of Strike Background

Palm Island off the coast of Townsville was, like other Aboriginal communities, under the highly restrictive Queensland Aborigines Act with their life controlled by white staff and the toll of the town bell. However, as it was set up as a penal colony or punishment island, it had particularly cruel supervisors, poor living conditions and harsh working regulations. Aboriginals from around Queensland were sent there for petty actions.

My son Michael's great grandfather, George Sibley, was sent there from Gugu (Kuku) Yalanji country for being "cheeky." That is, speaking up for himself. Michael's grandfather, Mick Miller Snr, was forced to go there from Waanji country for supposedly cattle duffing (stealing cattle) as a young man.

Palm Island was run by a particularly despotic Superintendent called Bartlam who ran the island by a bell to wake up to, be on parade, have lunch and dinner and go to bed with a 10pm curfew. If someone was late for parade, they were imprisoned. The punishment for young men and women seeing each other was the women would have their hair shaved off and have to sweep the streets with a stick-broom. The people had to work an 8-hour day and were paid $1-$2 a week. They queued for basic rations and had to salute white staff who passed by. The island living areas were segregated.

Families Arrive For 60th Anniversary

I miss the start of commemorations because of Norman's birthday. I arrive Wednesday for my 14-16 June visit by Hinterland Aviation just before 10am and am picked up by Lawrie Coutts as I am to stay with Lawrie and his wife Veronica. I am surprised to see a sign near the airport saying Kalkadoon Drive as this is the name of a tribe in the Gulf country.

Apparently, people from about 40 different tribes were moved here for punishment and they all had their different camps. The Kalkadoon mob must have camped near here. They are noted for having valiantly resisted European settlement. The original people of Palm Island are the Bwgcolman but those exiled to Palm are accepted by the local tribe and are known as Bwgcolman too.

Veronica and Lawrie live in a teacher's house on the esplanade because Veronica teaches special needs to grades 3, 4 and 5. She has a winsome smile and is a Torres Strait Islander with dreadlocks. Lawrie, hair starting to gray, is Aboriginal and does security work. They look after their grandchildren. It is a wooden house painted cream and they have a boat to enjoy fishing. With palm trees on the beach, it is a beautiful view. I sleep in the lounge and the next morning their granddaughter, Maymay, who is 3 years old, insists on brushing my hair and tying it back. She likes to sit on my lap. Her sister Lilly, 5 years old, is also a delight.

However, as soon as Lawrie drops me home with my gear, I walk straight over to the outdoor area near the council where the event is being held. It is a beautiful walk along the beach and past the jetty. The ocean is calm and beautiful. Marquees have been set up with tables, chairs, a stage, a microphone and video camera. Banners declare the 60th anniversary of the Palm Island strike.

The families of the seven strike leaders who were banned have come to commemorate this special occasion. For me, it is good to reconnect with the Sibley family, of which I am a part through my son. Many of the families don't live on island anymore and come from Woorabinda, Cherbourg, Mackay, Townsville, Cairns and the Torres Strait.

The 1957 Strike

I have a chat with Dulcie Isaro. She is a striking, confident figure in her blue dress, white lace shawl with her white hair swept back. Wearing sunglasses to protect from the glare, she leans on her red walker. Dulcie was 15 years old at the time of the strike and told NITV that her father,

Willie Thaiday, was sent to Palm Island for kissing a girl from another town. When Albie was to be deported from Palm Is for disobeying an order, it was the last straw. He refused to go and, with six other men, led the whole community in a strike in June 1957. They were Willie Thaiday, Albert Geia, Eric Lymburner, Sonny Sibley, Bill Congoo, George Watson and Gordon Tapau. My son's great uncle, Sonny Sibley, was one of them. As he is no longer here to tell the story, Dulcie Isaro does. She says,

> "I remember the fathers speaking up for their rights without fear ... it was something totally new to us. We couldn't believe that nobody would go to work."[47]

They took over the running of the island for five days but word got out to the mainland and police raided the homes of the seven men at dawn. Shackled and held at gun point, they and their families were forced on a boat and shipped to the mainland, banished forever. The seven families were exiled to Woorabinda, Cherboug and Bamaga.

Delphine Geia, a descendant of one of the strike leaders, opens in prayer and two Torres Strait Islander mayors, the Cherbourg mayor and Alf Lacy, the Palm Island mayor, speak of this important anniversary. The Torres Strait Mayors are touched at how Palm Island, an Aboriginal community, has integrated the descendants of Islanders sent there for punishment.

Then the Queensland Council of Unions (QCU) delegates speak. There is a union team from Townsville and Heath from United Voice in Cairns. Patrick from the Maritime Workers Union and Lara Watson, the ACTU Indigenous officer based in Brisbane speak. She's very passionate. She says the seven strike leaders on Palm Island paved the way for Indigenous workers' rights. The QCU representative tells the crowd they are lobbying re the Community Development Employment Program (CDEP) because it has no workers compensation or workplace health and safety and no sick or holiday leave. It is not a real job. Lara says a First Nations workers Alliance has been set up for CDEP workers but you had to be a union member.

Patrick from Badu says three of the strikers were from the Torres Straits – Willie Thaiday, Albie Geia and Gordon Tapau. The strike started on 10th June because Albie was to be exiled. Patrick talks about the Maritime strike in the Torres Strait in 1936 and the first council meeting in 1937 at Masig Island.

On Thursday 15th June, there is a moving wreath laying and flag lowering ceremony at 8.30am. The Lymburners are not here for this because of a family funeral in Townsville so I can't catch up with my son's sister Jenny Pryor. Jenny was the Aboriginal and Torres Strait Islander Commission (ATSIC) Commissioner for Palm. Lawrie Coutts is related to her. However, the reason I am staying with him and Veronica is through church connections. Veronica attended a conference I organized at Uluru in 2005 and Lawrie and Veronica are running a church fellowship on Palm Island.

The monument to the Thaidays was erected by Dulcie in 1999 and mentions all the family and the other six are erected for the 50th Golden Jubilee and just mention the men's names. Willie and Madge had a double wedding with Cissie Sibley and Mick Miller Snr, the latter being my son's grandparents.

Bill Congoo was one of the 1957 Palm Is Strike leaders and his family is laying a wreath at his memorial plaque and stone for the 60th anniversary of the strike. The Aboriginal flag which marks the monument is lowered to half-mast. Some of his family travel from Cairns to be here. The serene scene is in contrast to the harsh treatment and punishment metered out to an innocent people. A white stone on blue base marks the memorial to Bill with a plaque in his honor on the base. There is a row of memorials and similar ceremonies all along the shore.

After yarning with a few people, I am asked to do an interview with Dwayne and Farley, film makers from Townsville. Delphine Geia, the event organizer, has engaged them to cover the event. Dwayne is interested in my story that Palm Island contributed a large number of the signatures on William Cooper's petition to the King of England in the 1930's for better conditions for Australian Aboriginals.

The Palm Is strike is not just for better wages but is against the oppressive conditions of the Qld Aborigines Act. In 1981 Dulcie's father's book *Under the Act* was published by Shorty O'Neill of NQ Black Publishing, part of our North Qld Land Council, so I had an early copy. It is the first publication by both a black writer and a black publisher. On 16th June 2016, Dulcie launches her own book, *The Day Palm Island Fought Back* published by Jeanie Adams of Black Ink Press.

Griffith University has a display showing some of the history of Palm Island. I donate some books I have written on Aboriginal history to the Palm Island library.

Carol Doyle and the Sibley family lead a workshop on Emotional Well-being, helping families cope with the after effects of the government repression following the strike. It is a good opportunity for me to catch up with the Sibley family. Margaret Ah Kee and her sons live in Cairns, as I do, so it is easy to connect with them. Others have travelled from Mackay, Townsville etc., to be here. We gather near the store for a photo with the green and yellow Council logo and its palm trees atop the cream-colored building.

I am blessed by a gospel concert Wednesday night, organized by Delphine Geia with groups of Torres Strait Islander singers. I am surprised to get an opportunity to share briefly. I tell them of the vision and prophecy I received in 2003 about a revival on Darnley Island that would go north to PNG and south to the Aboriginal communities. Passionately, I say I believe it will affect Palm Island. Darnley Island was the first island in the Torres Strait to receive Christianity as I have discussed earlier.

Friday is now a public holiday to commemorate the strike and people are starting to go home. Veronica and Lawrie take me for a drive around the island and I am particularly interested in seeing Little Butler Bay where I camped with Mick in the 1970s. It is just after Big Butler Bay. Beautiful beach almond and oak trees abound. It is a very rough road even for a Land Rover. There is a lot of bush on each side. There are a few tin shacks for camping. To get there we pass Casement, where my son's father used to live, and there's a lookout and sign.

The Catholic church is now closer to town but at that time it was further out so it was a long walk to school for Mick and family. There is a memorial where the school was. It's near the panoramic beach. Casement is near the airport. I saw St Michael's Catholic primary school where Mick and his siblings went to school. The Catholic church and the priests and nun's quarters are on a hillside.

It is interesting to see the areas where the Luma Luma people live (Lawrie's mob) and Clump Pt mob, Babinda mob, Kuku mob etc. One of the beaches has holiday shacks but some live here permanently, waiting for housing. There is a lot of new housing but far out, so they'll need a car.

Palm Island is very honoring of its heroes and likes to acknowledge its history. It has a knowledge center, a war memorial and monuments to former councillors, to the 1957 strike leaders and to the Magnificent Seven who fought for award wages via a court case and won.

The main monument is a striking red ochre stone-like structure with a rectangular base rising up to a v-shape on the top right. It has three faces. In the background are the picturesque sea and the jetty. Palm trees adorn the beach and a shelter is near the jetty as protection for those who wait for the barge from Townsville on the mainland. There are flag poles nearby. The monument stands on a cement base and is surrounded by a black see-through fence. Outside the fence, the grassy area leads off to the sandy beach. Today the skies are a beautiful blue and the sun shines on this historic event.

There is a large plaque on each face of the monument. One of them is entitled "Footprint of Palm Island History." Various dates give a timeline starting in 1914 with Palm Island gazetted as an Aboriginal reserve and going to 2005 when Aboriginal Councils in Queensland start the transition to full Shire Council status. At the top left and right of the heading are the Aboriginal and Torres Strait Islander flags. At the bottom of the timeline, it says, "Our faith in God has kept us together during this time."

On another face of the monument is the heading "Strike '57" again with the Aboriginal and Torres Strait Islander flags on each side. There is a list of the seven strike leaders and on the bottom the theme of the 60th anniversary: "Go for broke."

The third face is about "The Magnificent Seven" and reads,

> "After 1968, the Queensland government began paying wages to all its employees on Aboriginal communities. Wages in the mid-1970's were only 57% of the basic wage and in the mid-1980's, only 72% of the basic wage.
>
> In 1985, Kitchener Bligh, Buller Coutts, Mavis Foster, Fred Lenoy, Jack Sibley and Jean Sibley began legal action against the Queensland government. This was through the Human Rights and Equal Opportunity Commission which declared the refusal to pay award wages breached the 1975 Racial Discrimination Act.
>
> The case was reactivated in 1995 through the Foundation for Aboriginal and Islander Research Action (FAIRA). The 7 plaintiffs described the humiliation of and struggle for survival of underpaid community workers. Evidence from government sources proved that the Queensland government had known since 1979 the underpayment was illegal. It also violated both State industrial as well as Federal racial discrimination legislation.
>
> In April 1997 on Palm Island, the Minister publicly apologized and handed over the $7,000 cheques to each of the plaintiffs (as compensation). This extensive fight for wage justice by "The Magnificent Seven" opened the gates for Aboriginal workers from around Australia."

Jack Sibley is a son of George Sibley and brother to strike leader Sonny Sibley and brother to my son's grandmother, Cecelia (Cissie) Sibley. There is certainly a tradition of working for justice in the family line.

Before the Sibley family returns home, we are invited to Lex and Cecelia Wotton's home for a wonderful meal. Cecelia is the daughter of

Jack and Jean Sibley. Some renovations have been done to their home as a result of compensation from a court case. I didn't ask Lex about the case at this family gathering as it was a time for a happy reunion of family members. However, the story is important as it reveals a lot about police-Aboriginal relations.

Death In Custody On Palm Island

On 19th November 2004, a 36-year-old Aboriginal man named Cameron Doomadgee, now known as Mulrunji, died in police custody on Palm Island. He had been arrested by Senior Sergeant Chris Hurley as a public nuisance after singing the Baha Men song *Who Let the Dogs Out?* as the officer drove past and swearing when challenged. Affected by alcohol, protesting and struggling, Mulrunji was brought into the Palm Island Police Station. Near the door to the police station, a struggle and fall with Senior Sergeant Hurley occurred. Mulrunji was then dragged limp and unresponsive into a cell. Within an hour, he was dead with no medical help called. He was considered an active and likeable person and it was a big shock to the community. The community was told on 26th November that he probably tripped on a step. He was the 147th Indigenous death in police custody since 1990. By June 2020, that number had risen to 434 since the Royal Commission into Aboriginal Deaths in Custody report came out in 1991.

A riot erupted after the release of a pathologist's report which found Mulrunji, whose liver had been cleaved in two, had died as a result of a fall and Sgt Hurley's mate was conducting the investigation. Later the Coroner's report found he had suffered four broken ribs, a ruptured spleen, a torn portal vein and his liver just about cleaved in two. Eyewitness Roy Bramwell told them earlier that week that after Mulrunji was arrested, Hurley had viciously assaulted him and left him to die without medical attention. Lex Wotton, a plumber, with previous stints as a local government councillor, was a leader of the rioters who burned down the police station and Chris Hurley's home on 26th November.

It seems Lex was meant to be there when the community erupted with anger over the treatment of Mulrunji as the *Guardian* notes,

> "On that fateful day of 26th November 2004, he was preparing to catch a plane to the mainland when he got a call from the Palm Island council chief executive.
>
> A water seal had broken on the main street of Palm Island. The council plumber had caught the previous plane out and Wotton was the only other person on the island with expertise. Wotton gave advice then went to the airstrip. Fate struck again: he'd forgotten to pack the key for his car on the mainland. He set up a later flight and went and fixed the pipe in front of the police station.
>
> Wotton noticed a community meeting nearby where a coroner's report into the death of Mulrunji was being read out at a community meeting …
>
> "I grabbed a big wrench and then went and smashed up the place," Wotton said. "That night I'm on television and I'm known right across the country and overseas. Some people rang up that knew of me and said, 'I saw you here in Times Square [New York]'."[48]

Lex told me by phone after I sent him the section in my book on Palm Island that he had wanted to be at the meeting where the pathologist's report was released. He agreed also agreed it was his fate to be there that day to stand up for his people.

A coronial inquest found Hurley had killed Mulrunji with three punches. He was tried for manslaughter and found not guilty in 2007. Three coronial inquests, a review by the Crime and Misconduct Commission in Queensland, two reviews by the Queensland Police Service (QPS), criminal proceedings against Senior Sergeant Chris Hurley in which he was acquitted of manslaughter, and litigation by police officers about potential disciplinary action against the police took place.

There were a large number of criminal proceedings against Palm Islanders, including Lex Wotton. Hurley admitted to the court accidentally causing Mr Doomadgee's death by falling on top of him with his knee protruding. Hurley was promoted and received a payout of $100,000 for damages. Thirty-four police officers who were on Palm Island during the protests were the recipients of awards or commendations for "bravery" including Detective Robinson, Hurley's mate, who was in charge of the initial investigation.

Instead of the police officer going to jail, the key Aboriginal protestor did for inciting the ensuing riot. In 2008, Lex was sentenced to six years jail and he got out in 2010 on parole because of time served awaiting court. However, he had a gag order which prevented him being a voice for his people. *Solidarity* writes,

> "During Wotton's trial (Detective) Robinson admitted that he had lied in previous investigations to help out his friend Hurley. One incident involved Hurley driving over Aboriginal woman Barbara Pilot's foot. He drove off, despite Barbara requiring surgery for a protruding bone.
>
> The Crime and Misconduct Commission (CMC) found Robinson had declared the woman's claims fictitious and refused to interview the witnesses to the incident. Although the CMC recommended action be taken against Robinson, the Queensland Police have yet to take any disciplinary action against him.[49]

What is particularly concerning is that the Queensland Police Union waged an aggressive campaign in support of Hurley heckling and putting pressure on the state government and the court system. Wilkins writes,

> "In the case of Chris Hurley, the first Australian police officer to be charged over an Aboriginal death in custody, support from the Queensland Police Union (QPU) was unwavering.
>
> Hurley was charged with manslaughter and assault over the death of Mulrunji Doomadgee on Palm Island in November

2004, sparking police across Queensland to brandish blue wristbands. He was acquitted in 2007.

But even before the trial began, the union lashed out at the coroner's findings that Mulrunji's death had been caused by Hurley. "She's [the coroner] used unreliable evidence from a drunk to support these claims," the then QPU president Gary Wilkinson reportedly said,"[50]

However, Lex, Cecelia and Agnes Wotton (Lex's wife and mother) led a successful class action of 447 residents, that the Palm Islanders had been treated in a racist manner. In the case of Wotton v State of Queensland (No 5) [2016] FCA 1457, the federal court said officers should not have "forced their way into houses occupied by unarmed families… pointing assault rifles at them and yelling at them to lie down" in a community that was not isolated and predominantly Aboriginal. (5th December 2016). In its judgement, Judge J Mortimer maintained,

> "Despite the entire population of Palm Island (including children) being less than 2000, between 88 and 111 police officers (including SERT[51] and the Public Safety Response Team) were on the island over the period covered by the emergency declaration. I have not accepted evidence suggesting the people to be arrested were reasonably suspected of having any weapons nor that there were any acts or threats of violence after the fires subsided on the evening of 26th November 2004.
>
> Yet, during the SERT operations, armed, masked SERT officers broke into the houses of 18 families on Palm Island, with assault rifles raised, confronting unarmed men, women and children in and around those houses. Mr Wotton was tasered in front of his family. I have found the use of SERT officers to effect the arrests was unnecessary, disproportionate and was undertaken as a show of force against local people who had protested about the conduct of police. Women and

children in and around the houses attended by SERT officers, who had nothing to do with the protests and fires, were terrified. Those women and children who gave evidence have suffered a lasting detrimental impact from the SERT operation." (5th December 2016), See the full judgement.[52]

Ironically, days earlier, Hurley was convicted of common assault in an unrelated court case despite the Queensland Police Union still protecting him and saying he didn't get a fair go. He also admitted assaulting a female police officer in another case. Hurley went into medical retirement.

Many locals say they are still traumatized by the episode. Tim Arvier reports on 7th May 2018 that,

> "Wotton's victory cleared the way for a class action involving 447 Islanders, with the Queensland Government agreeing to settle with a $30 million payment and to offer Palm Islanders an apology. [53]

However, the saga takes its toll on the community who are filled with grief. Gerry Georgatos writes,

> "One of the witnesses to Mulrunji's death was Patrick Nugent, he was in a nearby cell. Mr Nugent would soon be found dead. Mulrunji's death took its toll on his family. His son Eric, at only 18 years old, would be found hanging from a tree."[54]

The Queensland government confirmed in January 2017 that it was appealing the ruling handed down by the federal court that $30 million damages and costs be paid but would pay the $220,00 damages to the three members of the Wotton family. There was community relief when Attorney-General Yvette D'Ath announced the government was withdrawing the appeal on 28th February, having received legal advice about the State's prospects of success. Lex said they would accept the payout,

> "But thirty pieces of silver can't wash away the trauma which police caused to blacks on Palm Island twelve years ago.[55]

Lex's story is one of a life turned around that has made a difference. While in prison for the riot, he became a mentor for young Aboriginal offenders to help them see another way of life. Robertson writes,

> "In 1986, Wotton was a 19-year-old with a drinking problem and a conviction for domestic violence against his girlfriend.
>
> "I'm in a prison cell, doing a four-month stretch," he says. "I get on my knees and pray and say, 'God, this is not the life for me.' I woke up and said I have to take a different direction, so then I did."
>
> He got out of prison, broke off the relationship with his partner "because I didn't want to be destructive to her" and quit drinking cold turkey. He looked for a trade and found the only available apprenticeship was in plumbing. He took it and went to work.
>
> Nine years later Wotton rekindled his relationship with the woman who became his wife and life partner. They had four children. Wotton threw himself into his job, impressing a Townsville plumbing business owner who employed him. By 30, he was a councillor on the Palm Island Aboriginal Shire Council." [56]

Yes, a life turned around and a community healing.

Awareness Campaign with Award Wages Cheque at Cairns Esplanade and Munganbana Norman's Art in the Shape of a Dollar Sign, a Timeline of Significant Events 1897-2016

Book Launch at Knowledge Centre, Yarrabah, Barbara Henrietta Fourmile and Rev Dorita Wilson 31 Oct 2016

Families of Strike Leaders photo Barbara Miller

Family Members of Bill Congoo at his memorial stone and plaque photo Barbara Miller

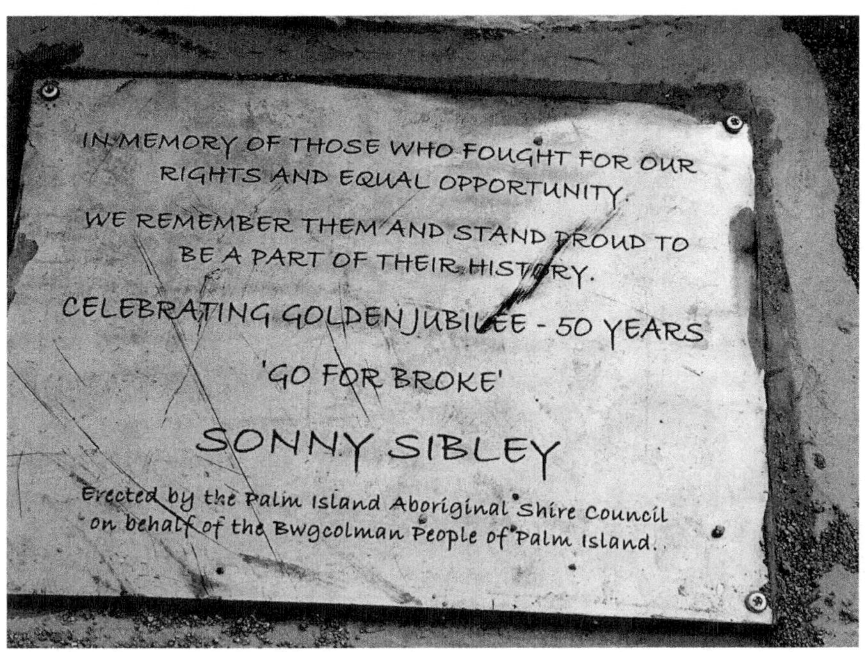

Plaque of Sonny Sibley photo by Barbara Miller

Sibley Family including Barbara Miller

Memorial to Palm Island's Heroes and History photo by Barbara Miller

Chapter 21

Mapoon Paanja Festival

Norman and I arrive at Mapoon Thursday night for the Paanja Festival 28-30 September 2018 which will start tomorrow. We fly in from Cairns to Weipa and hire a 4WD to take us to Mapoon. We cross a long narrow bridge over the Mission River with mangroves adorning the river bank. Rio Tinto Alcan has changed the landscape with their mining activities and heavy equipment. Trains carry the bauxite to the wharf in Weipa. The bauxite-red dust flies up as cars travelling to Weipa pass us. Pandanus trees and ant hills pepper the route.

Arriving at Mapoon, we stay at the home of Ricky Guivarra, an old friend who has been a Mapoon councillor. It is 55 years since the Aboriginal inhabitants were moved off by force to make way for mining and 44 years since I helped them return. They have become a very successful community. It is two years since Norman and I have been here talking to them about my proposed book *White Woman Black Heart: Journey Home to Old Mapoon, A Memoir*. This visit, I bring it with me.

It is a touching time for me. Many fond memories of the people who braved so much to move back to their land despite police and Queensland government intimidation. They did the hard yards of rebuilding from nothing; their community and homes having been burnt to the ground to stop them returning. The Paanja Festival commemorates this. The first

Paanja Festival was held in 2013 for the 50th anniversary of the removal. So as well as a cultural event, it is a celebration of survival, renewal and victory.

I have seen the advertising leading up to the event which includes a Mapoon Fishing Competition called the Cullen Point Barra Bash to take place on Sunday 30th sponsored by Rio Tinto, the mining company, the Mapoon Council and others. The first prize is $1,000, sure to lure some keen fishermen. It is ironic that the mining company is a major sponsor considering the people were moved off their land for proposed mining, mainly by Alcan and Comalco.

We head to the Jerry and Andrewina Hudson Community Hall where the main event is held. It is named after the leaders of the move back to Mapoon, Jerry and Ina, to honor them for their vision, leadership, sacrifice and hard work rebuilding the community. The hall is not airconditioned despite the tropical heat. It has fans and the walls are made of slats to have the maximum use of any natural breeze. The large sign “Out of the Ashes We Have Arisen” is a tribute to the courage and resilience of Mapoon people who rebuilt their community.

A large number of people have gathered and there are art and craft stalls, interactive information displays and food stalls around the edges. Aboriginal and Torres Strait Islander people have come in from many surrounding communities and many are camping. It is believed about 3,000 attended the festival which is now on the calendar with the Laura Dance Festival and the Cooktown Discovery Festival. There is a historical display by Mapoon council in the hall and a sound system has been set up with Trevor Tims of Cairns as the MC. Norman entertains them by singing “My Island Home” by Christine Anu.

Traditional games are played outside and sporting events, including spear throwing, are held. As well as a number of small tents for activities, I am surprised to find a carnival amusement area for the children outside the hall. Many of the participants are wearing a blue T shirt made for the festival.

As the hall is used for basketball, we see the markings of the basketball court. But for the next couple of days, traditional dancing will be performed here. Many dance groups come from the Aboriginal communities and the Torres Strait Islands including the Sundowner Dancers and Mapoon's own dancers.

The Badu Island dancers are very popular and they have travelled in dinghies and a bus from the tip of Cape York. The Badu women wear red dresses with white frangipani flowers on them, grass skirts, and rings of white flowers around their hair. The stamping of the feet of the Badu men dancers draws claps and whistles as they dance in white feather *dhari* (headdresses), red lap-laps covered with grass shirts *(zazi)* and white singlets. The men and women both wear decorations of white cloth around their wrists and ankles, the latter known as *muk muk*. The shakers create an exciting noise. *Kulap* shakers or rattles are a traditional musical instrument used for rhythm and beat. The Lockhart River dancers similarly thrill the crowd with adults and children in white body paint and long grass shirts doing shake-a-leg and traditional dances.

The descendants of the key families who moved back to Mapoon in 1974 to rebuild are honored in a ceremony of the presentation of plaques by Mayor Aileen Addo assisted by Council CEO Ms Naseem Chetty. Trevena Hudson receives a plaque for Jerry and Ina Hudson, Maggie Peter for Simon and Rachel Peter, and Linda Cooktown receives plaques for Jean Jimmy and Frank and Maggie Don. Harry Toeboys' family also receive a plaque. Norman and Jesse Wheeler's family may have as well. The plaques all have "Out of the ashes we have arisen" and "strength in unity" on them.

I am happy to meet Alma Day, niece of Rosina Toumese (Mamoose). Rosina and Ces moved back to Mapoon with the first group on 18th September 1974. I was with them that fateful day. Clarrie Grogan and Peter Noble, with the help of the Aboriginal Legal Service in Cairns, were with us too, to give the group extra courage and protection.

I privately give the Mayor and those who receive a plaque a copy of my Mapoon book. Aileen is keen for me to have my book available at the event for purchase. Some people do buy and I sign the books for them.

It is good to meet up with artist Zoe de Jersey, niece of Ina Hudson and on our final evening I am touched to catch up with Willie Hudson and his family. He is a brother to Jerry Hudson and we worked closely together leading up to the move back to Mapoon. I spend some time with Sharon Brown and John Mark, which is so good as I knew his father, Stephen, from my time at New Mapoon. It was so exciting to see descendants of the people I knew so well from days gone by. I chat with Bonnie whose parents Silva and Gina Blanco helped rebuild Mapoon, Gina being Jerry's sister and Silva being on the Mapoon council for many years.

I am interviewed by Bumma Bippera Media and National Indigenous Radio Service about my book and my work with the Mapoon people.

On the final night, there is rock concert and a large outdoor stage is set up with a colorful banner behind it. A number of performers entertain the enthusiastic crowd including Neil Murray, Cuzzie Bro, Sunset Rising, Gubil Markai and Royston Sagigi. The fireworks are a delight to all, especially the children, with fireworks shooting high into the night sky.

Church on the beach is to be held on Sunday and a fishing competition to end off the festivities. We turn up on the beautiful beach but the church service isn't held. Are they all out fishing? We are greeted by the organizer who tells us she was at the same conference as us in Israel in 2017 hosted by our Pacific family and Messianic Jewish congregations. Small world.

We watch the waves calmly lapping up on the sandy shore and enjoy the gentle breeze. The sun seems to lazily but warmly hug the beach almond trees. So peaceful - but time to return to our busy city life. We are sad to leave but happy we have come. It felt so good to reconnect.

Badu Island dancers Paanja Festival

Barbara with Trevena Hudson, Maggie Peter and Family and Linda Cooktown with Plaques

Chapter 22

Sorry, Journey of Healing & Constitutional Recognition

National Inquiry into the Stolen Generations

A National Inquiry into the Separation of Aboriginal and Torres Strait Islander Children from Their Families is established in May 1995 and takes evidence from 535 Indigenous people. In 1997 the Human Rights Commission releases its 689-page report accusing the government of genocide. It is called *Bringing Them Home*, and it calls the children "The Stolen Generation" though sometimes two or three generations had been removed. About 30,000 children are estimated to have been affected. International law defines genocide as including the forcible removal of children to a different cultural group "with the intent to destroy, in whole or part, the group."

The report calls for an official apology and financial compensation because thousands of Aborigines are involved in family breakdowns, mental health issues, drug and alcohol abuse and violence linked to the assimilation policy. Successive federal governments do not support such compensation.

The report triggers an unprecedented debate on black-white relations in Australia and a campaign to discredit the claim that generations of

Aboriginal children were stolen. Some sections of Australia cannot not face the shame of our history. Historian Robert Manne is a key defender of the claim while historian Keith Windshuttle is a key denier. Manne does claim that the *Bringing Them Home* report's numbers of three in ten Aboriginal children removed between 1910 and 1970 is wrong and it is closer to one in ten.

The ABC 7.30 Report arranges a debate on the Stolen Generation report with Manne, Associate Professor, La Trobe University and Ron Brunton on 29th March 2001. Brunton, an anthropologist, is working with the conservative think-tank, the Institute of Public Affairs and writes a scathing critique of the *Bringing Them Home* report. There is a debate on the numbers involved and reasons for removal:

To interviewer Kerry O'Brien's questioning, Brunton says,

> "I don't deny that there was the forced removal of children with no justification whatsoever."
>
> Manne asks, "I was going to say, Ron, do you accept that the Commonwealth had a policy of breeding out the color?"
>
> Brunton replies, "I accept there were a number of officials in the 1930's who spoke in these terms."

At another point in the interview, O'Brien asks:

> "Ron Brunton, what judgment do you make in the end about, for instance, the chief protector in the NT between '27 and '39, Mr Cook, who could approve or veto marriages between half-castes and full bloods?"
>
> Brunton replies, "I think it's appalling. I have made this point time and time again. I have said that we have to recognize that there was a degree of interference and surveillance of Aboriginal people that is absolutely unconscionable and Australians have to come to terms with that." (He agreed it was officially sanctioned).

Later in the interview, O'Brien asks Manne:

> "Robert Manne, you acknowledged yourself that there were many well-meaning people involved in the process. Do you accept that an unknown number of children, significant or otherwise, who did benefit in terms of education or other opportunity, from leaving their families, whether they were removed, whether there was some consent, whether that consent was as a result of pressure or otherwise, whose lives might have been saved by their removal?"
>
> Manne: "Well, can I say about the well-meaning – the point I make about this is that there were very many well-meaning people and very many brutes involved. The well-meaning people could not emancipate themselves from the racism of the time, up till the mid-50s. So, you find even the finest people thinking it was right to segregate half-castes and full bloods.
>
> I suppose there were some people who benefited; there must have been. But by-and-large, the overwhelming majority of the Stolen Generations suffered terribly because it's not fine to be brought up in an institution when the color of your skin is a matter for shame, and it's not fine to not know from where you come or who your parents are. It's a terrible thing."[57]

The White Australia Policy, the basis of Australian federation, has shades of eugenics. The first Prime Minister of Australia, Edmund Barton declared, "I don't think the equality of man was ever intended to include racial equality".[58]

However, while race appears to be a significant issue, separate races do not really exist. There is more genetic variation within what we call races than between them. This was borne out by a worldwide study commissioned by United Nations Educational, Scientific and Cultural Organization (UNESCO) in the 1950s.

Australian Reconciliation Convention

Norman and I go to the landmark Australian Reconciliation Convention 26-28 May 1997 (Reconciliation Week) in Melbourne where almost 1800 attend – Aborigines, government officials, religious leaders, lawyers, teachers, health workers, students etc. This is the culmination of a year of consultation and education events around the nation of which we are a part. While it is successful in many ways, the Melbourne conference is overshadowed by the opening address of then Prime Minister John Howard:

> "In facing the realities of the past, … we must not join those who would portray Australia's history since 1788 as little more than a disgraceful record of imperialism … such an approach will be repudiated by the overwhelming majority of the Australians who are proud of what this country has achieved although inevitably acknowledging the blemishes of its past history.[59]

Describing what happened to Indigenous people as a mere blemish, the Prime Minister dismisses centuries of dispossession and violence as insignificant and does it at a conference aimed to bring reconciliation. It is also the anniversary of the release of the *Bringing Them Home* report. Many Indigenous delegates in the audience turn their backs on John Howard in protest.

Nevertheless, much healing of relationships between Indigenous and non-Indigenous people occurred, and delegates reached fresh understandings. One commentator wrote,

> "But most telling I think is the sheer integrity of the Indigenous leaders … and people who can find it in their hearts to forgive. To witness the peace and tranquility emanating from those leaders, rather than the anger and rage emanating from our political masters, made me truly humbled in their presence." [60]

The Apology

As the debate continues, an election dramatically removes John Howard and his government from power. He had opposed the saying of sorry. The first item on the agenda for the incoming ALP government under Prime Minister Kevin Rudd is to apologize to the stolen generation of Aboriginal people. This is a bipartisan event in parliament with the new Leader of the Opposition, Brendon Nelson. The tide has turned.

Norman's Grandfather

Aborigines come from all over Australia to sit in Parliament House to hear the apology, wiping the tears from their eyes. Norman's grandfather, Thomas Miller, was taken from his mother in Nyleta, North Queensland in 1905 when he was about five years old. His mother was a full blood Aboriginal woman, and his father was Scottish. He was taken not only from his mother but his brothers and sisters. They were taken too, but the children were split up. He never saw his mother again, and in adult life, he was always searching for his brothers and sisters, finally finding some of them. It was too hard for him to talk much about it.

Removal of My Son's Grandparents

So, Norman stands in for his family in Canberra during the apology, and I am with him. When we arrive, we line up at the doors to Parliament House and meet Lydia and Marilyn Miller, my stepdaughters from my marriage to Mick. The Queensland government removed Mick's father to the penal settlement of Palm Island as a young man. Mick's mother, Cissie Sibley, was sent there with her parents. Her father, George Sibley had been "cheeky," in other words, was assertive and so had to be punished. It was a common thing in those days.

While Mick's parents, my son Michael's grandparents, were not stolen from their families as children, they were removed from family members, their land and their community to live in a penal settlement, an authoritarian, harsh, government-controlled environment.

The Nation Stands Still

It was 13th February 2008. Our local Member of Parliament, Jim Turnour, organizes for Norman and me to be sitting in the parliamentary gallery for the apology and to go to the reception afterwards. The gallery is full. The Great Hall which can seat about 1,000 is overflowing. The lawns in front of Parliament House are crowded, and schools and offices around the nation stop to watch and listen on TV. The only other thing that stops the nation is the Melbourne Cup horse race every year as we are a nation of horse race enthusiasts and gamblers. The only other thing that generates such excitement as the apology did is football matches which regularly fill stadiums. But this was the Parliament House of our nation – not dry old politics that day – and not a dry eye either.

It is such a momentous moment in the history of our nation when Kevin Rudd says sorry, Brendon Nelson says sorry, the country says sorry. A wave of tears is shed across the nation, washing away much pain, much hurt, much sorrow. Many non-Indigenous Australians stand with our government and share in saying sorry. It is not the end of the story, but a journey of healing starts, which is ongoing and real. Some Aboriginal people hold up signs saying, "We forgive you." Others say they are finally able to move on.

It is truly a historic moment, and it holds out a vision of what Australia can be. It is a new beginning. A page in history has been turned and a life-changing moment is experienced by many as tears flow around the nation.

From Sorry to Journey of Healing Painting

Norman is also an artist, and he paints a large canvas to record the apology. His wish is for it to sit in Parliament House to commemorate the event. We have some difficulty organizing this, however. Then we attend the

Parliamentary Prayer Breakfast in February 2011 and meet and became friends with Kevin Rudd's sister, Loree, a devout Catholic. Loree organizes for Norman to present the painting to Kevin Rudd who by then is Foreign Minister, after a leadership challenge. Norman presents the painting to him on the anniversary of the *Bringing Them Home* report's release, 26th May 2011. It is an important moment for Norman who wants to recognize and honor Kevin Rudd for what he has done.

26th May is celebrated each year as part of Reconciliation Week. Initially known as Sorry Day after the *Bringing Them Home* report came out, it changes to Journey of Healing Day so that people can work through their healing and move on.

Kevin Rudd tries to move the nation on from the history wars and is largely able to do so. His apology becomes the nation's apology. He inspires other governments to apologize to their Indigenous people.

There are arguments saying we should have practical not symbolic gestures towards reconciliation. We need both. Kevin Rudd follows the apology with upgrading the Closing the Gap program to reduce the considerable disparity in socio-economic indicators between Indigenous and other Australians. In the 10-year review of Closing the Gap in 2018, many of the targets are not met so they are refreshed and more targets added. The government is now working with a Coalition of Peak Indigenous organizations to bring about better future outcomes. This includes targets to reduce the high level of incarceration of Indigenous adults and youth.

Constitutional Recognition of Indigenous People 1990s

There is much talk in recent years about the recognition of Indigenous people in the Australian constitution as it basically sets out states' rights and commonwealth rights, Australian being a federation of sovereign states. Indigenous people were left out of the constitution at federation in 1901. With the centenary of federation coming up in 2001, the last decade of the 1990s, looks at two issues, becoming a republic rather than a constitutional monarchy and inserting a preamble to the constitution that will recognize Indigenous people and have some uplifting statements. For example, statements about hope in God, being a democracy, upholding freedom, tolerance, individual dignity and the rule of law, recognizing those who fought for Australia's freedom and the nation building contribution of immigrants etc.

Prime Minister Howard does not support a republic but supports a preamble and works on it with poet Les Murray and others but the wording is rejected for a number of reasons. The Aboriginal and Torres Strait Islander Commission (ATSIC), the Council for Aboriginal Reconciliation, the National Multicultural Advisory Council and the Constitutional Centenary Foundation support a preamble. The Mabo decision of 1992 also brings a focus on recognizing Indigenous Australians in the Constitution.

Constitutional Convention 1998

The 1998 Constitutional Convention votes to support 'in principle' Australia becoming a republic and is to discuss what model of a republic would be put to a referendum. Four working groups are set up, one of which includes ATSIC delegates and resolves that a separate referendum question be put on a new preamble at the same time as the referendum on the republic, and that such a preamble recognize 'Aboriginal peoples and Torres Strait Islanders as the original inhabitants of Australia who enjoy with all other Australians fundamental human rights'.

Indigenous National Constitutional Convention 1998

In March 1998, ATSIC organizes an Indigenous National Constitutional Convention and agrees on a Constitutional preamble recognizing Indigenous Australians and the fact of their original occupation.[61]

Referendum 1999

On 6th November 1999, a referendum is held on the following: whether Australian voters approve the proposal to establish Australia as a republic and the second change is whether they approve the proposal to insert a preamble in the Constitution. Both proposals are defeated. Why? The republican movement is divided on a model and Indigenous people are not properly consulted as to the wording of the preamble. An actual preamble was not put to the vote.

First Nations Australian leaders are vocal about recognition in the constitution but not many favor the preamble as a vehicle.

Expert Panel on the Constitutional Recognition of Indigenous Australians 2010

Time marches on. The political will for constitutional recognition of First Nations Peoples takes a big hit. The push resumes with Prime Minister John Howard promising on 16th October 2007 to hold a referendum on constitutional recognition. Labor Leader, Kevin Rudd agrees to give it bipartisan support.

However, there are still delays and on 8th November 2010, it is Labor Prime Minister Julia Gillard's turn to plan a referendum during the term of her government or at the next Federal election. On 23rd December 2010, Gillard appoints an Expert Panel to undertake public consultation throughout 2011. Co-chaired by Professor Patrick Dodson and Mark Leibler AC, it includes the Aboriginal and Torres Strait Islander Social Justice Commissioner Mick Gooda, Professor Marcia Langton AM, the Co-Chairs of the National Congress of Australia's First Peoples, Noel Pearson Founder of Cape York Partnership and MPs including Aboriginal MP Ken Wyatt AM.

The panel delivers its report *Recognising Aboriginal and Torres Strait Islander Peoples in the Constitution* on 19th January 2012, 45 years on from the landmark 1967 referendum which enabled Indigenous people to be counted in the census and the federal government to make laws for them. It is a surprise to me that there is still racial discrimination in the constitution. The report recommends the removal of Constitution sections 25 and 51(xxvi), and the insertion of new sections 51A, 116A and 127A. The new sections are:

Section 51A Recognition of Aboriginal and Torres Strait Islander peoples

> Recognizing that the continent and its islands now known as Australia were first occupied by Aboriginal and Torres Strait Islander peoples;
>
> Acknowledging the continuing relationship of Aboriginal and Torres Strait Islander peoples with their traditional lands and waters;
>
> Respecting the continuing cultures, languages and heritage of Aboriginal and Torres Strait Islander peoples;
>
> Acknowledging the need to secure the advancement of Aboriginal and Torres Strait Islander peoples;
>
> the Parliament shall, subject to this Constitution, have power to make laws for the peace, order and good government of the Commonwealth with respect to Aboriginal and Torres Strait Islander peoples.

Section 116A Prohibition of racial discrimination

> (1) The Commonwealth, a State or a Territory shall not discriminate on the grounds of race, color or ethnic or national origin.
>
> (2) Subsection (1) does not preclude the making of laws or measures for the purpose of overcoming disadvantage, ameliorating the effects of past discrimination, or protecting the cultures, languages or heritage of any group.

Section 127A Recognition of languages

(1) The national language of the Commonwealth of Australia is English.

(2) The Aboriginal and Torres Strait Islander languages are the original Australian languages, a part of our national heritage.

It proposes that the referendum be preceded by a well-resourced public education and awareness program and have all-party support and that of a majority of state governments. However, the Gillard government drops the ball on a referendum and opts to pass a recognition act instead. Insufficient community awareness and lack of bipartisan support are two reasons they give for deferring the referendum

On 12th March 2013, the federal parliament passes the Aboriginal and Torres Strait Islander Peoples Recognition Act 2013 which recognizes the Indigenous peoples of Australia and requires the establishment of a committee to advise on a suitable date for a referendum on these proposals. The process is given two years but provision is made to make it self-repealing on the 28th March 2018 when it winds up, no significant action having been taken.

Miller Boomerang Petition 2012-2016

Munganbana Norman Miller frames a petition around the recommendations of the Expert Panel and calls it the Miller Boomerang Petition, reminiscent of the Yirrkala Bark Petition. He travels Australia, with me accompanying him, and gathers, at his own expense, over 5,100 signatures from Indigenous and non-Indigenous people. As well as getting the signatures of the Mayors for Cape York Aboriginal communities, he gathers signatures at the Yabun Festival and Redfern in Sydney, NAIDOC events in Adelaide and Perth, street corners in Cairns and Sydney and events in Canberra, Brisbane and the Gold and Sunshine coasts.

Norman also makes a giant boomerang with the words "No Discrimination in the Constitution" and gains 360 signatures on the back of it. He presents it to then-Speaker Bronwyn Bishop on 27th November 2013. On 12th December 2013, the Hon Mr Entsch MP presents Miller's on-paper petition with 2115 signatures to Parliament.

Norman continues to gather signatures until over 5,100 have been collected and presents them to the Speaker Hon Tony Smith MP in the presence of the Clerk of the House and the Hon Warren Entsch MP on 8th February 2016. Mr Entsch then presents the petition to the Parliament. [62]

Norman receives a lot of press. He tells *The Cairns Post* on 8th January 2014,

> "Miller said the purpose of his campaign, which he will continue, is to prepare people for a yes vote in a referendum to be held on these issues in the term of the current parliament.
>
> My aim has been one of public education, raising community awareness and support and keeping the issue before government, bolstering its political will in this matter. While getting signatures for this petition I have met people from all walks of life, Indigenous and non-Indigenous, and found that there is little knowledge of this issue on the street and I have been able to discuss the issues and gain broad support."
>
> "I am encouraged" said Mr Miller "that this nation has come to the maturity to enable it to make changes to the constitution that will benefit the whole nation. It will also be an act of reconciliation. I have a strong desire to see justice done and I believe that the Australian people, at core, have a belief in a fair go for all."

I am pleased to assist Norman with research, press releases and administration in relation to this project to have First Nations people recognized in our constitution and have racial discrimination removed from it.

Recognise Campaign 2012-2017

Also, in response to the Expert Panel, the Gillard government funds Recognise in 2012 which is set up under Reconciliation Australia. Recognise is successful in raising awareness, but as there was no model for it to promote, the government closes Recognise in August 2017.

Reconciliation Australia website notes that in the five years of the Recognise campaign, awareness levels rose from 30% to over 75% of the population. These levels were higher amongst Aboriginal and Torres Strait Islander respondents from 60% to 84%. Reconciliation Australia says,

> "More than 160 community and corporate organizations partnered with Recognise to support change, and more than 18,000 Australians took part in the Journey to Recognition around the country. The Journey covered more than 38,000 km over a three-year period and held 386 community meetings as it toured across the country."[63]

Norman and I attend the launch of the Journey to Recognition in Melbourne in Reconciliation Week in 2013. Michael Long, famous AFL footballer, leads the walk from Melbourne which tours the nation. I am pictured walking with Michael Long and talking to Prime Minister Tony Abbott in separate photos. I am asking PM Abbott to sign a replica of William Cooper's 1930's petition which he does. Along with Uncle Boydie, Abe Schwarz and David Jack, we present the petition, on the 2014 anniversary of the 1967 referendum, to Governor General Sir Peter Cosgrove who presents it to the Queen. It was originally intended for the Queen's grandfather but the Australian government would not forward it because Australian Aborigines were not legally citizens of Australia.

A Joint Select Committee 2013

A Joint Select Committee on Constitutional Recognition of Aboriginal and Torres Strait Islander Peoples is established in 2013 to consider the recommendations of the Expert Panel report and delivers its report in June 2015.

Referendum Council 2015

The Referendum Council is jointly appointed by Prime Minister Malcolm Turnbull and Leader of the Opposition Bill Shorten on 7th December 2015. Its job is to advise on the next steps towards a successful referendum to recognize Aboriginal and Torres Strait Islander peoples in the constitution. Co-Chairs are Pat Anderson and Mr Mark Leibler AC.

The Referendum Council holds twelve Dialogues with Indigenous Australians around Australia between December 2016 and May 2017. They are by invitation only and capped at 100 persons to try to reach consensus. Feedback from these dialogues is given to a First Nations National Constitutional Convention at Uluru in May 2017.

Uluru Statement from the Heart at First Nations National Constitutional Convention 2017

Uluru, the large red rock in the center of Australia is an iconic image that often symbolizes Indigenous Australia and is a favorite spot for tourists. To the traditional owners, the Anangu, it is a sacred site. Many say it is the sacred heart of Australia. It is to Uluru, in the shadow of the rock, that the Referendum Council takes the First Nations Convention.

While there are sometimes heated discussions over whether sovereignty should be part of the outcome, they reach a consensus, and the lead constitutional lawyer for the process, Professor Megan Davis, reads out what becomes the Uluru Statement from the Heart on 26th May at the end of the Convention. The 250 Aboriginal and Torres Strait Islander delegates adopt it. Megan Davis is the first Indigenous Australian to sit on a United Nations (UN) body as Chair of the Permanent Forum on Indigenous Peoples, a significant achievement. Here is an excerpt from the Uluru Statement:

> "... we call for the establishment of a First Nations Voice enshrined in the constitution.
>
> Makarrata[64] is the culmination of our agenda: the coming together after a struggle. It captures our aspirations for a fair and truthful relationship with the people of Australia and a better future for our children based on justice and self-determination.
>
> We seek a Makarrata Commission to supervise a process of agreement-making between governments and First Nations and truth-telling about our history.
>
> In 1967 we were counted, in 2017 we seek to be heard ..."[65]

So, the Indigenous cry from the heart of Australia is VOICE TREATY TRUTH. Opposition leader Bill Shorten is supportive and commits to implementing it if he wins government.

Norman and I attend a treaty conference in Sydney around Australia Day 2018 and Norman signs the large canvas with the Uluru Statement on it. Thomas Mayor and others travel Australia raising awareness of it and getting the signatures of First Nations people. We also attend the 80th anniversary of the Day of Mourning on Australia Day 2018 at Australia Hall Sydney where the original Day of Mourning was held in 1938 on the 150th anniversary of white settlement.

Referendum Council Final Report 2017

The Referendum Council releases its Final Report on 30th June 2017 and is supportive of the Uluru Statement recommending:

> That a referendum be held to provide in the Australian Constitution for a representative body that gives Aboriginal and Torres Strait Islander First Nations a Voice to the Commonwealth Parliament. One of the specific functions of such a body, to be set out in legislation outside the Constitution, should include the function of monitoring the use of the heads of power in section 51 (xxvi) and section 122. The body will recognize the status of Aboriginal and Torres Strait Islander peoples as the first peoples of Australia.
>
> The second recommendation of the report is a Declaration of Recognition to unify Australians that sit outside the Constitution. This would be enacted by legislation passed by all Australian Parliaments.[66]

The establishment of a Makarrata Commission is outside its terms of reference.

On 26th October 2017, the Turnbull government rejects the voice as a third chamber of Parliament which is a misunderstanding of the proposal. So, the ball which has been kicked along for a number of years without reaching its goal is kicked along again to another Joint Select Committee.

The debate is continuing. Eminent former High Court Chief Justice, Murray Gleeson, who was on the Referendum Council, gives an address at a symposium and *The Australian* reports his views on 19th July 2019. He declares the voice is advisory and not a third chamber to Parliament and can be created through legislation. Its structure, function and composition can be determined through legislation with the possibility of change. At the same time, there can be minimal change to the constitution to ensure the Voice's continued existence and essential features.

Joint Select Committee 2018

Senator Pat Dodson and Julian Leeser MP co-chair the Joint Select Committee on Constitutional Recognition relating to Aboriginal and

Torres Strait Islander Peoples appointed in March 2018. It presents its final report on 29th November 2018. The first two recommendations are:

1. In order to achieve a design for The Voice that best suits the needs and aspirations of Aboriginal and Torres Strait Islander peoples, the Committee recommends that the Australian Government initiate a process of co-design with Aboriginal and Torres Strait Islander peoples.
2. The Committee recommends that, following a process of co-design, the Australian Government consider, in a deliberate and timely manner, legislative, executive and constitutional options to establish The Voice.

Indigenous Voice Co-design Process 2019

The Voice proposal languishes until the 18th May 2019 federal election when Prime Minister Scott Morrison says his government will support the Voice but it would be achieved through legislation rather be enshrined in the constitution. Ken Wyatt, elevated to Minister for Indigenous Australians in the Morrison government, the first Aboriginal to hold this position, sets up a Senior Advisory Group (SAG) to progress the co-design of the Voice and hopes to put it to a referendum in this term of Parliament if consensus can be achieved. Many Indigenous proponents of the Voice want it enshrined in the constitution however, so the government can't abolish it as they did ATSIC, the former national body.

The SAG is co-chaired by Professor Tom Calma AO, Chancellor of the University of Canberra, and Professor Marcia Langton of the University of Melbourne, both Indigenous. There is a subtle change in calling it a 'voice to government' rather than a 'voice to parliament' ".

The models for the Voice are planned to be developed in two stages:[67]

1. First, two groups, one local and regional and the other national, will create models aimed at improving local and regional decision-

making and identifying how best federal government can record Indigenous peoples' views and ideas. The groups consist mainly of Indigenous members.

2. Consultations will be held with Indigenous leaders, communities and stakeholders to refine the models developed in the first stage.

The National Co-design Group is announced on 15th January 2020, to be co-chaired by Dr Donna Odegaard AM and Ray Griggs AO CSC. On 4th March 2020 the Local and Regional Co-Design Group is announced. To be co-chaired by Peter Buckskin and National Indigenous Agency senior official Letitia Hope. The group meet for the first time in Sydney on 19th March 2020.

From the Heart is a group increasing awareness of the Uluru Statement From the Heart. They commission research which is conducted by the CIT Group in June 2020 and shows a majority of Australians support a Voice to Parliament that is constitutionally enshrined and that this support has increased.

Co-design Interim Report 2021

An interim report by the Senior Advisory Group on 9th January 2021 proposes that the government would be obliged to consult the Indigenous Voice to parliament re new legislation relating to race, native title or racial discrimination where it would affect Indigenous Australians. The Voice would not be able to veto the enactment of such laws, or change government policies however. The Voice would be made up of 16 or 18 members, who would either be elected directly or come from the regional and local Voice bodies. On 9th January 2021 Minister Wyatt announces a second stage of co-design meetings lasting four months with more consultation with Indigenous people. The final report will be ready between June and August 2021.[68]

The University of New South Wales Indigenous Law Centre's analysis of 1435 of the public submissions to the co-design found that 82%

supported the constitutional enshrinement of a Voice to parliament, while an additional 5% gave in-principle support.

Norman and I are able to attend the Cairns consultation of the co-design team of Marcia Langton, Donna Odegaard and, Mayor of Yarrabah, Ross Andrews in April 2021 where discussions are robust. Concerns are raised re the Voice being legislated not enshrined in the constitution and Marcia makes the point that generally the feedback around Australia is get what is politically achievable now and build on it later.

State Government Voice and Treaties

However, the state governments are not waiting for the federal government which has been very slow to act. In 2016, Victoria, sets up an Aboriginal Treaty Working Group to lead two rounds of community consultations, which leads to the creation of a First Peoples' Assembly. The role of the assembly will not be to negotiate treaties but will work with the state to develop a treaty framework for negotiations. Victoria also establishes a Treaty Advancement Commission to raise awareness among Victorians and promote a treaty.

In June 2018, the Northern Territory signs a memorandum of understanding with delegates of the four Indigenous land councils to work towards a treaty Mick Dodson AM, the former director of the National Centre for Indigenous Studies at the Australian National University, is appointed NT treaty commissioner and he is currently leading consultations with the Indigenous community.

On 16th July 2019, the Queensland government announces it will begin discussions with Indigenous people about a treaty called Tracks to Treaty. An independent Eminent Panel and Treaty Working Group, including Aboriginal and Torres Strait Islander and non-Indigenous representatives, spearheads the process with 22 consultation meetings across the state. Norman and I attend the one in Cairns and meet up with my old friend Cheryl Buchanan who is involved with consultations.

Norman's sister Joanne Radke is involved with consultations in SE Queensland.

The Treaty Working Group leads the formal public consultation process and provides a report to the Eminent Panel. There is significant support for a treaty. The recommendations to government in February 2020 are:

- The establishment of the First Nations Treaty Institute as an independent body to lead the Path to Treaty process
- The facilitation of a process of truth-telling and healing
- The building of capacity for First Nations to actively participate in the treaty process
- Deepening the understanding and engagement of the wider Queensland community in the Path to Treaty
- The adequate resourcing of these actions through the establishment of a First Nations Treaty Future Fund
- The placing before Parliament in the first half of 2020 a Bill to further the Path to Treaty, establish the First Nations Treaty Institute and the First Nations Treaty Future Fund.

On 14th February 2021, the Qld government announces a Treaty Advancement Committee with Dr Jackie Huggins AM and Mick Gooda as co-chairs. They were co-chairs of the Treaty Working Group. They consult with the Cairns community on 29th April. The government's August 2020 response to the Path to Treaty report includes initiatives in a number of areas towards reconciliation, healing from the wounds of the past and having a more just relationship. It notes that in 2010, they made an addition to the preamble to the Queensland Constitution to honor Aboriginal and Torres Strait Islander peoples as the First Australians.

SA to Adopt First Indigenous Voice

On 7th May 2021, South Australia's Premier Steven Marshall announces plans for his state to be the first cab off the rank for an Indigenous Voice to parliament. It will be chaired by the state's Aboriginal engagement commissioner Roger Thomas. He will be joined by 12 other Aboriginal members. First Nations South Australians will be able to vote for six of the committee members, with the government to appoint the remaining six. After three years of operation, the SA Electoral Commission will hold a statewide ballot to elect the 12 Voice members. Legislation to establish the Voice is to be introduced into parliament in 2021.

Agreement Making

A number of Indigenous Land Use Agreements (ILUAs) are negotiated between First Nations, government and corporations under the native title legislation. These can be used as a basis for treaty making. The most impressive of these is the Noongar agreement in WA. The South West Native Title Settlement, with six Noongar groups, involves around 30,000 Noongar people and covers approximately 200,000 square kilometers. The full details of the South West Native Title Settlement are recorded in six ILUAs.

Impetus to Remove Racial Discrimination from the Constitution Lost

Norman and I are surprised and concerned that recommendations from a number of bodies re removing racial discrimination from the constitution seem to have lost momentum as the debate has moved on to Voice, Treaty and Truth. The Expert Panel, the Boomerang Petition and the Joint Select Committee agree with the 1988 Constitutional Commission recommendation that s25 be repealed "because it is no longer appropriate to include in the Constitution a provision which contemplates the disqualification of members of a race from voting."[69]

The 1967 Referendum amends s51 by deleting the words "other than the Aboriginal race in any State," thereby giving the Commonwealth Government power to make special laws relating to First Nations people. This was a desired outcome by First Nations people at the time because of racist state legislation and policy. This power now underpins much legislation including the *Native Title Act 1993*. What is problematic is that s51 could be used to support a law that discriminates against First Nations people. There is now general agreement by the 1988 Constitutional Commission, the Expert Panel, the Boomerang Petition and the Joint Select Committee that it should be amended or repealed and replaced. The Expert Panel recommends the repeal of s51(xxvi) and the inclusion of a new s51A, with this new section outlined earlier.

Martin Hinton, QC, Solicitor-General of South Australia 2008-2016 writes, "The racist taint that ss 25 and 51(xxvi) bring to our Constitution is inextricably linked to our treatment of the First Australians."[70]

We are still waiting. It is a long haul. Momentum to deal with these issues of racial discrimination in our constitution needs to gather pace.

Australian Prime Minister Kevin Rudd (R) signs a card for an invited guest during a reception at Parliament House in Canberra on 13th February, 2008. Rudd had earlier on 13th February delivered an historic apology to the Aboriginal people for injustices committed over two centuries of white settlement. (Invited guest is Lorna "Nanna Nungala" Fejo whose story the PM quoted in his apology. Author is in photo also.) Photo GREG WOOD/AFP via Getty Images

Norman Miller Presents His Painting 'From Sorry to Journey of Healing' to Former PM Kevin Rudd in Reconciliation Week 26th May 2011 at Parliament House Canberra
photo Darren Coyne *Koori Mail*

Barbara with Prime Minister Tony Abbott at Launch of Journey of Recognition Melbourne 26th May 2013
photo supplied

Barbara with Michael Long at Launch of Journey of Recognition Walk Melbourne 26th May 2013
photo Norman Miller

L-R Abe Schwarz Barbara Miller Alf Turner (Uncle Boydie) Presenting Replica of William Cooper Petition to Governor-General Sir Peter Cosgrove Canberra, May 2014 photo David Jack

Munganbana Norman Miller Presenting His Boomerang Petition to MPs at Parliament House Canberra 27th November 2013 L-R Warren Entsch, Speaker Bronwyn Bishop and Ken Wyatt photo Geoff Bagnell *National Indigenous Times*

Munganbana Norman Miller and Author Presenting Final Signatures on Petition to the Hon Warren Entsch MP and the Speaker and Clerk of the House at Parliament House Canberra February 2016 photo supplied

Munganbana Norman Miller's Campaign for Voice Treaty Truth Cairns Festival 2019
photo Barbara Miller

Epilogue

Barbara and Norman in front of Dreams and Visions painting 2021
photo Lillian Miller

I want to conclude with the story of a large canvas three-piece painting of Norman's called *Dreams and Visions*. He paints under his Jirrbal name of Munganbana which means Mountain Water":

"I am the black face peering out. My wife is the white face looking back at me. We are a reflection of each other. Someone once said we are like twins; one black and one white, but one in spirit. Seeing the same vision. Dreaming the same dream.

Boomerangs symbolize a cycle of discovery. We continually venture out and try new things. Then we return and regroup before we go exploring again. Hands reach out to the sky as if reaching for the infinite possibilities of our imagination. The field of dreams and visions is broad and we need to be determined, committed and dedicated if we are to fulfil them. They give us purpose and direction and keep us on course in the face of obstacles.

Intricate patterns dance about either side of us. If we think outside the square, we can make a difference and have influence. We aspire to greater heights, align with our Creator, embrace humanity and hope to leave the world a better place for having been here."

I'd love a review on Amazon and/or Goodreads. Here is the amazon link to this book – https://www.amazon.com/dp/B095SDW3LY

And the link to my Goodreads page - https://www.goodreads.com/author/show/17901589.Barbara_Miller

Check me out on facebook - https://www.facebook.com/Barbara-Miller-Books-479991872149265/

Website - www.barbara-miller-books.com

Appendices

Press Articles Mentioning Author from 1974-1995 Plus one *NQ Messagestick* Article

ABORIGINAL RIGHTS

White light for black days

BARBARA MILLER is a quietly effective champion of Aboriginal causes

BY GREG ROBERTS

For the past 25 years, Barbara Miller has laboured tirelessly to improve the lot of Aborigines in remote northern Queensland communities. She has been a key figure in moves by displaced Aborigines to return to tribal lands and has been instrumental in highlighting domestic violence and other social problems in Aboriginal society.

The Cairns-based psychologist and social researcher has twice married Aborigines and has an Aboriginal child.

Few white activists have achieved the level of respect and affection that Miller, 44, enjoys in indigenous communities across the state. For several years, she was director of the state's peak Aboriginal body – the Aboriginal Co-ordinating Council (ACC). Successive governments have regarded her as one of the most articulate, if least public, exponents of Aboriginal and Islander causes.

Controversy: The life of Barbara Joyce Miller has seldom been without controversy. She was raised in the coal city of Ipswich, near Brisbane, and studied medicine at the University of Queensland for just 12 months before dropping out in 1970, effectively to become a full-time political activist. (She resumed studies much later, snaring degrees in sociology and psychology.)

Then Barbara Russell, she was a familiar figure around the university, handing out leaflets for a radical left-wing Christian group, Revitalisation of Christianity, which was the bane of mainstream churches at the time.

In 1972 she gave away almost all her possessions and hitch-hiked to Canberra where she set up the Canberra Christian Community, a commune that served as a base for the Aboriginal tent embassy demonstrations outside Parliament House. In an unrelated demonstration, she was arrested for inciting young men not to register for national service; her first aeroplane journey was spent handcuffed to a policewoman en route to Silverwater Jail in Sydney. She remains the only woman to be jailed for anti-conscription activities in Australia.

Miller was credited with persuading the ALP national conference on the Gold Coast in 1973 to vote for an end to Australian economic relations with South Africa. Bob Hawke, then the ACTU chief, was among delegates who were greatly impressed with the softly spoken but powerfully persuasive lobbyist. Miller later helped organise a campaign against the Portuguese colonial presence in Angola and Mozambique.

Miller moved to Cairns in 1974 to research Aboriginal issues for the aid group International Development Action. She became deeply involved in the plight of an Aboriginal community forced at gunpoint in 1963 to quit its traditional land at Mapoon, 80 kilometres north of Weipa, to make way for bauxite-mining leases. She lobbied hard for the Aborigines to be allowed to return to Mapoon from the far-flung reserves they had been sent to, and for federal funds to facilitate their return.

Counsellor Leslie Baird (centre) doing his rounds in Cairns

PHOTOGRAPHS BY DAVID MAY

Miller's campaign was vigorously opposed by the Bjelke-Petersen government at every step. Despite being invited by Aborigines to visit one Cape York reserve, she was placed under house arrest by a state official upon her arrival. Ultimately she prevailed. Mapoon today is home to a vibrant community of 60 people.

"The Mapoon story taught me a lot about the effect of racism on Aboriginal people," Miller says. "People who had been forced from their land had died in sorrow. It made me determined to remain involved and assist where I could."

While the Mapoon campaign was in full swing Barbara began living with, and later married, Mick Miller, a prominent Cairns Aboriginal leader. Mick had separated from his first wife, Pat O'Shane, who later became Australia's first Aboriginal magistrate. Barbara helped raise Mick's two daughters – the actor Lydia Miller, and Marilyn, an accomplished dancer – and the couple had a son, Michael, who is now 16.

Mick and Barbara Miller were a formidable combination. Together they established the North Queensland Land Council, which fought a series of pitched battles with the state government and mining companies over land rights. Their home in the leafy Cairns suburb of Edge Hill was a bustling hive of political activity and they scored some notable victories, such as persuading the Dutch company Billiton to forgo its Cape York bauxite leases in the late '70s.

Frequently, however, the council and its supporters – which at times included the federal government – found themselves outmanoeuvred by the Bjelke-Petersen administration. For instance, John Koowarta, an elder from the

Aurukun community, won a lengthy series of court battles to gain title to his clan's traditional land at the Archer River on Cape York, only to have the state declare the area a national park.

One of Miller's regular sparring partners was Bob Katter Jnr, former Aboriginal affairs minister in the state's National Party government. In an indication of the respect she commands on both sides of politics, Katter says he greatly admires Miller despite their differences. "She was one of the few white people in Aboriginal affairs who was really sincere and really cared," Katter says. "She wasn't in the do-gooder class. She stood out like a neon light in everything she was involved in."

Barbara's marriage with Mick ended in 1988 (they remain friends), but her work continued, albeit in a less activist fashion. In a ground-breaking report commissioned by the Royal Commission into Black Deaths in Custody in 1990, she chronicled an appalling level of domestic violence and child abuse and neglect in remote North Queensland communities. The report detailed how young children and grandmothers were being raped and how many women lived in constant fear of being bashed. It was a sensitive issue which few had previously dared to tackle.

Other major works by Miller include a comprehensive report funded by the Criminology Research Council on the legal system as it pertains to Aborigines. Her advice on Aboriginal relations has been sought out by groups ranging from the Wet Tropics Management Authority to the Queensland Police Service. Most recently, she completed an exhaustive study of the tenure of Aboriginal land in Queensland for the ACC.

Married: Barbara is now married to another Aborigine, Norman Miller, a distant relation of Mick's and a drugs and alcohol counsellor with the Bama Healing Centre in Cairns. Barbara helped Norman kick his own addiction to alcohol.

"She helped me understand how it had destroyed my self-esteem and was destroying the self-esteem of Aboriginal people," Norman says. "Aboriginal people trust her. They've never thought of Barbara as just another white person coming along to tell them what to do."

Barbara Miller: "I feel I have made a contribution"

Norman Miller (right) chats with Myrna Shortjoe, a member of the local community in Cairns

Barbara Miller's life has been so closely intertwined with Aborigines for so long that she does not always feel comfortable in white society. She has been told by Aboriginal friends and relatives many times that although her skin is white, her heart is black.

"I always seem to have had a tremendous empathy with Aboriginal people," she says. "I think and feel the same way they do, or at least the Aboriginal people I know." She nominates commitment to family and community as the Aboriginal traits she most closely identifies with.

Nonetheless, Miller says her involvement has "not always been a bed of roses". Her high profile has engendered hostility and jealousy among Aborigines. She was once accused of embezzling ACC funds, but was exonerated by an audit she requested. On odd occasions, she has felt that her physical safety was at risk.

Arrows fly from both sides, however. Her mother in Ipswich refused to attend either of her weddings and had great difficulty accepting both her Aboriginal sons-in-law. "She did not regard herself as racist and was fairly typical of Australians in that sense," Miller says. "She has changed now."

Miller, who has worked as a university lecturer since leaving the ACC in 1991 and now runs her own consultancy, is dismayed at what she claims is a high level of racism – much of it unconscious – in the wider community.

In one survey she undertook for a university thesis, she found that a large majority of Cairns residents regarded Aborigines as "dirty" and "lazy". She says such attitudes make it harder for Aborigines to break out of a "vicious cycle of violence" that prevails in many communities.

Miller is not optimistic about the immediate future. "It is easier to get changes to legislation than changes to the quality of lives," she says. "I have real fears about the situation in relation to domestic violence and other problems. There are lots of programs out there, but they aren't making a lot of headway ... I fear it will take generations to resolve."

Response: She adds, however, that the Keating government's response to the High Court's Mabo decision – the national land rights tribunal and social justice package – is a major step forward.

Miller is now scaling down her involvement with Aboriginal issues. "I feel I have made a contribution," she says. "I no longer believe that the [activist] role in this area is appropriate for non-Aborigines. "I think it is important for their self-determination that they do that themselves." ■

THE CAIRNS POST 15/5/91

New course for community police

By staff reporter
DIANE McKEAN

THE launch of a unique Aboriginal and Islander community police scheme could help curb rising crime rates by emphasising the need for "pro-active" methods of control, the Far Northern Assistant Police Commissioner, Mr Ken Strohfeldt, said yesterday.

Mr Strohfeldt said the two-week community police training course in Cairns was the first of its kind in the State and promised to establish career paths for community police.

The first block of the course, opened by the Deputy Police Commissioner, Mr Bob Kirkpatrick, yesterday, was attended by eight community police from Yarrabah, Aurukun, Lockhart River and Weipa South.

Mr Strohfeldt said community police previously had to operate with no training and a lack of opportunity.

He said the course not only covered theory but also involved practical work with State officers in beat duty, patrols and watch house duties.

He said the training would enable State officers to learn and respect the specific customs and laws of the communities while the community police received valuable insight into the practices and procedures of the Queensland Police Service.

Mr Kirkpatrick said community police had to deal with people on a grass roots level, with emphasis on keeping people out of jail and developing alternative social strategies.

Wherever possible, alternatives to the watch house or jail had to be used, he said.

He said social work was a large part of a police officer's job and community police had to be able to handle and solve a whole array of social problems.

Extra training would help community police to take up a historic role in the development of the Aboriginal and Islander communities.

The secretariat director of the Aboriginal Co-ordinating Council, Mrs Barbara Miller, said community police were an important step towards the process of communities governing themselves and increased training and career pathing would help facilitate this.

She said community police could be a part of the process of the community taking its own future back into its own hands. Increased training meant the adoption of crime prevention skills which would enable community police to tackle problems involving alcohol and juvenile crime.

Aboriginal and Islander community police were employed and selected by the local council and supervised by the State police, she said.

Aboriginal councils were in a unique situation in that they not only had local government responsibilities but also had to maintain law and order through the use of by-laws. A lack of funds for community police had led to frustration among its ranks, Mrs Miller said.

• Constable Leonard Graham — left — of the Yarrabah Community Police is pictured yesterday with the Deputy Police Commissioner, Bob Kirkpatrick, at the launch of the two-week community police training course in Cairns. In the background are community police from Aurukun, Lockhart River and Weipa South who are in Cairns to attend the first block of the course.

White woman, black heart

When the inquiry into Aboriginal deaths in custody wanted first-hand information on the plight of Aborigines in the Far North, there was only one person for the job, and she was white. **Desmond Zwar** reports.

IT is a sunny lunch-time in the Cairns Hilton. Barbara Miller is speaking quietly and unemotionally about her experience of the scattered Aboriginal communities of Cape York. What she is talking about would put most of the diners off their lobster or barramundi: alcoholism, self-mutilation, depression and despair. Aborigines, she says, as a powerless group, "have turned their rage in on themselves".

The result, she says, is the long list of cell suicides, self-injury, homicide, domestic violence, child abuse and neglect.

Ms Miller, 40, secretarial director of the Aboriginal Coordinating Council in Cairns, has been fighting for justice for black Australians since 1970. She married one — Mick Miller, a schoolteacher she met at a meeting on injustice. They have an 11-year-old son, but are no longer together.

Ms Miller appears preoccupied, speaks in a soft monotone and smiles for the first time when she confides that Aborigines in the communities her council represents call her "Aunty".

The Aborigines living in the scattered communities on Cape York trust her, and for her report they confided their problems, fears and despair as they never had before to a European. She had learned from the years with Mick, she says, how to understand their feelings. "They are very good at reading body language. They are different from Europeans in so many ways.

"They are more family oriented, less individualistic, less selfish; always prepared to share what they have.

"They have a spiritual level we do not begin to understand; they read a lot more into what is not said than is said."

Why do they trust her?

She smiled again. "I helped Mick set up the North Queensland Land Council in 1975 and they got to know me, I suppose. Even though we are not together any more, they give me the respect and recognition of the relationship. It began for him when a well-known Aurukun identity, Jack Spear, adopted him as a boy, and it remains, for both of us. I therefore have a whole network of relationships.

"I know I'm not Aboriginal," she says. "It's just that I feel in tune with Aboriginal people. I relate to them as my family.

"I have felt that I have a black heart — as people keep telling me — for the last 10 years."

She had not studied Aboriginal affairs academically. "My feeling is intuitive. It was always there. It was obviously one of the things that brought Mick Miller and I together.

"I speak a few words of Wikmunkan. I would particularly like my son, Michael, to learn his language."

It isn't only because she was married to an Aborigine that Ms Miller had an understanding of Aborigines, says Mick Connolly, 38, an Aboriginal councillor at Yarrabah community (population 800) on the opposite side of the bay to Cairns. He says of her report: "There are certain people who deal with Aborigines in a detached manner, whereas Barbara almost becomes an Aborigine; she can really feel for the people.

"She not only understands Aboriginal ways, but when she puts it on paper, all she has to do is reach within herself; she's got it all in her head, and has had it there for so long."

At a recent meeting at the council's Cairns office, Gladys Tybingoompa, 44, and Alison Woolla, 42, both from Aurukun community on Cape York, talked of "Aunty" Barbara's "black heart".

Gladys: "Her outside appearance is white. But she has a black heart and a black mind. Even though Aunty Barbara and Uncle Mick are not together now, she never put her back on us. She is loyal. We trust her and she trusts us. Some of the things that Aunty Barbara has done are personal and I would not speak to people outside the clan about them. Within the clan, yes. But not to you. It would be an embarrassment.

"When she brings Michael, her son, to Aurukun they give him gifts and take him fishing and hunting. They wait for him now. When she arrives it is like a queen arriving. A tribal leader."

Alison Woolla, looking steadily across at Ms Miller: "They say that maybe you were a child somewhere else, a black child; and your spirit died and you were born into another world from us and you have come again to us . . ."

Ms Miller, suddenly emotional: "Well I wasn't going to say it; but that's how I feel!"

BARBARA Miller, who the legal system turned to in 1990 for help, was not so popular with the authorities in the early 1970s. Then, she was listed by the police as a trouble-maker during the anti-Springbok demonstrations, where she received her first understanding of apartheid and how much of it paralleled what was happening to Australian Aborigines. She was arrested in Canberra for "inciting young men not to register for the draft for Vietnam". She went to jail in Sydney for refusing to pay a resulting fine.

At Queensland University, where she was supposed to be studying first-year medicine, she became friendly with the only Aboriginal girl student on campus and spent most of her time writing and distributing pamphlets. She later went back to her education and achieved degrees in psychology and sociology.

"In 1970 I went to an Assembly of God church service and something happened; an experience," she recalls. "I became a Christian. From around that time I found myself driven, I knew I had to work for Aboriginal justice for the rest of my life."

Today she is in charge of an office that is the "umbrella" of Cape York Aboriginal community councils; advising them on their socio-economic development, and acting as an on-the-spot observer of what is going wrong in the sometimes depressing rows of weatherboard houses.

Mr Lou Wyvill, whose royal commission hearings have run for more than a year, trying to get at the underlying reason Aborigines suicide, asked Ms Miller to go out among the people and get additional evidence for him.

What she found, she says, is that when anger and frustration at "seeing no light at the end of the tunnel" becomes too much, an Aborigine often smashes glass louvres in his house (which can be home for up to 20 people), deliberately cutting his wrists and his body. It is rage turned inward.

Black crime in Australia is not directed against whites as it is in the United States, but against other blacks, generally against the Aborigine's own family; his wife, girlfriend or de facto are the most likely victims. Men are fighting their brothers, fathers and uncles and bashing their mothers, she says. Women are running away from sons-in-law and grandmothers are being raped by their grandsons.

'They say that maybe you were a child somewhere else, a black child; and your spirit died and you were born into another world from us and you have come again to us . . .'

"One woman said: 'When I am angry, I reach the point where I can't get rid of anger any other way besides smashing things or getting stuck into somebody.'

"When an Aboriginal woman finds her home is not a safe place from assault and psychological violence, where does she go? Women's shelters do not exist on most of the communities. There's nowhere to go except hide in the bush overnight, seek refuge with friends or relatives (where she is sure to be found), or spend the night in the watchhouse or hospital."

Alcohol — consumed in canteens and bringing in $600,000 a year to some communities — or bought from sly-grog dealers, does not in itself, says Ms Miller, cause violence. "Alcohol is used by Aborigines as an anxiety reducing agent; to cope with the stresses attendant on colonisation and racism. Alcohol abuse has become a way of defying white authority.

"I have seen children hanging about outside the canteen drinking glasses of beer. It is nothing to see children with $20 notes in gambling games on pay or pension days. Children are neglected; they arrive at school or pre-school unfed or under-nourished, tired and with short concentration spans, especially after pay or pension nights. Some children have difficulty sleeping at night because of the noise of drinking and/or fighting. Neglect and lack of supervision are real problems.

"When I visited Community C I was told that cases of sexually transmitted diseases are dealt with every day, occurring in children as young as five. It is usually teenage boys who are the perpetrators, abusing young girls and boys. Some young boys are violated with sharp sticks. The children won't talk about it and are receiving no help besides medical treatment. The postmaster at Community C told me that between $4000 and $5000 in COD orders for pornographic videos came every week from Canberra at the request of both black and white viewers.

"In another Cape York community, two teenagers raped a five-year-old boy after watching a pornographic video."

Ms Miller's investigations have also brought suggested remedies — some already being put into action. "Because Aboriginal men no longer have initiation as a 'marker' between youth and manhood, young men are using a jail sentence as that marker. Initiation is now rarely practised in North Queensland and the first time a male Aboriginal gets drunk or goes to jail tends to fill that vacuum. We are hoping to get together with elders and young people to do something about a traditional marker; for some it might mean bringing back initiation."

Another suggestion: "dry" houses where alcohol may not be consumed. And "tough love", a scheme first tried among the American Indians "who have many problems matching Aborigines' problems".

"Most programs deal with the person who is the alcoholic," says Ms Miller, who does not drink. "'Tough love' is directed at the spouse. She needs to take responsibility for her own life and not be overly responsible for the alcoholic's life. Because that tends to happen; the cover up for the alcoholic, to save face. In 'tough love' the spouse is advised to say: 'OK, if you come home drunk, I'm not going to cook your dinner.' When he asks for money for grog, she won't give it to him. It means punch-ups; but they get punched up whether they cook the dinner or not; whether they give money or not.

"But we are finding that it is working; they are not always getting punched up. What is happening is that the spouse is getting her self-esteem back and is starting to take responsibility for herself, not just her husband. And this is forcing the husband to take responsibility for himself."

Ms Miller has been offered highly paid jobs. She has politely refused, preferring to work every day in an under-budgeted, understaffed office in Cairns that is looked on with respect by both Aboriginal communities and the Government.

"I guess it's my destiny."

Is she happy? "Oh," she laughs. "Very much so. And I have only recently found I am able to forgive the churches and the missionaries for what they did, possibly with the best will in the world, to the Aborigines in the early days. Children were separated into dormitories and taken away from their mothers. It was terrible. And now we have that legacy."

Family ties: Barbara Miller with her son, Michael, — "I feel in tune with Aboriginal people. I relate to them as my family." Picture: RUSSELL FRANCIS

September 1990: Barbara Miller visits Aborigines Valerie and Shirley Wolmby of Aurukun.

A horror story uncovered

This is part of the horror story Barbara Miller uncovered for the royal commission and outlined in her 107-page report.

- That in some communities the average death age for males is 44, 27 years younger than the average Queensland male dies. For women it is 43, 34 years earlier than Queensland women generally.
- That Aboriginal community children are seven times more likely to commit assaults than white children;
- That sexual offences are 11 times more likely to be committed; robbery is 26 times more prevalent; property damage nine times greater; weapon offences 41 times greater.
- Aboriginal children from the communities are 17 times more likely to appear before the courts for Liquor Act offences than Queensland children as a whole.

OCTOBER 14, 1990 The Sunday Mail

The blonde who dropped a bombshell . . .

'70s rebel is stirring for justice

By DESMOND ZWAR

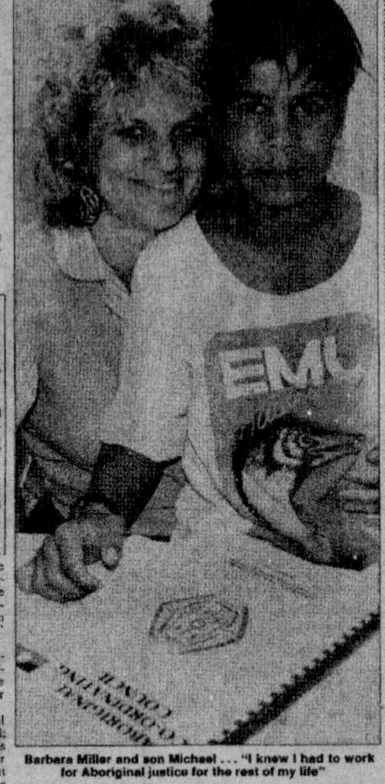

Barbara Miller and son Michael . . . "I knew I had to work for Aboriginal justice for the rest of my life"

SHE is white. She has intense blue eyes, cascading blonde curls and a beautiful face. The people she has devoted her life to are black.

It is lunchtime in the sunny Cairns Hilton, and Barbara Miller, secretariat director of the Aboriginal Co-Ordinating Council in Cairns, is quietly and unemotionally talking about alcoholism, self-mutilation, depression and despair; going over the shock report she has just delivered to the Royal Commission into Aboriginal Deaths in Custody, which has warned that Aborigines "as a powerless group, have turned their rage in on themselves".

As a result, she says, there has been the long list of cell suicides, self-injury, homicide, domestic violence, child abuse and neglect; and alcoholism.

Her face devoid of make-up apart from the highlighter intensifying the blue of her eyes, she looked to be in her late 20s or early 30s. She is 40, and has been fighting for justice for black Australians since 1970.

She married one — Mick Miller, a dashing, moustachioed school teacher she met at a meeting on injustice. They have an 11-year-old son, Michael, but are no longer together.

Barbara appears preoccupied, speaks in a soft monotone and smiles for the first time when she confides that Aborigines in the communities her council represents call her "Auntie".

This is the horror story "Auntie" Barbara uncovered in three weeks' intense investigation for the Royal Commission and outlined in her 107-page report:

- That in some communities there was an average age of death of 44 years for males — 27 years less than the average age of death for other Queensland males; and that the average age of death for females was 43 years — 34 years less than Queensland women generally.
- That assaults are seven times more likely to be committed by children from Aboriginal communities than white communities; that sexual offences are 11 times more likely to be committed; robbery is 26 times greater; break-and-enter 19 times more prevalent; property damage nine times greater; weapons offences 41 times greater.
- And Aboriginal children from communities are 17 times more likely to appear for Liquor Act offences than Queensland children as a whole.

"Queensland Aboriginal communities are clearly in a state of crisis," she concluded.

Because Aborigines living in the scattered communities on Cape York trust her, they had confided their problems, fears and despair, as they never had before to a European.

She had learned from the years with Mick how to understand their feelings. "They are very good at reading body language. They are different from Europeans in so many ways," she said, toying with her lunch.

"They are more family oriented, less individualistic, less selfish; always prepared to share what they have, often to their own detriment.

"They have a spiritual level we do not begin to understand; they read a lot more into what is not said than is said. However they can get stressed and uptight and have loss of sleep, just like we do."

Why do they trust her?

She smiled again. "I helped Mick set up the North Queensland Land Council in 1975 and they got to know me, I suppose. Even though we are not together any more, they give me the respect and recognition of the relationship.

"It began for him when a well-known Aurukun identity called Jack Spear adopted him as a boy, and it remains, for both of us. I therefore have a whole network of relationships."

Mick Connolly, 38, an Aboriginal councillor at Yarrabah (pop 900) community on the opposite side of the bay to Cairns, said when he read her report: "It isn't just because she was married to an Aborigine that Barbara has an understanding of Aborigines. Her attitude is such that even if she hadn't married Mick Miller, she still would have been accepted.

"She not only understands Aboriginal ways, but when she puts it on paper it is the skill of her research coming out. Her report is spot on.

"She is one of those white people who almost have more knowledge of us than we do ourselves."

Barbara Miller, the beautiful young blonde, was listed by the police as a troublemaker during the anti-Springbok demonstrations, where she received her first understanding of apartheid and how much of it parallele'd what was happening to Australian Aborigines.

She was arrested in Canberra for "inciting young men not to register for the draft for Vietnam" and went to jail in Sydney for refusing to pay a resultant fine.

At Queensland University where she was supposed to be studying first-year medicine, she became friendly with the only Aboriginal girl student on campus and spent most of her time writing and distributing pamphlets.

She later went back to her self-education and achieved psychology and sociology degrees.

"In 1970 I went to an Assembly of God church service and something happened; an experience. I became a Christian. From around that time I found myself driven. I knew I had to work for Aboriginal justice for the rest of my life."

Today she is in charge of an office that is the "umbrella" of Cape York Aboriginal community councils; advising them on their socio-economic development and acting as an on-the-spot observer of what is going wrong in the sometimes depressing row of weatherboard houses with broken louvres, often clustered around a canteen.

Is she happy? "Oh," she laughs. "Very much so. And I have only recently found I am able to forgive the churches and the missionaries for what they did, possibly with the best will in the world, to the Aborigines in the early days. Children were separated into dormitories and taken away from their mothers. It was terrible. And now we have that legacy."

Alcohol — consumed in canteens and bringing in $600,000 a year in some communities — or purchased from sly-grog dealers, does not in itself, says Barbara Miller, cause violence.

"Alcohol is used by Aborigines as an anxiety reducing agent; to cope with the stresses attendant on colonisation and racism. Alcohol abuse has become a way of defying white authority.

"I have seen children hanging about outside the canteen drinking glasses of beer. It is nothing to see children with $20 notes in gambling games at Aurukun on pay or pension days.

"Children are neglected; they arrive at school or pre-school unfed or under-nourished, tired and with short concentration spans, especially after pay or pension nights."

Barbara Miller has, with her qualifications and her experience, been offered highly-paid jobs. She has politely refused them, preferring to work every day in an under-budgeted, understaffed office in Cairns that is looked on with respect by both Aboriginal communities and government.

"I guess it's my destiny," she says.

A substitute for initiation

☐ BARBARA Miller found that many young Aborigines used a jail sentence as a sort of substitute for tribal initiation.

"Initiation is now rarely practised in north Queensland and the first time a male Aboriginal gets drunk or goes to jail, tends to fill that vacuum," she said.

"We are hoping to get together with elders and young people to do something about a traditional marker; for some it might mean bringing back initiation."

Where 'tough love' means 'tough, love'

☐ BARBARA Miller's suggestions to combat Aboriginal drinking include "dry" houses, where alcohol may not be consumed and "tough love", where boozers' wives go on strike.

"Most programs deal with the person who is the alcoholic," said Barbara. "Tough love is directed at the spouse. She needs to take responsibility for her own life and not be overly responsible for the alcoholic's life. Because that tends to happen, they cover up for the alcoholic, to save face.

"In tough love the spouse is advised to say, 'OK, if you come home drunk, I'm not going to cook your dinner'. When he asks for money for grog, she won't give it to him.

"It means punch-ups; but they get punched up whether they cook the dinner or not; whether they give money or not.

"But we are finding that it is working; they are not always getting punched up. What is happening is that the spouse is getting her self-esteem back and is starting to take responsibility for herself, not just her husband. And this is forcing the husband to take responsibility for nimself."

HUMAN Rights reformist Barbara Miller knows what prison is like: See page 3. FRONT PAGE

She knows what prison is like

THE EXAMINER 6/10/90

THE North Queensland woman, who wrote the comprehensive Aboriginal Co-ordinating Council submission on Aboriginal deaths in custody, has experienced racial discrimination firsthand.

By EUGENIE NAVARRE

• BARBARA and son Michael — A Russell Francis photograph.

She also knows what it is like to be behind bars.

Cultured, softly spoken Barbara Miller of Cairns has a son, Michael, by her former husband Aboriginal activist, Mick Miller.

The North Queensland psychologist, sociologist, mediator, mother and influential force in the Aboriginal rights movement wrote the comprehensive report in her spare time.

She said Aboriginal deaths in custody were now recognised as a national disgrace.

"When people are committing suicide at between three and 16 times the Qld average it is a human rights issue," she said.

"When I've gone to rent accomodation I've not taken him with me because of discrimination."

She says Aboriginal people are at a disadvantage when it comes to acquiring accomodation.

"People don't want Aboriginal people in their flats and apartments," she added.

Since 1989, Barbara has worked as Secretarial Director of the Aboriginal Co-ordination Council in Cairns.

Her Aboriginal deaths in custody submission released last week includes 211 submissions for Government action.

She says writing the submission was a traumatic experience — even more so than being thrown into prison for her humanitarian ideals as a student.

• CONTINUED P6

Reformist speaks out

• FROM P3

"The information was so horrific, even with all my experience in Aboriginal affairs, I was astounded at what I discovered. I burst into tears many times and found it hard to continue," Barbara said.

"When I looked at the childhood experiences of the Aboriginals who died in custody, their parents and family had died when they were just children.

"When arrested their life had entirely crumbled."

It was while the Springbox demonstrations were raging in 1971 that the then young student Barbara Russell recognised the plight of the black people of this country.

A sense of justice drove her on — she committed her life to the cause and there was no turning back.

She was arrested in Canberra in 1972 for inciting young men not to register for the Vietnam draft.

Barbara became the only woman in Australia ever to be arrested on a National Service related offence and was mobbed at Sydney Airport as she was taken to Silverwater Prison for a 10 day stay.

It offered personal knowledge of the horrors of life behind bars and would be a blueprint for the work that would follow including the recent Aboriginal deaths in custody submission.

The reformer puts Aboriginal deaths in custody down to violence perpetuated by white Australians over the last 200 years.

"It is a violence that continues today — a structural violence of race relations," she said.

"A violence that carries into many aspects of daily living from school trauma for non-white children to employment and accomodation problems."

The solution, she believes, is for the Aboriginal people to get in touch with their own spirituality, culture and identity through land rights, self determination and sovereignty.

"White Australians can offer 'respect' and opportunities for the Aboriginal people to run their own lives," she said.

'h. 52 6666 Classifieds 51 3333, 31 3333 109th YEAR FRIDAY, SEPTEMBER 28, 1990 48 PAGES No. 27,538

Aboriginals triple State death rate

THE death rate in Far Northern Aboriginal communities was three times the State average, according to an Aboriginal Co-Ordinating Council report released yesterday.

The 107-page report will be submitted to the Royal Commission into Aboriginal Deaths in Custody and includes 211 recommendations for action to prevent further Aboriginal deaths in custody and to generally improve conditions on Aboriginal communities.

The report says the overall death rate for Queensland was 6.81 per 1000 people in 1986 and 7.05 in 1987.

Figures for the period July 1986 to June 1987 published in the report show the death rate in the Aboriginal communities of Doomadgee, Yarrabah, Aurukun and Wujal Wujal was 22.39 per 1000 people.

This ranged from 27.11 per 1000 at Doomadgee, four times the Queensland rate, to 19.61 at Wujal Wujal.

In releasing the submission before about 50 Far Northern Aboriginal community and government representatives at the Pacific International Hotel in Cairns, the Member for Leichhardt, Mr John Gayler, said: "Here we are coming to the end of the 20th century where Aboriginal deaths account for almost three times the deaths in our European community. This cannot be tolerated."

The report said another major concern was the difference in average life expectancies between Aboriginals in communities studied and that of Queenslanders.

"On average, Aboriginal people from these communities have only 60 per cent of the lifespan of their Queensland counterparts to look forward to," the report says.

Written by ACC secretariat director Ms Barbara Miller, in consultation with Aboriginal communities, the submission suggested a permanent body be set up to oversee the recommendations of the Royal Commission.

The commissioner, Mr Lew Wyvill, QC, who conducted hearings into several Far Northern Aboriginal deaths in custody, said he was pleased with the submission's recommendations.

Mr Gayler said while he did not agree with the submission in its entirety, he supported the implementation of most of the recommendations and said everyone should be made aware of the facts.

The submission included the following major recommendations concerning Aboriginal community policing:

- An assessment needed to be made of whether Queensland Aboriginal communities were over-policed;
- Aboriginal councils should sit on interview panels to select State police who wish to work on Aboriginal communities;
- The Police Department should set up a single Aboriginal unit to have responsibility for Aboriginal policing throughout Queensland;and
- Drunkenness should be decriminalised and sobering up centres used instead of jailing drunks overnight.

The next section claimed because Aboriginal people were powerless compared to whites, they had turned their rage inward, resulting in suicide, self-injury, homicide, domestic violence, child abuse and neglect and alcoholism. The final section looked at Aboriginals and the justice system, quoting the high rate of crime by Aboriginals compared to Queensland averages.

• Pictured at yesterday's meeting which released the Aboriginal Co-Ordinating Council report are ACC secretariat director, Ms Barbara Miller, and Hopevale councillor and the meeting chairman, Mr Cedric Deeral.

Don't let racist police work with Blacks: group

C/Mail 6/12/1990

POLICE who work in Aboriginal communities should be screened to weed out racists, a State Government advisory group said yesterday.

The Aboriginal Co-Ordinating Council secretariat director, Ms Barbara Miller, said she welcomed Queensland Police Department moves to involve Aboriginal councillors on the interview panel to select state police applying to work in Aboriginal communities.

"There should be a screening process to weed out racist people who cannot be retrained so that they do not work in areas of high Aboriginal population," Ms Miller said.

At the Queensland Aboriginal Law and Spirituality Conference in Brisbane yesterday, Ms Miller said it was necessary for state police to be trained at the police academy with in-service courses in Aboriginal culture, history and inter-cultural communication by Aboriginal people.

Police also needed to build up a rapport with young people. All the Aboriginal communities she had visited had requested community police training.

THE COURIER MAIL 6-12-1990

Need to weed racist police out of force

BRISBANE — Police selected to work in Aboriginal communities should be screened to weed out racists, an Aboriginal leader told a conference here yesterday.

Barbara Miller is the secretariat director of the Aboriginal Co-ordinating Council, a statutory body which advises the Queensland government on Aboriginal affairs.

"There should be a screening process to weed out racist police who cannot be retrained so that they do not work in areas of high Aboriginal population," Ms Miller told the conference on Aboriginal law and spirituality.

The four day conference, titled "Two Laws", will include experts on legal, cultural and spiritual issues and aims to highlight inadequacies of western law as it relates to Aboriginal people.

Ms Miller said it was necessary that State police be trained at the Police Academy at Oxley in Brisbane, but with in-service courses in Aboriginal culture and history and inter-cultural communication by Aboriginal people.

"Courses should be designed and taught, where possible, by Aboriginal people," she said.

Ms Miller said the ACC welcomed moves by the Queensland Police department to involve Aboriginal counsellors on the interview panel to select police applying to work in Aboriginal communities.

Foundation for Aboriginal and Islander Research Action chairman Mary Graham said she hoped the four-day conference would mark the start of a better understanding of Aborignal law and culture.

She said Aboriginal laws and culture had for too long been unrecognised by European settlers but it was these which had kept Aboriginal people together for 40,000 years without wars or police.

Federal Race Discrimination Commissioner Irene Moss told the conference Federal law was the only recourse available to people living in Queensland who have been discriminated against.

She said Queensland was the only Australian state without its own law protecting human rights and outlawing various forms of discrimination.

The Cairns Post, Thursday, December 6, 1990

Aboriginal leader want racism test for police

BRISBANE (AAP) — Police selected to work in Aboriginal communities should be screened to weed out racists, an Aboriginal leader told a conference here yesterday.

Ms Barbara Miller, of Cairns, is the secretariat director of the Aboriginal Co-ordinating Council (ACC), a statutory body which advises the Queensland Government on Aboriginal affairs.

"There should be a screening process to weed out racist police who cannot be retrained so that they do not work in areas of high Aboriginal population," Ms Miller told the conference on Aboriginal law and spirituality.

The four day conference, titled "Two Laws", will include experts on legal, cultural and spiritual issues and aims to highlight inadequacies of western law as it relates to Aboriginal people.

Ms Miller said it was necessary that State police be trained at the police academy at Oxley in Brisbane, but with in-service courses in Aboriginal culture and history and inter-cultural communication by Aboriginal people.

"Courses should be designed and taught, where possible, by Aboriginal people," she said.

Ms Miller said the ACC welcomed moves by the Queensland Police department to involve Aboriginal counsellors on the interview panel to select police applying to work in Aboriginal communities.

She said police needed to make more use of pro-active policing with preventative programs.

These activities, such as blue light discos and other recreational activities, would build a rapport with young people.

Ms Miller said all Aboriginal communities she had visited had requested community police training.

Foundation for Aboriginal and Islander Research Action chairman Ms Mary Graham said she hoped the four-day conference would mark the start of a better understanding of Aboriginal law and culture.

She said Aboriginal laws and culture had for too long been unrecognised by European settlers but it was these which had kept Aboriginal people together for 40,000 years without wars or police.

Federal Race Discrimination Commissioner Ms Irene Moss told the conference Federal law was the only recourse available to people living in Queensland who have been discriminated against.

She said Queensland was the only Australian state without its own law protecting human rights and outlawing various forms of discrimination. Ms Moss said she welcomed the State Government's move to introduce legislation on these issues.

Sex stories cause fights

C/Mail 27/10 1990 or 91

By MADONNA KING

ABORIGINAL Councils and community police want the spreading of rumors about people's sexual habits to be an offence, a national conference was told yesterday.

The Aboriginal Co-ordinating Council secretariat director, Ms Barbara Miller, said the tales caused fights in Aboriginal communities.

Ms Miller told a national community policing conference in Brisbane that support also existed for an offence for people using the name of dead person.

This was against Aboriginal culture, usually happened when a person was drunk, offended relatives and caused fights, she said.

A further by-law proposal to go to the Queensland Government with the support of councils and community police includes curfews to keep children off the streets.

"The Queensland Government should allow the Aboriginal councils who request it, to put a curfew in their bylaws as to when children should be off the street at night," Ms Miller said.

The ACC is an Aboriginal community body which has a statutory authority to advise the State Government on Aboriginal Affairs.

Ms Miller said a major law and order crisis existed among the State's Aboriginal communities.

"Aborigines are seven times more likely to appear on homicide charges, 50 times more likely to appear on major assault charges, 37 times more likely to be charged with rape (and) 38 times more likely to be charged with burglary," Ms Miller said.

Wide sweeping reforms were needed urgently to lessen the number of Aborigines in custody, Ms Miller said.

A screening process was needed to weed out racist police who could not be retrained.

Drunkenness should be decriminalised and most Aboriginal community watchhouses should be demolished and rebuilt.

Ms Miller said drinking alcohol together gave Aborgines a way to experience group solidarity and identity.

25/10 1990 ~~or 1991~~ TOWNSVILLE BULLETIN

Black statistics quoted at crime conference

BRISBANE — Aborigines were seven times more likely to be charged with murder and 37 times more likely to be charged with rape than Queenslanders as a whole, an Australian Institute of Criminology conference was told yesterday.

They also were 50 times more likely to appear in court on serious assault charges, according to Aboriginal Co-ordinating Council secretariat director Barbara Miller.

Ms Miller said going to jail for the first time seemed to have become an initiation into manhood for young Aboriginal men.

She said that only about 4 per cent of all Queensland children under 15 were Aboriginal, yet they made up about 47 per cent of those under Children's Services Act orders.

"Assaults ... are seven times more likely to be committed by children from Aboriginal communities than in Queensland as a whole," she said.

Ms Miller was addressing a three-day conference on police and the community in the 1990s. She said Aborigines were more likely to vent their anger against other blacks than towards whites.

"Black crime in Australia is not directed against whites as it is in the USA but against other blacks," she said.

"In fact it is generally directed against an Aboriginal's own family — his wife, girlfriend or de facto are the most likely victims.

"Because Aborigines are not as individualistic as Europeans, the boundary between self and family is not as clearly defined and family violence may be perceived as similar to violence against self."

Aborigines were 40 times more likely to be placed in police custody than non-Aborigines and many felt they were "political prisoners", jailed by the laws of a racist society, Ms Miller said.

Nevertheless, Queensland Aboriginal communities were facing a law and order crisis of major proportions. She recommended that governments legislate to decriminalise drunkenness, establish sobering-up centres on settlements and introduce harsher penalties for sly grogging.

"Sly grogging should be dealt with severely by confiscation of vehicles and boats and laws need to be changed to assist Aboriginal communities to deal with the problem," she said.

Changes to outdated Aboriginal council by-laws also were necessary.

"Aboriginal Councils and police at a number of communities have told me that they want curfews to keep their children off the streets in the early hours of the morning to protect them," Ms Miller said.

"They also want it to be an offence for a person to 'cart tales' that a person is sleeping around because it causes fights.

The Sydney Morning Herald 28.9.90

What do Aborigines do more than most? Die

By GREG ROBERTS

BRISBANE: Aborigines in North Queensland communities died at between three and four times the rate of other Queenslanders, lived about 30 years less, and suicided up to five times as frequently, according to a report released yesterday.

The comprehensive report documents a growing crisis involving appalling health conditions, high infant mortality levels, AIDS, domestic violence, pornographic videos and alcohol abuse.

The submission by the Queensland Aboriginal Co-ordinating Council to the Royal Commission into Aboriginal Deaths in Custody was released at a function in Cairns.

The report makes 211 recommendations to address what its author, Ms Barbara Miller, the council's director and a psychologist, describes as "the rapidly increasing breakdown in the whole fabric of Aboriginal society and culture".

Among the report's findings:

- The death rate for Queenslanders in 1987 was 7.05 per 1,000. In four communities surveyed by Ms Miller it averaged 22.39.
- In the same year the median age at death for Queensland males was 70.6 years and for females 77.6. In communities it was 43.9 and 43.5 years.
- Aboriginal men are four times more likely to die violently than other Queenslanders, and women 6.5 times. Violence, motor vehicle accidents and drowning caused 26 per cent of deaths in communities.
- Suicides accounted for 3.1 (males) and 1.1 (females) per cent of Queensland deaths in 1987. In the Yarrabah community, 15 per cent of deaths were suicide.
- In Cairns Hospital, delivering mothers from communities had a peri-natal mortality rate of 35 per 1,000 live births; the Australian average was 12.9.
- Two children at Doomadgee near Mt Isa drowned in "great puddles" of sewage around homes caused by an overtaxed sewerage system.

The report said that in another community, postal orders worth between $4,000 and $5,000 of pornographic videos arrived weekly. Young boys were violated with sticks and girls as young as five sexually assaulted after teenage boys watched videos.

Aboriginal children were 26 times more likely to commit robbery and extortion than other Queenslanders. The rate of assault offences by community children was 5.2 per 1,000 compared to 0.7 in Queensland. Community teenagers were 11 times more likely be charged with sexual offences.

Adult Aborigines on communities are seven times more likely to be charged with homicide than other Queenslanders, 50 times for major assault, 37 for rape, and 59 for other violation-of-persons offences.

Alcohol abuse was a major problem. In one community, 20 per cent of the total fortnightly social security payments ($25,000) was spent in just four hours of "swilling".

The report said the imprisonment rate on the Lockhart River community was 2,153 per 100,000, or 18 times the State average.

"We cannot talk about black deaths in custody in isolation when three times as many babies from North Queensland communities die at or around birth than in the rest of the country," the report said.

FRIDAY, SEPTEMBER 14, 1990 COURIER MAIL

THE COURIER MAIL

14.9.1990

Hinze OK 'to bar in park'

By STEVE ROUS

ABORIGINES opened a bar in the middle of a children's playground in far north Queensland, an inquiry has been told.

A submission to the Royal Commission into Aboriginal Deaths in Custody said the canteen to sell alcohol was approved by the then-Local Government Minister, Mr Russ Hinze.

The 107-page submission by the Aboriginal Co-Ordinating Council said Mr Hinze had previously, in August 1985, visited the community of Aurukun and had been shocked by the conditions.

"This Government will not put up with sly grogging, women getting belted up and kids starving and not being educated," Mr Hinze had said.

He said the Government would allow the community to open a canteen if that would solve the problems and stop the daily flights of illegal alcohol coming in by light plane from Weipa.

The Aboriginal Co-Ordinating Council submission said the local residents had repeatedly voted against having a canteen for fear that it would increase problems.

"However, after Aurukun received local government status, Mr Hinze decided it was discriminatory for them not to have a canteen like other Queenslanders and seeing sly grogging went on anyway, they might as well keep the money in the community," the submission said.

"A canteen was built in the middle of the Centenary Park, in the midst of the children's playground equipment."

The submission said that on one Friday the total "work for the dole" payroll in the community had been $120,000 and the amount spent that night in the canteen had been $25,000.

"It is nothing to see children with $20 notes in gambling games at Aurukun on pay or pension days," the submission said.

The submission said many Aborigines turned to alcohol and violence out of frustration with what they saw as their low status.

"The traditional role of men in Aboriginal society has been eroded and there are few opportunities for men to develop a sense of achievement and self-worth.

"Men then tend to use violence on their women to reassert their authority."

The submission said the problem of the large number of deaths in custody was partly the result of the high incidence of crime by Aborigines and the large percentage of Aborigines sent to jail.

The number of Aboriginal deaths out of custody was equally disturbing, the submission said.

"We cannot talk about black deaths in custody in isolation when three times as many babies from north Quensland Aboriginal communities die at or around birth than in the rest of the country," it said.

The submission made 211 recommendations including calling for the creation of a body like the Criminal Justice Commission to oversee the implementation of the Royal Commission's recommendations.

The Royal Commission will report on the Queensland deaths in custody on September 30 and will present its national report on December 31.

The submission also said:

- There should be a special Aboriginal unit in the Queensland Police with as many Aborigines as possible recruited for the unit.
- Most watchhouses in Aboriginal communities should be torn down and re-built.
- There should be stricter control over hard-core pornographic videos coming into communities by post from Canberra.
- There should be curfews in communities to keep children off the streets.

THE CAIRNS POST 8.8.1990

Woman tells of body in car

A ROSSVILLE woman had to put her husband's body in the back of her car and take it to Cooktown because an ambulance was not available to do it, the public inquiry into medical services provided to Aboriginal residents in the Cooktown area heard.

The administrator of Tharpuntoo Aboriginal Legal Service and former Rossville resident, Mr George Villaflor, told the Human Rights and Equal Opportunity commission's Cairns hearing on Monday most members of the State Emergency Service were eligible to drive the Cooktown ambulance.

"Anywhere between 15 to 80 people were able to drive the ambulance but they were not always around," Mr Villaflor said.

"A steering group was formed in Cooktown to look at the feasibility of establishing a QATB there but we were told we didn't have the subscription rate to warrant an ambulance.

"The group eventually broke up although I believe there is another one now," he said.

Mr Villaflor said there was no guarantee the ambulance would be driven by a person with first aid training, although some of the eligible drivers had very basic training.

The secretariat director of the Aboriginal Co-ordinating Council, Ms Barbara Miller, said the Aboriginal Co-ordinating Council had made a submission to the Parliamentary select committee of inquiry into ambulance services asking for QATB centres to be set up in Cape York Peninsula.

The committee will report back to Parliament in December.

Ms Miller presented the submission to the inquiry for its information. She said each community had been asked what its requirements were for the submission.

"I believe a lot of communities are discriminated against because they don't have essential services such as ambulances," she said.

"I believe a QATB centre should be set up in those communities with vehicles set aside solely for emergencies and trained people to operate them."

Page 8 The Cairns Post, Wednesday, August 8, 1990

Inquiry told of Aboriginal deaths 'out of custody'

By staff reporter
ELIZABETH HINSHAW

A MAJOR thrust of the Aboriginal deaths in custody inquiry should be Aboriginal deaths out of custody, according to the Aboriginal Co-ordinating Council.

The secretariat director of the Aboriginal Co-ordinating Council, Ms Barbara Miller, told the Human Rights and Equal Opportunity Commission's public inquiry into medical services provided to Aboriginals in the Cooktown area on Monday that the Aboriginal Co-ordinating Council was very concerned about the overall state of health on Aboriginal communities.

Ms Miller told the inquiry's Cairns hearing the perinatal mortality rate for Aboriginals was three times the national average (includes stillbirths and deaths within the first month) and the birth weight of Aboriginal children born on the communities was three to five times lower than the national average.

She said this led to the stunting and wasting of children, some brain damage and was connected to heart disease in adults.

"There have been very little advances over the years to improve these rates," Ms Miller said.

A former Rossville resident, Mrs Bronwyn Villaflor, told the hearing the Hopevale cemetery was like a monument to infant mortality.

"I attended a funeral at Hopevale and noticed the number of baby graves and was shocked," Mrs Villaflor said.

Ms Miller said an Aboriginal man's life expectancy was 22 years less than a non-Aboriginal's and 15 years less for Aboriginal women.

"There is a serious problem with suicide, self injury and homicide," she said.

"Many of the problems relating to violence result from inter-family fighting and are alcohol related at times.

"The homocide rate on North Queensland Aboriginal communities is 12 times the State average and the violence rate is six times.

"Family breakdowns, such as the removal of children, are the reason for the high rate of violence.

"It is a serious problem and we are looking at doing research into law and order and social control issues.

"There is also a need to look at mental health and stress caused by white settlement.

"Health problems are not easy to solve because they are inter-related with other problems.

"A lot of health problems are related to environmental health such as the water supply being unfit for human consumption.

"There are sewerage problems in the communities . . . two children drowned in pools of sewage at Doomadgee."

FAMILY relationships sometimes broke up because women from remote areas in Cape York Peninsula had to come to Cairns for months at a time to give birth, according to the Aboriginal Co-ordinating Council (ACC).

The ACC secretariat director, Ms Barbara Miller, told the Cairns hearing of the Human Rights and Equal Opportunity Commission inquiry into medical service provided to Aboriginals in the Cooktown area on Monday that birthing centres were needed on Aboriginal communities.

"Mothers have to go to Cairns about two months before their baby is due whether it will be a difficult birth or not," Ms Miller said.

"It is a burden on the family and makes the women lonely — sometimes family relationships break up.

"If there are problems with the baby after the birth many mothers have to leave it at the hospital to go back to their other children."

Birthing centres needed

Ms Miller said the situation was the same all over the Peninsula.

She said Aboriginal people felt it took away their birth rights to have Cairns on their birth certificate instead of the community they came from.

Ideally, Ms Miller said she would like to see a birthing centre at every Aboriginal community which would mean about 10, but she said that was something to aim for in the future.

"There would have to be consultation at the community level because not every community would see it the same way," she said.

"If there are complications with the pregnancy they should still have the option of having their baby in hospital."

CP 11/4/84

Aboriginal board member urged

CAIRN POST

A WORKSHOP in Cairns on Aboriginal self-management and human rights has recommended an Aboriginal be appointed to the Cairns Hospital Board.

The workshop, which ended yesterday, was part of a study being sponsored by the Human Rights Commission and conducted by Cairns woman, Mrs Barbara Miller.

Mrs Miller said a delegation had been elected at the workshop to meet a representative of the hospital board to discuss the appointment.

She said the workshop also resolved to recommend to the board and the Commonwealth Department of Aboriginal Affairs that an extra two liaison staff be funded because of the need for interpreter services and the heavy liaison workload on the only Aboriginal welfare officer now employed.

In another move, the workshop voted to ask the Minister for Aboriginal Affairs, Mr Holding, to give money now going to state Aboriginal health programs to Aboriginal-controlled health services, particularly those on reserves.

Mrs Miller said some of the other recommendations passed at the workshop dealt with the Department of Aboriginal and Islander Advancement.

"These asked that all housing, accommodation and other facilities and assets under the control of the DAIA in urban areas be transferred to the ownership and control of local community-controlled Aboriginal organisations," she said.

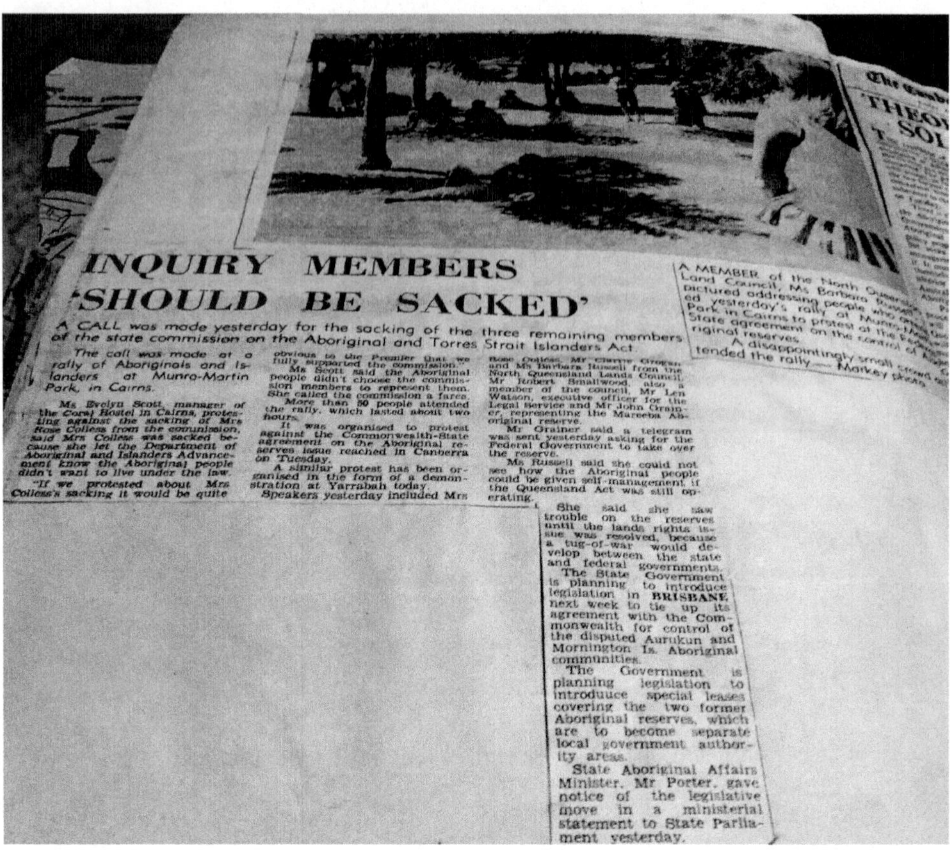

INQUIRY MEMBERS 'SHOULD BE SACKED'

A CALL was made yesterday for the sacking of the three remaining members of the state commission on the Aboriginal and Torres Strait Islanders Act.

The call was made at a rally of Aboriginals and Islanders at Munro-Martin Park, in Cairns.

Ms Evelyn Scott, manager of the Coral Hostel in Cairns, protesting against the sacking of Mrs Rose Colless from the commission, said Mrs Colless was sacked because she let the Department of Aboriginal and Islanders Advancement know the Aboriginal people didn't want to live under the law.

"If we protested about Mrs Colless's sacking it would be quite obvious to the Premier that we fully supported the commission."

Ms Scott said the Aboriginal people didn't choose the commission members to represent them. She called the commission a farce.

More than 50 people attended the rally, which lasted about two hours.

It was organised to protest against the Commonwealth-State agreement on the Aboriginal reserves issue reached in Canberra on Tuesday.

A similar protest has been organised in the form of a demonstration at Yarrabah today.

Speakers yesterday included Mrs Rose Colless, Mr Clarrie Grogan and Ms Barbara Russell from the North Queensland Lands Council, Mr Robert Smallwood, also a member of the council, Mr Len Watson, executive officer for the Legal Service and Mr John Grainer, representing the Mareeba Aboriginal reserve.

Mr Grainer said a telegram was sent yesterday asking for the Federal Government to take over the reserve.

Ms Russell said she could not see how the Aboriginal people could be given self-management if the Queensland Act was still operating.

She said she saw trouble on the reserves until the lands rights issue was resolved, because a tug-of-war would develop between the state and federal governments.

The State Government is planning to introduce legislation in **BRISBANE** next week to tie up its agreement with the Commonwealth for control of the disputed Aurukun and Mornington Is. Aboriginal communities.

The Government is planning legislation to introduuce special leases covering the two former Aboriginal reserves, which are to become separate local government authority areas.

State Aboriginal Affairs Minister, Mr Porter, gave notice of the legislative move in a ministerial statement to State Parliament yesterday.

A MEMBER of the North Queensland Land Council, Ms Barbara Russell, pictured addressing people who attended yesterday's rally at Munro-Martin Park in Cairns to protest at the Federal-State agreement on the control of Aboriginal reserves.

A disappointingly small crowd [illegible] tended the rally. — Markey photo

'purchase price' in return for reserve land

Courier Mail 5/4/78

BLANKETS, tea, sugar, flour and a hammer prepared for the Aboriginal and Islanders Advancement Minister (Mr. Porter) by (from left) Liz Johnson, Rosena Tourmese and Cheryl Buchanan outside Parliament House yesterday.

The women went to State Parliament yesterday to do a deal for aboriginal land rights.

Their offer was simple: "We return the purchase price, you give back the land of our ancestors".

They said the purchase price was flour, tea, sugar, tomahawks, blankers and boiled lollies given by Captain Arthur Phillip of the First Fleet for land at Sydney Cove in 1788.

They were unable to find any tomahawks to give back, but thought a plastic toy hammer was an adequate substitue.

Rosena and Barbara Russell, who was also present, are members of the North Queensland Aboriginal Land Council, Liz represented the Born Free Club, and Cheryl the Black Resource Centre.

They hoped to give the items to the Aboriginal and Island Affairs Minister (Mr. Porter), but he did not come out, despite a search by messengers and the Labor Member for Cook (Mr. Scott).

A letter with the items read: "You took our land from us by force and gave us flour, tea, sugar, tomahawks, blankets and boiled lollies as payment.

"Now we are returning them to you and we want our reserve land back.

"We want the Federal legislation to include land rights as well as self-management."

A copy of a petition to be sent to Federal Parliament was also sent to Mr. Porter.

It calls for full land rights in Queensland, the abolition of all State Government legislation and administration covering aborigines, enforcement of racial discrimination legislation, and the option for reserves to be self-governing with local authority status.

Ms Russell said there were about 10,000 signatures on the petition and expected the number to double by Friday.

Mr. Porter said later he was too busy to see the women.

"I am not interested in theatrical gestures anyway," he said.

Mark Noble (right) with Peter Kyle of Yarrabah.

THREE MOONS

Mrs. Jean Jimmy

Aboriginal's sacred calendar
And it holds traditional laws
From generation to generation
If you have broken the laws
Within the three Moon's
And what would you expect
If the laws are broken
It mean's death. From tribes
But if you abide in these laws
Then no harm will be done
Three moons are sacred to all
Aboriginals
Of course it even lets us know
About good and bad weather
Aboriginals judge by nature
Because Nature has civilized
Our ancestors in their own way.

AURUKUN AND MORNINGTON ISLAND

The stages are high. This fight is not just about the management of the two reserves but involves all that Queensland Aborigines have been fighting for since the fight began — land rights, self-determination, and the abolition of the Queensland Act.

by BARBARA RUSSELL

Since the Referendum of 1967 when the Australian Constitution was changed so that Aboriginal Affairs became a Federal Government responsibility, Queensland Aborigines have been pressuring for the Federal Government to takeover from the Queensland Government because of the racist legislation and administration under which Queensland Aboriginal reserve residents live.

When the Queensland Government announced its intentions to take over administration of Aurukun and Mornington Island from the Uniting Church, the Federal Government stepped in with promises of self-determination for the Aborigines of the two reserves and enacted self-management legislation for all Queensland reserves. This legislation should have but did not remove Queensland Aborigines from the racist Queensland Act.

There was talk by the Commonwealth of the possibility of acquiring the land on all Queensland Aboriginal reserves, particularly if the State Government would not co-operate with the Commonwealth Government. On April 11, Mr. Viner promised the Aborigines that if they were not happy with the State Government's legislation, the Commonwealth would acquire the reserves. However, Mr. Viner announced 17th May, 1978 that although the Aborigines were not happy with the State Government legislation, he was. It is nothing but a Commonwealth sellout!

Many Queensland Aborigines hoped that the Premier of Queensland would prove his usual stubborn self and that the Federal Government would be forced to come in in a heavy handed way and abolish the Queensland Department of Aboriginal and Islander Advancement completely.

However, the Federal Government, while it enjoyed considerable support from Queensland Aborigines when it supported the people on this issue, has now lost face badly.

It has gone from compromise to compromise and has reached agreements with the Queensland Government without consultation with the Aurukun and Mornington Island people. Not only that, the people were told by Mr. Fraser, the Prime Minister that discussions held between the two governments were confidential.

The Federal Government has ruled out the possibility of acquiring Aboriginal reserve land in Queensland not because of the cost but so as not to have a confrontation with the Queensland Government.

The Federal Self-Management legislation is virtually useless as it exists side by side with the Queensland Act. Also the Federal Government won't assume responsibility on reserves like Yarrabah, Mossman, and Mareeba that have elected to come under the Federal legislation.

The Yarrabah people have requested Mr. Viner or a Senior Departmental officer to have a meeting with them to explain the Federal legislation and to take some action to transfer responsibility for administration from the State Government to the Commonwealth.

However, the Federal Government is scared. The Queensland Director of the DAA was not prepared to face a meeting of the Area Advisory Committee representatives of all North Queensland reserves. This meeting was called by his department in Cooktown 17-18/5/78 to explain the Federal legislation.

Liberal Aboriginal Senator Nevelle Bonner has stuck by the Aurukun and Mornington Island people but his government has let him down badly.

Federal and State ALP members have also supported the people but they just do not have the numbers in Parliament.

The Uniting Church has been very vocal and active in support of the Aborigines on the two reserves on this issue, and has enlisted the support of the Catholic and Anglican bishops and archbishops.

Apart from physical resistance by the people themselves, and strikes and demonstrations in support of them, the only recourse is to international pressure.

On May 8th the Aurukun Council who were in Melbourne, appealed to the United States for aid. They tried to give the U.S. Vice-President, Mr. Mondale, a formal letter to President Carter asking him to stop the American-owned Tipperary Company attempting to mine bauxite near Aurukun.

However, Mr. Mondale's aides said the Vice-President would not pass on any messages from any Aboriginals. The N.Q. Land Council sent telegrams to the United Nations and the World Council of Churches to put pressure on the Federal Government. The Land Council is considering taking the dispute to the World Court and Amnesty International.

Various organisations in Britain, Europe, Canada and the U.S. have been kept in touch with the developments in the dispute through Land Council newsletters.

The Queensland Government are prepared to sell large areas of land to foreign landlords on favourable terms e.g. the Iwasaki tourist project at Yeppoon. However, any attempt by Aborigines to buy land e.g. Archer Bend at Aurukun has been squashed by the Queensland Government. The Queensland Premier has called opponents of the Iwasaki project racist but he is the biggest racist Australian has ever seen.

NOTE: This article should be read in conjunction with N.Q. Land Council newsletters No. 1 and 2.

N.Q. MESSAGESTICK was published in Cairns by the North Queensland Land Rights Committee. Responsibility for all material contained herein taken by B. Russell, 96a Lake Street, Cairns.

ENQUIRY — UNETHICAL ELECTORAL PRACTICES

by BARBARA RUSSELL

An enquiry should be held into the unethical electoral practices of the Queensland National/Liberal Party Coalition Government and its Department of Aboriginal and Island Advancement.

Remember the fuss kicked up by the Premier of Queensland about the Trachoma Project last November. Because this eye health team employed two Aboriginal field officers — Mick Miller and Clarrie Grogan — who had different political views to the Queensland Government, the Premier accused them of enrolling Aboriginal voters on the reserves, and put pressure on the Royal College of Opthalmologists to have them sacked. The Trachoma Project, a federally funded scheme was then suspended until after the State and Federal elections at the request of the Queensland Premier.

However, the Premier, Mr. Bjelke Petersen, authorized the Minister for Aboriginal and Island Advancement, Mr. C. K Wharton, and top public servants the Director of the DAIA Mr. P. Killoran and the National Party candidate, Mr. E. Deeral to go on a two-week campaign tour before the last State elections. (The Australian 10.11.77).

Just before the 1974 elections, workers at Bamaga reserve were advised that they would have the afternoon off to attend a political rally being conducted by Mr. Bjelke Petersen, but were told they'd get their pay docked if they didn't go. (Laurie Williams — 10.11.77). This is typical of the coercion, abuse of authority and political interference existing on reserves.

In the recent State elections, Rev. Hocking, Superintendant of Doomadgee Mission made Aboriginal voters fill their votes in out on the desk in front of him instead of letting them vote in the booths. He actually pointed out in what order squares were to be filled in. The ALP only got two votes.

At the small town of Coen during the Federal elections, the cowcockies sat on the voting desk with National Party tee-

cont. on page 6

CAIRNS POST

YEDINJI TRIBE MOVE BACK TO BUDDABADOO

By BRIAN GUNN

30/9/74

As part of a general determined movement by Aboriginals to return to their own tribal lands and live, members of the Yedinji tribe who were living at Yarrabah moved back to the old land they once occupied at Buddabadoo, about 30km south of Yarrabah, on Saturday.

The move by the Yedinji tribe follows closely the return last week of a party of Aboriginals to their old home grounds at Mapoon, about 84 km west of Weipa.

A research officer for International Development Action group, Miss Barbara Russell, has just returned after accompanying the Aboriginal families back to Mapoon.

Miss Russell told me the return of the Mapoon and Yedinji people was the start for many other Aboriginal tribes who were determined to return to their homelands and live permanently there.

All the land being re-occupied by the Aboriginals has strong spiritual ties for them. It is land many of them were born on and lived on over 30 years ago, she said.

"They need the land as an economic base for their future development, which they are determined to have," Miss Russell said.

There are about 100 members of the Yedinji tribe and all are signing a petition to the Commonwealth Government asking them to take over the Aboriginal and Island Affairs in Queensland, Miss Russell said.

Miss Russell said as the Yedinji tribe moved away from Yarrabah for Buddabadoo, a telegram was sent to Senator Cavanagh at Parliament House.

It read: "We wish to inform you of the return of Yedinji people to tribal land at Buddabadoo on Saturday, September 28, 1974.

"We urge you to take immediate action to stop Queensland DAIA from building road through Yedinji tribal ground at Buddabadoo to Pine Creek for tourist purposes also tourist development at Kundgurra on Yedinji land must be stopped."

The telegram was signed by Fred Mundraby and Parmines Mundraby, tribal elders, and Mark Noble, chairman, Yedinji Tribal Council.

Miss Russell said the journey by the Aboriginals to their old land at Mapoon was completed without incident.

A large ex-Army truck drawing a converted railway carriage formed the advance party, which included six Aboriginals, all former residents of Old Mapoon.

They left Weipa last Wednesday and arrived at Batavia out-station early the next morning.

Miss Russell said the vehicles negotiated the narrow bush track without incident.

The bush track is inaccessible in wet weather.

The remainder of the Mapoon people arrived in convoy later on Thursday and joined up with the advance party.

The Aboriginals have set up camp a short distance from where their original homes were burnt down in 1963.

Miss Russell said the transformation in the Aboriginals when they returned to their old home area was remarkable.

They immediately erected tents, made bush tables and a bush bathroom and even utilised remnants of old corrugated iron roofing that remained from their old burnt-out homes to use on their new homes.

Hunting and fishing parties were organised and they ate that night on freshwater turtle, ducks, wild pig, salmon and barramundi.

Return

"It's the complete return to their real life and you only have to look at them to see how happy they are," Miss Russell said.

The Mapoon people have formed a company—Marpuna Company.

Mr Jerry Hudson is managing director. Mr Hudson is an experienced stockman and is already organising horses for some of the men to use in rounding up about 2000 head of cattle which are running wild in the area.

Miss Russell said the Mapoon people intend to start a fishing, prawning and crabbing industry there.

She said huge oyster beds could be seen.

The first priority for the party on arrival was a working bee to clean the old air-strip of small saplings and bushes.

The air-strip is registered and was originally built by the Aboriginals by hand during the war years when they supplied the northern defence forces with meat, vegetables and fruit.

Miss Russell said a boat containing many more families from New Mapoon and Thursday Is. was expected to arrive at Old Mapoon yesterday.

She said she expected that in about two weeks time a mass exodus of all Mapoon people, including several who have intermarried at New Mapoon and Thursday Is., will join the remainder already settling down in their new homes.

Endnotes

[1]Gray, S. 2009 Bjelke-Petersen clashes with church, *Brisbane Times* https://www.brisbanetimes.com.au/national/queensland/bjelke-petersen-clashes-with-church-20090101-geap4u.html

[2] Ibid.

[3] MacDougall, David and MacDougall, Judith (1979) *Takeover* Canberra: Australian Institute of Aboriginal and Torres Strait Islander Studies

[4]Commonwealth, Parliamentary Debates, Senate 15 March 1978, 31 http://historichansard.net/senate/1978/19780315_senate_31_s76/#subdebate-23-0

[5] Ibid.

[6] Queensland, Parliamentary Debates, Legislative Assembly 27 April 1978 https://www.parliament.qld.gov.au/documents/hansard/1978/1978_04_27.pdf

[7] Pritchard J and Pelissier, L (1979) "Aurukun and Mornington Island (1978)" an extract from Queensland Dossier *Radical Times* https://vimeo.com/246620629

[8]Commonwealth, Parliamentary Debates, Senate 10 May 1978 http://historichansard.net/senate/1978/19780510_senate_31_s77/#debate-34

[9]Commonwealth, Parliamentary Debates, Senate 16 August 1978 http://historichansard.net/senate/1978/19780816_senate_31_s78/#debate-30

[10] Williams, G (1979) "Mobilising World Opinion and Aboriginal Votes" *Sydney Morning Herald* 16th March 197

[11] Sanders, D.E. (1977) *The Formation of the World Council of Indigenous Peoples* IWGIA Document no 29 Copenhagen.

[12] O'Neill, Shorty (ed) "Action Against RTZ" interview with Les Russell *N.Q. Messagestick* August 1981 Vol 6 No 3

[13] North Qld Land Council papers

[14] North Qld Land Council papers

[15] Tribune (1985) "Confronting Racism on Film – Dennis O'Rourke's 'Couldn't Be Fairer' 1985" *Tribune. 11th December 1985 https://printedshadows.wordpress.com/2012/02/06/confronting-racism-on-film-dennis-orourkes-couldnt-be-fairer-1985/*

[16] Ibid.

[17] Ibid.

[18] Austin, Allan (1981) *Report on Cape York Trip* Victorian Baptist Social Justice Working group and the Division of Social Justice of the Uniting Church of Victoria

[19] Mulligan, M. (1980) "Mick Miller Speaks on Noonkanbah," *Direct Action* 1st October 1980

[20] Russell, B. (1977) "National Trachoma and Eye Health Programme Forced Out of Qld for Political Purposes" *NQ Messagestick*, Vol 2 No 5 November 1977

[21]Gray, S. (2008) "Sir Joh 'expelled' Fred Hollows" *Brisbane Times* https://www.brisbanetimes.com.au/national/queensland/sir-joh-expelled-fred-hollows-20081212-gean9t.html

[22] Ibid.

[23] Miller, Barbara (1994) *Options for the Future, Local Government and Native Title on Queensland Aboriginal Communities*. Aboriginal Coordinating Council, P59.

[24] Keon-Cohen, B A (2000) "The Mabo Litigation: A Personal and Procedural Account" [2000] MelbULawRw 35; 24(3) *Melbourne University Law Review* 893, http://www.austlii.edu.au/au/journals/MelbULawRw/2000/35.html

[25]Chesterman, John and Villaflor, George (2000) *Mr Neal's Invasion: Behind an Indigenous Rights Case*, http://www.austlii.edu.au/au/journals/AUJlLawSoc/2000/1.pdf

[26] Nicol, Emily (2018) "Warrior Spirits: The Wik Women Who Stood Up for Their Land and Communities" 26th June 2018 *NITV* https://www.sbs.com.au/nitv/article/2018/06/12/warrior-spirits-wik-women-who-stood-their-land-and-communities

[27] Zwar, Desmond (1990) "White Woman, Black Heart" in *Sunday Age* 2nd December 1990

[28] Zwar, Desmond (1990) "70's rebel stirring for justice" in *Sunday Mail* 14th October 1990

[29] Adams, J, Miller, B, Venables S. P. Aurukun Support Group (1991) *Woyan Min Uwamp Aak Ngulakana or Finding the Right Road Ahead*, Townsville: Yalga-Binbi Institute for Community Development

[30] Miller, B. (1992) "A Community Development Approach to Crime Prevention in Aboriginal Communities," Australian Institute of Criminology Conference, Cairns. Printed in "Proceedings of the Australian Institute of Criminology Conference in S. Killop (ed.), *Aboriginal Justice Issues*, Canberra 23-25 June 1992 P17-23. www.aic.gov.au/publications

[31] Ibid. P22

[32] Human Rights Commission (1993) *Mornington: A Report by the Federal Race Discrimination Commissioner*, Canberra P56

[33] Ferguson, Martin (1998) 7th April Hansard P2704 https://parlinfo.aph.gov.au/parlInfo/search/display/display.w3p;db=CHAMBER;id=chamber%2Fhansardr%2F1998-04-07%2F0066;query=Id%3A%22chamber%2Fhansardr%2F1998-04-07%2F0070%22

[34] Zohar, D. and Marshall. I (2004) *Spiritual Capital, Wealth We Can Live By*, San Francisco: Berrett-Koehler Pub Inc. P4

[35] Transformations - Almolonga Guatemala - Revival produces Gigantic Vegetables! https://www.youtube.com/watch?v=QTDK_L-X6tk

[36] 'Cor van Keuk, (2007) *On the Reconciliation Process; In-between the Netherlands and the Aboriginal Nations of Aurukun and Yolngu; Part One,* http://wititjhealing. yolasite. com/r1-on-the-reconciliation-process-dec-07. php

[37] Ibid.

[38] Sayers, B.J. (1998) *A fair go: Aboriginal living and learning in the dominant Australian culture*, Darwin: Australian Aborigines and Islanders Branch, Summer Institute of Linguistics P80

[39] Carney, M. (2011) "Return to Aurukun", *Four Corners* 27th Apr 2011, https://www.abc.net.au/4corners/4c-full-program-aurukun/8961288

[40] Ibid.

[41] Ibid.

[42] Robinson, N. (2016) "'*Aurukun needs to be awakened': Local pastor hopes town at 'turning point' after difficult past,*" *ABC* https://www.abc.net.au/news/2016-05-27/aurukun-in-deep-crisis-after-difficult-past/7451556

[43] Ibid.

[44] Ibid.

[45] Overs, Marge (2012) *In Fred's Footsteps: 20 Years of Restoring Sight* Rosebery, NSW: Fred Hollows Foundation Australia P85

[46]Kidd, Ros (undated) *Held to account: governments and Indigenous interests*, http://www.linksdisk.com/roskidd/tpages/t29.htm)

[47] Archibald-Binge, Ella (2017) "60th Anniversary of Palm Island Strike" *NITV* 15.7.17

[48] Robertson, Joshua (2016) "'You're my warrior': Lex Wotton and the fight for justice after the Palm Island riots" *The Guardian* 7th December 2016 https://www.theguardian.com/australia-news/2016/dec/07/youre-my-warrior-lex-wotton-and-the-fight-for-justice-after-the-palm-island-uprising

[49] Solidarity (2008) "Lex Wotton found guilty, Racism rules in Queensland courts" *Solidarity* 4th November 2008 https://www.solidarity.net.au/mag/back/2008/9/lex-wotton-found-guilty-racism-rules-in-queensland-courts/

[50] Wilkins, Georgia (2020) "The Thin Blue Line: Fine Balance Between Police Union Power and Justice" *Crikey* 12th June 2020 https://www.crikey.com.au/2020/06/12/are-police-unions-preventing-justice-when-it-comes-to-aboriginal-deaths-in-custody/

[51] Special Emergency Response Team

[52] Federal Court of Australia (2016) *Wotton v State of Queensland (No 5) [2016] FCA 1457 Summary* https://www.judgments.fedcourt.gov.au/judgments/Judgments/fca/single/2016/2016fca1457/summary/2016fca1457-summary

[53]Arvier, Tim (2018) "Why Palm Islanders still live in the shadow of 2004 riots," *9News* https://www.9news.com.au/national/palm-island-2004-riots-lex-wotton/abedd89c-d30e-429d-8728-281c6206fb7c

[54] Georgatos, Gerry (2014) "An interview with Lex Wotton – social justice warrior," *The Stringer* 2nd August 2014 https://thestringer.com.au/an-interview-with-lex-wotton-social-justice-warrior-8173#.YCIlq-gzbIU

[55] NITV (2017) "Money won't wash away Palm Island's trauma, Lex Wotton says" *NITV* 2nd February 2017 https://www.sbs.com.au/nitv/nitv-news/article/2017/02/02/money-wont-wash-away-palm-islands-trauma-lex-wotton-says

[56] Robertson, Joshua (2016) "'You're my warrior': Lex Wotton and the fight for justice after the Palm Island riots" *The Guardian* 7th December 2016 https://www.theguardian.com/australia-news/2016/dec/07/youre-my-warrior-lex-wotton-and-the-fight-for-justice-after-the-palm-island-uprising

[57] O'Brien, Kerry (2001) "Bringing Them Home Report" *ABC 7.30 Report* 29th March 2001

[58] Woorama (2007) *Eugenics and Aborigines, Genetic Science – Its Role in Indigenous Policy, Identity, Genocide* http//suite101.com/article/eugenics-and-aborigines-a22972, P2

[59] State Library of Victoria (2011) *Reconciliation Convention 1997* http://ergo.slv.vic.gov.au/explore-history/fight-rights/indigenous-rights/reconciliation-convention-1997 P1

[60] Ibid.

[61] Aboriginal and Torres Strait Islander Commission (1998) *ATSIC News*, May 1998

[62] Warren Entsch MP Presents the Boomerang Petition to Parliament on Behalf of Cairns Indigenous Leader Norman Miller https://www.youtube.com/watch?v=4LSEErGV1rI&feature=youtu.be

[63] Reconciliation Australia https://www.reconciliation.org.au/

[64] Yolgnu Aboriginal word for treaty or peace after conflict

[65] Uluru Statement From the Heart (2017) https://fromtheheart.com.au/explore-the-uluru-statement/

[66] Referendum Council (2017) *A Voice To Parliament Key Recommendation Of Referendum Council's Final Report* 17th July 2017 https://www.referendumcouncil.org.au/node/1000.html

[67] Grattan, Michelle (2019) "Proposed Indigenous 'voice' will be to government rather than to Parliament" *The Conversation*, 29th October 2019

[68] SBS (2021) "Indigenous Voice to Parliament will get no veto power under interim proposal" *SBS News* 9th January 2021 https://www.sbs.com.au/news/indigenous-voice-to-parliament-will-get-no-veto-power-under-interim-proposal

[69] Hinton, Martin QC "Is Australia's Constitution Racist?" in the Law Society of South Australia *Bulletin* March https://www.lawsocietysa.asn.au/LSSA/Lawyers/Publications/Articles/Is_Australias_Constitution_Racist.aspx

[70] Ibid.

References

Aboriginal and Torres Strait Islander Commission (1998) *ATSIC News*, May 1998

Adams, J. Miller, B, Venables S. P. Aurukun Support Group (1991) *Woyan Min Uwamp Aak Ngulakana* or *Finding the Right Road Ahead*, Townsville: Yalga-Binbi Institute for Community Development

Archibald-Binge, Ella (2017) "60th Anniversary of Palm Island Strike" *NITV* 15.7.17

Arvier, Tim (2018) "Why Palm Islanders still live in the shadow of 2004 riots," May 7 2018, *9News* https://www.9news.com.au/national/palm-island-2004-riots-lex-wotton/abedd89c-d30e-429d-8728-281c6206fb7c

Austin, Allan (1981) *Report on Cape York Trip* Victorian Baptist Social Justice Working group and the Division of Social Justice of the Uniting Church of Victoria

Carney, Mathew (2011) *Return to Aurukun: Material from the Four Corners archives, 'Our cultural leadership is being taken from us'* 27 April 2011 https://www.abc.net.au/4corners/4c-full-program-aurukun/8961288

Chesterman, John and Villaflor, George (2000) *Mr Neal's Invasion: Behind an Indigenous Rights Case*, http://www.austlii.edu.au/au/journals/AUJlLawSoc/2000/1.pdf

Commonwealth, Parliamentary Debates, Senate 15 March 1978, 31 http://historichansard.net/senate/1978/19780315_senate_31_s76/#subdebate-23-0

Commonwealth, Parliamentary Debates, Senate 10 May 1978 http://historichansard.net/senate/1978/19780510_senate_31_s77/#debate-34

Commonwealth, Parliamentary Debates, Senate 16 August 1978 http://historichansard.net/senate/1978/19780816_senate_31_s78/#debate-30

Commonwealth, Parliamentary Debates, Senate 7th April 1998 Ferguson, Martin speech P2704 https://parlinfo.aph.gov.au/parlInfo/

Cor van Keuk, (2007) *On the Reconciliation Process; In-between the Netherlands and the Aboriginal Nations of Aurukun and Yolngu; Part One* http://wititjhealing. yolasite. com/r1-on-the-reconciliation-process-dec-07. Php

Carney, M. (2011) "Return to Aurukun," *Four Corners* 27th Apr 2011, https://www.abc.net.au/4corners/4c-full-program-aurukun/8961288

Dorante, Karen (1990) "Royal Commission into Aboriginal Deaths in Custody" *ABC* Cairns 5th October 1990

Elias, David (1980) "Quietly Flow the Words of Anguish," *The Age* September 1980

Engel, Mathew (1982) "Queensland Police Arrest 200 in Aboriginal Rights Protest" *The Guardian* 8th October 1982

Family Responsibilities Commission Annual Report 2019-2020 https://www.frcq.org.au/resources/publications/annual-report-2019-20/

Federal Court of Australia (2016) *Wotton v State of Queensland (No 5) [2016] FCA 1457 Summary* https://www.judgments.fedcourt.gov.au/judgments/Judgments/fca/single/2016/2016fca1457/summary/2016fca1457-summary

Forsyth, Chris (1979) "Globalizing Aboriginal land rights," *The Nation Review,* 12th April 1979

Georgatos, Gerry (2014) "An interview with Lex Wotton – social justice warrior," *The Stringer* 2nd August 2014 https://thestringer.com.au/an-interview-with-lex-wotton-social-justice-warrior-8173#.YCIlq-gzbIU

Grattan, Michelle (2019). "Proposed Indigenous 'voice' will be to government rather than to parliament" *The Conversation*, 29th October 2019

Gray, S. 2008 "Sir Joh 'expelled' Fred Hollows," *Brisbane Times* https://www.brisbanetimes.com.au/national/queensland/sir-joh-expelled-fred-hollows-20081212-gean9t.html

Gray, S. 2009 "Bjelke-Petersen clashes with church," *Brisbane Times* https://www.brisbanetimes.com.au/national/queensland/bjelke-petersen-clashes-with-church-20090101-geap4u.html

Hinshaw, Elizabeth (1990) "Inquiry told of Aboriginal deaths out of custody," *The Cairns Post* 8th August 1990

Hinshaw, Elizabeth (1990) "Birthing centers needed," *The Cairns Post* 8th August 1990

Hinshaw, Elizabeth (1990) "Woman tells of body in car," *The Cairns Post* 8th August 1990

Hinton, Martin QC "Is Australia's Constitution Racist?" in the Law Society of South Australia *Bulletin* March https://www.lawsocietysa.asn.au/LSSA/Lawyers/Publications/Articles/Is_Australias_Constitution_Racist.aspx

Human Rights Commission (1993) *Mornington: A Report by the Federal Race Discrimination Commissioner*, Canberra

Human Rights Commission (1997) *Bringing Them Home: Report of the National Inquiry into the Separation of Aboriginal and Torres Strait Islander Children from Their Families* https://humanrights.gov.au/our-work/bringing-them-home-report-1997

Keon-Cohen, B A (2000) "The Mabo Litigation: A Personal and Procedural Account" [2000] MelbULawRw 35; 24(3) *Melbourne University Law Review* 893, http://www.austlii.edu.au/au/journals/MelbULawRw/2000/35.html)

Kidd, Ros (undated) *Held to account: governments and Indigenous interests* http://www.linksdisk.com/roskidd/tpages/t29.htm

Koowarta, John (1980) Interview in *NQ Messagestick* Vol 5 No 2 September 1980

Lodi News-Sentinel (1980) "Aborigines' lizard god to be defended at U.N," *Lodi News-Sentinel* 27th August 1980

MacDougall, David and MacDougall, Judith (1979) *Takeover* Canberra: Australian Institute of Aboriginal and Torres Strait Islander Studies

Miller, Barbara (1990) "Submission to Royal Commission into Aboriginal Deaths in Custody" Aboriginal Coordinating Council.

Miller, Barbara (1992) "A Community Development Approach to Crime Prevention in Aboriginal Communities," Australian Institute of Criminology Conference, Cairns. Printed in "Proceedings of the Australian Institute of Criminology Conference in S. Killop (ed.), *Aboriginal Justice Issues*, Canberra 23-25 June 1992 P17-23, www.aic.gov.au/publications

Miller, Barbara (1994) *Options for the Future, Local Government and Native Title on Queensland Aboriginal Communities*. Aboriginal Coordinating Council.

Miller, Barbara (2005) *Building Spiritual Capital at Aurukun* unpublished paper

Miller, Barbara (2012) *William Cooper, Gentle Warrior: Standing Up for Australian Aborigines and Persecuted Jews* Xlibris

Miller, Barbara (2014) *The European Quest to Find Terra Australis Incognita: Quiros Torres and Janszoon* Barbara Miller Books

Miller, Barbara (2018) *White Woman Black Heart: Journey Home to Old Mapoon, A* Memoir Barbara Miller Books

Miller, Barbara (2018) 2nd ed. *The Dying Days of Segregation in Australia: Case Study Yarrabah* Barbara Miller Books

Miller, Barbara (2019) *White Australia Has A Black History: William Cooper and First Nations Peoples' Political Activism* Barbara Miller Books

Miller, Barbara (2020) *Shattered Lives Broken Dreams: William Cooper and Australian Aborigines Protest Holocaust* Barbara Miller Books

Mulligan, M. (1980) "Mick Miller Speaks on Noonkanbah" Direct Action 1st October 1980

Nicol, Emily (2018) "Warrior Spirits: The Wik Women Who Stood Up for Their Land and Communities" 26th June 2018 *NITV* https://www.sbs.com.au/nitv/article/2018/06/12/warrior-spirits-wik-women-who-stood-their-land-and-communities

NITV (2017) "Money won't wash away Palm Island's trauma, Lex Wotton says" *NITV* 2nd February 2017 https://www.sbs.com.au/nitv/nitv-news/article/2017/02/02/money-wont-wash-away-palm-islands-trauma-lex-wotton-says

NQ Messagestick Jan 79 Vol 4 No 1

Oakes, Laurie (1978) "Aurukun Deal Blocked, Viner: We will block Joh." *The Sun* 30th March 1978

O'Brien, Kerry (2001) "Bringing Them Home Report" *ABC 7.30 Report* 29th March 2001

O'Neill, Shorty (ed) "Action Against RTZ" interview with Les Russell *N.Q. Messagestick* August 1981 Vol 6 No 3

Overs, Marge (2012) *In Fred's Footsteps: 20 Years of Restoring Sight* Rosebery, NSW: Fred Hollows Foundation Australia

Pritchard J and Pelissier, L (1979) "Aurukun and Mornington Island (1978)" an extract from Queensland Dossier *Radical Times* https://vimeo.com/246620629

Queensland, Parliamentary Debates, Legislative Assembly 27 April 1978 https://www.parliament.qld.gov.au/documents/hansard/1978/1978_04_27.pdf

Queensland, Parliamentary Debates, Legislative Assembly 21 April 1998

Reconciliation Australia https://www.reconciliation.org.au/

Referendum Council (2017) *A Voice To Parliament Key Recommendation Of Referendum Council's Final Report* 17th July 2017 https://www.referendumcouncil.org.au/node/1000.html

Roberts, Greg (1990) "What do Aborigines do more than most? Die." *The Sydney Morning Herald* 28th September 1990

Roberts, Greg (1995) "White Light for Black Days" *The Bulletin* 24-31 January 1995

Robertson, Joshua (2016) "'You're my warrior': Lex Wotton and the fight for justice after the Palm Island riots" 7th December 2016 *The Guardian* https://www.theguardian.com/australia-news/2016/dec/07/youre-my-warrior-lex-wotton-and-the-fight-for-justice-after-the-palm-island-uprising

Robinson, N. (2016) "'*Aurukun needs to be awakened': Local pastor hopes town at 'turning point' after difficult past*", *ABC* https://www.abc.net.au/news/2016-05-27/aurukun-in-deep-crisis-after-difficult-past/7451556

Rous, Steve (1990) "Hinze OK 'to bar in park'" *The Courier Mail* September 1990

Russell, Barbara (1977) "National Trachoma and Eye Health Programme Forced Out of Qld for Political Purposes" NQ Messagestick, Vol 2 No 5 Nov 1977

Sanders, D.E. (1977) The Formation of the World Council of Indigenous Peoples *IWGIA Document* no 29 Copenhagen.

Sayers, B.J. (1998) *A fair go: Aboriginal living and learning in the dominant Australian culture*, Darwin: Australian Aborigines and Islanders Branch, Summer Institute of Linguistics

SBS (2021) "Indigenous Voice to parliament will get no veto power under interim proposal" *SBS News* 9th January 2021 https://www.sbs.com.au/news/indigenous-voice-to-parliament-will-get-no-veto-power-under-interim-proposal

Solidarity (2008) "Lex Wotton found guilty, Racism rules in Queensland courts" *Solidarity* 4th November 2008 https://www.solidarity.net.au/mag/back/2008/9/lex-wotton-found-guilty-racism-rules-in-queensland-courts/

State Library of Victoria (2011) *Reconciliation Convention 1997* http://ergo.slv.vic.gov.au/explore-history/fight-rights/indigenous-rights/reconciliation-convention-1997

The Age 20th February 1978

The Australian (1978) "Aurukun Threatens Appeal to World Court," *The Australian* 13th April 1978

The Australian 21st April 1978

The Canberra Times (1978) "Bjelke-Petersen to use force" *The Canberra Times* 3 April 1978

The Canberra Times, 31st August 1978

The Cairns Post (1978) "Policy conflict reason for mission takeover" *The Cairns Post* 15th March 1978

The Cairns Post, 22nd March 1978

The Cairns Post, 29th March 1978

The Cairns Post (1978) "Protest Rally a Great Success" *The Cairns Post* 10th April 1978

The Cairns Post 14 April 1978

The Cairns Post (1978) "Aurukun Aboriginals want freehold land," *The Cairns Post* 18th April 1978

The Cairns Post (1978) "Miller rejects 'communists' tag," *The Cairns Post* 22nd April 1978

The Cairns Post (1978) "Porter's claims refuted," *The Cairns Post* 27th April 1978

The Cairns Post (1978) "Black leaders blast claim as racist" *The Cairns Post* 28th April 1978

The Cairns Post (1978) "Disillusioned with Canberra, ANGERS AURUKUN, Ministers accused of siding with Qld" *The Cairns Post* 8th May 1978, Canberra (AAP)

The Cairns Post (1978 "Back to Old Mission Days" *The Cairns Post* 16th August 1978

The Cairns Post (1978) "Land Rights Body Blames State Government," "Health Move Attacked," and "Issue and Excuse To Throw Church Out," *The Cairns Post* 31 August 1978

The Cairns Post (1978) "Aurukun Council Seeks Land Tenure" *The Cairns Post* 30th August 1978

The Cairns Post 22nd November 1978 AAP report from London

The Cairns Post, 6th September 1980

The Cairns Post 11th April 1984

The Cairns Post (1990) "Aboriginals Triple State Death Rate," *The Cairns Post* 28 September 1990

The Cairns Post (1991) "Aboriginals Launch Policy" *The Cairns Post* 13th April 1991

The Cairns Post on 8th January 2014

The Courier Mail, 21st March 1978

The Courier Mail (1978) "The law takes a long look," *The Courier Mail* 15th April 1978

The Courier Mail, 21st April 1978

The Sun (1978) "Aurukun Deal Scrapped, Viner: We will Block Joh" *The Sun,* Melbourne 30th March 1978

The Sydney Mornington Herald 30th March 1978

The Sydney Morning Herald (1978) "Qld Abolishes Reserves to Block Fraser" *The Sydney Morning Herald* 8th April 1978

The Townsville Bulletin (1990) "Need to weed racist police out of force" *The Townsville Bulletin* 6th December 1990

The West Australian (1980) "Arrests in the North … but convoy pushes on" *The West Australian,* 11th August 1980

Transformations, *Transformations - Almolonga Guatemala - Revival produces Gigantic Vegetables*! https://www.youtube.com/watch?v=QTDK_L-X6tk

Tribune (1985) "Confronting Racism on Film – Dennis O'Rourke's 'Couldn't Be Fairer' 1985" *Tribune. 11th December 1985 https://printedshadows.wordpress.com/2012/02/06/confronting-racism-on-film-dennis-orourkes-couldnt-be-fairer-1985/*

Uluru Statement From the Heart (2017) https://fromtheheart.com.au/explore-the-uluru-statement/

Williams, G (1979) "Mobilising World Opinion and Aboriginal Votes" *Sydney Morning Herald* 16th March 1979

Wilkins, Georgia (2020) "The Thin Blue Line: Fine Balance Between Police Union Power and Justice" *Crikey* 12th June 2020 https://www.crikey.com.au/2020/06/12/are-police-unions-preventing-justice-when-it-comes-to-aboriginal-deaths-in-custody/

Zohar, D. and Marshall, I (2004) *Spiritual Capital, Wealth We Can Live By*, San Francisco: Berrett-Koehler Pub Inc

Zwar, Desmond (1990) "The blonde who dropped a bombshell … 70's rebel stirring for justice" *Sunday Mail* 14th October 1990

Zwar, Desmond (1990) "White Woman, Black Heart" *Sunday Age* 2nd December 1990

Author Bio

Barbara Miller has been involved in Aboriginal politics and history first hand for about 50 years working for Aboriginal organizations such as the North Queensland Land Council as newspaper editor and research officer and the Aboriginal Coordinating Council as CEO. She is a psychologist, sociologist, historian and social justice advocate. Author of ten books and part of an Aboriginal family, she brings an insider view to her writing.

Barbara's first memoir, *White Woman Black Heart: Journey Home to Old Mapoon, A Memoir* was short-listed in 2018 for the Queensland Literary

Award for the major award, the Premier's Award for a "Work of State Significance."

Professor Henry Reynolds FAHA FASSA University of Tasmania, eminent historian and award-winning author described Barbara's writing as "essential reading for anyone interested in political and social change over the last 50 years."

She lives in Cairns, Australia with her husband Norman and son Michael.

Books by the Author

Miller, B. (2020) "The Power of Vision" in Brehm, R. et al *Success Code*, Dauntless

Miller, B. (2020) *Shattered Lives Broken Dreams: William Cooper and Australian Aborigines Protest Holocaust*, Barbara Miller Books

Miller, B and Miller, N. (2020) "Birthing a New Call to Protect Our Judeo-Christian Heritage," in Mahlburg, K. and Marsh, W. (eds) *The Blessing of Almighty God: The Canberra Declaration Story and the Call to Revitalise Australia,* Australian Heart Ministries

Miller, B. (2019) *White Australia Has A Black History: William Cooper and First Nations Peoples' Political Activism*, Barbara Miller Books

Miller, B. (2019) *If I Survive: Nazi Germany and the Jews, 100-Year Old Lena Goldstein's Miracle Story*, Barbara Miller Books

Miller, B. (2018) *White Woman Black Heart, Journey Home to Old Mapoon, A Memoir*, Barbara Miller Books

Miller, B. (2018) *The Dying Days of Segregation in Australia: Case Study Yarrabah.* 2nd ed. Barbara Miller Books (1st ed 2016)

Miller, B. (2014) *The European Quest to Find Terra Australis Incognita: Quiros, Torres and Janszoon.* Barbara Miller Books

Miller, B. (2012) *William Cooper, Gentle Warrior: Standing Up for Australian Aborigines and Persecuted Jews*, Xlibris.

Miller, B. (2006) 'The Re-Founding of Australia' in Maeliau, M., Maki, J., Miller, B. and Siilata, M. *Uluru: the Heart of Australia*, Honiara, Solomon Is.

Miller, B. (1992) 'A Social-Historical and Psychological Perspective on Aboriginal Intra-Cultural Aggression' in Thomas, D. and Veno, A. (Eds) *Psychology and Social Change, Creating an International Agenda*, The Dunmore Press: Palmerston North, New Zealand.

Roberts, J.P., Russell, B., and Parsons, M., (1975) (Eds) *The Mapoon Story by The Mapoon People, Volume 1*, International Development Action: Fitzroy, Victoria and printed by Amber Press, Sydney.

Roberts, J.P., Parsons, M., and Russell, B. (1975) *The Mapoon Story According to the Invaders: Church Mission, Queensland Government and Mining Company, Volume 2*, International Development Action: Fitzroy, Victoria and printed by Amber Press, Sydney.

Read about one of Australia's early Indigenous activists who met with Prime Ministers and petitioned Kings & who championed the cause of Jews at Kristallnacht in 1938

WILLIAM COOPER, GENTLE WARRIOR

This book is the history of Indigenous Australia in a nutshell

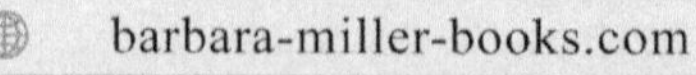

Printed in Great Britain
by Amazon